DEFENDING WHITE DEMOCRACY

Defending White Democracy

THE MAKING OF A SEGREGATIONIST

MOVEMENT AND THE REMAKING OF

RACIAL POLITICS, 1936–1965

JASON MORGAN WARD

THE UNIVERSITY OF

NORTH CAROLINA PRESS

Chapel Hill

This book was published with the assistance of the
Thornton H. Brooks Fund of the University of North Carolina Press.

The paper in this book meets the guidelines for permanence
and durability of the Committee on Production Guidelines for
Book Longevity of the Council on Library Resources.

The University of North Carolina Press has been a member of
the Green Press Initiative since 2003.

Library of Congress Cataloging-in-Publication Data
Ward, Jason Morgan.
Defending white democracy : the making of a segregationist movement and the remaking
of racial politics, 1936–1965 / Jason Morgan Ward.
p. cm.
Includes bibliographical references and index.
ISBN 978-0-8078-3513-5 (hardback)
1. Segregation—Southern States—History—20th century. 2. Segregation—Political
aspects—Southern States—History—20th century. 3. Southern States—Race relations—
History—20th century. 4. Southern States—Race relations—Political aspects—History—
20th century. 5. Whites—Southern States—Politics and government—20th century.
6. Whites—Southern States—Attitudes—History—20th century. 7. African Americans—
Segregation—Southern States—History. 8. Civil rights—Southern States—History—20th
century. 9. Government, Resistance to—Southern States—History—20th century. I. Title.
F220.A1W37 2011
305.800975—dc22   2011015513

15 14 13 12 11   5 4 3 2 1

For Alison

CONTENTS

ILLUSTRATIONS

ACKNOWLEDGMENTS

Peter Jocys taught U.S. history from the last chapter *backwards* so that his students at South Granville High School would finally make it past the Civil War. I have been stuck in the twentieth century ever since. Down the road from Creedmoor, I spent as much time as possible in the embarrassment of riches that is the Duke History Department. John Herd Thompson, Raymond Gavins, Sydney Nathans, Charles Payne, Larry Goodwyn, and Kristen Neuschel taught me to think and write like a historian. Paul Ortiz and Wayne Lee, two freshly minted Duke Ph.D.s, showed me how to put together a research project in their seminars. Bob Korstad and Bill Chafe took time from their duties elsewhere on campus to offer encouragement. John Hope Franklin graciously took me to lunch and listened to me yammer on about my senior thesis. My good fortune astounds me more each day.

The history faculty at Yale provided sage advice and steady encouragement from the day I arrived in New Haven. The first professor I met, Jon Butler, also taught my first class and always took time to share his peerless good sense. David Blight's example as a teacher and scholar remains an inspiration. John Demos's zero-tolerance policy for gratuitous alliteration made me a better writer. John Mack Faragher not only allowed me to write a southern history paper in his U.S. West research seminar, but also kept after me until I finally submitted it to a journal. Stephen Pitti taught me twice and scared up timely research support through Yale's Program on Ethnicity, Race, and Migration.

Well before this book project took shape, Beverly Gage challenged me to push beyond my regional focus and never slack off on my writing. Generous, insightful, and razor sharp, Bev is the best thing to happen to the Yale History Department in a good while. When I was not meeting with Bev, I was distracting Jonathan Holloway from his many duties at Calhoun College. Jonathan has provided unflagging encouragement and a steady stream of good counsel as I made my way from New Haven to Mississippi. No one has left a greater mark on this book than Glenda Gilmore, but it pales in comparison to her impact on my thinking, my teaching, and my life. Her vision shaped this project before I even knew what it was about, and I am profoundly grateful for her patience, wisdom, and advocacy on my behalf.

When I arrived in New Haven, Kat Charron, Aaron Wong, Françoise Hamlin, and Adriane Lentz-Smith looked after me. The Y'all University

Southern History crowd—especially Robin Morris, Sam Schaffer, Steve Prince, and Julie Weise—continue to make New Haven, Connecticut, a hotbed of Dixie-ology. A few years after I inherited her old room on Mansfield Street, Tammy Ingram hosted me during multiple research trips. Bill Rando gave me a great job, and Yvette Barnard's quick thinking helped me get my current one. In ways big and small, Eden Knudsen, Grace Leslie, Caitlin Casey, Julia Irwin, David Huyssen, Brenda Santos, Dana Schaffer, Sarah Haley, Sarah Hammond, Kamil Redmond, Rebecca McKenna, Julia Guarneri, and Kathryn Gin left their mark on my life and work in New Haven. I thank them all.

I received generous and timely support from various archives and institutions. The Joel Williamson Visiting Scholar Grant from the Southern Historical Collection at the University of North Carolina, the Elison Durant Smith Research Award from the South Caroliniana Library, and a research grant from the Institute for Southern Studies at the University of South Carolina allowed me to plumb remarkable repositories and enrich my project. More recently, the Mississippi State University Department of History provided course relief and research funds that accelerated the publication process. My department head, Alan Marcus, made this book a priority, and Pam Wasson, Patsy Humphrey, and Lonna Reinecke have helped me juggle its completion with various other duties. I am lucky to work with brilliant and collegial historians on a daily basis. Expect big things.

Talented folks who did not know me from Adam nonetheless lent their time and insight. Claire Potter, Joseph Lowndes, John Dittmer, David Chappell, Jane Dailey, and several anonymous readers shared advice that stuck. Charles Eagles read a draft cover to cover and whipped the prose into shape. Kevin Kruse signed on as an honorary reader and offered a timely critique. The term "reader" is a poor measure of Joe Crespino's mark on this manuscript—the road map that he provided has guided me through many rounds of revision. David Perry's decision to put the manuscript in Joe's capable hands was the first of many smart moves, and I could not have asked for more from an editor. David and everyone at the University of North Carolina Press make book publishing look easy. I could not have been in better hands.

My family made this undertaking possible. On my first trip to an archive, I thumbed through crumbling newspapers for twenty dollars and lunch. My employer that day, Tim Tyson, hooked me on history, cheered me on, and read every word of this manuscript. He and Perri Morgan, along with my other Chapel Hill relatives—Phil Morgan and Susan Evans—let me write large chunks of this book in their respective basements. Several dozen other aunts, uncles, and cousins from both sides make me proud and grateful to be a Morgan *and* a Ward. My grandmothers, Doris Perry Morgan and Evelyn Strickland Ward, and my late grandfathers, Sam Morgan and Max Ward, have handed down a history and opened doors for me along the way.

My sister Brooke teaches more classes in a day than I do in a week and still manages to read more books. My parents, Mike Ward and Hope Morgan Ward, have stood by me all the way. Professing is a weak amalgam of preaching and teaching, but I learned both from the best in the business. Speaking of teachers and preachers, Margaret and Larry Greene are an inspiration and a rock of support. They treated me like a son, and Miranda treated me like a brother, years before it became official. Because she believes in me, Alison Collis Greene kept me focused and grounded long enough to get this book out. Her encouragement, perspective, and integrity give life and work purpose. For these reasons and a thousand more, I dedicate this book to her with love and gratitude.

According to Birmingham columnist John Temple Graves, the civil rights movement arrived during World War II. And he was not happy about it. The son of a prominent Georgia newspaperman and a great-grandnephew of John C. Calhoun, Graves watched nervously as the black press launched a "Double V" campaign—victory over fascism abroad and racial discrimination at home—in the months following Pearl Harbor. Before the war, Graves considered himself a "southern liberal." He championed education and economic development as a formula for easing racial tensions. He denounced bigoted demagoguery for poisoning the politics of his native region. But during the war, Graves discovered the limits of his tolerance.[1]

Civil rights activists exploited the wartime emergency, Graves complained, with "the most intensive campaign ever launched against any and every differential, minor or major, between white man and black." Yet even as African Americans entered World War II determined to topple Jim Crow, Graves warned that white southerners would not abandon the racial status quo without a fight. Gloomily predicting a "domestic war" over segregation, Graves lamented the untimely return of "the race issue." He had thought the matter settled.[2]

For many white southerners of Graves's generation, black subordination affirmed a natural order. Yet, for their fathers, Jim Crow marked the culmination of a regional white supremacy campaign. During the final decade of the nineteenth century, white counterrevolutionaries overthrew the remaining biracial state governments in the South and inaugurated the Jim Crow era with a barrage of discriminatory legislation. Viewing the racial turmoil of the 1940s through the lens of this earlier struggle, an aging architect of the white supremacy campaign shared Graves's apprehension. Eighty years old in 1942, North Carolina newspaperman Josephus Daniels applauded Graves's vilification of wartime agitators and predicted greater trouble ahead. Yet unlike Graves, Daniels knew firsthand that the race question had never been settled for good.

Writing to Graves in 1942, Daniels recounted a confidential exchange with incoming governor Charles Brantley Aycock in the wake of North Carolina's bloody white supremacy campaign. After overthrowing a biracial fusion coalition of Republicans and Populists in 1898, North Carolina

Democrats had enacted a variety of disfranchisement measures. "When Governor Aycock was elected . . . and we adopted the Grandfather Clause," Daniels confided, "I said to him that I was very glad that we had settled the Negro question for all times." Aycock's answer reverberated four decades later, and Daniels shared it with Graves. "Joe, you are badly mistaken," the governor had replied. "I hope we have settled it for 25 years. Every generation will have the problem on their hands, and they will have to settle it for themselves." The turn-of-the-century white supremacist campaign, one of its key leaders quietly admitted, had achieved only a temporary answer to "a question that will not stay settled."[3]

By the outbreak of World War II, southern conservatives had mobilized to resist racial change once again. Tracing the resurrection of the race question to the rise of the New Deal, the defenders of the segregated status quo lamented the influx of northern black voters into the Democratic Party and the stirrings of a national civil rights movement. Convinced that the New Deal coalition of liberals, labor, and northern blacks threatened "the white democracy of the South," the descendants of the white supremacy generation mounted a new counterrevolution.[4] Responding to outside pressures and black initiative, they attempted once again to "settle" the race question before the federal government settled it for them. As the civil rights movement picked up steam during and after World War II, white southerners launched a preemptive campaign aimed at preserving their embattled social order even as the foundations of legalized discrimination crumbled.

From the rise of the New Deal to the climactic civil rights legislation of the 1960s, a consciously "segregationist" countermovement emerged in tandem with the African American freedom struggle. Rather than a knee-jerk insurgency, white opposition to the civil rights movement was a carefully constructed political project. Massive resistance—the campaign that stymied school desegregation and captivated national attention in the wake of the *Brown* decision—grew out of a longer struggle to defend the color line in the face of domestic turmoil and global war. If there was a "long civil rights movement," there was also a long segregationist movement.[5]

When southern conservatives spoke of defending "white democracy," they referred simultaneously to a racial worldview and a political order. They considered black disfranchisement and segregation essential to maintaining a society governed by and for whites. The survival of this racial order rested upon regional allegiance to the Democratic Party, which had long been the refuge for Jim Crow's architects and guardians. As an outspoken white supremacist argued in the 1940s, "orthodox" southerners traced their political heritage back to Thomas Jefferson's vision of "constitutional government and individual liberty." But they rejected any attempt to update Jefferson's qualified egalitarianism with "the newly evolved theory" that "men of all races have been found to be equally capable in every respect and . . . should be merged without distinction." From its inception, the ideal of a "white democracy" rested upon allegiance to the "White Democracy" envisioned by the party founders.[6]

As the Democrats evolved from a Dixie-dominated "white man's party" to a fountainhead of civil rights bills, southern conservatives struggled to maintain racial unity and regional power. With the rise of the New Deal, these southerners first confronted a nationally viable civil rights campaign and an increasingly pivotal black electorate. From the moment that African Americans entered Roosevelt's New Deal coalition, white supremacists warned of dire consequences down the road. Reeling from a 1936 Democratic National Convention that featured unprecedented black participation and a successful attempt to limit southern veto power over presidential nominations, a South Carolina newspaperman anticipated "increasing embarrassment in regard to the negro." While Roosevelt did little to directly challenge Jim Crow, some southern whites warned that federal expansion and liberal social programs would erode white supremacy. From the end of the president's first term through the outbreak of war, Jim Crow's defenders increasingly linked "Rooseveltianism" to racial revolution.[7]

After the Japanese attack on Pearl Harbor, white supremacists attempted to align their cause with the war effort. Contrasting Axis totalitarianism with white democracy, Jim Crow's defenders likened federally mandated racial reform to a Nazi invasion. Attempting to shape the war's meaning to their advantage, racial conservatives responded to wartime egalitarianism with a patriotic affirmation of the southern status quo. Faced with federal fair employment initiatives and attacks on southern disfranchisement tactics, southern conservatives defined Americanism in their own terms. In 1942, the Mississippi chairman of Fight for Freedom, Inc., a national patriotic association, argued that wartime turmoil offered an opportunity to stand up for "white supremacy, strict interpretation of the Constitution, and freedom in our domestic affairs." Even as African Americans fought for freedom at home and abroad, their southern adversaries deployed a segregationist vision of Double Victory.[8]

Thus, as civil rights activists attacked racial discrimination as a social evil and diplomatic liability, a "segregationist" identity emerged among their adversaries. The volatile postwar transition accelerated this trend, and many defenders of the segregated status quo foreswore militant white supremacy for a refined rationale for racial separation. The black-belt elites and right-wing industrialists who had spearheaded white resistance in the 1930s and 1940s contended with a business-minded ruling class. A new breed of southern leadership shed the hard-line rhetoric of white domination for a refined language of states' rights and racial integrity.[9] Yet the tension between militancy and moderation persisted as a diverse coalition fought to save segregation while securing the South's share of postwar prosperity.

Segregationists entered the 1950s armed with a well-honed rhetoric of responsible resistance. Deep South governors preempted a looming school-desegregation mandate with reformist schemes and extremist threats. Even as they spent millions of dollars to "equalize" black schools, veteran foes of civil rights such as governors James Byrnes of South Carolina and Herman Talmadge of Georgia threatened to abolish public education in the event of a desegregation order. In the wake of the *Brown* decision, segregationists could not resolve the tension between radicalism and respectability. Like equalization before it, massive resistance suffered from longstanding tensions that its architects never fully resolved.[10]

As the civil rights movement captured national attention and legislative victories in the late 1950s and 1960s, segregationists struggled to maintain unity and direction. The legislative climax of this struggle—the Civil Rights Act of 1964 and the Voting Rights Act of 1965—dramatized the intertwined fears of social equality and political parity that had fueled white opposition for three decades. As their ability to bottle up civil rights legislation and restrict black voter registration slipped away, so too did their shaky rationale for white political unity. The segregationist response to civil rights reveals how profoundly southern conservatives disagreed about their political future.[11]

By providing a longer timeline of white opposition to the civil rights movement, this study downplays the *Brown* decision as an anchor date for southern resistance. The roots of this opposition movement lay not only in the shallow soil and emotionally volatile politics of school desegregation. They pushed more deeply into the two preceding decades.[12] If some white southerners clung to myths of settled questions and contented African Americans during this era, many abandoned those fantasies years before National Guard troops and northern volunteers arrived.[13] Extending the timeline of segregationist opposition contextualizes African American initiative by showing that the civil rights campaigns of the 1930s and 1940s did more than break ground and sow seeds for the struggle ahead. These pioneering efforts also provoked a white response, one more preemptive and multifaceted than current scholarship conveys.[14]

Historians have not ignored the precedents for segregationist resistance in the volatile racial battles of the New Deal era. Recent studies have shown how powerful southern elites used their disproportionate influence on Capitol Hill to stymie civil rights legislation from the New Deal onward.[15] Other scholars have chronicled the rightward drift of southern politics during the 1940s, arguing that wartime civil rights controversies forced many southerners to privilege racial concerns above all else.[16] The decade's most substantial expression of organized southern opposition to civil rights, the Dixiecrat revolt, is by far the most studied. Disillusioned by Truman's unprecedented civil rights program, Deep South diehards bolted the Democratic Party in 1948 and set an important precedent for regional protest politics.[17] Yet the Dixiecrat movement was only one avenue for southern racial conservatives who differed fiercely over the surest strategy for preserving segregation. Placed alongside other attempts to stave off racial reform and reassert regional clout, the Dixiecrats' failure to unite the South in defense of white supremacy underscores the complexity and contingency of southern racial politics. At the same time, the movement's vision of a national, racially motivated reawakening of the Right profoundly influenced civil rights opponents in future decades.[18]

Although southern segregationists pushed racial politics rightward from the New Deal to the rise of massive resistance, scholars of "the generation before the civil rights movement" have paid more attention to the minority of white southerners who pushed back. These accounts contend that the New Deal era represented a window of opportunity for racial and economic justice before red-baiting and racial reaction slammed it shut.[19] By looking beyond massive resistance to a longer campaign against the civil rights movement, this study questions how large that window was. More important, a longer view of white opposition to racial change puts the courage and audacity of these pioneers in sharper relief. In their struggles to change the South, interracial activists faced a committed segregationist majority that envisioned a very different future. Rather than a sleeping giant awakened by the Soviet Union and the Supreme Court, conservative opposition represented a premeditated and complex countermovement that hindered racially progressive ventures from the New Deal onward.

Despite pioneering scholarship on southern racial politics before *Brown*, the era is usually presented as prologue in recent work on southern whites and civil rights. By connecting the slow but steady demise of Jim Crow to the story of those who fought to save it, this study carves out a new periodization that complicates the linear narrative of scholarship that dates organized segregationist opposition from the 1950s. Some of the most perceptive new work on southern whites and civil rights suggests that segregationists adapted strategically and successfully to the world wrought by the civil rights movement. By toning down the racial rhetoric of their predecessors, the opponents of black advancement reasserted their influence in national politics while retaining their power and privilege back home. Moving beyond caricatures and easy generalizations, this new scholarship challenges historians to examine what southern whites stood for as well as what they stood against.[20]

A longer view of resistance politics reveals more fully the uneven evolution of southern white opposition. Rather than a steady progression from racial militancy to respectability, the white countermovement of the 1950s and 1960s inherited a mixed legacy from earlier decades. During the years immediately preceding and following the *Brown* decision, segregationists shifted emphasis and refined strategy but also clung to bedrock beliefs about race and democracy. The politics of "strategic accommodation" and coded conservatism that outlasted segregationist militancy represented more than a response to, or refinement of, massive resistance. Likewise, the tension between radicalism and restraint did not spring directly from *Brown*. It reached back further, intensifying with the reemergence of the race question on the national stage during the New Deal era.[21]

By linking the "early" history of white opposition to the upsurge in segregationist activity after *Brown*, this account also complicates the dichotomy between elite resistance in the New Deal era and grassroots rebellion in the civil rights years. Neither portrayal fully captures the complexity of white opposition politics nor offers a satisfactory explanation for the emergence and unraveling of massive resistance. From Georgia governor Eugene Talmadge's race-baiting "Grass Roots Convention" of 1935 to the invocation of "grassroots" credibility by the segregationist Citizens' Councils two decades later, the defenders of the racial status quo claimed the common man's allegiance. The complicated interaction between political leaders, economic elites, and everyday white southerners renders either a "top-down" or "bottom-up" characterization of segregationist opposition insufficient. Meshing the more familiar stories of political campaigns and legislative maneuvering with foot soldiers' efforts to forestall racial change and rally their neighbors, the chapters that follow reveal that southern elites were not the only shapers of the segregationist movement.[22]

Rather than a backlash against the unthinkable, the segregationist movement was a coordinated revolt against the foreseeable. A longer view of massive resistance denaturalizes white opposition to civil rights by broadening the story beyond the volatile politics of school desegregation. White opposition to racial reform did not spring spontaneously from some innate repulsion to the idea of black boys sitting beside white girls in school. Examining massive resistance from both ends reveals that opposition to school desegregation was neither an irrational outburst nor a predetermined last stand. A fuller picture of white opposition to civil rights in the tumultuous decades preceding the *Brown* decision expands our view beyond the legal and constitutional arguments of segregationists to their longstanding anxieties over black civic equality, racial egalitarianism, and the federal government's role in promoting both.[23]

The popular depiction of massive resistance as a prairie-fire rebellion sparked by backstabbing federal judges is in part a creation of the segregationists themselves. Portraying their movement as a patriotic crusade against tyrannical government, segregationists deployed a compelling rhetoric of reflexive defiance. "To resist," as Mississippi senator James Eastland warned in the wake of the *Brown* decision, "is the only answer I know."[24] Drawing on a mythology of Yankee persecution, Jim Crow's defenders invoked the resilient image of the embattled and long-suffering South. In the process, they obscured their years of struggling and strategizing in an attempt to recast their movement as a spontaneous, even instinctive, racial uprising.

While a broader regional coalition rallied to save Jim Crow, the Deep South clung most fiercely to the tenets and tactics of white democracy. Despite important differences, the swath of southern states from South Carolina to Louisiana retained proportionally large black populations and disproportionately powerful conservative coalitions. In each state, the defense of segregation was inseparable from the maintenance of a political order and a racialized labor system. South Carolina, Mississippi, and Georgia—the three states that historian Numan Bartley identified as "the original hard core of resistance"—figure prominently in this regional account of the segregationist movement.[25] In each state, the convulsions of the New Deal and World War II forced a showdown between militant white supremacists and pragmatic segregationists. What emerged in each state was a conservative regime that balanced postwar progress with racial retrenchment. Despite significant differences in state-level politics, the postwar period witnessed an increasingly coordinated effort to defend the racial status quo from internal and external threats. Apologists and activists from a broader swath of southern states, particularly Alabama, Louisiana, and Virginia, attempted to promote a regional identity and present a united front for the sake of saving segregation.

Focusing on particular states within a subregion of the South is an imperfect compromise between a local case study and an exhaustive regional analysis. Yet the chapters that follow reveal important continuities in southern racial politics even as each state's unique experience highlights important themes. Mississippi's reputation as the last bastion of white supremacy is measured against its attempts to tamp down its extremist image and act preemptively to stave off racial reform. In South Carolina, refined forms of segregationist resistance proceeded apace with the relatively early emergence of a viable two-party system. Despite the moderating effects of urbanization, a loyalist Democratic establishment, and a rapidly growing black electorate, Georgia remained a hotbed of segregationist resistance from the New Deal to the 1960s. By interspersing the evolution of racial politics in these states with the emergence of a regional countermovement, this study highlights how Deep South segregationists connected their local civil rights struggles to national politics. Even as the legal foundations of their racial order crumbled around them, Jim Crow's defenders clung to white democracy as the nation's last best hope.

AGITATING FALSELY THE
RACE PROBLEM

1

On 24 October 1932, over 200,000 onlookers choked Atlanta's streets. They hoped to catch a glimpse of their next president. Franklin Delano Roosevelt, just two weeks shy of a landslide victory over sitting president Herbert Hoover, waved at the surging crowd from the back seat of a convertible. The New York governor's visit to Atlanta, according to a local newsman, had attracted "the greatest multitude ever assembled below the Mason and Dixon line." National guardsman scheduled to march in the procession were pressed into service to bolster the unprecedented yet overwhelmed police detail. The huge crowds forced parade planners to cancel a stop at the Henry Grady monument, where Roosevelt's daughter was to lay a wreath at the feet of the "Spokesman of the New South."[1]

Southern dignitaries and everyday folks converged on Atlanta to cheer on Georgia's "adopted son." Indeed, Roosevelt's connections to the state and his affections for the South ran deep. Since the 1920s, Roosevelt had spent a considerable portion of his life in the same Georgia spa village where John C. Calhoun had convalesced a century before. Roosevelt's time at his Warm Springs retreat helped him to recuperate from polio and strengthen his southern ties. Georgia politicians and journalists celebrated the presidential hopeful as one of their own. The *Atlanta Constitution*, which claimed to be the first major newspaper to endorse Roosevelt, cheered the ascent of a part-time "Georgia Farmer" to the presidency.[2]

Elected officials from across the South descended upon Atlanta for Roosevelt's visit. Governors and senators headed delegations from Mississippi, Alabama, Florida, Tennessee, and the Carolinas. Roosevelt's popularity and the urgency of the economic crisis temporarily overwhelmed the rivalries and factions of southern politics. Every delegation, reported one correspondent, "brought to [Roosevelt] assertions that their States were solidly behind him." At the postparade rally, enthusiastic Georgians and their out-of-state guests frequently interrupted Roosevelt's speech "with ringing rebel yells."[3]

Roosevelt was not the only "Georgian" on the rise in 1932. Riding with him in the parade was sitting governor and senator-elect Richard Russell. During his 1930 gubernatorial campaign, Russell promised a departure from "personal and factional politics" and a program of "conservative progress."[4] Russell's reputation for honest and efficient government earned him Georgia votes and national clout. Once in Washington, Roosevelt would rely on southerners like Russell to rally behind him.

Eugene Talmadge, Georgia's governor-elect, trailed Russell and Roosevelt in the parade. Realizing that he stood no chance against Russell in a Senate race, the three-term state agriculture commissioner had set his sights on the governor's mansion. Talmadge had earned the loyalty of Georgia farmers through a skillful mix of policy and propaganda. A master of the county-unit system, which inflated the power of rural Georgia in statewide elections, Talmadge had built a formidable political machine by 1932. It would continue to grow.

Like Russell, Talmadge lined up behind Roosevelt. After riding in the Atlanta parade and sitting beside the honored guest at a luncheon, the governor-elect attended a fundraiser sponsored by the city's Roosevelt Business and Professional League. Climbing atop a 400-pound cotton bale, the celebrity auctioneer "sold" the donated crop to raise money for the homestretch of the presidential race.[5]

If any cracks existed in the southern wall of support for Roosevelt, they were difficult to discern in the early 1930s. "I don't imagine you could have found a white man in Georgia," Talmadge's son Herman recalled years later, "that would have admitted publicly in '32 that he was against Roosevelt."[6] Yet, just three years later, Herman's father emerged as the president's most notorious southern critic. Even in 1935, Eugene Talmadge risked political ostracism for breaking with Roosevelt. When he lashed out at the president and his Georgia allies with provocative racial warnings, Talmadge connected the rise of the New Deal to the decline of Jim Crow. While few prominent southern politicians were ready to take that leap with him, Talmadge and other militant white supremacists foreshadowed a broader confrontation between southern racial conservatives and the national Democratic Party. By 1936, even as Roosevelt cruised into his second term, serious divisions arose among white southerners over the New Deal and its implications for the region. The scattered racial confrontations of the New Deal years convinced more than a few white southerners that they would have to fight to maintain their racially exclusive brand of democracy.

Although some white southerners recognized the threat that the New Deal posed to the color line, those who voiced their fears risked ridicule. The southern political establishment initially dismissed these warnings as irresponsible rabble rousing. Nevertheless, the line separating demagoguery from respectable white supremacy blurred as a burgeoning civil rights movement forced the white South to ponder the New Deal's racial implications. Confrontations over the color line challenged the notion that white supremacy was a settled issue rather than a topic for public discussion. In a society where most whites regarded legalized segregation and systematic discrimination as affirmation of a divinely ordained social order, subjecting white supremacy to political debate denaturalized Jim Crow. Diehards faced an uphill battle convincing their fellow southerners that the New Deal endangered white supremacy, but their early battles forged the way for future defenders of the segregated status quo.

While demagogues such as Talmadge captured the most attention during the 1930s, they were not the first southerners to question the racial implications of the New Deal. Less than a year into Roosevelt's first term, conservative businessmen founded the Southern States Industrial Council (SSIC). President John Edgerton, a Tennessee mill owner and former president of the National Association of Manufacturers, argued that Roosevelt's recovery program undermined the southern labor system. By attempting to standardize wages and working conditions with a litany of codes and regulations, the National Recovery Administration (NRA) destabilized a racialized labor ladder that assigned southern blacks to the lowest rungs. "Colored labor has always been paid less than whites," declared an Alabama industrialist, "and for good reason."[7]

Southern industrialists cited southern blacks' inefficiency and "subnormal capabilities" as rationale for their discriminatory wage scale, but they prized the competitive advantage that cheap black labor provided. In their conservative vision of progress, a segregated, low-wage labor system provided the South a path to modernization and prosperity. In addition, as John Edgerton argued, discriminatory wage rates and segregated workplaces would "preserve labor's racial purity." Southern leaders successfully pressured the Roosevelt administration to accept a lower wage scale for southern industry and to avoid any public demands for equal pay for black workers. However, as NRA codes and regulations led to shorter hours and better wages for southern workers of both races, their employers caught a glimpse of the federal government's growing reach.[8]

Even if their early protests did little to diminish popular support for Roosevelt, southern industrialists mobilized to undercut the disruptive potential of New Deal regulations and reforms. The president, who realized that conservative southern Democrats could derail his reform agenda, bartered away the more aggressive provisions of his New Deal programs. Meanwhile, southern politicians made sure that their constituents reaped the benefits of the New Deal's agricultural subsidies, relief programs, and rural development initiatives. Confident that they could keep the money flowing without undermining the racial status quo, the southern political establishment maintained an overwhelmingly united front during Roosevelt's first term.

At first, Eugene Talmadge seemed the exception that proved this political rule. The Georgia governor had little patience for the establishment, whether in Atlanta or Washington. Unlike Senator Richard Russell, whose conservative vision of regional modernization meshed with Roosevelt's pragmatic approach to recovery and reform, Talmadge traded in a politics of localism and resentment. If Russell represented "conservative progress," then Talmadge perfected his own brand of reactionary populism.[9] Having built a powerful base among the farmers and courthouse cliques of rural Georgia, Talmadge lashed out at urban elites, organized labor, and distant bureaucracies. He overrode the legislature with executive orders, replaced uncooperative state officials, and even declared martial law to impose his will. Critics called him a dictator and a demagogue, but the governor cruised into a second term in 1934 with the greatest landslide in Georgia history.[10]

Like most southern politicians of his day, Talmadge initially lined up behind Roosevelt. Yet, almost immediately after his resounding reelection in late 1934, the governor abandoned his campaign slogan of "Roosevelt and Talmadge" and launched an all-out attack on the New Deal. "The only way to have an honest government is to keep it poor," he declared. "You can't help the people by giving them something. You weaken their soul and their heart, and dry up their muscles."[11] After informing his state legislators that there would be no more New Deal initiatives passed in Georgia, Talmadge launched a national crusade against the Roosevelt administration. With the assassination of Louisiana governor Huey Long that same year, Talmadge took his place as the most notorious southern critic of the Roosevelt administration. But unlike Long, Talmadge attacked from the right and aimed below the belt. Calling the president a "radical in the extreme form," Talmadge painted Roosevelt as a pampered elitist and even mocked his physical handicap. "The next President who goes into the White House will be a man who knows what is to work in the sun fourteen hours a day," declared Talmadge. "That man will be able to walk a two-by-four plank, too."[12] A few weeks later, the governor traveled to Washington to kick off an anti–New Deal speaking tour.

Talmadge and many of his critics credited this new insurgency to the governor's loyal "wool-hat" followers. Indeed, the governor's populist standing rested on his credibility among rural Georgians. But Talmadge's revolt also caught the attention of right-wing industrialists who feared the New Deal's potential to disrupt the region's racialized capitalism. A smattering of southern businessmen quietly bankrolled Talmadge's crusade against the president. Even a few northern millionaires, eager to nurture an anti-Roosevelt revolt in the solidly Democratic South, sent money to the Georgia governor. Their most ambitious collaboration, the National Grass Roots Convention, convened in Macon, Georgia, on 29 January 1936. Over 3,000 pro-Talmadge backers, mostly Georgia farmers, gave the elite production a populist feel. The governor hyped the event as the launching pad for a nationwide campaign to block Roosevelt's renomination, and the convention attracted a couple hundred diehards from other states. But the meeting was hardly national.[13]

Talmadge's misnamed convention dramatized the racial anxieties of the South's most vocal New Deal opponents. When delegates filed into the Macon auditorium, they discovered a copy of the Talmadge-published *Georgia Woman's World* in each seat. On the tabloid's front page, a convention organizer bragged, was "a picture of Mrs. Roosevelt going to some nigger meeting, with two escorts, niggers, on each arm." In the Roosevelt White House, the paper reported, blacks worked as appointed advisers, attended banquets, and slept in guest bedrooms. With a gigantic Confederate battle flag draped behind him, Texas lumberman and oil tycoon John Henry Kirby departed from his prepared remarks to highlight the tabloid's revelations concerning the president's "friendly attitude towards Negroes." Aging novelist Thomas Dixon lashed out at the NAACP, while multiple speakers stressed Roosevelt's hostility toward "states' rights."[14]

As his national crusade lost momentum, Talmadge took aim at his state's most prominent New Dealer. In 1932, Richard Russell's successful Senate bid had cleared Talmadge's path to the governor's office. By 1936, Richard Russell had emerged as one of Roosevelt's most loyal southern supporters and most influential regional power brokers. Even as insurgents back home questioned administration policies, Russell remained firm in his support for the New Deal. Talmadge's inability to turn Georgians against the president confirmed the political wisdom of Russell's stance. Nevertheless, Talmadge continued to portray the junior senator as a "rubber stamp" for federal programs and policies that would ultimately unleash a social revolution in Georgia and across Dixie. Talmadge allies charged early and often that the New Deal imported "social equality" to Georgia, and they sought to link Senator Russell to this conspiracy at every turn. White supremacy's survival, Talmadge warned, was at stake.[15]

In challenging Russell's 1936 Senate bid, Talmadge stepped up his racially charged attacks on the New Deal. Through his self-promoting weekly, the *Statesman*, and the inflammatory *Georgia Woman's World*, the governor cataloged the racial apostasies of the Roosevelt administration. Both tabloids included regular reports of blacks dining at the White House, consorting with administration officials, and infiltrating Georgia under the auspices of New Deal agencies. The *Woman's World* was particularly preoccupied with interracial sexuality, from its pictures of Eleanor Roosevelt mingling with black men to its defense of lynching. Most of the editors and contributors to the *Georgia Woman's World* claimed membership in the Women's National Association for the Preservation of the White Race (APWR), founded in the early 1930s to counter a homegrown campaign against lynching. As the group's president, Mrs. J. E. Andrews, informed the Association of Southern Women for the Prevention of Lynching (ASWPL) in 1932, "an organization of white mothers has arisen to defend our girls, both against negro men and you." The growing antilynching movement, the *Woman's World* warned, encouraged the "permissive ravishment" of white mothers and daughters.[16]

By 1936, the Talmadge-backed women's group had broadened its agenda. Accusing the Roosevelt administration of promoting "social equality," these militant women meshed their white supremacist critique of the New Deal with explicit appeals for white mothers to resist racial change. On one occasion, the group's president burst into an interracial student conference held at Atlanta's Gammon Theological Seminary to show white Georgians that "our college girls sat elbow to elbow with Negro men." When seminary president Willis King requested that Andrews and her entourage of reporters leave, she slapped the distinguished black clergyman across the face.[17]

The Talmadge tabloids publicized real and imagined clashes between white Georgians and racial subversives. The governor attempted to trap Senator Russell in his rumor web by spreading lurid allegations. In one instance, Talmadge sent Russell testimony from "a Mrs. Holmes," who described her experience working for a Works Progress Administration (WPA) project in Atlanta. According to the sensational account, New Deal officials had forced this "refined and educated" white woman to work on a black college campus. When she and her white counterparts arrived at Morris Brown College, they discovered phrases such as "all white women are sons of bitches" scribbled on the sidewalks. Inside, they found "perfectly and unspeakably horrible" dormitory conditions, from bedbugs to filthy toilets. When one woman started to walk down the street to use a filling station restroom, the report alleged, "the one in charge said you can use the negro toilet here or not go at all." Rather than establish separate break times for the white and black workers, the program's nonsouthern administrators forced the women to intermingle as they exited adjacent buildings. While the WPA project provided relief work, the report concluded, "the main idea is to break the will of our people and force social equality with the negro."[18]

Russell resented the indirect attacks on his commitment to the color line. Dutifully informing Talmadge that he would demand yet another investigation, Russell noted that none of the governor's previous complaints had turned up any damning evidence. He informed Talmadge that he had recruited his own "informants" to gather "concrete illustrations and facts to support the charge of a tendency toward social equality with the negro" in Georgia New Deal programs. Instead Russell found ample proof that the governor fabricated rumors for political gain. "To my amazement," Russell chided Talmadge, "I found that practically every one of my informants relied upon the same individual for their evidence, and strange as it may be, this individual was not on relief and had no actual knowledge of the facts himself, though he seemed to spend quite a bit of his time going around alarming others about efforts to foster social equality in Georgia."[19] Talmadge made no reply.

Such repudiations notwithstanding, the racial reality lay somewhere between Talmadge's lurid rumors and Russell's unflappable faith in the segregated status quo. Talmadge had harbored a grudge against alphabet agencies ever since Harry Hopkins, head of the Federal Emergency Relief Administration (FERA), federalized Georgia's New Deal programs in early 1935. Tired of watching Talmadge obstruct costly relief programs and dole out patronage posts, Hopkins stripped him of administrative control and put state welfare director Gay Shepperson in charge. While Shepperson routinely denied Talmadge's accusations and fended off Russell's obligatory inquiries, she also defied traditional gender and racial customs by employing mostly women, white and black, to administer relief programs. Georgia WPA officials did not force white women to use black restrooms, but they routinely addressed black clients as "Mr.," "Mrs.," and "Miss" and occasionally held interracial staff meetings.[20] While this disregard for Jim Crow orthodoxy fell far short of the aggressive egalitarianism described by Talmadge, it also belied Russell's cool denials of racial change.

Russell roundly denounced Talmadge's attempts to inject race into their political rivalry. "Any southern white man worth a pinch of salt would give his all to maintain white supremacy," Russell argued, "and it is a disgrace that some should constantly seek to drag the negro issue into our primaries, where as a matter of fact they do not in any way participate and cannot." Russell made clear his commitment to Jim Crow. "As one who was born and reared in the atmosphere of the Old South," he wrote to Talmadge, "I am willing to go as far and make as great a sacrifice to preserve and insure white supremacy in the social, economic, and political life of our state as any man who lives within her borders." According to Russell, real white men stood united in their opposition to social and political equality, and the respectable ones knew the difference between true threat and political ploy. "Should some real menace from the negro present itself," Russell assured a political supporter, "I still believe that the white manhood of not only Georgia, but the entire South, would rise en masse immediately and again assert itself."[21] While Talmadge traded in fear, Russell rested his political fortunes on confidence in the racial status quo.

Despite Russell's initial avoidance of the race issue, Talmadge kept up his attacks as the primary campaign heated up. During the summer, Talmadge forces circulated reports that the Works Progress Administration had assigned a black instructor to a local canning program. While the senator responded with his customary protest letter to the local WPA office, Talmadge blasted "Rubber Stamp" Russell for welcoming subversive New Deal programs into his state. "Would the Senator stand for a black negro wench coming into his mother's home to dictate to her how she should run her domestic establishment?" the *Georgia Woman's World* taunted. "No he wouldn't, but he would and did permit this to happen to a lot of unfortunate relief workers in Fulton County." By September 1936, the warnings had escalated. The *Georgia Woman's World* claimed that Russell had "done more to cause racial equality in the State of Georgia than any man who has ever been in the United States Congress from Georgia." Charging that "Russell prefers that the Negro race be predominant," the Talmadge tabloid warned: "If we send him back to the Senate we may expect to see the homes of Southern white people taken from them and turned over to the blacks."[22]

Russell deplored Talmadge's "despicable" racial appeals. "He does what every candidate who is about to be beaten does," Russell declared: "He comes in crying nigger." Although he maintained a restrained and genteel public stance, Russell privately prepared to counter Talmadge blow by blow. In an unused speech draft entitled "The Negro Question," Russell outlined his white supremacist record. He touted the passage of the 1927 "Racial Purity Law" during his tenure as Georgia Speaker of the House. Talmadge, Russell claimed, was "the only white man in the confines of the State of Georgia who raised his voice against this measure." Russell also recalled an instance when Governor Talmadge had ordered National Guard troops "to protect a black brute guilty of an unmentionable crime" even as Gainesville residents suffered from the ravages of a fierce storm.[23] That Russell needed no such speech to defeat Talmadge lent credence to his claim that specious racial appeals distracted Georgians from more pressing issues. But he kept the speech on file, just in case.

Russell deflected Talmadge's attacks with unflappable confidence, but privately he harbored his own racial concerns. In Russell's mind, race-baiters posed as great a threat to the segregated status quo as civil rights activists. Both groups inflamed race relations and made challenges to white supremacy more likely. "In my opinion," Russell wrote in his unused "Negro Question" speech, "the action of the Governor in financing and circulating a scurrilous sheet called the 'Georgia Woman's World' over the State, filled with slimy and obscene matter, has done more to foster an arrogant spirit in the benighted negroes of Georgia than every act of every public official I have ever known of in Georgia since Carpet Bag Days."[24] Irresponsible rabble-rousing, rather than federal aid, inspired black insurgency.

No longer confined to race-baiting demagogues and wealthy industrialists, racial anxieties animated political rivalries across the South. Other New Deal critics followed Talmadge's example and attempted to race-bait Roosevelt's southern allies. In South Carolina, junior senator James F. Byrnes fended off two challengers who argued that he was too friendly with the Roosevelts. Thomas Stoney, a former mayor of Charleston, and William Harlee, a retired Marine colonel, both contended that Byrnes's loyalty to the New Deal jeopardized white supremacy. When Roosevelt invited a black minister to offer the opening invocation at the 1936 Democratic convention in Philadelphia, South Carolina senior senator Ellison "Cotton Ed" Smith furnished Byrnes's opponents with more ammunition.

Smith, who had served in the Senate since 1909, stormed out of the convention hall as the black minister took the podium. "Get outa my way," he fumed. "This mongrel meeting ain't no place for a white man!"[25]

After Smith's notorious "walk," Byrnes's opponents criticized the junior senator for not following his colleague out of the convention hall. They circulated postcards that blasted the "Roosevelt-Nigger Democratic Party" and urged South Carolinians to "kick Roosevelt and Byrnes out of power forever." These cards warned that a vote for Byrnes would lead to "negroes rubbing shoulders" with white women in buses, trains, theaters, and churches. "From this," they warned, "it will only be a step when negroes will be allowed to propose wedlock to white girls."[26]

Even as he publicly condemned the racial attacks, Byrnes privately conceded that the hardliners had a point. "F. D. R. has done more for the negroes than all other Presidents," he admitted, but only because the rising tide of federal aid lifted all boats. On the campaign trail, Byrnes urged voters to ignore the racial threats. "I have no respect for the man who, for political gain, will seek to arouse the prejudices of the people," he declared to a Charleston crowd. In South Carolina, as in Georgia, the strategy of brushing aside such attacks proved smashingly successful. On primary day, Byrnes carried all but one precinct in the state. Back in Georgia, Russell received nearly twice as many votes as Talmadge.[27]

Many contemporary observers interpreted the elections in Georgia and South Carolina as a triumph for respectable politicking and a repudiation of demagoguery. But both campaigns also portended more racial controversy ahead. Southern loyalty to the New Deal remained strong, but it weakened as conservatives in the region pondered the racial consequences of New Deal policies and programs. The Byrnes campaign painted its challengers as lowdown demagogues, but some powerful South Carolinians shared the growing fear that the New Deal spelled trouble for the racial status quo. William Watts Ball, the unapologetically aristocratic editor of the *Charleston News and Courier*, quietly coached Thomas Stoney in his challenge to Byrnes's reelection. While Ball stopped short of any public endorsement, he privately warned that Byrnes's "Rooseveltianism" would eventually "ruin the country." Even as Byrnes's opponents circulated lurid racial rumors, Ball revealed broader concerns about black political influence. Months before Roosevelt's landslide reelection in 1936, Ball warned, "the able and astute Negro politicians of the northern cities have captured both national parties." He pointed to attempts by both Democrats and Republicans to reach out to the growing and increasingly pivotal black vote

After incumbent senator Richard Russell defeated Eugene Talmadge in the 1936 primary, mock graves such as this one in Cherokee County prematurely celebrated the demise of the race-baiting Georgia governor. (Richard B. Russell Papers, Richard B. Russell Library for Political Research and Studies, University of Georgia, Athens, Ga.)

in cities such as Philadelphia and Chicago. Over a decade before the Dixiecrat revolt of 1948, Ball considered the situation dire enough to ponder a massive political defection. "The question," Ball concluded, "is whether we Southerners shall accept the negro in politics, let him vote, or form an independent Southern white man's party."[28]

But Ball's dreams of political defection, like Talmadge's predictions of racial revolution, failed to resonate in the solidly Democratic South. Neither race-baiting populists nor right-wing industrialists significantly weakened regional support for Roosevelt. For most white southerners, the New Deal's tangible benefits temporarily drowned out provocative racial warnings. In August 1936, a handful of southern lawyers and businessmen joined other disaffected "Jeffersonian Democrats" in Detroit. But while the southerners concurred with other delegates that Roosevelt's policies were "anti-Democratic and anti-American," they blocked a proposal to endorse the Republican ticket. Jeffersonian Democrats organized branches across the South over the next couple months, a southern journalist reported, "but without any appreciable chance that they can seriously affect the outcome in November." Despite scattered signs of "Democratic Doubt" during the 1936 campaign, Richmond newspaperman Virginius Dabney concluded, "the Roosevelt administration is far out in front in Dixie."[29]

The provocative 1936 primaries ultimately mattered less to southern conservatives than subtle shifts in party politics. While Talmadge tabloids fanned the flames of racial resentment, more credible sources cited political changes that had monumental implications for the southern status quo. If the racially charged Senate contests in Georgia and South Carolina unsettled a few, the presence of African Americans in national Democratic Party politics rattled many more. Southern conservatives interpreted the participation of northern African Americans in the 1936 Democratic National Convention as an ominous concession. The flap over Cotton Ed's "walk" overshadowed more consequential, if less provocative, developments. A black preacher calling the 1936 convention to prayer mattered less than the elimination of the two-thirds rule for nominating candidates. By voting to approve presidential tickets by a simple majority, convention delegates stripped southern Democrats of veto power over party nominees. Faced with unprecedented challenges, southern conservatives lamented the shifting regional and racial character of the party. For those who failed to connect an interracial Democratic Party to the decline of white civilization, Cotton Ed traced a startlingly short path. "The doors of the white man's party have been thrown open to snare the Negro vote in the North," he warned in the wake of the 1936 convention. "Political equality means social equality, and social equality means intermarriage, and that means mongrelizing of the American race."[30]

More temperate southern observers stopped short of forecasting white extinction, but they concurred that the Democratic Party's unprecedented interest in black votes portended trouble ahead. Three days after Roosevelt's resounding reelection, Birmingham columnist John Temple Graves warned that "the shift of the Negro to Democratic ranks" could shake southern white devotion to the party of the Solid South. Declaring the black vote "a prize to be sought in every election," Graves predicted, "the future of the Democratic party here may depend upon what it is willing to pay for this prize." If the price was federal intervention in racial matters, Graves warned, the Democratic Party would forfeit its most loyal base. "The South has remained politically solid largely because the Democratic party has been an asylum for its sensibilities on the Negro question,"

Graves explained. If the national party could no longer tolerate Jim Crow, it would remove the "sole reason" for white southern loyalty.[31]

The 1936 election provided ominous statistics for apprehensive southerners. The economic appeal of the New Deal had shaken African Americans' historical loyalty to the party of Lincoln. As southern migrants swelled the ranks of the northern black electorate, Democratic politicians paid greater attention to African American voters. In 1934, black Chicago Democrat Arthur Mitchell defeated black Republican congressman Oscar De Priest with the campaign slogan, "Forward with Roosevelt." The first black Democrat elected to Congress, the Alabama-born Mitchell had been a GOP loyalist as late as 1932. Across the urban North, African Americans made similar defections. Whereas only 25 percent of African Americans had voted for Democrat Al Smith in the 1928 presidential election, 75 percent of black ballots cast in 1936 went for Roosevelt. Conservative southern Democrats did the electoral arithmetic. Some worried openly that a subversive alliance of uppity blacks and slick urban politicians had seized control of their party.[32] After the 1936 election, these anxieties coalesced around the fight over federal antilynching legislation.

By the mid-1930s, the crusade for federal antilynching legislation had emerged as the first civil rights cause with traction on Capitol Hill. Leading the charge was Walter White, a blond-haired, blue-eyed African American whose light skin and remarkable courage allowed him to investigate dozens of lynchings for the NAACP. In 1929, White succeeded James Weldon Johnson as the organization's executive secretary and made the crusade against lynching the NAACP's primary legislative objective. Sympathetic congressmen had introduced antilynching bills since 1922, but the upsurge in lynching during the early 1930s galvanized a formidable coalition of civil rights advocates, national religious organizations, and southern liberals in the Commission on Interracial Cooperation (CIC) and the Association of the Southern Women for the Prevention of Lynching. Despite growing national sympathy and polls showing that a slight majority of southerners favored the legislation, filibustering southern senators stood in the way of a landmark civil rights victory.[33]

Southern politicians' ability to thwart antilynching legislation bolstered their claims that they could fend off federal meddling. Yet the campaign against vigilante violence boosted the credibility of southern diehards who warned that white supremacy was under renewed attack.[34] The South had not faced a similar challenge to home rule since 1890, when Republicans abandoned their attempts to send federal election supervisors south to prevent black disfranchisement. But now the threat emanated from inside the Democratic Party, with northern congressmen and representatives willing to sponsor legislation that would dispatch federal agents to intervene in southern racial matters.

No southern state embodied the contradictions of the lynching debate more vividly than Mississippi. By any measure, the Magnolia State was the lynching capital of the United States. From 1885 to 1925, one in every seven recorded lynchings occurred there. As mob violence declined dramatically after World War I, the proportion of lynchings occurring in the Magnolia State increased. Fifty blacks, roughly 40 percent of all U.S. lynching victims in the 1930s, died at the hands of Mississippi mobs. Despite their failure to stamp out vigilante violence, white Mississippians maintained their right to handle the problem and scoffed at northern congressmen's attempts to police southern lynch mobs. Even after Mississippians committed half of the twenty recorded lynchings in 1936, the *Jackson Daily News* confidently predicted, "Congress will never pass an anti-lynching bill . . . providing a form of Federal jurisdiction." Noting that the nation's lone black congressman, Arthur Mitchell of Chicago, had introduced a revised antilynching bill in the House, editor Frederick Sullens confidently dismissed the campaign as "another one of those time wasting measures."[35]

Just two days after Sullens deemed the Deep South immune from federal intervention, vigilantes undercut his claim that Mississippi had its lynching problem under control. In April 1937, angry whites abducted Roosevelt Townes and "Bootjack" McDaniels from the Montgomery County Courthouse in Winona. Both men stood accused of killing a white merchant in nearby Duck Hill. After their arraignment, a mob of one hundred men seized the prisoners and forced them into a waiting school bus. A second busload of vigilantes and several dozen automobiles followed the lead bus back to the murdered merchant's store. The mob chained both men to trees before torturing them with a blowtorch until they confessed their guilt. After both men admitted to participating in the murder, members of the mob built a brush fire around the alleged triggerman, Roosevelt Townes, and burned him alive. Another vigilante dispatched McDaniels with a single shot to the head.[36]

The Duck Hill lynching grabbed headlines from New York to Nazi Germany. The calculated spectacle harkened back to the turn of the century, when hundreds of onlookers would gather for lynchings on the town square.[37] Mississippi newspapers condemned the killings but gloomily predicted that it would provide new momentum for antilynching legislation on Capitol Hill. The Duck Hill lynching, predicted one editor, "furnishes ammunition that the enemies of the south will not be slow in using." Another newspaperman predicted that the lynching would stoke "the racial and anti-South feeling which always is smouldering in some section of the United States where there is no racial question and where conditions are entirely dissimilar." The Duck Hill lynchings would encourage enemies of the South to "threaten us with the Federal Government, as in Reconstruction days, when they forgot their White Brothers for others."[38]

Seizing on the national reaction to the Duck Hill lynchings, New York Democrat Joseph Gavagan offered a revised antilynching bill. In addition to allowing federal prosecution of lynchers, the proposed legislation would fine or imprison local lawmen who failed to protect prisoners from lynch mobs. The bill also included a provision that would make a county liable for damages if a lynching occurred within its borders. Just three days after the double lynching in Duck Hill, the House overwhelmingly passed the Gavagan bill. In the Senate, however, the companion bill languished for months. When sponsors Robert Wagner and Frederick Van Nuys finally presented the bill in January 1938, southern senators staged the longest filibuster in five decades. For six weeks, Texas senator Tom Connally orchestrated a steady rotation of southern speakers. While one Mississippian celebrated the "blast of old-fashioned southern oratory," it took more than fiery speeches to fill up over 200 hours of filibustering. Louisiana senator Allen Ellender spoke for six days straight, but his central premise could be summed up in a sentence. "We shall at all cost," he vowed, "preserve the white supremacy of America."[39]

The recently reelected senators from Georgia and South Carolina closed ranks with their southern colleagues. Having effectively brushed aside challengers who had raised the racial threat of the New Deal, Russell and Byrnes suddenly sounded quite similar to their critics back home. Echoing the charges of his recent primary opponents, South Carolina's James Byrnes argued that the Democratic Party had sold out loyal southern whites in exchange for northern black votes. "The South may just as well know . . . ," announced Byrnes, "that it has been deserted by the Democrats of the North." Byrnes facetiously suggested that the name of the bill should be changed to "a bill to arouse ill-feeling between the sections, inspire race hatred in the South, and destroy the Democratic Party."[40]

Byrnes vented some of that "race hatred" on Walter White. A constant presence during the antilynching filibuster, the NAACP executive secretary observed the proceedings from the Senate gallery and lobbied majority leader Alben Barkley. Angered by White's presence and perceived influence over the proceedings, Byrnes complained, "Barkley can't do anything without talking to that nigger first."[41] As he concluded his portion of the southern filibuster, Byrnes turned and pointed his finger at White. "For years this man White has worked for this bill," Byrnes fumed. "Now that he has secured the balance of power in so many states, he can order its passage." As he continued the personal attack, Byrnes warned that White had more "demands" yet to make. Byrnes wondered aloud if White would push for "the right to stop at hotels where white persons are entertained" or even "laws providing for the supervision of elections within the states." Foreshadowing the emergence of the modern civil rights movement and a Democratic Party increasingly responsive to its concerns, Byrnes warned that "those who are willing to vote for this bill will acquiesce to his subsequent demands."[42]

Like Byrnes, Russell connected the antilynching fight to a far-sighted civil rights agenda. He had fought off racial agitation from the Right, but now he outlined a more sinister plot emanating from the Left. Just two years after Eugene Talmadge launched a crusade against "Negroes, the New Deal, and . . . Karl Marx," Russell described a strikingly similar alliance. He blamed vote-hungry northern politicians for remaking the party of Jefferson and Jackson into an "Afro-Democratic Party." Reading from a Communist tract, "The Road to Liberation for the Negro People," Russell lumped together black activists, northern liberals, and revolutionary Marxists in a plot to destroy Jim Crow. Echoing Byrnes's predictions of federal intervention in southern elections and challenges to segregation, Russell envisioned "a bill which will strike down the laws . . . which prevent the intermarriage of whites and blacks."[43] Antilynching legislation, he warned, sat atop a slippery slope.

Just over two weeks later, Robert Wagner withdrew his bill. Despite southern senators' defeat of the latest antilynching bill, the recurrent debate over vigilante violence worried the defenders of white supremacy. The antilynching campaign embodied the gathering threat of politically influential black voters and their northern allies. The sponsors of antilynching bills, southern lawmakers readily pointed out, hailed from states such as New York and Illinois with large and growing black populations. At the same time, antilynching legislation raised the threat of federal interference in southern racial matters. While early opponents of the New Deal struggled to convince fellow southern whites that New Deal reforms could disrupt the racial status quo, antilynching legislation clearly threatened white supremacy. Any outside interference in local racial relations, southern lawmakers warned, would only worsen problems. If the federal government could overrule local law enforcement and punish lynchers, civil rights groups would have a precedent for future assaults on the color line.

Despite the resounding defeat of the latest federal antilynching bill, some prescient white southerners predicted that their struggle was far from over. Even as she praised the southern senators for their "splendid defense of white supremacy," an anxious Mississippian warned that greater battles lay ahead. "I believe you men will see," she warned, "that the fight *has just started*." [44]

The fight, of course, had not started with the antilynching battle. But that showdown confirmed fears that the New Deal challenged white supremacy. The majority of white Georgians and South Carolinians had stood by New Dealers such as Russell and Byrnes in 1936, despite the race-baiting tactics of their challengers. At the same time, southern whites faced the sobering reality that Roosevelt could have been reelected that year without a single southern electoral vote. An administration hostile to Jim Crow could use its unprecedented power to overhaul the entire region. Anxious southern conservatives cringed when Roosevelt attempted to pack the federal judiciary with sympathetic judges in 1937. In editorials, resolutions, and political speeches, southern conservatives condemned the court-packing plan on racial grounds. Virginia senator Carter Glass blamed the scheme on "visionary incendiaries" who hoped "to see the reversal of those decisions of the Court that saved the civilization of the South." [45]

Southern conservatives eyed another round of legislation with disdain and looked for allies in their opposition to extending the New Deal's reach. Joining forces with a loose but growing coalition of Republican partisans, conservative businessmen, and rural taxpayers alarmed by the consolidation of power in Washington, conservative southerners melded their defense of white supremacy with a wider assault on the New Deal. After the 1936 election, North Carolina senator Josiah Bailey quietly drafted a "statement of principles" after deliberating with right-wing businessmen and conservative colleagues from both parties. Championing free enterprise, fiscal restraint, and "state rights," the ten-point declaration helped to formalize the bipartisan "conservative coalition" that would hold the balance of power in Congress for several decades. The only southern senator to tout his role in drafting the Conservative Manifesto, Bailey put a defiantly southern spin on his criticism of the New Deal. Keynoting a Southern States Industrial Council banquet in early 1938, Bailey lauded his homeland's "unchangeable character," its "ability to withstand criticism," and its determination "to repel the advances of uplifters." Southern businessmen clapped and crowed as Bailey likened New Dealers to carpetbaggers. "They can't reform us," he boasted, "and they can't reconstruct us." [46]

The mounting southern hostility toward "uplifters" reflected Roosevelt's preoccupation with the region. The president and his closest advisers considered the South crucial to their broader goals. The federal government, New Dealers argued, had to subsidize southern modernization and integrate the region into the national economy. Calling the South "the Nation's number one economic problem," Roosevelt commissioned a study that outlined an ambitious program of regional development. Released in 1938, *The Report on Economic Conditions in the South* promoted what historian David Kennedy has called "a kind of regionally targeted New Deal." [47] But as the Roosevelt administration paid greater attention to the South, the president boosted the credibility of those who had argued all along that the New Deal meant to make over the region. As the New Deal's conservative opposition gained strength, its southern faction increasingly used race to discredit Roosevelt's reform program.

With his legislative agenda stalled, Roosevelt took aim at the southern conservatives who bolstered his formerly puny opposition. Two years after senators Russell and Byrnes cruised to victory on Roosevelt's coattails, the president traveled south to punish their senior colleagues for stalling his regional reform goals. Stopping in Gainesville, Georgia, on his way to his Warm Springs retreat, Roosevelt likened the southern "feudal system" to European fascism. "If you believe in the one," Roosevelt declared, "you lean to the other." As the midterm elections drew nearer, Roosevelt criticized the conservative congressmen who stood in the way of his legislative agenda. After calling out the southern "Copperheads" in one of his fireside chats, Roosevelt headed south to oppose incumbent senators Walter George of Georgia and "Cotton Ed" Smith of South Carolina. [48] At an August rally in rural Georgia, Roosevelt shocked the crowd by declaring that he and George did not "speak the same language." With the veteran senator sitting just a few feet away, Roosevelt endorsed a reluctant young attorney tapped by the New Dealers to unseat George. "Mr. President," the courtly senior senator responded, "I want you to know that I accept the challenge." [49]

A polished and powerful statesman, Walter George was, according to one historian of Georgia politics, "the essence of establishment." But after his confrontation with Roosevelt, George embraced his role as an outsider. By week's end, George was blasting an ominous alliance of labor bosses, Communists, and African Americans in front of raucous crowds. "I wear as a shining emblem the condemnation I have received from James Ford, the Negro Vice-Presidential nominee of the Communist Party," George declared at a Waycross rally. When he finished his speech, the American

Legion band played a rousing rendition of "Dixie." Responding to the senator's racially charged rhetoric, the NAACP accused George of "using Walter White to help scare the white people of Georgia." At a campaign stop in Barnesville, George took a shot at the NAACP secretary and warned audiences that civil rights advocates wanted "to send a Connecticut judge down here . . . to try you on an anti-lynching charge." As a local political insider later remarked, it was "one of the neatest niggah-baiting tricks you ever saw."[50]

In South Carolina, Cotton Ed Smith campaigned largely on his already infamous "Philadelphia Story." He reminded voters that he had walked out of the 1936 Democratic convention to protest black participation. "Senator Smith is a white supremacy Democrat," announced a campaign pamphlet, "his reelection will be a wholesome warning to the East." On election day, several hundred Smith supporters in Orangeburg County donned red shirts as a tribute to the white terrorists who had helped overthrow an interracial state government in 1876. Over four decades later, the new Red Shirts hovered around polling places to intimidate white neighbors whose support for the New Deal threatened another Reconstruction. Or at least that is what Cotton Ed told them. After patrolling several polling places in the Orangeburg area, the new Red Shirts caravanned to Columbia to join Smith at the capitol building. Gathering under the statue of the original Red Shirt candidate, General Wade Hampton, Smith and his supporters waited for the election returns. After learning that he had trounced former governor and ardent New Dealer Olin Johnston, Smith donned a red shirt and posed for photographers. "We conquered in '76 and we conquered in '38," Smith boomed. "We fought with bullets then, but today, thank God, we fought with ballots."[51]

Rejecting Roosevelt's plea to elect leaders "whose minds are cast in the 1938 mold and not the 1898 mold," South Carolina voters stuck with Smith. But if Smith played the conquering hero, Roosevelt was, if by accident, the better historian. With his Red Shirt theatrics, Smith compared his victory to South Carolina's overthrow of an interracial Reconstruction government in 1876. Roosevelt alluded to a longer campaign against interracial democracy that climaxed in an 1898 white supremacist coup in Wilmington, North Carolina. Across the South, white Democrats fought for decades to build a social and political order that excluded African Americans. They had mobilized in violent defense of white supremacy and cemented their victories with a litany of codes and laws meant to stamp out black political participation forever.[52]

If few white southerners in the New Deal era could remember Reconstruction vividly, the racial lessons of the late nineteenth century still reverberated in the 1938 campaign. Before white supremacy became an accepted fact of southern life, it was a political project fueled by white fears of black domination. With the renewed threat of black political influence in 1936, those anxieties roared back. The racially charged campaigns in Georgia and South Carolina dramatized the link between southern disillusionment with the New Deal and concerns about the color line. Junior senators Byrnes and Russell won in 1936 by fending off racial allegations and riding the coattails of an immensely popular president. Two years later, their senior colleagues, Smith and George, triumphed by championing white supremacy and fending off challengers publicly endorsed by a popular president.

The resounding victories in Georgia and South Carolina compelled Turner Catledge, a Mississippi-born correspondent for the *New York Times*, to conclude that "white supremacy has returned as a political issue in the South." Roosevelt considered the South "the nation's No. 1 economic problem," Catledge noted, but his attempts to remake the region had aggravated the region's "No. 1 social problem." The attempted "purge" of conservative senators, along with the influx of black voters into the Democratic Party, had heightened white anxiety about the racial implications of the New Deal. The fear of black political power was no longer "the reasoning . . . of demagogues alone," Catledge warned, "but also of many thoughtful Southerners who had hoped the day had come when candidates no longer could ride into office on the race issue." That hope, however fervent, "was based upon the assumption that white supremacy was permanently established."[53]

The racially charged confrontations of the New Deal called that mythical permanency into question. But the rightward lurch in southern politics worried Catledge more. As statesmen embraced rumors and accusations previously dismissed as demagogic, southern moderates found themselves increasingly on the defensive. Meanwhile, white supremacists stepped up their crusade to rally resentment and demonize reform.

Rather than reassure southerners of their power, the successful filibuster of the antilynching bill and the rejection of the "purge" attempt raised unsettling questions about the racial struggles that lay ahead. As southern conservatives warned of continued agitation, a few diehards offered bloody visions and radical solutions for avoiding an impending racial disaster. This new sense of crisis fueled southern unease with the changes, rumored and real, taking place around them.

No public figure better embodied the tension between the New Deal's popularity and the concern for its racial implications than Mississippi senator Theodore Bilbo. While factions in other states wrangled over their allegiance to Roosevelt's reform program, Bilbo seemed at war with himself. Over a long and turbulent career in state politics, the former governor had championed progressive reforms. In 1935, Bilbo thundered into the Senate during the Depression with a populist, pro–New Deal platform that drew intense opposition from the state's conservative elite. Though never one to mince words on white supremacy, Bilbo had not used racial appeals in his rise to the Senate. In a black-majority state with virtually no registered black voters, Bilbo focused instead on the intense regional and class rivalries between hill-country farmers and aristocratic planters.

Yet, at the slightest hint of racial controversy, Bilbo championed white supremacy with the same gusto he had earlier reserved for Roosevelt. Taking his turn during the 1938 filibuster, the Mississippi senator blamed "Negro lovers, Negro leaders, and Negro voters" for the unprecedented agitation. Like his more temperate colleagues, Bilbo deemed antilynching legislation a thinly veiled attempt "to promote the entering wedge to the bill of civil rights and social equality by the Negroes." But Bilbo went a step further when he proposed the "deportation or repatriation" of African Americans as the solution to this looming racial disaster.[54]

By the time Bilbo mentioned this scheme, southern senators had filibustered for nearly three weeks. They had said, and would continue to say, nearly anything to delay a vote on the antilynching bill. But if most ignored Bilbo's vow to ship "the entire Negro race" back to Africa, the Mississippi senator made unlikely friends. Letters trickled in from black nationalists, many of them veterans of Marcus Garvey's Universal Negro Improvement Association (UNIA), who were lobbying Congress for funds to resettle in Africa. With the help of a Richmond-based white separatist, Earnest Sevier Cox, they had persuaded the Virginia legislature to pass resolutions endorsing federal aid for black colonization. This minor victory prompted *Newsweek* to profile a "vast new Back-to-Africa movement" that was "growing in strength."[55]

As the willing sponsor of a colonization bill, Bilbo was an unlikely ally who could take the Back-to-Africa crusade to the Senate floor. When the UNIA convened in Toronto in August 1938 for its annual convention, Marcus Garvey urged his followers to endorse Bilbo's Back-to-Africa legislation. Mentored by Cox and supported by a loose network of black fringe groups, Bilbo composed the Greater Liberia Bill of 1939. The legislation authorized the United States to negotiate with the European powers for expanded territory in West Africa, provide federal grants to black settlers, and establish a temporary military government for "Greater Liberia." When Bilbo presented the bill on 24 April 1939, nearly 500 black supporters poured into the Senate gallery. Black nationalists followed Bilbo's speech with several mass meetings in New York City and vigorous membership drives throughout the northeastern states. Bilbo quickly printed 100,000 copies of his speech and began making plans for a unified Negro Nationalist Movement administered from Washington. Privately, he wanted to see "a million negroes" marching on the nation's capital.[56] Ultimately, infighting among his coterie of black allies and the outbreak of war in Europe undermined Bilbo's grand designs. More important, his colonization scheme failed to resonate with southern colleagues who viewed Bilbo's plan as a crude and counterproductive stunt.

Dismissed as a particularly absurd expression of southern bigotry, the Back-to-Africa scheme revealed a persistent strain of racial pessimism that fueled diehard resistance to the New Deal order. The clashes between the Roosevelt administration and the South's old guard provided an opening for militant white supremacists to engage in some racial agitation of their own. If most white southerners doubted the feasibility and political expediency of massive black resettlement in Africa, more than a few shared the sense of impending racial disaster that drove the colonization movement. At its base, the Back-to-Africa argument rested on the assumption that Jim Crow was at best an uneasy truce. With the race issue "revived" by the late 1930s, militant white supremacists forecast a future that most white southerners could scarcely imagine. Their more moderate counterparts invoked racial warnings occasionally to beat back an immediate threat. The diehards, by contrast, used apocalyptic warnings to rally white southerners to the barricades.

Few embodied the racial pessimism that bolstered the colonization movement more vividly than Thomas Dixon. Seeing only violence and destruction in store for a multiracial America, the aging novelist brought the Armageddon to life. One of the most popular writers of the early twentieth century, Dixon had promoted his deeply conservative and highly romanticized view of the South for four decades. His turn-of-the-century novel *The Clansman* had inspired D. W. Griffith's *The Birth of a Nation*, which vilified southern blacks and celebrated the triumph of white supremacy over Reconstruction. From his first novel, *The Leopard's Spots*, in 1902, Dixon had portrayed African Americans as fundamentally inferior and dangerously degenerate. Along with the *The Clansman* and *The Traitor*, Dixon's "Trilogy of Reconstruction" emphasized the folly of black political participation and the need for white racial purity. But even before he had completed his Reconstruction trilogy, Dixon had launched another series of novels aimed at exposing the threat of socialism. By the 1930s, he had linked leftist subversives and black degenerates together.

Dixon's unrelenting hostility toward socialism, communism, and black equality compelled him to abandon the Democratic Party in the early 1930s. After concluding that communists had infiltrated the New Deal, Dixon joined Eugene Talmadge at the Grass Roots Convention and later campaigned for Roosevelt's Republican challenger Alfred Landon in 1936. A Republican judge rewarded Dixon with a patronage post in Raleigh, North Carolina, and the aging novelist used his federal paycheck to finance his latest project, *The Flaming Sword*. Lifting his title from his longtime nemesis, W. E. B. Du Bois, Dixon aimed "to give an authoritative record of the Conflict of Color in America from 1900 to 1938." Referring to the project as "the most important thing I have ever done," Dixon worked as much as sixteen hours a day on the novel.[57]

In *The Flaming Sword*, Dixon updated his familiar narrative of racial turmoil by portraying New Dealers, African Americans, and other assorted radicals as the enemies of white America. *The Flaming Sword*, Dixon explained, was "more than a novel." It was a call to arms. He introduced the book as "the foundation and justification of a crusade to rid our country of influences and activities which, for years, have been secretly dynamiting the pillars of the nation." Determined to settle old scores in *The Flaming Sword*, Dixon cast his longtime critics as villains. In the opening section of the novel, a poem written by NAACP leader James Weldon Johnson inspires a black man in South Carolina to rape and murder a white woman. In the second part of the book, Dixon portrays the futility of the interracial cooperation movement and the sinister intent of the "Negro Junta" led by Du Bois. Angela, the sister of the raped and murdered woman in part one, travels north to study the race question, only to discover that it was "an unsolved and insolvable problem." She becomes a proponent of the colonization movement because she fears that if blacks do not leave the United States the Communists will arm them and overthrow the American government. Angela and the rest of Dixon's band of white protagonists form an underground organization, the Patriot Union, to protect the country from the looming revolution. Meanwhile, the Communists and their legion of black devotees decide to begin their coup during one of Roosevelt's fireside chats. On that cue, the black Nat Turner Legion overruns the South, torches cities, and rapes white women. By the end of the novel, Dixon's white freedom fighters pledge to reclaim their homeland from the newly established "Soviet Republic of the United States."[58]

Despite Dixon's ambitious plans for his final novel, the "nightmare melodrama" marked neither a literary triumph nor a successful call to arms for southern white supremacists. Released in early 1939, Dixon's race-war saga competed with a very real conflict sweeping Europe. Having previewed *The Flaming Sword* as the "sequel" to *The Birth of a Nation* in late 1938, Dixon's hometown paper panned the novel as "a preachment of conservative patriotism and an indictment of the liberal concept in race relations which the author scores as an invitation to the radicalism he seems to fear with something like hysteria." But another southern editor lauded the book as "an American epic" and "an authoritative narrative of the race problem" that would "assuredly furnish food for much reflection." With war raging in Europe, and the recent signing of a nonaggression pact between Nazi Germany and the Soviet Union, even a New York book critic conceded that *The Flaming Sword* was "not as wildly incredible today as it might have seemed a few short weeks ago."[59]

The unexpected truce between Hitler and Stalin provided a window of opportunity for diehard white supremacists. Just as civil rights activists compared Jim Crow with the fascist regimes sweeping Europe, southern white supremacists equated fascism, Communism, and all other "isms" as threats to traditional "Americanism." Lumping "New Dealism" with "socialism, fascism, collectivism, bolshevism, communism, [and] Nazism," a Talmadge ally in Georgia concluded, "all these isms are essentially the same." Another Talmadge supporter lashed out at domestic subversives who would force social change on the South. Arguing that "Hitler and Mussolini apply it from the top, Stalin from the bottom, and these American Socialists . . . from our middle class," the Talmadge camp contended that the end result of any one of these movements would be "a Christless, regimented, controlled state of slavery." The only alternative was "to preserve Americanism as our fathers knew it."[60]

Temporarily seizing their dubious moral high ground, white supremacists redoubled their efforts to root out subversives of various stripes. Increasingly alarmed by New Deal reforms, labor agitation, and black protest, southern conservatives joined with hard-line anticommunists to expose the interwoven menace of radical infiltration and racial rebellion. East Texas congressman Martin Dies, chairman of the newly established Special House Committee on Un-American Activities, led the charge. Dies, like many of his southern colleagues, concluded during the late 1930s that an urban North "politically controlled by foreigners and transplanted Negroes" had seized control of the Democratic Party. Convinced that the New Deal was leading the nation away from white supremacy and constitutional democracy, Dies launched investigations in the late 1930s aimed at exposing Communist sympathizers in civil rights groups, organized labor, and New Deal agencies. In 1940, a Dies Committee report branded Communism a "Trojan Horse for Negroes."[61]

That same year, the hard-line anticommunist Constitutional Educational League (CEL) distributed *The Fifth Column in the South*. Based in New Haven, Connecticut, the league had established a southern headquarters in Birmingham at the invitation of antilabor industrialists. "A dangerous alien-bred and alien-minded Fifth Column has invaded an unsuspecting Southland," warned the CEL. This subversive movement would bring "economic ruin, moral bankruptcy, and the destruction of time-honored Southern traditions." Putting a southern spin on its militant anticommunism, the CEL warned that alien subversives and their homegrown converts intended to spark "race riots" and "mass violence" that "would make Sherman's march to the sea seem tame and trivial."[62]

Communists and their fellow travelers would stop at nothing, the CEL warned, to overturn southern society. They would even poison young minds. According to the CEL, subversives indoctrinated southern children through nursery schools and traveling puppet shows "on the problems of Negro farmers." Eugene Talmadge, who returned to the governor's mansion in 1940, argued that this indoctrination plot had infiltrated Georgia universities. Barred from running for a third consecutive term in 1936, Talmadge had spent four years trying to unseat both sitting Georgia senators. Sailing into his old office, Talmadge turned his racial barrage on a new target. Arguing that "there is no whit difference in the Communism of Stalin, the Nazism of Hitler, the Fascism of Mussolini, and the Socialism of . . . radical professors," Talmadge went after suspected racial agitators in the classroom.[63]

Seizing on a disgruntled history instructor's testimony, Talmadge charged that the dean of the University of Georgia's College of Education, Dr. Walter Cocking, had advocated the establishment of an integrated branch campus near Athens. Ignoring a report by the chairman of the University System Board of Regents that there was no concrete evidence for the charges, Talmadge roared ahead with his plans to purge Cocking and any other university official who promoted "social equality" on campus. When a skeptical board of regents voted by a margin of one to retain Dean Cocking, Talmadge quickly dismissed his staunchest opponents from the committee and replaced them with political allies. Meanwhile, Talmadge allies in the Ku Klux Klan abducted Cocking's black house servant and forced him to sign an incriminating typed statement. The kidnappers also tried to force the frightened employee to unlock the Cocking home for them and offered him money to steal or fabricate correspondence between his boss and black educators.[64]

When the board of regents reconvened at the state capitol in July, Talmadge put on a rollicking show for the packed house. Dean Cocking, newly installed board chair James S. Peters charged, worked with the philanthropic Julius Rosenwald Fund to undermine segregation. "Negroes will ride in the same railroad cars, sit in the same schools, go to the same lavatories as white men," Peters warned. "They won't do it," Talmadge shouted on cue. The crowd cheered. Reversing its earlier decision, the packed board of regents voted to dismiss Cocking, and then turned to another target, Georgia Teachers College president Marvin Pittman.[65]

During the lunch break, Talmadge instructed Peters to "hit the chair and holler" as he grilled Pittman. Waving a book snatched from the Georgia Teachers College library, Peters demanded that Pittman explain a page from *Calling America*. The volume contained an image of a shackled black man alongside a passage that criticized "the American habit of forgetting the Negro in talking about democracy." Pittman responded that he had never seen the book, but the board of regents dismissed him in short order. With the majority of the regents squarely behind him, Talmadge swiftly fired eight more university officials. In an act previewed by the literary lynching of President Pittman, Talmadge allies in the State Board of Education banned twenty-three "off-color texts" from Georgia schools. Historian Albert Bushnell Hart made the blacklist for suggesting in his popular textbook that "Southern whites have an unfounded and unformulated fear that somehow white supremacy is in danger." The board also banned a children's book that contained an illustration of a white and black boy sharing a soda at a corner drug store. Such a "visual object lesson" for impressionable Georgia youth, Talmadge's weekly tabloid charged, "gets them ready for racial intermixing."[66]

With disloyal educators and subversive literature out of the way, the Talmadge camp heralded their historic victory. "The upheaval about Dean Cocking," announced the Talmadge-published *Statesman*, "was only the eruption of a volcano that has smoldered ever since Harriet Beecher Stowe slandered our Southern forefathers in the pages of 'Uncle Tom's Cabin.'" But even as Talmadge promoted himself as the savior of segregation, many Georgians questioned the costs of his crusade. The national press com-

Non-Partisan Picture Of Race Mixing In The South

Read The Editorials Reproduced In This Pamphlet And See Whether Racial Equality Is Being Demanded

The Best Way to Keep Negroes Out Of White Schools Is To Keep Educators Who Condone It Out Of School System. — Eugene Talmadge.

RE-ELECT

EUGENE TALMADGE

GOVERNOR

Democratic White Primary
September 9, 1942

In 1942, Eugene Talmadge lost his bid for a fourth term as governor after attempting to purge Georgia universities of "subversive" administrators, faculty, and textbooks. But Talmadge defended his actions in campaign literature that outlined a plot to break down segregation in southern schools. (Eugene Talmadge Pamphlets, Special Collections, McCain Library and Archives, University of Southern Mississippi, Hattiesburg, Miss.)

pared Talmadge to Hitler, and many southern papers joined in the attack. The Southern University Conference voted unanimously to expel Georgia, and the Southern Association of Colleges and Secondary Schools threatened to revoke the accreditation of the state's white colleges. Fearing for their potentially discredited degrees, hundreds of students at the University of Georgia hanged and burned three effigies of Talmadge. Then they piled into more than one hundred cars and caravanned to Atlanta carrying signs reading "Gene Don't Be Mean" and "Talmadge, Phooey!" By the time they turned back toward Athens, thousands of Atlantans had lined the streets to applaud their rowdy procession.[67]

Unfazed, Talmadge lashed out at his critics. In response to *Atlanta*

Constitution editor Ralph McGill's claim that "there is no issue of 'white supremacy,'" Talmadge pointed out threats to segregation at every turn. "Brother McGill," he argued, "apparently has never heard of the Chicago and Pittsburgh negro papers which daily scream out against the South in an effort to drive an opening wedge for inter-racial social equality." Equating racial reformers with foreign saboteurs, Talmadge forces raised the specter of totalitarianism. "Inter-racial movement is an insidious thing," warned a pro-Talmadge columnist, "something like the infiltration of the communists and fascists who work subtly until they are in position to begin demanding, whereupon business picks up." Real Georgians, Talmadge declared, rejected "those who come here seeking to bring the 'new order' as outlined by the selfish, tyrannical crackpots who have enslaved the minds of the Russians and the Germans."[68]

The Talmadge propaganda machine churned out rapturous praise for the university purge, but the accreditation crisis sparked a backlash that ultimately drove the Georgia governor out of office. Promising to restore academic freedom without jeopardizing segregation, challenger Ellis Arnall defeated Talmadge in 1942.[69] Southern moderates cheered the defeat as a referendum on race-baiting. According to Birmingham columnist John Temple Graves, Talmadge had committed "the two greatest sins that can be done against the South—the sin of laying unholy hands on the educational system and the sin of agitating falsely the race problem." Graves concluded that "an electorate turned to its best lights" had punished Talmadge for his demagoguery. Most Georgians saw through the ploy, Graves explained, because segregation "was not a genuine issue" before the United States entered World War II. "Talmadge," he claimed, "was simply putting on a one-man show."[70]

From his post–Pearl Harbor perch, Graves looked back on the prewar years as a time of relative racial calm. He scolded demagogues such as Talmadge for inflating for immediate political gain the long-term threat posed by civil rights activists. Implicitly, Graves also highlighted the very real constraints that outspoken white supremacists operated under in the prewar years. Despite the racially charged skirmishes between New Dealers and southern conservatives, the Roosevelt administration still had strong ties to the South's Democratic establishment. Loyal southern Democrats, even if they harbored grave suspicions about the New Deal, recognized that racial agitation cut both ways. "Agitating falsely the race problem" goaded the Democratic Party's liberal wing and spurred greater black militancy, consequences that Graves and other southern elites worried would hasten far more serious confrontations down the road.

But Talmadge was not the only southerner to argue that the battle had already begun. Despite his attempts to spark a white supremacist revolt, racial reaction had been scattered at best in the prewar years. Isolated elites, rather than everyday folks, provided much of the energy behind the white supremacist critique of the New Deal order. Yet by the end of the 1930s, nervous southerners connected changes on the ground to tectonic shifts in national politics. As plantation owner and writer Archibald Rutledge complained in 1940, relief work had "morally debased" his black neighbors in lowcountry South Carolina. "They regard the government as some easygoing Santa Claus," Rutledge complained, "and they will take all that they can get." New Dealers engaged in "arrant bribery" by using taxpayer money to "to make the Negro a complete political turncoat." For Rutledge, the New Deal's limited yet undeniable impact on African Americans had sparked a political realignment that would shake the pillars of southern civilization. "Nothing more revolutionary in American politics has ever occurred," he argued, "than the defection of the Negro from the Republican party."[71]

For far-sighted white supremacists, race was no false issue. After Pearl Harbor, the southern political mainstream echoed many of their warnings. Discussion of the "race question" dismissed before 1941 as demagogic suddenly seemed rational, responsible, and urgently relevant. When Talmadge declared segregation under attack in the 1930s, critics dismissed the warnings as rabble-rousing. But after Pearl Harbor, John Temple Graves accused civil rights activists of "looking everywhere for trouble" without jeopardizing his authority as a southern voice of reason.[72] If African Americans entered the war convinced that the time for full equality had come, white southerners encountered mounting evidence that their way of life faced serious threats. During the war, white supremacy moved from the sidelines to the center of southern politics. But the war provided the tinder, not the spark.

THE WHITE SOUTH'S "DOUBLE V"

2

A few weeks after the Japanese attack on Pearl Harbor, the NAACP proclaimed itself "On Guard Against Racial Discrimination." Under a picture of black men in uniform, an NAACP pamphlet announced, "if racial discrimination under Hitler is wrong, racial discrimination in America is wrong." The war effort, civil rights activists asserted, necessitated a domestic drive to stamp out segregation. "The dictator armies may be defeated by a Jim Crow Navy, a Jim Crow Army, a Jim Crow Air Corps," argued the NAACP, "but the dictator idea will never be defeated by Jim Crowism." Segregation was now enemy ideology, and the wartime civil rights movement demanded that white southerners choose sides. "Policies of racial discrimination divide us and aid the enemy," declared the NAACP. "The man who discriminates against Negroes is a Fifth Columnist."[1]

W. M. Burt saw things differently. The white Mississippian worked at an ordnance plant that produced powder bags for artillery shells. He spent 10 percent of his income on war bonds, and his only child was a bomber pilot. Burt watched with apprehension as civil rights activists and northern politicians took aim at the underpinnings of segregated society. In the fall of 1942, the House of Representatives voted overwhelmingly to outlaw the poll tax. As the bill moved to the Senate, Burt cheered on the anticipated southern filibuster. "I claim in every way to be a 100% American and as patriotic as any man in the United States," he declared, "but I want to say that if we win this War against the Germans, Italians, and Japs, and yet have this Poll Tax bill rammed down our throats, we of the South will have won only HALF a victory, and the remaining half will have to be won all over again."[2]

The poll tax fight was only one of several episodes in which white southerners reconciled their racial convictions with the fight against the Axis. Even as the wartime civil rights movement mobilized a "Double V" campaign for victory over fascism abroad and discrimination at home, white southerners linked their own racial struggle to the war effort. Like their adversaries, they rallied behind appeals to freedom and democracy. They too argued that the global struggle against fascism had domestic implications. Yet defenders of segregation articulated their own vision of Double Victory. Championing white supremacy and demanding freedom from outside interference, southern conservatives deemed federal encroachment and black insurgency to be as dangerous as an Axis invasion. White southerners, like African Americans, had entered the war fighting on two fronts.

Even before the attack on Pearl Harbor, African Americans accelerated their campaign against vigilantism, systematic disfranchisement, and segregation. Stressing the liability of racial discrimination in the global struggle against fascism, Asa Philip Randolph announced in early 1941 that he would lead 10,000 marchers to the nation's capital to demand the desegregation of the armed forces and defense industries. As the movement gained momentum, eager activists and anxious observers multiplied Randolph's estimate by ten. Faced with the prospect of 100,000 black protesters flocking to Washington on July 1, Roosevelt issued Executive Order 8802 to prohibit discrimination in "defense industries or government." The directive also established the Fair Employment Practices Committee (FEPC). In response, Randolph cancelled the March on Washington with less than a week to spare.[3]

By authorizing an interracial committee to investigate workplace discrimination, Executive Order 8802 threatened to undermine a racial caste system that relegated African Americans to the lowest rungs of the labor ladder. Military mobilization and out-migration disrupted an abundant supply of cheap black labor, and antidiscrimination orders would only make matters worse. Maintaining the color line in the workplace, argued the mayor of Shreveport, Louisiana, mattered as much to the South as the struggle against the Axis. "Of equal importance with winning the war," he declared, "is the necessity for keeping Negroes out of skilled jobs." As the fledgling FEPC struggled to handle the hundreds of complaints flooding its offices, discouraged observers conceded that such war analogies accurately portrayed the mood in Dixie. "The grim truth is, the South has thrown down the challenge to the federal government," explained African American journalist Roi Ottley, "It regards Executive Order 8802 as the initial assault on its way of life."[4]

The establishment of the FEPC precipitated one of many wartime confrontations between civil rights advocates and segregation's defenders. While the tiny federal task force failed to make much headway in the South, the war effort exposed Jim Crow to other threats. On military bases in the South and tours overseas, white southern servicemen encountered breakdowns in segregation. Racial clashes, real and imagined, preoccupied southern leaders and everyday folks on the home front. For many white southerners, racial unrest threatened fiercely guarded freedoms and privileges. "Are we fighting this war to destroy everything we inherited from our forefathers?" asked a Mississippi Delta planter. "This is a conservative war. . . . It is not a war for Fascism, Nazism, Communism, Socialism, New Dealism or Democracy." The only "ism" worth fighting for, declared a likeminded Mississippi legislator, was the "100% Americanism" embodied by "the white democracy of the South."[5] Faced with unprecedented threats to the southern status quo, the defenders of segregation lumped together their foreign and domestic foes under the umbrella of totalitarianism.

Wartime challenges to local political control posed the most immediate threat to white democracy. Faced with campaigns to abolish the poll tax and invalidate the white primary, Jim Crow's defenders demonized racial reform as a domestic manifestation of fascist aggression. And white southerners, concerned observers repeatedly warned, were ready to fight back. As John Temple Graves argued in 1943, southern white opposition to racial change embodied the very essence of American war aims. He declared the struggle against the Axis "a war for states' rights, for the right of individual lands not to be invaded by outsiders, not to be dictated to or aggressed against."[6] Even as Jim Crow's defenders fought Hitler abroad, they battled a totalitarian menace back home.

In the months following Pearl Harbor, race tension rose with the temperature on the southern home front. Civil rights advocates had declared war on white supremacy, and many southerners quickly recognized the war's potential to undermine the racial status quo. Less than a year after Pearl Harbor, a federal field agent reported that many Georgia whites feared that "going all out" for the war effort would result in "a revolution in Southern society and . . . racial relationships." As Roosevelt proclaimed the Four Freedoms and government officials trumpeted the war for democracy, white Georgians noticed that such appeals "were not exclusive of Negroes." They cringed as African Americans harnessed the war rhetoric of freedom and democracy to their civil rights campaign. The war had the potential to turn the southern social order on its head, and Georgia whites "had revolting visions of what the new society may be like." They were not fighting for a new world, the federal official concluded, but to keep things "as they have been in America."[7]

For whites in Georgia and across the region, the sight of armed and uniformed African Americans portended racial trouble. As black soldiers poured into southern army bases in early 1942, alarmed locals protested to military officials and southern politicians. White southerners frequently claimed that black troops were abusing their military privileges, but these allegations often revealed little more than a steadfast refusal to grant black servicemen any semblance of authority. After a convoy of black troops rolled through Lincolnton, Georgia, in the spring of 1942, angry whites alleged that the soldiers blew kisses and showered catcalls on white women. A Lincolnton lawyer claimed that one soldier cursed out a white road crew for refusing to salute him. Town officials notified Senator Richard Russell, who demanded a War Department investigation of the "outrageous conduct" in Lincolnton. "No stone will be left unturned," he pledged, "to mete proper punishment to those guilty." Military inquiries, however, failed to turn up evidence of misconduct. The all-white Georgia Motor Police escort that had accompanied the battalion, according to one military investigator, "reported that it was the most orderly convoy of soldiers, either white or colored, with which they had ever come in contact."[8]

White Army officers offered their own interpretation of the incident. As their convoy passed through Lincolnton, they had assigned some black troops to direct civilian traffic. The site of uniformed blacks halting white motorists apparently sent some residents over the edge. "Their displeasure," concluded the investigator, "resulted in unfounded reports of misconduct on the part of these colored soldiers." The local newspaper, which churned out editorials blasting the "insidious work" of civil rights activists, primed whites for such a protest. "It is not necessary to go to Atlanta, Detroit, or New York, or any other metropolitan city, with their large negro populations, to see the changes taking place," warned the editor. "It can be seen right here in Lincolnton and in hundreds of other rural towns." Arguing that the campaign for "FULL EQUALITY" was on the march, the newspaperman stressed the urgent need to keep African Americans in their place. "The negro has his rightful place in the American way of life, and he has no friends who are as good to him as the white people of the South," he argued, "but as for accepting on a plane of equality, as is being advocated by some negro leaders—it must and shall not be done."[9]

While many southern whites resented the black troop presence, others complained that too few African Americans entered the service. Georgia whites circulated rumors that the military rejected nine out of ten southern blacks due to venereal disease. Others warned against leaving too many black men on the southern home front. Fearing that blacks would "steal, kill, [and] worse, rape white women," a Georgia woman offered to "furnish a long list of names" for the draft board. A father of two girls reported that African Americans in Georgia and South Carolina were "becoming more and more brazen day by day and gloat over the day when all the [white] male population will be taken away to fight for them." He complained that his black laundrywoman sent her daughters to a boarding school with the money that her three sons earned in northern defense jobs. Unable to afford such tuition for his own daughters, the man resented the fact that none of the woman's sons served "in the armed service of the country that avails more for them than some white folk of the very best and purest American people."[10]

Resentment quickly boiled over into disrespect and intimidation. The army's Fourth Corps Area, headquartered in Atlanta, received scores of complaints as black recruits flooded into southern army installations. "Incidents have occurred recently," reported the regional commander, "which have led the War Department to believe that the negro in the uniform of the United States Army has not always received the equitable treatment which is due him by virtue of the fact that he is a soldier." Arguing that mistreatment undermined morale in southern camps, the general implored local leaders to protect black servicemen. At the same time, he pledged to "to maintain pleasant relations between its garrisons and the adjacent civilian communities with due regard to the local and state and community laws and customs."[11]

As the top brass balanced appeals for tolerance with deference to southern "customs," some particularly anxious whites clashed with military officials. In July 1942, just one week after 20,000 enthusiastic Georgians in Moultrie helped Governor Eugene Talmadge kick off his unsuccessful reelection campaign, a feud erupted between the city council and officers at nearby Spence Field. "Negro soldiers congregate and block our streets on Saturday so that white ladies cannot get by," complained a council member. "They are demanding to eat at the same places white people do and drink at the same fountains, and we have every reason to believe that this view is fostered by the officers in charge of the base." Warning that "there is going to be some killing of negroes unless the officers at the Air Base change their views," the councilman declared that city officials would "not permit any negro soldier to commit any breach of peace or show disrespect to white people whether the Army likes it or not." The commanding officer at Spence Field implored local authorities to treat black soldiers with courtesy and respect. In response, city leaders reminded their police force that "a negro soldier is just another negro with a different sort of clothes on."[12]

Moultrie police chief Tom Bell quickly acted on that premise. On a

Saturday night in midsummer, a white blacksmith complained that black servicemen were arguing outside his shop. Within minutes, Chief Bell had bloodied three soldiers with his blackjack. Although Bell claimed that the servicemen were drunk and disorderly, two white military policemen who had accompanied the chief on his rounds told a different story. They, along with the medic who stitched up the soldiers, denied that the victims were intoxicated. In sworn testimony, the white servicemen and the three beaten black soldiers all reported that the chief had threatened to kill them.[13]

City officials alleged that, in the days after the beatings, a white officer at Spence Field "threatened to put machine guns on our street corners and mop up the City Police force if his negro soldiers didn't get the treatment he thought they ought to have." Incensed at the demands and alleged threats of the northern officers, the mayor called a special hearing at City Hall. Police Chief Bell claimed that he had simply subdued the drunk and defiant black soldiers for cursing and threatening whites. Charging that uncooperative northern officers and white military policemen were making his job infinitely more difficult, Bell offered a solution: "Southern boys on the Military Police force." Responding to city officials' denials of mistreatment, a colonel from Spence Field interrupted: "It is a well known fact that you don't treat the colored people like the white." The mayor responded flatly, "We don't expect to do so." A hostile city councilman interjected that another officer, Lieutenant Colonel Dan Moler, "said that when you put a uniform on a negro he is not considered a negro anymore." Moler was sitting a few feet away. "That is a bad statement to make," the councilman continued. "You put a Lt. Colonel's uniform on a jackass and it is the same."[14]

The feud in Moultrie revealed that southern whites frequently resisted attempts to adapt Jim Crow to wartime exigencies. The dissonance between southern custom and wartime necessity also brought underlying racial anxieties to the surface. "Is it true," the mayor grilled the officers, "that they take our southern negro soldiers up north and teach them the same as the northern soldiers in way of equality?" Spence Field officers denied that the military indoctrinated black soldiers with subversive racial ideas, but Moultrie officials persisted with complaints and investigations. Later claiming that base officials had dismissed two civilian employees for disrespecting black soldiers, the city council concluded that "the teaching of social equality is bringing on all this trouble with the negroes here in Moultrie."[15]

Confrontations in Georgia reflected wider concerns about black servicemen. Unsympathetic military officials offended some whites, but defiant black soldiers spelled disaster. In South Carolina, Governor Richard Manning Jefferies closely monitored the black troop presence. In tandem with Senator Burnet Maybank, Jefferies worked behind the scenes to minimize the number of black servicemen entering the state. "I want you to know," Maybank reported in April 1942, "that I protested to the Air Corps in reference to the sending of negro troops to guard the air bases in South Carolina." A few months later, Jefferies apprised Maybank of "widespread rumors" that the military planned to establish "a large Negro army camp" near Columbia. Jefferies confided that South Carolinians feared "that white troops will be displaced at Fort Jackson with Negro troops and that the Fort will become a Negro camp." While the War Department assured Maybank that no such plan existed, he reported that his Washington office had also received "many reports in reference to colored troops and colored officers in the South."[16]

Warning that "the situation in Alabama and Georgia is even worse than in South Carolina," Maybank suggested a coordinated effort to meet the problem. Georgia senator Richard Russell claimed that he had received "protests from nearly all of the cities which have camps against having negro soldiers stationed there." After a summer of complaints and clashes, Alabama senator John Bankhead implored General George C. Marshall to keep black servicemen out of the South. "Our people," Bankhead declared, "feel that the government is doing a disservice to the war effort by locating Negro troops in the South . . . at a time when race feeling among the Negroes has been roused."[17]

Southern whites chafed at reports that military officials frequently placed African Americans in positions of authority over whites. "I have been watching the Negro situation in this part of the country," reported one Mississippian, "and trying to figure out just what is causing the negroes to attempt to do the things that they are trying to do." He pointed to "things happening in this Army of ours" as the source of racial unrest and blamed "Yankee officers" for the trouble. The sight of black soldiers guarding white prisoners on work detail incensed him. "I know," he wrote to his senator, "that you would not stand for a negro to stand on the roads with a rifle and give your boy orders."[18]

Fears of empowered black soldiers meshed with concerns about the military's adherence to Jim Crow. While the armed forces remained officially segregated throughout World War II, southern officials and civilians protested whenever southern military officials blurred the color line. To the chagrin of many white southerners, the region's military installations often permitted or overlooked de facto integration. Responding to reports that black and white servicemen shared cafeteria tables at a Mississippi army base, an alarmed Georgian deemed it "unfair to draft a white boy in the Army and force him to associate with negroes." Such a situation angered and offended him. "I am willing for my boy to fight for our country," he declared, "but I don't think he should be humiliated."[19]

Many grievances focused on military medical facilities. At Mississippi's Keesler Field, reported a civilian employee, "right in the Hospital the Damn Negro is Bed by Bed in the same ward with white Soldiers and eat in mess Halls together." In Georgia, alarmed parents and relatives complained of integrated hospital wards at Camp Lawson. An Atlantan with a nephew at the hospital alleged that "negroes have to use same mess and toilet facilities as whites use," and another claimed that black patients were ordering white volunteer nurses to make their beds. "I do not believe that the exigencies of war make this necessary," declared another Atlantan, "or that patriotism should be used as a cloakroom for embittering the white people of the South and bringing about disunity."[20]

The thought of white nurses working in these integrated hospital wards alarmed southern whites. The prospect of nursing in racially mixed wards compelled some women to steer clear of military hospitals. In southern Mississippi, Red Cross volunteers deemed Camp Van Dorn insufficiently segregated. When the women realized that "their duties would have to be performed in a mixed environment and they might even be expected to render the same services to each of the races," they balked. "The white ladies of this section are willing and anxious to render whatever services they can," reported a local lumberman, "but to enable them to do so it would be necessary that their work be confined entirely to the white environment to which they are accustomed."[21]

Southern leaders passed along their constituents' complaints about the military's lukewarm commitment to segregation. When Senator Russell protested the "terrible mistake" of racial mixing to the War Department, military officials replied: "It is not practicable to provide separate wards for white and colored patients in our hospitals." While the War Department affirmed its commitment to segregation where adequate facilities existed and when "local hospital conditions and capacity so warrant," the top brass asserted that "hospital capacity must be utilized to care for the sick and wounded no matter what their race or color may be." Discouraged by his investigation, Russell informed his concerned constituents that he "was surprised to find that in practically all of the Army hospitals white and colored soldiers are being treated in the same ward."[22] Thus integration seeped slowly into South, courtesy of the federal government.

For southern white servicemen who shipped off to war, unsettling incidents on the home front paled in comparison to the violations of the color line abroad. While the military maintained segregated fighting units, the top brass had neither the intent nor the resources to police the color line to some soldiers' satisfaction. In a confidential memo, the U.S. Army Headquarters in the European Theater of Operations outlined its "Policy on Negroes." Military officials insisted "that discrimination against the Negro troops be sedulously avoided" and refused to impose segregation on the communities that black and white servicemen would visit on pass and furlough. As a military official in Europe concluded, "it would be a practical impossibility to arrange for segregation so far as welfare and recreational facilities are concerned." Army commanders predicted "a variety of problems," including access to "dances and other social activities," but refused to "issue any detailed instructions" to officers. "Local Commanding Officers will be expected to use their own best judgment in avoiding discrimination due to race," announced Assistant Adjutant General Fred Meyer, "but at the same time, minimizing causes of friction between White and Colored troops."[23]

The breakdown of strict segregation overseas alarmed many white southerners, and they could do little to stop it. Some white soldiers pointed to the mildest antidiscrimination directives and scattered pockets of de facto desegregation as signs of a federal plot to break down racial barriers. Their criticisms reflected the growing concern that any ground ceded during the war emergency would have to be won back. The uproar over interracial offenses in the military also highlighted the international implications of southern segregation. As the military sent white and black southerners abroad, Jim Crow orthodoxy collided with foreign assumptions about race and place. White southerners had to justify their racial values and navigate social situations that did not conform to Jim Crow. While these experiences forced some whites to change their worldview, others recoiled at the racial laxity within the military and in foreign countries. Faced with unprecedented challenges, Jim Crow's defenders pointed to racial abominations abroad to refute civil rights agitation back home.[24]

The criticism of creeping integration in the military revealed the mounting anxieties of southern whites more than it reflected any firm stand against racial discrimination by the American military. Two years after the army's European headquarters issued its ambiguous antidiscrimination directive, black war correspondent Roi Ottley reported that "the noose of prejudice is slowly tightening around the necks of American Negro soldiers, and tending to cut off their recreation and associations with the British people." By relying on the "best judgment" of local commanding officers, Ottley argued, the U.S. Army had in many cases left the policing of the color line to men who were "still fighting the Civil War—this time on British soil."[25]

After several weeks traveling around Great Britain, Ottley offered "ample evidence to prove that racial prejudice is encouraged by such officers, a group often dominated by Southerners." Many white personnel resented British hospitality toward African American soldiers. They fumed at press reports that black troops were "being welcomed with the utmost cordiality, even to English homes" and "sharing accommodation with white American and British troops." According to Ottley, "they lost no time in attempting to discipline the British people" because "in the back of the Southerner's mind here is the belief that on his return the Negro will be mighty difficult to remold in the Jim Crow pattern."[26]

This "discipline" took various forms. Some white officers maintained segregation by restricting passes to black troops until they could inspect surrounding towns and designate certain restaurants, theaters, and hotels for white troops only. "This has proved an effective strong-armed instrument for establishing the Jim Crow pattern in public places," reported Ottley, "and, incidentally, relegates Negroes to the worst sections on the outskirts of town or along the waterfront." When African Americans crossed the impromptu color line, white soldiers occasionally reacted violently. Some black Red Cross workers carried baseball bats to ward off ambushes. According to Ottley, white troops formed "gangs" that would declare nearby towns "their" territory and run off any black troops that wandered in while on pass. Harassment occasionally led to minor riots and even armed standoffs. In Lancaster, England, black troops barricaded themselves in an arsenal and fired on white officers after a military policeman shot a black GI in the back. Just before Ottley filed his report, white and black troops in Leicester clashed in two weeks of sporadic rioting, leaving five dead and dozens wounded.[27]

Ambiguous policies and irregular enforcement resulted in recurrent discrimination and violence, but the lack of detailed guidelines and the exigencies of war also allowed room for ad hoc integration. Military service forced many white southerners into unprecedented and unwelcome interactions with black soldiers. A retired colonel from Brunswick, Georgia, complained that "white men and Negros often stand in line to get to the same latrines, Mess, and Canteens." After reading in *Stars and Stripes* that military leaders had attached black platoons to white companies on the front lines, the Georgian protested to Washington. "I had rather die than live under such conditions," he complained, "and many of my friends feel likewise." The practice of inserting black combat units into formerly all-white regiments, argued a Mississippian on the German front, degraded southern fighting men. "We are told on entering a foreign country to re-spect the customs and traditions of the people," he argued, "yet those things dear to the heart of a Southerner are completely ignored."[28]

The most jarring interracial encounters occurred when southern sol-diers encountered black servicemen in positions of authority. While visit-ing a Tunisian city after the North African campaign, South Carolina sol-diers ran into black military policemen who told them "where we could go and what we could and couldn't do." Already concerned about reports of racial trouble back home, the soldiers resented taking orders from Afri-can Americans. "This scene will always be in the minds of the Southern boys . . . ," recalled a sergeant. "I have heard lots of them say that these Negros, and their leaders and Northern white liberals who are causing all this trouble are worse enemies to us, than the Germans will ever be."[29]

Segregation on the high seas also proved inadequate for some south-erners. A Mississippian who spent sixteen months in the Pacific detested the racial mixing aboard crowded troop ships. "It was necessary for me to eat at the same table with niggers or die," he recalled. "Needless to say, I'm still living." But while the sailor reluctantly submitted to integrated dining, he refused to sleep next to black soldiers. "Two yankee buddies and I slept for 39 nights on a hatch," he recalled, "in preference to sleeping down in a foul smelling hole saturated with negro stench." On behalf of "clean living white men," another southern sailor complained to his superiors about intermingling aboard ship. When the officers replied that they could do little to enforce strict segregation, the sailor requested a transfer. "The rearing I had in Miss. and Ala.," he explained, "won't allow me to live in these conditions very long."[30]

Embarrassed and offended by interracial contact abroad, southern whites argued that integrated military service would lead to trouble back home. Worried that the "racial mixup" corrupted southern blacks, a Geor-gia veteran warned, "the Devil has been put in their heads." The "Devil" was racial equality, and reports of black men socializing with European women put that threat in sharp relief. Even as southern white soldiers shunned interracial contact, they lamented the failure of foreign whites to follow their lead. "The British, French, and seemingly none of the other countries' 'white women'," a Chattanooga soldier complained, "seem to know colors very well."[31]

Like rampant claims of black sexual assaults on the home front, reports of black soldiers dating European women confirmed warnings that the clamor for civil rights veiled a desire for "social equality." Southern conservatives feared the return of black veterans corrupted by their interracial experiences. "It was nothing strange in Australia to see a negro walking proudly down a street with a beautiful 'Aussie' girl, who knew no better, who did not care," reported a South Carolinian serving in the South Pacific. "What's to happen when those fellows get back, after having been with white girls?"[32]

Aware of the racial controversies back home, a few black troops taunted southern whites with evidence of their newfound social liberty. In the midst of a southern filibuster, Senator Bilbo received a photograph of a uniformed black soldier and an Italian woman locked in a deep kiss. "I am sending you this picture because I know that it will be making you happy . . . since you are strictly for democracy," read the attached note, signed "R.H. and many others."[33]

While the thought of the Senate's most outspoken white supremacist receiving this photograph may have amused those soldiers, interracial sex remained a deadly serious matter. Long a southern justification for lynching, sexual fear fueled the crusade against wartime civil rights legislation. In Washington and across the South, white supremacists collected and circulated lurid reports of interracial sex abroad. One account that crossed the desk of Georgia senator Richard Russell described Tombolo, a sprawling pine grove outside of Pisa, Italy, whose reputation as a meeting place for black soldiers and local women had reached mythic proportions. The report described "strange huts" deep in the forest where "white women live in promiscuity with colored soldiers." One account described "Babel camps of American negroes in Tombolo," where homeless Italian women wandered around the thickets "looking for a negro who will let them sleep in a tent and in his arms during the night." Military police regularly raided the area and seized by the hundreds dirty and disheveled women who looked "more like animals than human beings." Women in Tombolo allegedly "sold themselves tens and tens of times a day" and frequently wandered around naked during the summer. At night, according to horrified investigators, "frantic orgies can suddenly be seen while the diabolic

During the fall of 1942, as Mississippi senator Theodore Bilbo fought legislation to outlaw the poll tax, African American soldiers sent him this postcard from Italy. (Theodore G. Bilbo Papers, Special Collections, McCain Library and Archives, University of Southern Mississippi, Hattiesburg, Miss.)

boogie woogie is danced around the fire."[34] Southern leaders entered war-time civil rights battles armed with similar accounts, supplied by worried whites from the home front to the battlefield.

When the defenders of segregation criticized the military or denigrated black soldiers, the national media, government officials, and many southern editors denounced their attacks as demagoguery run amuck. Yet southern servicemen and civilians fed their elected officials enough provocative stories to keep the diatribes coming. "If you need any information to prove that the 'niggers' stationed here during the war lived up to their true characters of being shiftless, contemptible, and arrogant," a sergeant informed Bilbo. "I shall be able to furnish you proof." Another southern soldier offered "true reports of the mutinous conduct of the negroes in the places where they have been camped around me." Offering "the factual situation on the majority of the colored troops," a southern white officer serving with a black battalion listed acts of insubordination, sabotage, and criminal behavior. Worse, the major reported, black soldiers had developed a militant racial outlook. "These misfits and agitators often write to the President of the United States and his wife citing petty and imagined grievances," the officer complained. "They read and circulate negro newspapers bearing large headlines of white aggression on negroes."[35]

Throughout the war, southern white supremacists disparaged African American soldiers to undermine demands for equality. "In spite of all the ballyhoo that has been put out about Negroes making good soldiers," Mississippi congressman William Colmer declared, "any Army officer will tell you that they do not." Colmer argued that ample evidence from both world wars proved "that the Negro soldier will not stand up under combat pressure." He suggested that politicians forced African Americans into combat roles to satisfy civil rights activists. "If the Army officers had their way, they would use the Negro soldiers entirely in labor battalions," he claimed. "But, again, unfortunately for the war effort, we run into the political problem."[36]

Such slanderous attacks embarrassed southern moderates, yet overt praise for black servicemen posed political risks as well. In a racially charged wartime environment, southern leaders felt substantial pressure to avoid such gestures. South Carolina congressman Joseph Bryson, attempting to moderate an anti–civil rights speech, included praise for black soldiers in an initial draft. "Large numbers of Southern Negro youth have been called to the colors and are acquitting themselves with honor in our armed forces on land, on the seas and in the air," he wrote. "We of the South are proud of them and gladly pay them tribute." Yet, by the time Bryson delivered the speech, he had marked through those lines with a pencil. Instead of praising black servicemen, Bryson complained that the "liberal family allowances" provided by the army had made it "almost impossible to obtain domestic or other needed help in the South." He hoped, however, that blacks would "proudly slip back into their normal pursuits" when the war ended.[37]

More than a demagogic ploy to stave off civil rights legislation, the uproar over race in the military reflected a collision of grassroots anxieties with elite resistance strategies. Whether complaining to military officials or criticizing black soldiers, southern leaders amplified the wartime anxieties of their constituents and deployed them to refute the demands of civil rights activists. If the uproar over northern black troops and creeping integration in the military bolstered the recurrent southern argument that racial agitation was a foreign import, the white South feared internal threats as well. Even as South Carolina governor R. M. Jefferies monitored black troop activity in his state, he mobilized his state constabulary to investigate black subversion. Responding to rampant rumors that black South Carolinians were buying up firearms and ammunition, Jefferies ordered lawmen to gather information quietly from local merchants.

While the constables uncovered little evidence to suggest that black South Carolinians hoarded guns and ammunition en masse, many reported even the slightest suggestion of subversive activity. A Bethune constable named a black man who tried to buy five boxes of shotgun shells from a hardware store. Another officer in Sumter furnished a list of two dozen African Americans who had purchased guns from a pawn shop. After visiting local merchants, the constable informed the governor, "they are willing to co-operate with us 100 per cent, in not selling shells or ammunition, or any kind of firearms to negroes."[38]

Although confronted with armed and uniformed black soldiers, white lawmen attributed much of the agitation to shadowy organizations of cooks and maids. The dragnet in South Carolina also targeted the "Eleanor Clubs" allegedly sweeping the South during the war. Rampant rumors of this imaginary organization reflected white southern contempt for the first lady as well as widespread fears of black rebellion. Encouraged by Eleanor Roosevelt, this vast network supposedly fomented revolution by encouraging black domestics to enter white homes through the front door, sit with white families at the dinner table, and skip work without notice. "I understand that already they are advising colored servants to demand higher wages and to refuse to do certain kinds of work," reported a Charleston resident. "Perhaps this movement is connected with the plans of the Communists to foment a 'black revolution' in the South. It probably is worth investigating."[39]

Governor Jefferies agreed. At his request, the State Law Enforcement Division scoured South Carolina for any sign of Eleanor Club activity. Most constables uncovered only hearsay, but some provided detailed evidence to substantiate the widespread rumors. A Cheraw constable reported the date, time, and address of an "Eleanor Society" meeting in his town. "At this meeting," he claimed, "they decided that cooks and nurses would not work for less than $6 per week." An officer in Chester reported that a black North Carolinian came down from Charlotte to organize local chapters, while another lawman identified white liberals as agents of the "Eleanor Roosevelt Society." A Gaffney constable provided the name and address of "a great lover of negros" who allegedly entertained black guests at her home and ate with them at her dinner table. The Iowa-born woman, he reported, ran her county's Eleanor Club and encouraged its members to strike for shorter work hours and higher pay. S. J. Pratt, the head of the state constabulary, reported to the governor that the investigation served the added purpose of intimidating racial liberals. "I am of the opinion that when the officers are continuously traveling around," he noted, "that the white people who might be the kind that would sympathize with the negroes know that we are on the lookout for any disturbance, they are not so apt to be involved with the negro question."[40]

While several South Carolina constables turned in troubling reports, others candidly admitted that they could find no evidence of black insurrection. But they did find plenty of white anxiety. A Beaufort constable discovered firearms sales "far below normal" and Eleanor Club activity nonexistent. "I would not, however, have you to infer that the matter of inter-racial relations is exactly normal," he added. "There is too much talk about it among the white people." In the absence of any immediate local threat, the constable concluded that the apprehension "seems to be entirely about what is supposed to have happened elsewhere—trouble between the races in Charleston, 'every white woman in her own kitchen in Christmas' in Columbia and all that sort of thing." Rather than pin the unrest on rabble-rousers, the constable reported that the growing racial tension transcended class lines. "This situation does not seem to be restricted to any particular group but is found in all social groups," he concluded. "The white people appear to be considerably disturbed."[41]

Across the South, wartime rumors spurred predictions of racial disaster.

The details varied from community to community, but the basic themes remained the same. Like Governor Jefferies, University of North Carolina sociologist Howard Odum took the rumors seriously. In *Race and Rumors of Race*, Odum catalogued fantastic tales of black insurrection and impending race war. Introducing his study as "an appeal for genuinely realistic education rather than revolutionary action," Odum wanted to show the nation just how volatile southern racial tensions had become in the first year of war. By presenting "abundant evidence in the catalogue of rumors, tensions, conflicts, and trends," Odum aimed to prove that civil rights activists bore responsibility for the "greatest crisis since the days of the reconstruction." In preparing his book, Odum solicited reports from over one hundred southern white college professors. Through interviews with students, community leaders, and everyday folks, the professors helped Odum compile a list of over 2,000 race rumors. Half of the professors who sent in rumors feared that publishing them "would do more harm than good," but Odum persisted with his portrayal of "a solid South again highly motivated for self-defense."[42]

For John Temple Graves, the South's fighting spirit represented a double-edged sword. Like Odum, the syndicated southern columnist deemed the white South "unwavering and total in determination not to have race segregation abolished." In his 1943 book, *The Fighting South*, Graves attempted to reconcile the white South's fervent support for the war effort with its allegiance to Jim Crow. A self-described "Woodrow Wilson Democrat," Graves had enthusiastically supported American intervention in World War II even before Pearl Harbor. While he celebrated the South's role in military mobilization and its unrivaled patriotism, Graves reminded the nation that the region's whites put their own spin on the stakes of the war effort.[43]

Graves pointed to ominous signs that the "no-compromise leadership among the Negroes" was goading the white South into a race war. Less methodical than Odum, Graves presented his own collection of threats and predictions as "a genuine voice of race trouble below the Potomac." In an entire chapter devoted to "the bigotries, implacables, fierce arguments, dark passions, and impossibles that divide Negro and white man in Southern states," the columnist quoted from letters sent by black and white southerners. Graves followed a letter from a white Alabama newspaperman predicting "hangings, shootings, [and] burnings" with a black correspondent's poem: "Why should I grovel and take the bones, He throws to me as to a dog he owns?" A Virginia woman reported that whites in her community had stopped buying war bonds in response to federal racial reforms, while a black South Carolinian wished Hitler would "drop bombs on every damn southern town in the United States."[44]

Such ominous rhetoric, coupled with mounting reports of racial clashes, convinced embattled southern moderates that reckless black activists were provoking white reactionaries into open conflict. Mark Ethridge, the Mississippi-born editor of the *Louisville Courier-Journal*, warned that African Americans were "impregnated with the feeling that now is the time to make our move for the break-down of segregation." Black militants, he warned, were "moving on every front." Like Graves, Ethridge chided "all or nothing" black leaders for "giving cruel and disillusioning leadership to their people" and "playing into the hands" of militant white supremacists. "Their breed is not dead," Ethridge warned, "it still flourishes in the South [and] it can bring a reaction that will destroy many of the gains that have been made by the colored race."[45]

The rising fortunes of southern demagogues, who had been relatively easy to marginalize in the prewar years, frightened the region's moderates. "Undoubtedly the Old Guard is back in control," reported North Carolina newspaperman and White House advisor Jonathan Daniels. "Also at present a process is in operation which may push New Dealers and liberals more and more to conservative opinions and into conservative ranks." Daniels, who had moved to Washington to advise Roosevelt on wartime racial problems, agreed with Graves that white southerners had their own vision of Double Victory. "Even if mistaken," Daniels explained to presidential secretary Marvin McIntyre, "Southerners feel that they fight for a 'moral issue,' too."[46]

While Daniels sympathized with the plight of Southern moderates, he cringed at the rightward drift of southern politics. The retreat of level-headed leaders in the face of black protest and white reaction, Daniels worried, would create a vacuum of leadership that demagogues would eagerly fill. "When Negro or any other leadership, in trying to go too fast, pushes [southern moderates] out of what we used to call liberalism," he warned, "I am afraid equally dangerous people on the reactionary side will be able to get away with things they wanted to get away with all along." Graves argued that the wartime civil rights movement had only strengthened southern white commitment to segregation. "The centripetal force" of race, Graves explained, "had brought them all home at once and lined them up together." But if Graves claimed that wartime turmoil had forced a racial "homecoming" for southern whites, Daniels pointed out that many had never left. He worried that by rallying to defend segregation, moderates would align with "a company of Southerners who aren't drawn back on racial questions to Southern thinking by any centripetal force but have been pretty close to Talmadge . . . all along."[47]

With the region's moderates in rapid retreat and federal officials reluctant to offend powerful southern conservatives, a pessimistic Daniels offered a bleak prognosis. "More and more in recent months," he noted early in 1943, "I have been impressed with the similarity of our situation to that in the last century when the extreme abolitionists and the violent secessionists almost collaborated to leave sensible people helpless in the middle." After the Detroit riots left two dozen dead and scores wounded in the summer of 1943, Daniels prepared the president to expect more of the same. "The race riots in Detroit," he warned Roosevelt, "must be recognized, it seems to me, as a climax in what amounts to an epidemic of racial tensions in the United States—an epidemic still spreading."[48]

At the Office of War Mobilization, former South Carolina senator James Byrnes interpreted the Detroit riot as an indication that "in many northern cities the resentment of the white people is greater than in the South." While he dutifully avoided public comment of racial issues, Roosevelt's "Assistant President for the Home Front" complained that "radical Negro leaders" had sparked a domestic crisis. "We can not fight a war abroad," Byrnes warned, "and have a race war at home."[49]

As his constable corps scoured South Carolina for Eleanor Clubs and stockpiles of weapons, Governor Jefferies headed to Washington to ward off another looming threat. In late 1942, the Senate held hearings on a bill to abolish the poll tax in the handful of southern states that still required it. The tax's defenders claimed that it provided needed funds for education, but opponents decried its effectiveness as a disfranchisement tactic. For poor southerners, black and white, a tax of one or two dollars represented a large slice of their weekly wages. Several Deep South states levied a cumulative tax. An older voter might have to pay more than fifty dollars to cover the previous decades' unpaid levies.[50]

The fight to end this practice had become a liberal cause célèbre. The National Committee to Abolish the Poll Tax coordinated a campaign that brought together civil rights organizations, labor unions, and progressive church groups. Opponents of the practice pointed out that, in non–poll tax states, two-thirds of the voting-age population cast ballots in the 1940 elections. In the poll tax states, however, less than a quarter of adults voted. While defenders of the poll tax claimed a higher turnout in primaries, the only elections that mattered in the solidly Democratic South, southern journalist Stetson Kennedy demonstrated that the general election drew larger numbers of voters.[51]

In addition to disenfranchising an estimated 11 million southerners, the poll tax gave the region's voting minority a disproportionate influence in national politics. As poll tax opponents pointed out, more Rhode Islanders cast ballots for their two representatives in the House than the combined voters of Mississippi, Alabama, Georgia, and South Carolina cast for their thirty-two. Once the seventy-eight poll tax congressmen reached Washington, their road to seniority was much easier than that of their colleagues. In the three congressional elections between 1938 and 1942, the turnover among congressmen from "free voting states" was 70 percent greater than among the poll tax representatives. With their congressional seats safe and their seniority insured, southern Democrats enjoyed disproportionate control of congressional committees. Poll tax Democrats headed seventeen of forty-three committees in the House and ten of thirty-three in the Senate. As conservative southern Democrats turned against Roosevelt and the New Deal, they used their lopsided influence on Capitol Hill to kill progressive legislation. "When Polltaxia is 'agin' a bill," lamented Stetson Kennedy, "the United States is often forced to do without it."[52]

The poll tax embodied for many Americans the fundamentally undemocratic nature of Jim Crow politics, but the campaign to abolish it represented a call to arms for southern conservatives. At the Senate hearings on anti–poll tax legislation, South Carolina's governor invoked patriotism and states' rights in defense of voting restrictions. "I respectfully submit," declared Jefferies, "that the eight poll-tax States are inhabited by true Americans willing and ready to make every sacrifice for the protection of our national existence." At the same time, Jefferies argued that the South stood ready to defend its sovereignty in the face of federal interference. By abolishing the poll tax, he warned, Congress would be headed down a slippery slope of totalitarian legislation. "When you get through with that then South Carolina will have no rights whatsoever," argued Jefferies, "we might as well turn over the elections to the Federal Government." South Carolina was "sort of democratic," Jefferies argued, and that was good enough.[53]

The poll tax controversy revealed the continuity between charges of outside agitation and demands for local control. When Congress passed a bill in September 1942 that waived poll tax requirements for American servicemen, fears of emboldened black soldiers collided with concerns over federal encroachment. The Soldier Voting Act of 1942, passed several weeks after the southern party primaries, posed no immediate threat to Democrats in poll tax states. But the ominous precedent invited howls of protest from Deep South diehards. Alabama congressman Sam Hobbs deemed the bill "an attack on our southern way of life and on white supremacy" and an attempt "to cater to the soldier vote at the expense of the very foundation of our democracy." The average white soldier, he contended, "does not wish to vote at such a price." The House's most notorious Negrophobe, John Rankin of Mississippi, blamed the bill's poll tax amendment on "a long range communistic program to change our form of Government and . . . to take the control of our elections out of the hands of white Americans."[54]

After Rankin and company failed to derail the bill, National Negro Council president Edgar Brown vowed to make the infamous race-baiter its first victim. Noting that the number of active-duty black servicemen from Mississippi's First Congressional District outnumbered the votes cast for Rankin in the recent primary, Brown announced a write-in campaign to oust the congressman. Hailing the soldier-vote bill as "the greatest contribution to democracy since Lincoln signed the Emancipation Proclamation," Brown nominated a black Mississippian fighting under General Douglas MacArthur in the South Pacific: Private Abraham Lincoln Brooks.[55]

Despite civil rights activists' high hopes, the Soldier Voting Act's practical impact fell far short of its promise. Rankin's hometown paper chided black "misleaders" for stirring up false hopes. Denouncing the write-in campaign as "Utter Foolishness," the *Tupelo Daily Journal* warned it would be "many, many years before Negroes will even vote — much less elect congressmen." The paper's stance seemed enlightened compared to Rankin's hard-line white supremacy, which grew shriller as the poll tax fight continued on Capitol Hill. Just five weeks after exempting soldiers from the poll tax, the House of Representatives voted three-to-one to abolish the requirement altogether. "You are now creating a second front," Rankin warned his colleagues moments before the vote. "You are waging war against the white people of the Southern States."[56]

Unbeknownst to Rankin, a few Mississippians had already struck back. The same day that the House approved the anti–poll tax bill, newspapers across the country announced a brutal double lynching in Mississippi. Early on the morning of October 12, vigilantes had stormed the Clarke County jail and seized two black fourteen-year-olds charged with attempted rape. The next morning, authorities found Ernest Green and Charlie Lang hanging from a bridge near Shubuta. Just five days later, a much larger mob dragged forty-nine-year-old Howard Wash from a jail in nearby Laurel. A local jury had just convicted Wash of murdering his white employer but had declined to recommend the death penalty. That same night, one hundred armed men hung Wash from a local bridge.[57]

Mob violence refocused national attention on the state long regarded as the nation's lynching capital. Yet even as regional and national press blasted the state's ambivalent reaction to mob violence, many white Mississippians blamed northern politicians and civil rights activists for the lynchings. "Chickens come home to roost!" declared the *Meridian Star*, arguing that "cheap and dirty national politics" had inspired the vigilantes. The *Star* pointed out that the lynchings followed Rankin's prediction that an anti–poll tax bill would spark violence across the South. "Vote-hungry national leadership has purposefully stirred up the issue of race prejudice," the editor declared. "Washington is sowing tragic seed. We must harvest bitter fruit."[58]

Civil rights activists agreed that the poll tax fight on Capitol Hill had spurred mob violence. A black weekly in New York called the Mississippi lynchings a "Poll Tax Rout." The editor deemed no southern blacks safe from the white supremacist onslaught. "On the eve of the congressional action on the Anti-Poll Tax bill to 'enfranchise' some 4,000,000 Negroes in eight Southern States," he warned, "the South opened the first gun of its reprisal by lynching two 14-year-old colored boys." Alongside reports of the Mississippi lynchings, the New York weekly reported that Talmadge allies in Georgia had launched "the Vigilantes, Inc.," in response to the poll tax vote. This secretive new organization, the paper warned, was "designed to take over the unfinished work of the Klan."[59]

In Birmingham, John Temple Graves pinned the blame for mob violence on civil rights advocates. Moderate leadership had Talmadge and his ilk on the run, Graves lamented, as evidenced by the Georgia governor's recent defeat at the hands of liberal challenger Ellis Arnall. But "the continuing agitation of the Negro" had "given new leases" to the diehards. Advocates of racial equality, Graves argued, traded in an equally dangerous brand of demagoguery: "Talmadge had been beaten, for the time being, but his soul was marching on—by courtesy of the National Association for the Advancement of Colored People, the Northern Negro press, the politicians and sentimentalists in high places at Washington, and the devoted but cross-eyed humanitarians." By attacking "something as vital to white Southerners as the war itself," misguided militants had goaded their adversaries into open revolt. "I think the impartial historian," Graves concluded, "will place the greater blame for the disgraceful scene on the incorrigible domestic crusaders who forced the poll tax issue, with all the bitter irreconcilables it involved, at a time of greatest war."[60]

The poll tax controversy, which erupted amidst mounting fears over the domestic implications of World War II, exposed the vision of white democracy that the defenders of segregation fought to save. But marauding vigilantes were not the most powerful force in this counteroffensive. The formidable southern Senate bloc, whose filibuster ultimately killed the anti–poll tax bill, posed the greatest threat to the wartime civil rights campaign. Senator Bilbo, while personally opposed to a disfranchisement tactic that cut into his traditional support base of hill-country whites, decried federal interference in state elections. Like the antilynching bill before it, Bilbo branded the anti–poll tax bill as an "entering wedge" for "the 'full equality' program which the Negro leaders have launched in this time of war." Fashioning himself as a freedom fighter, Bilbo aligned his filibuster with the war effort. "In making this fight against the unconstitutional anti-poll tax bill," he declared, "I feel that I am as much a soldier in the preservation of the American way and American scheme of Government as the boys who are fighting and dying on Guadalcanal."[61]

Such a declaration would have seemed laughable if enthusiastic supporters had not echoed the sentiment. "You are receiving these congratulations," declared a young state legislator, "from one who over a month ago joined the United States Marines, and who is willing to fight and die for his country, but who does not want his country depriving him of the freedom he is fighting for." For anxious white southerners, the stakes of the global struggle against the Axis echoed their traditional hostility to outside interference. Even as civil rights advocates compared lynch mobs to Nazi storm troopers, some white southerners considered the anti–poll tax bill as perilous as a Panzer division rolling across the Mason-Dixon Line. Responding to the anti–poll tax bill, an anxious Alabama lumber dealer argued that "such legislation is so very dangerous in that it seeks to destroy the individual state and make Federal control over all things." Civil rights legislation, he feared, would "rapidly lead to the destruction of individual rights and Liberties and make of us a Dictator controlled people, the very thing which we are now supposed to be fighting to destroy in other Nations and to keep America free."[62]

The lessons of Reconstruction figured prominently in this white supremacist expression of wartime patriotism. The poll tax fight, warned the mayor of Vicksburg, marked "the beginning of another carpet bag era and a knife plunged into the very heart of local self government by what we thought was our party." By backing such legislation, northern politicians played into the enemy's hands. "No action which the congress of the

United States could take would please Hitler, Hitlerites and the Quislings more than this or any similar action calculated to stir up strife and divide the Nation," the mayor declared. "Perhaps it is being encouraged by some who would benefit by such a result." Protesting the anti–poll tax bill, another Vicksburg resident blamed "German sympathizers" for attempting "to cause another civil war in this country."[63]

Reconstruction and its aftermath, which some elderly southerners still remembered vividly, surfaced repeatedly in white supremacists' wartime rhetoric. If southern whites cringed at the thought of racial change, their resistance was not based on blind nostalgia. Wartime resistance reflected not just fear for the future but also an abiding awareness of the past. Praising the defeat of the anti–poll tax bill, a lawyer from the Arkansas Delta paid tribute to the lessons of white supremacy handed down from his father. An eighty-seven-year-old retired judge, E. D. Robertson remembered a time when black freedmen would "line up for two blocks long to vote." When the Ku Klux Klan failed to keep black voters away, local whites would stage a "fake pistol fight" in front of the polling place to confuse and frighten the freedmen. Ultimately, legal barriers achieved what costumes and gunfire could not. "He said that they soon caught on to these things," noted the judge's son, "but when they put the $1.00 poll tax to them they faded out of politics like dew in August before the morning sun." The living link to an era of black political participation made the threat of the wartime civil rights movement that much more urgent. "They do not know how seriously the people in the South consider the negro question," argued the judge's son. "Lots of Southern people would die and go to Hell lots of times before they would become subject to the negro race."[64]

In their descriptions of the wartime threats facing the South, the defenders of white democracy often cursed African Americans and the Axis in the same breath. Some even tried to tie them together in a grand conspiracy. But given that Hitler sympathizers were no more numerous on the southern home front than committed integrationists, many white southerners regarded Nazism and NAACP-ism as a dual threat to the southern way of life. Faced with a homegrown campaign for interracial democracy, some whites flatly admitted that they would rather take their chances with the Nazis. "We the people of the south are as patriotic and determined to win this World War as any body, and are working diligently to cooperate with all groups to win the war," declared one Mississippian, "but we might as well be under Hitler rule as to be under the rule of these bone-headed niggers here." The "outrageous invasion of States Rights" discouraged a father with two boys in the service. "It might be better to lose this war," he declared, "than to have victory with Negroe equality and black domination."[65]

As southern conservatives assessed the wartime threats to their political and economic power, they pondered the racial implications of global war. Some charged that enemy agents exploited domestic racial turmoil to undermine the American war effort, and others predicted that an Axis victory would turn Jim Crow on its head. When a poll tax defender predicted that newly enfranchised black voters, seething with "inborn hate of the white man," would elect Hitler president, he revealed the connection that racial conservatives drew between Axis totalitarianism and civil rights activism. Charles Wade, a Mississippi Delta lawyer, linked black protest to the multiethnic Axis alliance. "The Jap side of this war is strictly a race matter," he argued. Given the racially charged confrontation in the Pacific theater, this argument was neither novel nor exclusive to southern white supremacists. However, Wade's notion of a global "race war" provided a counterpoint to African American attempts to parallel Axis totalitarianism with southern racial practices. "The negro question in the South is not as local as the Government wishes to believe," he warned his senators. "It's going to be a world wide race movement, and you people who call the turns had better get your ears to the ground if you wish to continue to enjoy the advantages of white supremacy."[66]

In the Mississippi Delta, where blacks heavily outnumbered whites, local elites took such warnings to heart. Even in an area long regarded as a bastion of white domination, regional power brokers interpreted any hint of black assertiveness as an attack on the social order. When a committee of the Delta Council sponsored an interracial meeting in Greenville in early 1943, some alarmed locals protested the concession. "I see nothing good to come out of such meetings," argued a Delta Council leader, "except further demands for social and political equality . . . which they are craving and we all know it." Deeming blacks "unfit at this time to exercise the ballot from both a mental and cultural standpoint," the local attorney argued that whites should continue to decide policies and reforms "without having to be goaded by the negroes."[67]

Unnerved by black initiative, Delta whites quickly organized "active Vigilance Committees to protect our rights, our civilization and our way of life." Committee leaders in Leflore and Sunflower Counties stood ready to assist other Delta communities in forming their own chapters. Hoping to discourage local blacks from pushing for racial change, white elites also launched the Southern Crusaders to "Keep America Safe for Americans." Carrying endorsements from the governor as well as prominent planters and businessmen, the Southern Crusaders advocated "teaching the negroes the advantages of the American form of government" while warning them "to shun that class of persons who would have them accept some foreign teachings." By urging their black neighbor "to keep his ear to the ground and his eyes open," the organizers hoped to enlist a network of black "Crusaders" who could help keep racial agitators at bay.[68]

Despite mounting challenges to their racially exclusive brand of democracy, southern conservatives regarded themselves as the inheritors of sacred American traditions. Deep South elites worried that the wartime civil rights drive would penetrate the last bastion of true Americanism, defined by one Mississippian as "white supremacy, strict interpretation of the Constitution, and freedom in our domestic affairs." But southern African Americans increasingly challenged this racially exclusive definition of democracy. During World War II, southern politicians appealed to "democracy" and the "American way of life" so often, and so interchangeably, that black activists felt compelled to draw a distinction between the two. "Which Do You Want," asked the Negro Citizens' Committee of South Carolina, "Democracy or 'The American Way of Life'?" Responding to a rhetoric that conflated white supremacy with authentic Americanism, these southern activists defined democracy as "equal rights and privileges for all—and not the so-called 'American Way of Life' which often compromises, discriminates, or even denies where Negroes are concerned."[69]

By early 1944, African Americans in South Carolina and across the region had reason to believe that they had white democracy on the run. Southern senators could protect the poll tax, but they could not prevent the federal judiciary from ruling on an explicitly racial disfranchisement tactic: the white primary. By legally barring blacks from participation in the Democratic primary, Deep South states effectively nullified any black political challenge. The Supreme Court had previously upheld the white primary, ruling that the Democratic Party was a private organization that could restrict membership by race. But in 1943, the NAACP took up the case of Lonnie Smith, a black Houston dentist who had sued a Texas election official for denying him a ballot in the state's 1940 Democratic primary.[70]

Southern African Americans anticipated the U.S. Supreme Court's decision with unprecedented organization. Hopeful but not counting on a favorable court ruling in *Smith v. Allwright*, the Negro Citizens Committee of South Carolina raised $300,000 for future court battles. Meanwhile, black activists in the state organized a pro-Roosevelt "Colored Democratic

Party" as a grassroots challenge to whites-only politics. Renamed the Progressive Democratic Party, the organization enlisted 45,000 members, sent protest delegates to the Democratic National Convention, and nominated a black Senate candidate. While neither the seating challenge nor the Senate campaign succeeded, grassroots activists served notice that the political status quo faced internal as well as external threats.[71]

The reality of homegrown protest provoked South Carolina's particularly strident condemnation of *Smith v. Allwright*. The state legislature preempted an unfavorable decision by adopting a resolution demanding that "the damned agitators of the North leave the South alone" and proclaiming "our belief in and our allegiance to established white supremacy." Like previous wartime protests, the resolution linked the defense of the racial status quo with the struggle against the Axis. The resolution accused Northern politicians and civil rights activists of "taking traitorous and treasonous advantage" of wartime upheaval and adopting a "Nazi philosophy of conquest."[72]

When the Supreme Court struck down the Texas white primary on 3 April 1944, South Carolina fired off another round of defiant declarations. In an impassioned appeal to the South Carolina legislature, governor and Senate candidate Olin Johnston revisited the "immorality" of Reconstruction. "Where you now sit," he reminded them, "there sat a majority of negroes." Invoking the spirit of the late South Carolina senator and white supremacist icon Ben Tillman, Johnston declared: "History has taught us that we must keep our white Democratic primaries pure and unadulterated so that we might protect the welfare and homes of all the people of our State." Johnston urged South Carolinians to employ all "necessary methods" to exclude blacks from the Democratic Party. "White supremacy will be maintained in our primaries," he vowed. "Let the chips fall where they may!"[73]

For a decade, southern diehards had attempted to link the rise of Roosevelt with the downfall of white supremacy. After *Smith v. Allwright*, as one national news magazine put it, "the lid came off the race problem." While "U.S. Negroes had won a considerable moral victory, and had gained a little political ground," the South was "still solid" on white supremacy. With unprecedented furor, white supremacists equated Roosevelt with racial revolution. "Everywhere south of the Potomac," *Time* concluded in the wake of *Smith v. Allwright*, "the New Deal had lost a little more ground."[74]

Combining the wartime threat of enemy subversion with the specter of federal tyranny, southern conservatives portrayed the New Deal as the domestic wing of a worldwide totalitarian offensive. With racial tensions at the boiling point, white southern leaders contrasted their vision of Americanism with the federal activism and social engineering of the Roosevelt administration. "The duties and ideals of loyal Americans, true Democrats, and patriotic Southerners are not inconsistent," declared former Mississippi governor Mike Connor after *Smith v. Allwright*. New Dealers, on the other hand, had embraced "un-American and undemocratic philosophies of government." They sought, Connor charged, "to change the very form of our government from a republic to an absolute, totalitarian state of communism or national socialism, which would destroy at home everything our armed forces abroad are fighting to preserve." For Connor, the racial stakes of this struggle had never been more clear. The national Democratic Party, he argued, had become a "New Deal Party" that would continue to "traffic with northern negroes to place the black heel of negro domination on our necks." Connor called on Democrats to reclaim the traditional values of the "white man's party" and reject the New Deal. "America is White, not Red, not Black," Connor declared, "and the time has come for the Democratic Party to tell the New Dealers, with all the force at our command, that we [propose] to keep it White."[75]

For Roosevelt's reinvigorated southern critics, the demise of segregated primaries forecast the breakdown of other racial barriers. "It is abundantly and increasingly clear," declared former Louisiana governor Sam Jones, "that the New Deal high command hopes to use the war as an instrument for forcing the social 'equality' of the Negro upon the South." Echoing Jones's warnings, a North Carolina industrialist distributed anti-Roosevelt pamphlets during the 1944 campaign. Because the president "has done more to give [blacks] social equality than all men and political parties combined," the pamphleteer announced, "I Can't Vote for Mr. Roosevelt in November." The front page featured a photograph of an interracial wedding party: "The picture on the front is the result of these teachings and preachings," he warned, ". . . when this white boy gets married, in Connecticut, he gets a negro for best-man."[76]

The white supremacist revolt against Roosevelt fueled a broader southern attack on the New Deal. Clayton Rand, a Mississippi newspaperman, melded his critique of totalitarianism with his own interpretation of southern history. Speaking before civic groups and business leaders in Alabama, Mississippi, and Louisiana in the spring of 1944, Rand warned that the New Deal portended a "New Slavery" far worse than anything the South had imposed on African Americans. "The most human type of slavery," Rand argued, had existed on the antebellum plantation. The "lenient masters" allowed their slaves "more or less personal freedom," while the New Dealers sought to destroy individual liberty through bureaucracy. "The cruelest

I Can't Vote For Mr. Roosevelt In November

Wartime racial controversies convinced some southern conservatives that President Roosevelt and his New Deal allies wanted to dismantle segregation. During the 1944 presidential campaign, a North Carolinian distributed an anti-Roosevelt pamphlet with an interracial wedding party on the cover. (Richard B. Russell Papers, Richard B. Russell Library for Political Research and Studies, University of Georgia, Athens, Ga.)

form of slavery is that in which the individual is under the complete control of the state," Rand declared. "Much rather would one be owned by an individual than become a chattel under the regimentation of a totalitarian state."[77]

During World War II, the defense of Jim Crow evolved from scattered protests and rumormongering to a rival interpretation of Double Victory. More than an elite rhetorical strategy but less than an authentic grassroots rebellion, the attempt to reconcile Jim Crow with the war effort involved and invigorated racial conservatives from all walks of life. From the battlefield to the home front, southern whites experienced the convulsions that shook the region and confronted the racial stakes of the global conflict. World War II raised the expectations of civil rights advocates, but it also emboldened a countermovement that perceived no conflict between American war aims and the segregated status quo. Thus southern conservatives, like their adversaries, moved into the postwar years convinced that theirs was the true patriotic crusade.

FROM WHITE SUPREMACISTS TO "SEGREGATIONISTS"

3

In late March 1944, Theodore Bilbo traveled home with a warning for his fellow Mississippians. With the "joy and happiness of the prodigal son returning to loved ones and the old homestead," the senator stood before a joint session of the state legislature. After reflecting on his long and stormy tenure in state politics, the former governor assured the packed gallery and a radio audience of ultimate victory over the Axis. Triumphant forecasting gave way to foreboding, however, as the senator turned his attention to race. "I wish to discuss with you this grave race problem fully and frankly," Bilbo announced. "In the interest of our Nation, our Southland and our own State of Mississippi," he continued, "I shall be forced to make startling revelations to you. Such action I have decided is absolutely necessary at this time."[1]

By early 1944, what Bilbo had to say would have shocked few white Mississippians. He had battled anti-lynching and anti–poll tax legislation with unmatched fervor and had denounced the FEPC and attempts to open Democratic primaries to black voters. His constituents had every reason to expect a white supremacist harangue, but Bilbo spoke with a heightened sense of urgency. "We in the Southland," he announced, "being fully aware of the attempts to break down segregation and implant social equality of the races throughout the Nation are ready to do some plain talking." The senator reminded the packed gallery and the radio audience of their sacred duty to maintain racial integrity and defend white civilization. "We people of the South must draw the color line tighter and tighter," Bilbo declared, "and any white man or woman who dares to cross that color line should be permanently and forever ostracized."[2]

As the war abroad wound down, Jim Crow's defenders rallied to the barricades. Convinced that assaults on the white primary and the poll tax served the ultimate goal of breaking down segregation, southern racial conservatives increasingly focused their energy on defending and justifying its continued existence. As a self-identified "segregationist" conceded in 1945, "Southern people are not so much concerned with the Negro's voting per se — they are concerned with the results of that voting." Faced with a wartime civil rights campaign that called the question on segregation, southern racial conservatives mobilized explicitly in its defense. As the nation transitioned from war to peace, affirmations of segregation overtook calls for white supremacy as the battle cry of southern racial conservatives.

The rise and demise of Washington's most notorious racist proceeded apace with this uneven transition. Theodore Bilbo earned his well-deserved reputation as a southern demagogue and a Capitol Hill pariah. Yet as Jim Crow faced unprecedented threats during World War II, the political mainstream in the South shifted toward Bilbo's hard-line stance. At the same time, Jim Crow's most militant defenders recognized that egalitarian war rhetoric and black political pressure had transformed the national landscape. Even Bilbo realized that World War II rendered "white supremacy" insufficient and imprecise as a rallying cry for white southerners. While "Bilboism" became an umbrella epithet for crude bigotry and violent repression, the Mississippi senator also fought desegregation in the nation's capital, penned a segregationist manifesto, and attracted allies who had previously shunned him.[3] Bilbo's strange career reveals that even Jim Crow's most diehard defenders recognized that segregation demanded a multifaceted defense. As they mobilized to redeem the color line as a social necessity and a fundamentally American institution, Bilbo and his allies broadened their critique of wartime egalitarianism.

Bilbo's Mississippi legislature speech marked no significant departures in his racial thinking. What had changed, he believed, was his newfound authority. Bilbo addressed his constituents, he proudly announced, as the new "mayor ex-officio" of Washington, due to his recent appointment to the chairmanship of the Senate Committee on the District of Columbia. If his new title sounded impressive, Bilbo's promotion was hardly a coup. The death of Indiana senator Frederick Van Nuys opened up a more attractive committee assignment for District Committee chairman and Nevada Democrat Pat McCarran. By virtue of seniority, Bilbo assumed chairmanship of the least prestigious standing committee in Congress. The Mississippi senator headed a congressional institution long regarded, in the words of one Washington journalist, as "a proving ground for junior members or a dumping ground for embarrassing ones." But in the hands of the

Senate's most fervent white supremacist, the District Committee became a bully pulpit for segregation and a lightning rod for the wartime civil rights movement.[4]

Speaking for his fellow southerners, the senator would later write that "the Negro problem is neither academic nor hypothetical; we live in the midst of it."[5] In the nation's capital, perhaps more than in his home state, Bilbo and his southern colleagues caught a glimpse of the coming civil rights revolution. During World War II, African Americans in the District of Columbia launched campaigns against discrimination and disfranchisement that foreshadowed the southern protests and boycotts that would grab headlines in future decades. At the same time, a few farsighted white southerners anticipated opportunities to garner the sympathy of northern whites threatened by campaigns against residential segregation. During his brief tenure as the "Mayor of Washington," Bilbo fought hard to keep Jim Crow in the nation's capital.

From the moment Bilbo assumed the District Committee chairmanship, African Americans fought back. The nation's capital held strategic and symbolic significance for the wartime "Double V" campaign. As "the head and front and nerve center of the world," argued A. Philip Randolph, "Washington is the political symbol of the greatest power on earth today." For segregationists and civil rights leaders alike, however, the nation's capital held more than emblematic importance. Washington was a symbol, but it was also a city. In the eyes of many African Americans and their allies, that city retained its decidedly southern accent. "Washington is not only the capital of the nation," Randolph lamented. "It is the capital of Dixie, of 20th century Copperheaded Confederacy."[6]

By Bilbo's estimation, however, Washington was not southern enough. The nation's capital, Bilbo explained, "while sometimes called a southern city, is on the borderline."[7] For the Mississippi senator, the nation's capital lost more of its southern twang with every wartime challenge to racial discrimination and white supremacy. More than a few of his southern supporters heartily agreed. The relatively lax color line in wartime Washington shocked a visitor from the Arkansas Delta. "It was with a mixed surprise and disgust," G. B. Deane reported, "that I saw so many things that we of the South hold so high, trampled under foot." When Deane stepped off the train, he immediately noticed the "utter disregard for color at the station." Recounting his initial shock and the many that followed on his trip to the nation's capital, Deane congratulated Bilbo "for having certain people in Washington shivering." Deeming Bilbo's appointment "a defeat for Mrs. Eleanor Roosevelt," another enthusiastic southern supporter hoped that the new "mayor" could "stop some of that social equality that has ruined our nation's capital."[8]

In his appeals to fellow southerners and the nation as a whole, the Mississippi senator warned that civil rights advances in the District of Columbia would fan outward. From local campaigns for voting rights to desegregation in federal agencies, Bilbo pointed to racial skirmishes in the district as harbingers of a civil rights revolution. Using the same language he had invoked in filibusters against antilynching and anti–poll tax legislation, Bilbo warned that racial reform in Washington would provide an "entering wedge" for future encroachments on white supremacy throughout the South.[9] If civil rights advocates hoped that Washington would serve as a showcase for interracial democracy, the defenders of segregation wanted the nation's capital to conform to Jim Crow orthodoxy.

Although the district committees lacked prestige on Capitol Hill, their southern members had long wielded substantial power over local affairs. Since Congress had ended a short experiment with home rule in the late nineteenth century, the District Committee managed municipal matters in the nation's capital. Bilbo was the most notorious white supremacist to serve on the committee, but he was not the first. During the Depression, former Mississippi attorney general and longtime Bilbo rival Ross Collins became chairman of the House Subcommittee on District Appropriations. When the congressman slashed funding for municipal improvements, the head of the district's welfare department visited his office to request additional funding for black facilities. "If I went along with your ideas," Collins declared, "I'd never keep my seat in Congress. My constituents wouldn't stand for spending all that money on niggers."[10]

The lack of adequate housing and municipal services did not slow the influx of southern black migrants into Washington. As the black population of the District of Columbia ballooned to 200,000, new arrivals crowded into shantytowns in the broad alleys sandwiched between row houses. The residents of Washington's alleys endured wretched living conditions. When Malcolm Little first visited the capital in 1941 as a dishwasher on a passenger train, he reacted with shock and disgust. "I was astounded," Malcolm X later recalled, "to find in the nation's capital, just a few blocks from Capitol Hill, thousands of Negroes living . . . in dirt-floor shacks along unspeakably filthy lanes with names like Pig Alley and Goat Alley." Native North Carolinian David Brinkley, who arrived in Washington in 1943 to work as a radio broadcaster, remembered that the Health Department once tallied 15,000 privies in the alleys, each one shared by as many as thirty people.[11]

Assuming the District Committee chairmanship in early 1944, Bilbo took aim at the district's black enclaves with a barrage of law-and-order rhetoric. "The criminal element has made Washington a haven of safety long enough," he declared. "But from now on it's going to be moving day." Bilbo pushed for an expanded police force, programs to curb juvenile delinquency, and slum clearance. Vowing to transform Washington into a "model city," Bilbo also pledged to renovate hospitals and improve the local water system. If his earlier reform efforts in Mississippi indicated anything, African Americans would reap few benefits from these progressive proposals. "On the basis of Bilbo's record and statements," Washington NAACP president Arthur Gray announced, "Negroes cannot expect any kind of fair treatment under his administration of District affairs." While the black press lamented Bilbo's appointment, they deemed his appropriation of the "mayor" title frightfully accurate. "The man schooled in the rope and faggot tradition of Mississippi," the *Chicago Defender* lamented, "will hold in his hands the administration of the capital of the nation supposed to be the 'world's greatest democracy.'"[12]

True to form, Bilbo offered black Washingtonians little more than a free ticket out of town. The senator assumed the chairmanship in the midst of a prolonged series of committee hearings on public housing in Washington. Wartime migration magnified the housing shortage, particularly in the district's appallingly overcrowded black ghettos. Although Bilbo endorsed long-delayed plans for slum clearance, he opposed any proposals for expanded public housing in the "Negro heaven" of Washington. Instead, Bilbo recommended that local authorities deliver the 20,000 black inhabitants of Washington's alleys to planters in Maryland and Virginia. "The farmers are begging for labor," Bilbo declared. "There's not an occupant in an alley who can't find a place in which to live or work to do."[13]

Bilbo's plan to "free a lot of people from the bright lights of Washington" reflected his sympathy for southern white employers and their struggle to maintain control over an increasingly mobile black workforce. The senator's constituents lamented their own labor woes, as Mississippi blacks fled northward in search of better wages and improved living conditions. The president of the Hattiesburg Compress Company complained that "[labor] recruiting in our local area does not amount to a hill of beans, with local and other Mississippi newspapers carrying large ads for out of state common labor." The lure of lucrative wartime employment, he reported, "keeps our local labor dissatisfied with wages and working conditions."[14]

Bilbo's relocation scheme reflected broader anxieties about black migration. It also earned him a chorus of ridicule from Washingtonians. A black columnist observed that Bilbo "has more plans and places for relegating Negroes than a dog has fleas—first to Africa, and now to the basements of white 'bourbons' where they can eke out a starvation or to a more 'airy' starvation on nearby 'Virginny' farms." The papers that had largely ignored Bilbo in the past now roundly condemned his recommendations. "Senator Bilbo has begun his career as District 'mayor' with all of the finesse that might be expected of a rhinoceros in the National Gallery of Art," declared the *Washington Post*. "His proposal . . . reeks of prejudice, social backwardness, and Hitlerian technique."[15]

Shrugging off the scorn of the Washington establishment, Bilbo regularly reminded his constituents of his efforts to defend segregation in the nation's capital. In his 1944 address to the Mississippi state legislature, Bilbo portrayed Washington's color line as the front line in the wartime assault on white supremacy. The March on Washington Movement had forced the president to order the desegregation of government buildings. "In the Federal offices in Washington," Bilbo declared, "whites and Negroes work in the same rooms, the same offices, eat together at the same cafeterias, use the same rest rooms and recreational facilities." Workplace desegregation, Bilbo repeatedly pointed out, forecast the racial chaos yet to come. Bilbo spoke of partitions, sinks, and toilets "wrecked and removed" to emphasize the integrationists' reckless zeal. "Destroying racial barriers," he explained, "is the aim of these Negroes; they want to see white girls working for Negro men and Negro girls working for white men, and to some small extent, they have been successful in bringing about this deplorable condition in the Nation's Capital." According to Bilbo, "the mixing of the races has gone so far that southern girls, going to the capital city to work, have returned home." Those who remained, he added, "find such conditions almost unbearable."[16]

Bilbo based his accusations on letters received from resentful southern whites working in the nation's capital. "Conditions at the Bureau are getting rather bad," complained a Georgia woman at the Bureau of Printing and Engraving. "The negroes now eat at tables formerly reserved for whites," she reported, "and are now using the toilet rooms of the white dressing rooms." At the War Production Board, another federal employee quit her job rather than share restrooms with her black coworkers. "It is irritating to a white woman of any refinement," she complained, "to go to a washroom to clean up a bit before lunch and find a husky negress before the mirror with her cosmetics spread out, smoking like a chimney and refusing to budge an inch."[17]

Such reports convinced Bilbo that white Washingtonians stood behind him, but the cries to revoke his committee chairmanship grew louder in the wake of his Mississippi legislature speech. The following month, 3,000 Washington residents packed the main auditorium at the historically black Asbury Methodist Episcopal Church. In one of the largest integrated meetings in Washington's history, the "Sponsoring Committee to Oust Senator Bilbo" condemned the Mississippian's "undemocratic opposition to those ideals for which we are fighting and . . . his demonstrated inability to act for or on behalf of the voteless citizens of the nation's capital."[18]

Yet, when faced with demands for his removal, Bilbo insisted that he spoke for Washington's imperiled white majority. He argued that unchecked in-migration, coupled with the increasing assertiveness of African Americans, undermined law and order. While thwarting attempts to expand housing options for black residents, Bilbo also assailed the attempts of African Americans to move into white areas of the district. The senator boasted that local whites had turned to him for protection from blockbusting African Americans and "unethical and unprofessional white real estate agents." Bilbo suggested that this new "menace" represented "a concerted move on to break up white sections throughout Washington."[19]

By raising the issue of residential segregation, Bilbo tapped a wellspring of racial turmoil across the urban North. In Detroit and dozens of other industrial centers, African American migrants faced fierce resistance from white homeowners and tenants determined to keep them out of their neighborhoods. Protesting the construction of a housing project for black war workers, a Detroit neighborhood association posted a sign reading, "We Want White Tenants in Our White Community." On the day that the first black families moved into the Sojourner Truth housing project, white protestors rioted.[20]

Such outbreaks convinced southern observers that white northerners shared their racial anxieties, and politicians more temperate than Bilbo took note. Hoping to furnish Richard Russell with fodder for another filibuster, moderate Atlanta mayor William Hartsfield passed along a pamphlet on restrictive covenants published by the Chicago Federation of Neighborhood Associations. "The race question is not confined to the South alone," Hartsfield wrote, describing the federation's campaign "to uphold property values in Chicago which are being ruined by promiscuous mixture by the races."[21]

Bilbo counted white Chicagoans among his northern admirers. "We in 'Little Africa' are so pushed around by the colored . . . ," reported a woman on Chicago's South Side, "that we have become as numb and apathetic as were the Europeans enslaved by Hitler." Another Chicagoan assured Bilbo that there was "as much feeling against interracial mixture in the North as there is in the South, but, somehow, we are misrepresented in Congress by a few fanatics." White northerners, she argued, demanded protection from "the Blacks who would like to move into their drawing room and then into the sanctuary of their bedroom." As Bilbo took his segregation crusade before a national audience, he discovered newfound sympathizers. "Some of us northerners laughed at you Southern fellows when you talked against Communism and for race preservation," another Chicago supporter noted. "They are now coming around to your point of view."[22]

Spurred on by a nationwide network of admirers, Bilbo lined up behind Washington's white neighborhood associations in their war on blockbusting. The district's homeowners responded enthusiastically to Bilbo's support. As soon as the senator assumed the chairmanship of the District Committee, the head of the Home Builders Association of Metropolitan Washington praised Bilbo for his "very good understanding of the problems of the District of Columbia" and predicted he "would make a most excellent chairman of the committee." The president of the district's Federation of Citizen's Associations also praised the new "mayor." Speaking on behalf of sixty-seven neighborhood associations with a combined membership of nearly 100,000, the president claimed Bilbo as a valuable ally in preserving "good government" in the district. "You have already made an auspicious beginning in assisting us to this end," he announced, "for which we are very gratified."[23]

In the midst of the media firestorm surrounding his appointment, Bilbo received enthusiastic congratulations from local neighborhood associations. "We feel we have a real friend at the helm," declared the president of the Logan-Thomas Circle Citizens' Association. Another neighborhood leader visited Bilbo in person to protest "the Colored invasion of white property" in Northeast Washington. Like southern white supremacists, some neighborhood activists connected their struggle to the war effort. One flier urged white residents to protect the homes and neighborhoods of fighting men overseas. "It is up to YOU, Mr. and Mrs. Property Owner, not to destroy their homes and neighborhoods . . . ," the flier warned, "Never let it be said that you helped in any way to destroy a white block or community."[24]

According to Bilbo, the blockbusting campaign operated in tandem with the drive for black political power. "These Negroes are willing to pay $2,000 or $3,000 in excess of the market value of the property," he claimed, "in order to carry out their scheme to drive the white people from the white sections of Washington so that they may take possession of them." He cited this assault on white Washington neighborhoods as one of the main reasons that he adamantly opposed home rule for Washington. In a Senate speech, he warned that the district was threatened by "a concerted movement to drive the white people out of Washington into Virginia and Maryland, and to flood the town with Negroes, so in case the citizens of Washington are given the right to vote there will be a Negro administration in the Nation's Capital."[25]

Bilbo's opposition to black political power surprised no one. "I am not interested in the Negro voting," Bilbo announced from the Senate floor. "The Negro does not vote in my State, and he is not going to vote within a long, long time." Opposition to self-government in the district, however, represented more than an extension of southern white supremacy. As with the housing controversy, Bilbo seized on the ambivalence of white Washingtonians in his crusade against home rule. He pointed to District Committee hearings on the establishment of an elected municipal government, in which prominent white Washingtonians discouraged black suffrage. Clinton Howard, the great-nephew of the white namesake of historically black, federally funded Howard University, argued that wartime racial tension rendered home rule a recipe for disaster. He warned against enfranchising "the under-privileged, illiterate, proletarian class who would at once possess the balance of power and, in the near future, a majority of the voting citizenry." With a shrinking white majority, Howard predicted that "the laws of fecundity" would rule Washington. "The alley," he warned, "will dominate the avenue."[26]

Howard considered himself "a lifetime friend of the colored race," but his testimony bolstered Bilbo's contention that most white Americans shared an aversion to black political power. "This is not a question of race prejudice," Howard argued, "but a question of Negro domination, always distasteful to the white race whether in the South or the North." Enfranchising the district's black residents at a time of heightened racial tension, he warned, was as volatile as "a cigarette dropped in a powder mill." Despite his humanitarian appeals for peace and understanding, Howard's parting shot sounded like vintage Bilbo. "If anyone doubts this advice," Howard concluded, "let him tune in on any Sunday night at 10:30 P.M. over station WINX and listen to the so-called services of a certain church and hear the savage howls that hark back to the jungle . . . and ask himself whether he thinks the group there represented intelligent enough to exercise the right of suffrage and decide the future of the well-being of the Capital City."[27]

Bilbo seized upon Howard's testimony in his fight against self-government in Washington. In his trip to Mississippi shortly after his promotion to the District Committee chairmanship, Bilbo repeated Howard's warning that "the Negroes would soon have control of the city and the alleys would be completely outvoting the avenues" if Congress granted home rule. "If the affairs of this District were turned over to the local people, knowing the population as I do . . . ," Bilbo warned the Senate a few weeks later, "I am afraid Congress would rue the day it had released the control of the government of the District."[28] Political power, Bilbo contended, would lead to further breakdown of segregation and white supremacy in the nation's capital.

For tangible proof of black Washingtonians' growing assertiveness, Bilbo could point to a local nonviolent direct action campaign. By the time he took over the District Committee, Howard University students had already organized a sit-in at the Little Palace cafeteria. "There's No Segregation Law in Washington, D.C.," read one picket sign, "What's Your Story, Little Palace?" Emboldened by this first attempt, fifty-six students entered Thompson's Restaurant on 22 April 1944 and requested service while supporters picketed outside. Although the management agreed to serve the demonstrators, they made no promises about long-term changes to their discriminatory practices. The president of Howard University, Mordecai Johnson, intervened in the sit-in campaign for fear that it would aggravate Bilbo and his southern allies. The university relied on the District Committee for funding, which often forced administrators to balance student activism with practical concerns.[29] Nevertheless, such protests only strengthened Bilbo's conviction that African American activists desired more than voting rights and workplace desegregation.

Bilbo deemed miscegenation the inevitable outcome and underlying motivation of civil rights activism. "Back in the heart of every Negro in America who is behind movements of this kind," Bilbo declared, "is the dream of social equality and intermarriage between whites and blacks." For proof, he referred again to events in the nation's capital. In his Mississippi legislature speech, Bilbo reported that the Congress of Industrial Organizations (CIO) had opened an integrated canteen in Washington for servicemen and -women. He described the scene on opening night, with white and black servicemen dancing and mingling with an interracial group of hostesses. "Can you picture such social affairs taking place in our Nation's Capital?" Bilbo asked his Mississippi constituents. He quoted an equally incredulous southerner, Louisiana congressman Charles McKenzie, who pondered, "How can anyone be a party to encouraging white girls into the arms of Negro soldiers at a canteen while singing Let Me Call You Sweetheart?" From integrated federal offices to interracial dancing, Bilbo warned, black militants would not rest until they had erased any semblance of racial distinction from American life. "Behind it all," he argued, "is the drive of A. Philip Randolph to force social equality, to force the intermingling of the races, and do away with segregation in Washington and throughout the entire Nation."[30]

If Washington was not southern enough for Bilbo, his adversaries considered it a bastion of white supremacy and segregation. "Is Jim-Crow in Washington?" A. Philip Randolph asked in 1943. "What a question! Is water wet? Is fire hot? Is Mississippi's Senator Bilbo anti-Negro?" That a committed segregationist could wield control over the nation's capital embarrassed the United States on the world stage. But Bilbo's reign also dramatized the fundamentally undemocratic southern political system and served as a frightening indicator of the extent of southern influence on federal policy. For civil rights advocates, Bilbo's stint as "mayor" underscored the national reach of poll taxes and white primaries. The senator, declared the *Chicago Defender*, "is no more representative of Mississippi than Mussolini was of Italy," yet he wielded substantial power over the "very heart" of American democracy. Bilbo's District Committee chairmanship heightened black fears that "the undemocratic hand of the Dixie poll taxers is not limited or restricted by state lines."[31]

While Bilbo worried that civil rights gains in Washington would spread southward, Randolph feared the reverse. "Our federal government in Washington," he argued, "has become an official carrier of the germ of Jim-Crow throughout the length and breadth of our land, and is infecting the body politic everywhere and poisoning the blood stream of national public opinion." While Bilbo blasted the increasing interference of the federal government in racial matters, Randolph condemned both states' rights and increased federal power in "a Jim-Crowized and segregationized federal system." Unless America stamped out discrimination on the national level, Randolph warned, "the South won't need states' rights anymore. They will have control over Federal rights."[32]

The district held symbolic and strategic significance for civil rights proponents and opponents alike, but the racial confrontations in Washington also highlighted how contentious the color line had become. By the end of World War II, diehards such as Theodore Bilbo continued to champion white political domination, but the showdown over segregation took center stage. Controversies over residential segregation, public accommodations, and especially workplace discrimination forced militants and moderates to rally in defense of the color line. Bilbo deemed Washington a crystal ball for Jim Crow's future. By the time the Mississippi senator returned home with his racial warnings, the skirmishes he witnessed in Washington had already spread south.

More than any single racial controversy, the battle over fair employment accelerated the emergence of a self-consciously "segregationist" movement. While racial conservatives warned that abolition of the poll tax and the white primary would lead to "social equality," federal efforts to combat workplace discrimination represented a more direct assault on the color line. The Fair Employment Practices Committee, an agency pressured into existence by the wartime civil rights movement, fixed the spotlight on racial separation rather than political repression. Furthermore, the establishment of the FEPC brought together the fears that had fueled southern white protest since the New Deal's inception: the disruption of the South's racialized labor system through the erosion of racial segregation. By pushing African Americans up the labor ladder and forcing them into direct contact with whites, the FEPC took aim at the economic and social imperatives that drove Jim Crow.[33]

In the battle against the FEPC, southern conservatives fought explicitly as segregationists. Rather than championing white supremacy in politics or advocating states' rights in principle, they affirmed their right to maintain the color line in employment and everywhere else. Diehards had previously warned of scattered assaults on segregation in New Deal programs and military installations, but the federal stand against institutionalized discrimination dramatized the threat like never before. "The FEPC," Richard Russell warned, "is the most sickening manifestation of the trend that is now in effect to force social equality and miscegenation of the white and black races on the South."[34]

The FEPC controversy, which raged throughout the war and into the immediate postwar months, also presented an opportunity to reconcile the segregationist position with a more transcendent rhetoric of individual liberty. Sectional issues such as the poll tax and the white primary riled white southerners, but they failed to resonate with potential sympathizers elsewhere. While southern conservatives made no bones about the FEPC's dire implications for the region, they recognized that fair employment policies affected employers nationwide. As segregation's defenders shaped the war's meaning and the very definition of Americanism to their advantage, the FEPC battle broadened their options. Melding freedom of association with free enterprise, these southerners nurtured new alliances as they fought the latest and greatest "totalitarian" threat. The more they focused on segregation, the clearer the link they drew between their regional racial priorities and their broader vision of conservative Americanism.

From its inception, the FEPC faced unbridled hostility in the South. At first, the controversy over Roosevelt's nondiscrimination directive seemed yet another excuse for demagoguery. However, prominent white supremacists mixed bluster with blunt assessments of fair employment's ultimate outcome. When, in 1942, Alabama governor Frank Dixon turned down a federal war production contract rather than accept its nondiscrimination provision, he warned that desegregation would not stop at the shop floor. "Under cover of this clause," Dixon declared, the federal government sought to "break down the principle of segregation of races" in all spheres of southern life. "The social structure of the South," the governor continued, "has been built, and can endure, only on the principle of segregation . . . a ruling basic principle, without which there can be no orderly society below the Mason-Dixon line."[35]

When the FEPC held hearings in Birmingham, the Alabama press mocked the "Roosevelt racial experts" and "halo-wearing missionaries of New Deal socialism." In Georgia, Eugene Talmadge harassed the FEPC's Atlanta field office while the city council lobbied the state's congressional delegation to run the committee out of town. When a life insurance agent dropped by the Atlanta office, he encountered two black secretaries. "I truly believe," the agent fumed, "that if it were possible to get enough leaders from the various business communities and towns in Georgia to Atlanta and let them look in this office, see the Negro secretaries working for white men . . . the State would vote Republican in November."[36]

Ominous predictions aside, southern resistance limited the wartime FEPC's scope and enforcement powers. With the initial FEPC in disarray, Roosevelt issued another executive order in May 1943 that redefined and temporarily broadened the agency's scope. But the southern congressional bloc chipped away at the committee's appropriations and limited its enforcement powers. As the president distanced himself from the "political hot potato," one black journalist lamented, the committee devolved "from an independent agency responsible to the President himself to one . . . dependent for funds on Southern politicians in Congress." Civil rights activists and their liberal allies fought back with a campaign to upgrade the FEPC from a wartime taskforce to a permanent government agency. In early 1945, FEPC supporters in the House and Senate introduced numerous bills toward that end. When Harry Truman took office after Roosevelt's death in April 1945, the former Missouri senator surprised southerners by publicly calling on Congress to renew the committee for another year.[37]

But even as FEPC supporters promoted the agency's survival as another nail in Hitler's coffin, southern conservatives derived different lessons from the war. In the weeks after Germany's surrender, civil rights opponents invoked the struggle against fascism in their FEPC fight. Informing his constituents that he had never encountered legislation "more serious in its implications . . . the anti-poll tax and anti-lynch bills not excepted," veteran Mississippi congressman William Colmer declared, "Hitler in his heyday put through nothing in Germany more vicious than this." As Colmer and his colleagues fought to strip the struggling agency of funding and enforcement powers, they equated antidiscrimination orders with Nazi racial policies. Attempting to "legislate against prejudice," Colmer contended, was no better than legislating for it. In its attempts to referee the hiring and firing of minority groups, the FEPC had stolen a page from the Nazi playbook. "Its provisions are no different in principle than the edicts of Hitler, et al. to ostracize and deny employment to Jews, Negroes and other minorities to be employed," Colmer argued. "While the objectives are diametrically opposed, the principle is the same."[38]

Mocking federal attempts to "legislate love," southern conservatives conjured up images of secret police and government thugs enforcing racial equality at gunpoint. The FEPC, southern opponents warned, would unleash an American "Gestapo" that could raid offices, seize private records, and haul businessmen off to a "kangaroo court." Allusions to Nazi persecution resonated with alarmed constituents back home. Branding the FEPC "un-Constitutional, un-American and anti-Christian," a Methodist men's club in Savannah resolved that a permanent fair employment agency would "make the now defunct German Gestapo weak and feeble by comparison." In another resolution, the Lions Club of Port Gibson, Mississippi, blasted the FEPC "for subjecting good American citizens to Gestapo persecution and intimidation."[39]

The Nazi metaphors reached their zenith in May 1945, when a freshman North Carolina congressman called the FEPC "a concentration camp for all Americans." Speaking for over an hour, Joseph Wilson Ervin warned that the FEPC would "operate with the weapon of fear" by hauling off employers to trial at the hands of "carpetbagger personnel." Noting that the majority of FEPC employees were black, the younger brother of North Carolina judge and future senator Samuel James Ervin added that most of the agency's white staff belonged to the "lunatic fringe." He read the FEPC employees' names aloud, noting the preponderance of "interesting" surnames such as Asepha, Castenada, Wazem, and Zeidman. "How would you like for one of these birds to try your case?" he asked his colleagues. "How would you like for this court to try the Governor of your State, or your local school board?" Under the guise of civil rights reform, Ervin warned, radicals within the government would shackle the national economy with oppressive regimentation and "subject the minorities of America to certain bitterness and recrimination." Hitler could lose the war in Europe, Ervin declared, and still see his "greatest ambition achieved" on American soil. "Shall we send millions of our young men to war and spill their blood in an effort to abolish concentration camps abroad," Ervin concluded, "and let them return to find that we have established a concentration camp in America?"[40]

When the concentration camp analogies failed to keep the House from attaching FEPC funds to an omnibus defense bill, Mississippi senator James Eastland invoked other wartime lessons. During an anti-FEPC filibuster in June 1945, Eastland railed against black troops and claimed common cause with white men across America. "In Europe the Negro has crossed the color line," announced Eastland. "He has gone with white girls of the very lowest caliber, and I know how the northern white boy feels about that." Furthermore, the senator alleged, "Negro soldiers have disgraced the flag of their country." Black cowardice, insubordination, and criminal behavior, Eastland fumed, had caused the United States to "lose prestige all over Europe." Eastland claimed that black soldiers in Italy deserted their posts "without cause, rhyme, or reason," while their counterparts in Normandy raped French women at gunpoint. The senator reported that white soldiers were "openly and avowedly" seeking revenge. "The soldiers are mad," he warned. "We talk of racial tolerance. The agitation for social equality has destroyed racial tolerance." Eastland reasoned that white soldiers had won the war, and they alone deserved the spoils. Thus, he concluded, "there will be no FEPC, there will be no social equality, there will be no such un-American measures when the soldier returns."[41]

Eastland's tirade, roundly scorned by southern moderates as well as national observers, was an exceptional outburst in a measured counteroffensive. Attempts to link racial concerns to issues of free enterprise and employer rights enjoyed greater success. No group melded white supremacy and capitalism more enthusiastically than the Southern States Industrial Council, which attempted to unite the region's elites and open lines of communication with likeminded allies across the country. The council had fought federal interference with the South's segregated labor system since the earliest New Deal initiatives, but its leaders deemed the FEPC "the most dangerous piece of legislation ever introduced in Congress." Meeting in New Orleans in April 1945, SSIC members worried aloud that a permanent FEPC "would destroy white supremacy in the South, and upset completely the amicable working arrangements which now exist between the races."[42]

Although the SSIC made no bones about the racial stakes of the FEPC fight, its members reached out to conservative businessmen across the country. Soliciting donations from its 6,000 members, the council expanded its propaganda campaign beyond its regional support base. By mid-1945, an SSIC executive reported, the council had "contacted every trade association in the United States, some 2,800 in number, in an effort to enlist their assistance." The FEPC, council propaganda warned, "would deny the employer his traditional American right of using his own sound judgment in selecting loyal and capable employees."[43]

The rhetoric of employer rights and over-reaching government resonated with business groups and right-wing industrialists across the country. Bombastic southern filibusters overshadowed the substantial opposition to fair employment laws among conservative Republicans. Likewise, the regional composition and segregationist rhetoric of the Southern States Industrial Council obscured the ambivalence of the National Association of Manufacturers and the Chamber of Commerce toward antidiscrimination directives. The campaign against the FEPC lacked the bipartisan coordination and national cohesiveness that its southern opponents had hoped to inspire, but enough ambivalence existed across the nation that the agency's backers failed to overcome congressional opposition.[44]

Whether ranting about black soldiers or making constitutional arguments, southern segregationists invoked common cause with other conservative white Americans in the FEPC fight. Rather than obscure their defense of the color line, they grounded it in a rhetoric of conservative Americanism. At the same time, they pointed to the national scope of racial tension at every turn. When a Republican congressman from California presented a petition protesting the return of interned Japanese Americans to their West Coast homes, Mississippi congressman John Rankin took another swipe at fair employment. "Not only are they going to return the Japanese to California . . . ," Rankin warned his Republican colleague, "but the chances are the F.E.P.C will try to make you accept them on terms of equality."[45]

For southern racial conservatives, the FEPC fight fixed a spotlight on segregation. Battles over lynching and the poll tax reflected African Americans' unprecedented political clout, but the FEPC revealed a more unsettling reality. Faced with racial turmoil at home and abroad, the federal government adopted a wartime rhetoric of tolerance and egalitarianism that directly challenged the southern caste system. More than any previous civil rights controversy, the FEPC fight convinced segregation's defenders that legislative maneuvers and rhetorical gymnastics alone would not save the status quo. The war effort had stirred racial tensions, but it had simultaneously unleashed an ideological offensive. Egalitarianism was on the move, and it demanded a response.

Compared to their headline-grabbing confrontations over poll taxes, white primaries, and fair employment, attempts to beat back egalitarian "propagandizing" remained scattered and developed slowly. Southern conservatives refuted not only the wartime rhetoric of tolerance but also decades of scholarship that undermined the academic respectability of white supremacy. These trends converged in a manual on race and prejudice commissioned by the United Service Organizations (USO) in the wake of the 1943 Detroit race riot. Prepared by Columbia University anthropologists Ruth Benedict and Gene Weltfish, the slim and straightforward pamphlet explained the common origins of all people. The military ordered 50,000 copies of The Races of Mankind for soldier orientation. "No matter whether a man is round-headed, or long-headed, whether his hair is kinky or straight," Benedict and Weltfish explained, "any head can house a good brain." To demonstrate that environment rather than biology determined intelligence, Benedict and Weltfish included a table showing that African Americans from New York, Illinois, and Ohio outscored white southerners from Mississippi, Arkansas, and Kentucky on the military intelligence test.[46]

The pamphlet provided a foothold for segregation's defenders. When the chairman of the House Military Affairs Committee, a Kentuckian, discovered the embarrassing content in The Races of Mankind, he led a successful campaign to keep the pamphlet out of military training programs. One of his fellow committee members claimed that the booklet was "filled with Communist propaganda," and a Georgia editor urged southern congressmen to "utterly destroy the crawling vermin who are responsible for things like this." While the pamphlet's sponsors pondered why elected officials would suppress materials "that completely refute the enemy's contention of a super race," the committee chairman warned that he and other outraged southern congressmen "would have plenty to say" if military officials ignored their demands. "That booklet," he declared, "has no place in the army program."[47]

Despite the attempts to smother the pamphlet, *The Races of Mankind* popped up in unlikely places. Just days after the House Military Affairs Committee banned the pamphlet's distribution, the *Atlanta Journal* reported that schoolchildren in nearby Sand Hill had discussed the controversial publication. "All blood is the same," the teacher summarized. "The color of the skin has nothing to do with the blood type." She explained to her class that the Red Cross segregated its plasma banks because some whites feared African American blood "might turn them black" but pointed out that the pamphlet refuted this notion. "Maybe Negroes would appreciate getting white blood," suggested a student. "I bet they'd like that." While the *Atlanta Journal* dismissed the lesson as a provocative but poorly chosen critical thinking exercise, Talmadge's *Statesman* blasted the "cruel hoax on innocent children" as a brazen assault on the color line.[48] Given that southern schoolchildren had read a pamphlet that politicians deemed unsuitable for American soldiers, the Talmadge tabloid seemed more credible than ever.

The lack of an effective intellectual response to wartime egalitarianism frustrated diehard white supremacists. John Irwin, a banker's son from Sandersville, Georgia, lamented his fellow southerners' apathy in the face of an equalitarian onslaught. Angered by political and academic assaults on Jim Crow, Irwin churned out his own race pamphlet. In "Let's Keep the United States White," Irwin dreamed of the day "when segregation will not be seen as discriminatory and unfair, but as a plan whereby the racial integrity of both the whites, and the blacks, can be maintained and forever perpetuated in conformity to God's intent and design." Irwin was no scientist, just a foot soldier in the fight to save segregation. Rather than offer "a biological or an anthropological discussion," Irwin penned "a plain, common sense statement of facts and conditions that the crackers and the common herd and the women may read with understanding." Irwin mailed hundreds of his pamphlets "indiscriminately" across the country. "The reaction has been gratifying," he reported, "but our people do not seem to be able to unite in a solid front, or form organizations to combat the sentiment that we are all equal."[49]

In Washington, Bilbo worked on a more thorough retort to the egalitarians. Following the uproar over *The Races of Mankind*, the senator demanded a copy from Gene Weltfish. "Let me assure you," she replied, "that it is a sincere attempt to present the facts of science as we now know them so that our people may be armed against the lies of Hitler and his henchmen, for Hitler fights with ideas as well as with guns." Some of those guns, however, were aimed at southern soldiers who could not so easily abandon white supremacy. "For many months I was just burned up sitting around in England listening to all this racial propaganda," a Mississippi serviceman complained to Bilbo. "In my opinion everyone seems to think only the Southern white people should associate with the Negro on an equality basis."[50]

Back home, Bilbo urged racial separatist Earnest Sevier Cox to distribute a rebuttal to *The Races of Mankind*. Cox's scathing review argued that Benedict and Weltfish promoted "nuptial-couch race harmony." Radical Republicans had promised the freed slaves forty acres and a mule, Cox scoffed, but "the new Carpetbagger proposes to throw in a white woman with the mule and the land." *The Races of Mankind* posed a threat, Cox warned, because Benedict and Weltfish interwove "miscegenation ideals" with denunciations of race prejudice. "If [miscegenation] is not disengaged from our war ideals, but left with them, it could be truly said that if our soldiers, white and black, return from the war and find that in their absence their sisters have not conceived a mulatto child they will feel that their sacrifices have been in vain," Cox concluded. "Could an excess of zeal carry a group to a more pathetic conclusion?"[51]

Convinced that the court of public opinion, rather than Congress, would decide the fate of white civilization, Bilbo pledged to "propagandize the American people with the slogan of physical separation of the races." As the war effort wound down, Bilbo devoted more time to his own segregationist manifesto. He was not the only one. Other authors—a school principal in Georgia, a widow in Mississippi, a "Southern White Friend" in Alabama—worked on their own tracts. Homer Loomis Jr., a Princeton dropout and World War II veteran who moved south to start a white nationalist organization, discovered budding propagandists wherever he went. "I have been traveling all over Georgia," he reported to Earnest Sevier Cox, "speaking with various people who have started movements, or written books and pamphlets, on this race question."[52]

Before war's end, a New Orleans businessman-turned-publisher submitted his "majority report" on behalf of the white South. "Little is being done to offset the propaganda of those who are trying to establish racial equality," lamented Stuart Omer Landry. "It would seem that the equalitarians are winning their case before the court of public opinion by default." In *The Cult of Equality*, Landry argued that there was still a place for the "age-old idea of the inequality of races" in postwar America. The alternative, he warned, was the demise of white civilization. Landry argued that the "equalitarian stream of thought" represented "a Gulf Stream in reverse, that, instead of warmth and life, brings cold and eventual death to superior peoples."[53]

While no bestseller, *The Cult of Equality* constituted a groundbreaking achievement for the defenders of segregation. Landry offered a comprehensive defense of segregation that combined timeworn justifications for racial separation with an updated attack on the "theory" of racial equality. He invoked history, eugenics, and personal observation to prove that "militant equalitarians" were as wrong as they were rash. Taking on the building scientific consensus that racial intermingling posed no dangers, Landry countered that "common sense tells us that it would be a biological mistake." To prove that blacks were of an inferior stock, Landry offered a catalogue of "Negro Delinquencies and Deficiencies." He deemed African Americans irresponsible, dishonest, and shiftless. They spread poverty, crime, and disease wherever they settled. Landry attributed these problems not to discrimination, but to mental, physical, and cultural primitiveness. While he trotted out statistics to bolster his defense of Jim Crow, Landry also invoked the white southern mantra of personal interracial experience. At one point, Landry recalled a "very black" nurse from his childhood. When she played with Landry's baby sister, the nurse would sometimes nibble her fingers. Looking back, Landry interpreted this as proof of "cannibalistic tendencies," yet another sign that blacks were "not far removed from the culture and habits of the jungle."[54]

Landry did not deem all primal urges undesirable. "The prejudice against people of a darker race is inborn," he declared, "a protective instinct instituted by Nature." Suggesting that there might be "something to be said for intolerance," Landry deemed racial chauvinism "an attitude of mind which stems from determination" to resist intermixture and degeneration. "Racial prejudice is a form of racial pride, and it is difficult to believe that the expression of it comes only from a selfish spirit, that it evidences a desire to dominate other people, or that it is immoral," argued Landry. "Whatever may be said against it, insofar as it keeps the race pure, race prejudice is admirable and even necessary."[55]

Segregation was not only natural. It was American. Combining timeworn arguments for segregation with the conservative southern vision of wartime patriotism, Landry lashed out at the FEPC. Fair employment laws, he warned, represented "a trend toward dictatorship or totalitarianism."

Furthermore, they threatened to rob loyal and patriotic Americans of their personal liberties. "The right to segregate is a natural right, and when it is abrogated we are no longer free," Landry declared. "America is the land of segregationists."[56] Years before the title became both an epithet and a badge of honor in the civil rights struggles of the 1950s and 1960s, Landry proudly proclaimed the United States a "segregationist" nation. In one of the first published appearances of the term, Landry deployed "segregationist" not to explain southern peculiarity but to declare racial integrity the most fundamental of American values.

Landry's patriotic affirmation of segregation, and his denunciation of the egalitarian "cult," made less of a splash than he had hoped. Northern reviewers gave Landry "the silent treatment," a Charleston newspaper complained. "The evidence is that the highbrows in the Big Burghs are afraid to mention Landry and his book." But if the academic community scorned Landry or simply brushed him aside, black sociologist E. B. Reuter argued that *The Cult of Equality* could not be ignored. While concluding that Landry showed "no understanding of racial realities and no insight into the nature of race relations," Reuter argued that scholarly merit was beside the point. Landry, he noted, "seems to embody and reflect racial beliefs and attitudes that prevail in his social class and community." Most white southerners stood solidly behind their segregated status quo, Reuter warned, and they would develop new strategies to defend it. "In the American South the Negro has generally been excluded by force and fraud," Reuter argued. "But now the need is felt for a body of supporting doctrine, and the ideology must be pitched at various levels of literacy and sophistication."[57] While Landry had shown little restraint in his musings about cannibalistic house servants, he had attempted to provide a comprehensive and respectable response to the egalitarian establishment.

As Bilbo prepared for his third Senate race, he put the finishing touches on his own manifesto. Bilbo's mentor in this project, Earnest Sevier Cox, had spent decades churning out separatist propaganda from his Richmond apartment. Cox and Bilbo had collaborated for several years on black colonization legislation, and the aging racial propagandist eagerly embraced Bilbo's new project. In *Take Your Choice: Separation or Mongrelization*, the man who had built a career as a fiery demagogue claimed the mantle of academic respectability. "In dealing with those who desire to maintain race," noted Cox in a glowing introduction, "Senator Bilbo is exceptionally considerate. Here, there will be found no harshness in ideal or statement." While Bilbo sorely tested this appraisal, he traded his coarsest racial epithets for denunciations of integrationists and, especially, academics. "The damnable and blighting teachings of these disciples of Boas," warned Bilbo, "are being disseminated and inculcated into the minds of the pure-blooded Anglo-Saxon students of Dixie."[58]

The reluctance of white southerners to defend their racial order alarmed Bilbo even more. "In the past four or five years over two hundred books have been written by Negroes and white Quislings pleading for Negro equality," Bilbo declared, "while only five or six books have been written in behalf of the preservation of the white race and white supremacy." A subversive wartime civil rights campaign, Bilbo charged, had challenged the moral and academic justifications for segregation. In *Take Your Choice*, Bilbo attempted to refute as many egalitarian arguments as possible. Two chapters, "False Interpretations of Democracy" and "False Concepts of the Christian Religion," took on constitutional and moral arguments for racial equality. Bilbo borrowed liberally from classic, if outdated, eugenics studies to demonstrate "The Dangers of Amalgamation" before ending with nearly one hundred pages promoting his black colonization scheme.[59]

At stake in this racial debate, Bilbo argued, was the very survival of American civilization. "Although the race problem may seem to lie dormant at times, it continually exists, lives on and on and sometimes rages with all the fury of a jungle beast," he warned. "It gnaws at the very vitals of our existence, in time it will sap our strength and destroy the greatness of our American way of life unless solved properly and permanently." Claiming that he would prefer destruction at the hands of an atomic bomb to "the maelstrom of miscegenation, interbreeding, intermarriage, and mongrelization," Bilbo presented the racial threat in apocalyptic terms. In doing so, he borrowed not only from white supremacist propaganda and outdated eugenics literature but also from the dire wartime warnings of southern moderates. Echoing John Temple Graves's recent book title and central premise, Bilbo vowed, "the fighting South will defend her position."[60]

Just as less reactionary counterparts had attempted to differentiate southern segregation from Axis fascism, Bilbo attempted to counter comparisons of Jim Crow and Nazism with his own analogy. "It seems as if these full equality advocates have taken the advice of Adolph Hitler," Bilbo argued, "who once said that if you make the lie big enough, tell it often enough and emphatically enough, it will appear to the masses of people as the truth."[61] Dismayed by the outpouring of egalitarian rhetoric during the war years, Jim Crow's most outspoken defenders laid the groundwork for segregationist apologetics in the wake of the *Brown* decision. Responding to a "Cult of Equality" that had exploited a war emergency for its own subversive purposes, farsighted segregationists sought to awaken white southerners to the gathering threat to their way of life. At the same time, propagandists sought to affirm segregation even as the sympathies of the nation seemed to be slipping away.

As the nation transitioned from war to peace, the white supremacist stance evolved to meet changing conditions. Long regarded as a hard-line defender of white political domination, Theodore Bilbo reflected the white South's increasing preoccupation with racial separation itself. Concerns about the color line, though ever present, gradually overtook white supremacy as a nationally viable and politically tenable proposition in the postwar era. As the Mississippi senator geared up for his 1946 reelection campaign, he took to the stump armed with battle stories from his wartime racial crusade.

Bilbo had spent his political career advocating a progressive platform that had put him at odds with Mississippi's planter elite. The rivalry between the aristocratic Delta and the poorer hill country, V. O. Key explained in his landmark 1949 study of southern politics, dominated Mississippi's political culture. Better than anyone, Bilbo exploited that divide. Yet during World War II, racial controversies united white Mississippians. After railing against the FEPC in the 1945 filibuster, Bilbo received enthusiastic praise from the previously inhospitable Delta. An insurance agent from the Delta town of Cleveland assured Bilbo that he had "gained friends by the thousands" for his stand against fair employment. I have heard numbers say that they are for you . . . ," he reported, "who have never been that way before." As African Americans attempted to build on their wartime momentum, the Delta and the Hills united to defend the color line. "You have most definitely earned my support and I am sure the support of all other thinking white people who do not wish to lose their birthright . . . ," declared a Greenwood city official. "Your friends, supporters, and non-supporters are all for 'the man Bilbo.'"[62]

Despite their personal misgivings about their "redneck liberal" senator, Delta whites understood the political stakes of disunity in the face of an egalitarian onslaught. "With the 'damn yankees,' Eleanor, the New York and Chicago nigger congressmen and Hollywood fighting you for your position on the F.E.P.C and as mayor of Washington, your defeat would indicate that your home folks repudiated your stand for white supremacy and *agin* social equality . . . ," explained a Leland physician. "You will get votes in Washington County you never got before." When it came to race, campaign manager A. B. Friend confidently asserted, "Mississippians are probably more thoroughly in accord with Senator Bilbo on this issue than upon any other question or policy."[63]

Owing his newfound momentum to wartime civil rights battles, Bilbo fanned the flames of racial reaction throughout his reelection campaign. "The race question is far from dead," he thundered at a Eupora rally. "It is the keenest, livest question that confronts the South today." In Meridian, Bilbo regaled the crowd with stories from his stint as the mayor of D.C. and urged them to send him back to "keep Washington a segregated city." The Mississippi senator garnered national attention for encouraging violent reprisals against potential black voters. While the FEPC controversy had overshadowed *Smith v. Allwright*, the 1946 election marked Bilbo's first campaign since the abolition of the white primary. "Do not let a single nigger vote," he bellowed. "If you let a few register and vote this year, next year there will be twice as many, and the first thing you know the whole thing will be out of hand." Bilbo bragged that he could provide county registrars "at least a hundred questions no nigger can answer," but added, "the proper time to manage the nigger vote is the night before the election."[64]

Despite the headline-grabbing appeals for political terrorism, which spurred election-day violence across the state, Bilbo's primary campaign represented more than white supremacy's last gasp. The shift toward a consciously segregationist backlash was readily apparent even in the Deepest South. After Bilbo racked up more votes than his four challengers combined, Bilbo's critics attempted to explain "Mississippi's Verdict" to the world. "The Senator is not a credit to his state or to his section," explained the editor of the *New Orleans Times-Picayune*. Claiming that many voters would rather support "a candidate of finer character and better qualifications," the editor argued that "outside extremists and propagandists of demagogue stripe" had forced white Mississippians to back Bilbo. His "outside traducers and unintentional aids," according to the editorial, "centered their attack against a feature of his senatorial record that is impregnable—his stubborn and defiant opposition of the FEPC bill conceived for political purposes, tyrannous in its methods and ulterior motives violative of the constitutional guarantees of individual liberty." Rather than a vote for demagoguery, the Mississippi primary was "an emphatic verdict against FEPC and the inciters of racial strife."[65]

Steeped in traditions of white democracy and racial separation, many southerners would not easily abandon these convictions in the postwar world. Like Bilbo, they had reacted to the wartime civil rights movement with shock, resentment, and, in some cases, explosive defiance. Even as the expedient egalitarianism of the war effort demoted white supremacy from southern custom to social ill, racial conservatives reaffirmed and re-articulated their dedication to the segregated status quo. Even after "The Man" succumbed to cancer shortly after his primary victory, his staunchest foes hesitated to equate Bilbo's death with the end of Bilboism. More than a prophet of "hate and violence and crime," the Mississippi senator defined the stakes of the segregation struggle even as he provided a cautionary tale of the embarrassing excesses and political liabilities of militant bigotry. Though "Bilboism" became shorthand for the pathological excesses of white supremacy, the Mississippi senator had helped to make this transition possible.[66]

Whatever died with Bilbo, plenty did not. By lashing out early and often at a nascent civil rights movement, Bilbo articulated a litany of threats to segregation and emphasized the necessity of a deliberate and multi-pronged defense. As southern racial traditions encountered opposition at home and abroad, Bilbo proved that you could take white supremacy anywhere. Postwar segregationists would fare better at dressing it up.

NATIONALIZING RACE & SOUTHERNIZING FREEDOM

4

On a Saturday afternoon in August 1946, the Massey brothers staggered out of the Ritz Café in Athens, Alabama. Ben, a recently discharged veteran, and his younger brother Roy, an active-duty Army private, were already drunk. As they stumbled onto the street, the Massey boys collided with L. C. Horton, a black World War II veteran. An argument ensued. It ended when Horton knocked Ben Massey to the ground and ran away. When police arrived at the scene of the scuffle, they arrested the bloodied brothers for drunken and disorderly conduct. White bystanders, angered by the policemen's apparent lack of interest in chasing down Horton, followed the policemen back to the city jail. Bolstered by rural whites on their Saturday trip into town, the mob quickly swelled to several hundred. When a white real estate broker implored the crowd to disperse, mob members bloodied him with their fists. The mayor, hoping to avert a riot, dropped the charges and handed the brothers over to the crowd in the courthouse square.[1]

With the Massey boys freed, the mob turned its wrath on the town's black residents. Climbing atop a dairy truck, a mob leader called on his comrades to "get the nigger" who had knocked down Ben Massey. Approximately 2,000 rioters, hoping to "clear the streets of Negroes," attacked black residents with fists, clubs, and makeshift whips. Fifty highway patrolmen and a company of the state guard restored order but detained only nine "hoodlum leaders of the mob." Eight of the nine arrested were teenagers, including a thirteen-year-old who reportedly "carried a club and knocked Negroes down." Assuring outsiders that the situation was under control, local authorities pledged to "turn the fire hose" on any future rioters. In an earnest stand against mob violence, circuit court judge James Crowe called a special grand jury hearing to investigate the Athens riot. The judge's "distracting name" notwithstanding, prospects for justice seemed slim, black reporter Vincent Tubbs lamented, "in a State infamous for its anti-co. attitude."[2]

The Athens riot was an exceptionally large outburst in a surge of p war violence, but it was far from the bloodiest. As wartime anxieti spilled over into a postwar campaign of intimidation and abuse, white supremacists attempted to force African Americans back into their pre-war place. Just weeks before the Athens riot, Theodore Bilbo in Missis-sippi and Eugene Talmadge in Georgia race-baited their way to primary victories. Like Bilbo, Talmadge advocated terrorism from the stump. Geor-gia vigilantes took him at his word, and they responded with a series of racial slayings. In the most notorious incident, a mob waylaid and mur-dered two black couples near Monroe, Georgia, in July 1946. Although the black press lumped the violent outbreaks together under the banner of "Talmadgism-Bilboism lynch terror," racial tension boiled over just as fre-quently in states that embraced political moderation at the polls. Even as white Alabamians gave the nod to populist Jim Folsom in the 1946 guber-natorial election, rural vigilantes and Birmingham policemen racked up a list of atrocities that rivaled occurrences of racial violence in Mississippi and Georgia.[3]

In Alabama and elsewhere, racial violence defied easy categorization. Race riots in Tennessee and mob slayings in the Carolinas proved that postwar racial violence was no Deep South anomaly. The Athens incident occurred near Alabama's northern border, closer to the site of a 1946 riot in Columbia, Tennessee, than to the Black Belt. With a white majority com-prised mainly of small farmers and mill workers, north Alabama preferred the economic populism of "Big Jim" Folsom to the conservatism of Black Belt planters and Birmingham's "Big Mules." Those planters and industri-alists lined up behind the reactionary Boswell Amendment, a 1946 refer-endum aimed at curbing black voter registration. By strengthening vot-ing restrictions as a substitute for the recently invalidated white primary, the state Democratic Party chairman explained, the Boswell Amendment would help local registrars to turn away "those elements in our commu-nity which have not yet fitted themselves for self-government." While poor farmers and urban workers voted against the new suffrage restrictions, planters and business elites enthusiastically backed the measure.[4]

When rallying cries of "White Supremacy" and "Negro Domination" failed to unite white Alabamans politically, moderate leaders advocated a compelling agenda of economic modernization and racial retrench-ment. Bristling at black criticism in the wake of the Athens riot, outgoing

Alabama governor Chauncey Sparks refuted reports of "a reign of terror" in the South. "With cooperation rather than hostile criticism," Sparks declared, "those of us of both races down South who are trying to live together in peace and justice could do a better job."[5] Like other southern moderates, Sparks publicly promoted law and order as prerequisites for economic progress. His successor, Jim Folsom, was wrapping up a successful gubernatorial campaign notable for its lack of white supremacist rhetoric. In South Carolina, former judge and decorated World War II paratrooper J. Strom Thurmond employed a similar strategy in his successful gubernatorial bid. Even as Bilbo and Talmadge advocated terrorism from the stump, politicians such as Folsom and Thurmond glossed over the racial turmoil around them while emphasizing political reform and economic development.

But modernization provided no panacea for explosive tensions and brutal repression. As in Alabama, the rhetoric of law and order did not exempt South Carolina from the racial violence sweeping the South. In February 1946, a white assassin gunned down a black tenant farmer after an altercation in Elko, the hometown of Thurmond's bride-to-be. The same month, the vicious blinding of black veteran Isaac Woodard shocked the nation and fueled a national campaign against mob violence. Just weeks after Thurmond's January 1947 inauguration, a South Carolina mob capped eighteen months of unabated southern violence by torturing and murdering an epileptic murder suspect named Willie Earle.[6]

In language that more closely approximated African American "Double V" rhetoric than states' rights apologia, Thurmond offered no quarter to white vigilantes. "Mob rule is against every principle for which we have recently sacrificed so much," the new governor declared, "and we intend to fight it with the same determination." In an impressive display of federal muscle and southern cooperation, the FBI helped state authorities round up thirty-one suspects and obtain twenty-six signed confessions. Thurmond's stance garnered praise from national observers and black South Carolinians alike. "It has been a very long time," local black activist Osceola McKaine declared, "since a Governor of South Carolina has shown by his actions that he would really fight for even-handed justice." Yet, just three months later, a Greenville jury acquitted Earle's self-confessed murderers. The defense attorneys, who had urged the jurors to return a verdict that would rebuke the "meddling of the North," stood on courtroom tables to accept the handshakes of the crowd.[7]

Disillusioned civil rights advocates blasted the "token trial" in South Carolina, but the prosecution of Earle's lynchers marked a turning point for segregationist politics. By early 1947, the militant rhetoric of "Bilbo-ism" had run headlong into the modernizing South's law-and-order ethos. Racial terrorism demanded a response not only from the federal government but also from white southerners who promoted segregation as the guarantor of interracial harmony and order. Hoping to reign in the embarrassing excesses of white supremacy, southern leaders attempted to articulate a defense of segregation that would garner sympathy rather than scorn. Some contemporary observers, and subsequent historians, interpreted these developments as signs of racial progress. Yet moderate candidates succeeded not by shaking up the segregated status quo but rather by reassuring white voters that economic growth could proceed apace with racial retrenchment.[8] In the late 1940s, moderation and militancy did not seem incompatible to many white southerners. Together, these impulses held together a loose regional coalition united in its opposition to racial change.

The crackdown on mob violence yielded no resounding victories, but it marked an attempt by moderates to seize back some of the ground ceded to racial militants during World War II. Despite their differences, all but the most diehard white supremacists wanted to cultivate an image of progress, civility, and order. During the war, the zealots had drowned out voices of racial moderation. From prominent liberals to ardent conservatives, prominent white southerners placed the blame for deteriorating race relations squarely on the shoulders of "radical" black leaders. While they deplored demagoguery and violence, the more temperate defenders of segregation declared themselves powerless to rein in their reactionary brethren as long as black militants persisted with their demands. But as racial violence reached a crescendo in the immediate postwar months, leading southern whites realized the urgent need to chart a course between mob rule and racial reform. Violent outbreaks across the region undercut the timeworn argument that segregation provided the blueprint for social progress and interracial harmony. With one eye toward northern investment and the other on the federal government, southern leaders calculated the high costs of racial turmoil.

Hoping to extend the unprecedented prosperity of the war years, southern advocates of law and order viewed racial violence as a hindrance to economic growth and modernization. While the Piedmont region of the Carolinas stood out as a shining example of southern industrialization, the campaign for economic growth extended beyond the urban upper South. Across the region, leading whites responded to agricultural mechanization with industrial development schemes. Despite its national image as the last bastion of southern feudalism, Mississippi had pioneered business incentives in the late 1930s with the Balance Agriculture with Industry program. This initiative attempted to lure firms and factories south with promises of cheap land and labor. As war mobilization picked up, other states followed suit. By the end of World War II, as historian James Cobb has argued, "a southern governor's obligation to recruit new industry was second only to his obligation to defend segregation." Although this campaign for economic development heightened the need to clamp down on the brutal excesses of white supremacy, southern industrialization proceeded within Jim Crow's parameters. As Cobb has argued, "plantation-style industrial development persisted even as traditional plantation agriculture was fading away."[9]

Increasingly uneasy with the Democratic Party's concessions to labor and civil rights groups, southern industrial elites clung to a conservative philosophy of economic growth. None promoted this vision more fervently than the Southern States Industrial Council, a regional network of right-wing businessmen that emerged from the war trumpeting the twin goals of economic growth and racial retrenchment. Founded to battle New Deal labor reforms, the SSIC had focused increasingly on civil rights since the wartime battles over the FEPC. Abandoning the "passive resistance" of the prewar years for an aggressively segregationist economic agenda, the SSIC boasted more members and larger coffers than ever before. Research director Thurman Sensing distributed a weekly column that reached 2.5 million southern subscribers. The seventh-largest lobby in Washington by 1947, the SSIC spent nearly as much on Capitol Hill as the American Legion and the Farm Bureau combined.[10]

The war boom, Sensing argued, offered the South an unprecedented opportunity to emerge from the shadow of the industrialized North. The Civil War had ravaged the region and set the stage for decades of economic stagnation. Eighty years later, another war presented an opportunity to cast off the stigma of colonial dependence. While some greedy Yankees selfishly wished for the region to "remain a furnisher of raw materials and an importer of manufactured goods," Sensing explained, the proud and prosperous South would no longer remain "a subordinate economic region." Southern industry was on the move.[11]

Even as he urged the South to embrace economic modernization, Sensing denounced other postwar trends. "In attaining its rightful prosperity," Sensing cautioned, "the South must be careful not to trade its birthright for a 'mess of pottage.'" Some things, he reminded his southern readers, were more important than money. Sensing counted chief among those values the "belief in the soundness of racial segregation and the solution of race problems on a local basis rather than by national legislation." Seeing no conflict between segregation and economic development, Sensing believed the South could have both. Indeed, it could not accept an alternative path. *"While promoting its prosperity,"* Sensing declared, *"the South must at the same time preserve its principles."* Hoping "to advance the industrial progress . . . of the South along sound lines," the ssic promoted "economic advancement" through "the development of parallel civilizations."[12]

The ssic narrative of southern progress revealed a wider truth about postwar racial politics. For most white southerners at midcentury, modernization and segregation seemed neither incompatible nor antagonistic. Promoting himself as a candidate of the people, South Carolina gubernatorial candidate Strom Thurmond curried favor with voters who had little in common with the wealthy industrialists who dominated the ssic. But even as Thurmond touted the "unlimited possibilities" of postwar prosperity throughout his 1946 campaign, he stood firm against any potential changes to the segregated status quo. "I will never favor mixing the races in schools, in churches, theaters, restaurants and elsewhere," Thurmond vowed in his only campaign statement on the subject. "I will never sign a bill to mix the races." Like the ssic, Thurmond embraced a segregated view of southern modernization.[13]

Thurmond tempered his firm stance on segregation with a hopeful message of economic advancement for white and black South Carolinians alike. Arguing in his inaugural address that prosperity should spill across the color line, Thurmond urged increased funding for black education. Separating economics from race in his optimistic modernization pitch, Thurmond strengthened his moderate credentials while ignoring the fact that whites reaped most of the benefits of segregated industrialization.[14]

Business-minded southern moderates also ignored, or at least underestimated, the contradiction of welcoming federally subsidized development while spurning outside interference in southern racial matters. New Deal programs and war mobilization spurred southern modernization and expanded the federal presence in the region, but a government strong enough to subsidize economic development could also push unwelcome reforms. The threat of federal intervention in racial affairs drove southern attempts to tamp down violence as much as the desire to encourage outside investment. Yet as they balanced allegiance to the past with pledges of a prosperous future, moderate elites often seemed weak-willed and ambivalent when juxtaposed with militant white supremacists.

The inability of southern leaders to curb racial violence and punish its perpetrators, combined with black demands for federal intervention, compelled the Truman administration to take unprecedented steps on civil rights. During the months of mounting atrocities, hundreds of members of the National Association of Colored Women had picketed the White House and thousands more had marched to the Lincoln Memorial to demand that the resurgent Ku Klux Klan be outlawed. The National Emergency Committee against Mob Violence, composed of leaders from more than forty civil rights, labor, and religious organizations, lobbied the president to take a stand against vigilantism and police brutality. By the end of 1946, Truman had established the President's Committee on Civil Rights (PCCR). This interracial taskforce included businessmen, labor leaders, clergy, educators, and government officials—including white southern liberals Frank Porter Graham and Dorothy Rogers Tilly. Truman charged the PCCR with investigating civil rights violations across the country, but from the outset southern racial problems dominated the agenda.[15]

In pressing Truman on civil rights, African Americans and their allies wielded unprecedented leverage in national politics and international diplomacy. Although northern blacks had flooded into the Democratic Party during the New Deal, many had drifted back to the GOP during the 1946 congressional elections. Picking up fifty-five seats, mostly in northern battleground states, Republicans regained control of the House of Representatives for the first time since 1928. For Democratic strategists, shoring up the black vote was more important than ever. In his influential study of the increasingly pivotal black electorate, NAACP official Henry Lee Moon pointed out that the combined electoral votes of New York, Pennsylvania, Illinois, and Michigan exceeded that of the entire South. In each state, urban black voters constituted a balance of power that could spell victory, or defeat, for the Democratic ticket. Presidential aide Clark Clifford urged President Truman to speak out on civil rights despite southern objections. "As always," Clifford predicted, "the South can be considered safely Democratic. And in formulating national policy, it can be safely ignored."[16]

If political strategists could disregard protests by southern conservatives, it was increasingly clear that the world paid attention to southern racial discrimination. "We cannot escape the fact that our civil rights record has been an issue in world politics," reported the PCCR. "The world's press and radio are full of it." The PCCR warned that southern lynchings furnished grist for the Soviet propaganda mill. "Those with competing philosophies," warned the PCCR, "have stressed—and are shamelessly distorting—our shortcomings."[17] If the United States wished to serve as a beacon of democracy, the PCCR advised, the federal government had to take steps to curb racial violence and discrimination.

Compelled to action by racial violence, political calculus, and diplomatic imperatives, Truman adopted an unprecedented civil rights agenda. In June of 1947, he became the first president to address the NAACP's annual convention. In his first public endorsement of racial reform, Truman emphasized the need for federal civil rights protections. Three months later, the PCCR released its landmark report, *To Secure These Rights*. In its indictment of "the shortcomings and failings of American democracy," the PCCR focused on lynchings, police brutality, and widespread discrimination against African Americans and other minorities. Concluding its report with a "program for action," the PCCR proposed a comprehensive federal civil rights agenda. In its recommendations, the PCCR outlined the key issues that had galvanized the opponents and defenders of Jim Crow for over a decade. In addition to federal antilynching legislation, the PCCR urged the Department of Justice, FBI, and state investigative agencies to devote more resources to civil rights enforcement. The committee also urged Congress to pass fair employment legislation, outlaw the poll tax, and enact federal penalties for police brutality. Calling for the desegregation of the armed forces, the District of Columbia, and interstate transportation, the committee endorsed "the elimination of segregation . . . from American life."[18]

Many white southerners regarded the report as an insult rather than an outright attack. Keeping cool for the time being, Thurmond stressed modernization while mocking the PCCR's misled idealism. "A little more practical help on economic lines, and a little less fallacious racial theory," Thurmond declared, "would accomplish a great deal more for the improvement of the level of life and opportunity of all our people of whatever race." SSIC columnist Thurman Sensing chided the committee, and particularly its two white southern members, for proposing reforms that were not only "impractical" but also "inimical to the American way of life." Claiming that segregation was not discrimination but rather "a law of nature," Sensing concluded: "Those who actually understand the relationship between the races know that nothing would be worse for the Negro race than enforced abolishment of segregation."[19]

Southern critics of the PCCR recognized, of course, that a presidential committee could not enact or enforce anything. But the president could. On 2 February 1948, just three months after the release of *To Secure These Rights*, Truman outlined a ten-point program for racial reform that included most of the major recommendations of the President's Committee.

He called for the repeal of the poll tax, federal penalties for lynching, and a permanent FEPC. Acknowledging the national reach of racial discrimination, Truman endorsed home rule for the District of Columbia and compensation for Japanese Americans interned during World War II. While he did not echo the committee's call to end segregation in schools and public accommodations, Truman pledged to desegregate interstate transportation and the armed forces.[20]

The president's address electrified southern racial politics. The PCCR report had unnerved white southerners, but even its harshest critics tended to dismiss *To Secure These Rights* as a dangerous pipe dream rather than an imminent executive agenda. Truman's unprecedented civil rights address, on the other hand, fueled fears of a federally backed racial revolution. "Almost to a man," historian John Egerton has noted, "the Southerners in Congress took it as a declaration of war." If southern liberals and moderates agreed in principle with some of Truman's proposals, they overwhelmingly denounced federal intervention as a means to achieving them. To their right, southern conservatives scorned the president as a "political whore" and a closet communist. "This proves," Mississippi senator James Eastland declared, "that organized mongrel minorities control the government." Texas senator Tom Connolly, who had coordinated southern filibusters against federal antilynching legislation, called Truman's civil rights program "a lynching of the Constitution."[21]

From the late 1930s through the end of World War II, white southerners had debated the extent and urgency of the civil rights revolution. But in the late 1940s, the immediate threat of a comprehensive federal civil rights program transformed this debate. Instead of convincing their fellow southerners of the looming threat of racial reform, the defenders of segregation now debated the most effective strategies for warding off federal intervention. For Deep South conservatives, electoral insurgency provided the surest path back to national influence. Yet the diehards chose as their standard-bearer a governor who had built a reputation as a moderate. Trading party loyalty for sectional militancy, Thurmond blazed a short trail to the head of the states' rights, or Dixiecrat, revolt.

Rather than a prairie-fire rebellion, the Dixiecrats represented a consequential yet highly controversial phase in the slow burn of segregationist politics. The majority of white southerners refused to equate electoral insurgency with a commitment to segregation, and most southern leaders questioned the tactical value of a regional revolt.[22] From the early months of 1948, white southerners on both sides of the Dixiecrat divide debated the most effective means for preserving segregation. If they emerged from the election year with no conclusive answers, some believed that the civil rights struggle presented newfound opportunities for the southern crusade to save segregation and, in the process, redeem America. But even as the protest ticket siphoned off Deep South voters from Truman, the majority of southern voters did not bolt the national party in 1948. The emerging rivalry of southern Democrats and Dixiecrats, like the earlier response to mob violence, revealed that a steadfast commitment to segregation rendered militancy and moderation inseparable.

Although a South Carolinian eventually received the Dixiecrat presidential nomination, Mississippians fired the opening shots of the states' rights revolt. In his inaugural address on 20 January 1948, Governor Fielding Wright preempted Truman's upcoming civil rights address with a call to arms. Declaring that "vital principles and eternal truths transcend party lines," Wright proclaimed that "the day is now at hand when determined action must be taken." As southern elites elsewhere debated the most effective response to Truman's civil rights plan, 4,000 Mississippians poured into the Jackson city auditorium on 12 February to urge "all true white Jeffersonian Democrats" to join together in a regional revolt. Energized by this early show of enthusiasm and eager to help spread it, a Yale-educated Mississippi circuit court judge named Thomas Pickens Brady declared "The South at Bay." Incensed by "traitor Truman's Civil Rights Program," Brady attempted to capture the outrage of the "white Jeffersonian Democrat" at his abandonment by "Iscariotic" northern liberals. Declaring that the national party leaders had dropped the "emblem bearing the donkey" and replaced it with a "black panther," Brady warned that federal civil rights laws would force southern states "to abandon their rights regarding suffrage, education, health, recreation, wages, police powers, profits, and all rights to regulate the life of their citizens." While Deep South Democrats made explicit the connection between their racial convictions and their political ideology, this invocation of states' rights overtook white supremacy as the battle cry of southern conservatives. And the most imperiled and most precious of these states' rights, the Dixiecrats argued, was the right to segregate.[23]

Building on the work of Jim Crow apologists such as Stuart Omer Landry and Theodore Bilbo, states' rights propagandists blended their critique of the civil rights movement with a broader appeal to constitutional conservatism. Born and raised on a cotton plantation in the Alabama black belt, Maryland lawyer Charles Wallace Collins deemed white supremacy "the very fibre of the southern soul." Yet, Collins warned, subversive racial reformers were "attempting to drive the South into a corner of moral isolation on the Negro race question." Harnessing the egalitarian rhetoric that emerged from the war years, civil rights advocates used "political profanity" to defame the white South. "What is the sense of calling a Southerner a Fascist," Collins complained, "for holding the same views which have been held by generations of his ancestors?"[24]

Hoping to awaken "the orthodox Southerner" to the interwoven threats of racial reform and federal totalitarianism, Collins penned a handbook for southern insurgency. More than a catalogue of complaints, 1947's *Whither Solid South?* outlined the plan that Deep South Democrats would soon embrace in their defection from the national party. If the southern states could pool their 127 electoral votes to deadlock the upcoming presidential election, Collins argued, they could force the election into the House of Representatives. There, white southern congressmen, rather than northern African Americans, would hold the balance of power in picking the new president.[25]

Lamenting their abandonment by the Democratic Party, southern diehards invoked the protests and prophecies of Roosevelt's earliest critics. Collins traced the betrayal back to 1936, which he branded as "a black year for southern politics." As Brady explained, "A few far-sighted Southern Democrats realized in 1936 that the great Democratic river was beginning to split into two forks." One of those prescient southerners was Nelson T. Levings, a Mississippi Delta planter and veteran convention delegate. Levings had protested the elimination of the two-thirds rule in 1936 and walked out of the next two Democratic National Conventions. Fellow Mississippians had ridiculed him, Levings recalled, "for opposing Roosevelt's plan to leave the South out of the Democratic Party." The events of 1948 offered grim vindication for diehards such as Levings. "1936 was the time we should have stopped the nationalization of our own civil and states' rights, and retained at least a semblance of a voice in our own affairs . . . ," Levings reflected in 1948. "I say NOW is about our last chance for CONCERTED and EFFECTIVE ACTION."[26]

By raising the specter of "nationalization," Levings and other states' righters framed their fight as a reaction against the centralization of power in Washington. Warning that "the whole Negro problem is infected with the deadly virus of stateism," Collins argued that any proposed racial reform was part of "a broad scheme for national planning which, if it became the law of the land, would nationalize all civil rights and thus effectively deprive the States of their republican form of government." From the outset, the Dixiecrat hardcore looked beyond their regional revolt to a burgeoning national campaign for limited government and constitutional conservatism. "We, both Democrats and Republicans, are now reaping the whirlwind of our association with the New Deal," argued Southern States Industrial Council president R. Kirby Longino. It was time, he argued, to sever those ties.[27]

Recognizing the necessity of weaving their racial convictions into a broader conservative agenda, the more farsighted Dixiecrats envisioned their regional protest movement as the catalyst for a conservative reawakening. "A strong, pure, Jeffersonian Democratic Party will arise," Brady predicted in early 1948, "a conservative Democratic Party into whose ranks all true conservative Americans, Democrats and Republicans alike, will be welcomed who are most solemnly sworn and determined to relentlessly oppose the radical elements of this country who arrogantly call themselves Liberals." Even as he outlined the Dixiecrat strategy, Collins envisioned a political coalition that could counter the civil rights revolution. Two decades before Richard Nixon's "Southern Strategy," Collins foresaw "the conversion of the present Republican-Southern Democratic coalition into a new conservative party."[28]

Before they went national, however, Deep South elites had to expand their appeal among southern whites. Despite its grassroots aspirations, the Dixiecrat movement remained an elite endeavor. In the wake of Truman's civil rights address, organizers anticipated the difficulty of recruiting ordinary white southerners to the movement. "The task of upper bracket organization and financial support should not be too difficult," predicted New Orleans Dixiecrat J. J. Kramer, "but from the middle classes down the picture is not so bright." An assistant to New Orleans businessman and Dixiecrat leader John U. Barr, Kramer believed that Truman's civil rights program had angered white southerners from all walks of life. "Our check in the grass roots of several of the states shows that the little fellow is ready to 'join' something if our leaders can form something for him and his woman to join." Nevertheless, Kramer complained, ordinary southerners seemed "bewildered" by the racial controversies that had erupted over the past few years. "They can't quite digest the published news and editorial comments on 'FEPC', 'anti-lynch' and 'poll tax'," Kramer reported. "They certainly are not clear on the significance of 'States' Rights.'"[29]

While southern elites plotted and promoted revolt, their rhetoric of monolithic outrage outpaced their ability to rally everyday southerners to the cause. The southern industrialists who bankrolled the Dixiecrat revolt claimed to represent "the most unified region of the country," but worried about the lack of unanimity on the ground. "I can assure you that this thing is not synthetic," a Louisiana Dixiecrat warned the SSIC's legal counsel in early 1948, "It is much stronger at this moment at the top." Southern industrialists responded with a trickle-down propaganda strategy. David Clark, the right-wing publisher of the *Textile Bulletin*, translated the Dixiecrat message for those who worked for his subscribers. "A vote for Truman," Clark warned, "is a vote for white mill employees to work side by side with Negroes upon the basis of social equality." [30]

The preoccupation with the little people persisted as the states' rights movement gathered steam. Just as the defenders of segregation had invoked their constituents in earlier battles against the wartime civil rights movement, the Dixiecrats wanted and needed to speak for everyday southerners. Keynoting the Dixiecrats' July convention in Birmingham, former Alabama governor Frank Dixon addressed "those who are of the opinion that this is not a 'Grass roots' movement." Claiming to have received "hundreds of telephone calls" from everyday southerners, Dixon warned, "our people are more aroused than they have been in many, many years, and they will repay by retirement to private life the efforts of so-called southern leaders who hope to carry them into the camp of Harry S. Truman in the coming election." [31]

Despite these lofty ambitions, the Dixiecrats lacked the ideological coherence, organizational capacity, and time necessary to mount a serious challenge to Truman. When Frank Dixon argued that nominees Thurmond and Wright needed no platform other than their opposition to the president's civil rights program, he pointed out both the Dixiecrats' strength and fatal weakness. The pairing of an economic progressive with a Black Belt conservative on the Dixiecrat ticket suggested that the states' righters offered little to voters beyond a commitment to the racial status quo. The challenge of shaking white southern loyalty to the Democratic Party proved even more daunting than cobbling together a comprehensive platform. Despite their misgivings about Truman's civil rights agenda, most southerners ultimately heeded the advice of Virginia attorney general and future governor J. Lindsay Almond Jr. "The only sane and constructive course to follow is to remain in the house of our fathers," Almond declared, "even though the roof leaks, and there be bats in the belfry, rats in the pantry, a cockroach waltz in the kitchen and skunks in the parlor." [32]

Many southerners simply did not believe that a regional bloc could deadlock the Electoral College, and Dixiecrat organizers had a precious few months to convince them otherwise. Many prominent southern moderates ridiculed the Dixiecrats as much for their tactical delusions as for their reactionary racism. North Carolina newspaperman Jonathan Daniels deemed the Electoral College scheme "utterly fantastic and ridiculous" and warned his readers that the "bush-league secessionists" would deprive the South of "any effective participation in the making of national decisions on the questions of race."[33] As Daniels's dismissive comments suggest, the Dixiecrats spurred little debate among white southerners over the morality or feasibility of segregation. They did, however, push their detractors to articulate alternative strategies for defending and legitimizing southern racial practices from inside the Democratic Party.

Whatever they accomplished, Dixiecrats failed to stalemate the election and throw it into the House of Representatives. Capturing a mere thirty-nine electoral votes with victories in Louisiana, Mississippi, Alabama, and South Carolina, the Dixiecrats could not rally substantial support in the remaining southern states. With 1.1 million ballots received, the Dixiecrats barely edged out Progressive Party candidate Henry Wallace to finish third in the popular vote count. Despite the Democratic votes picked off by the Progressives on the left and the Dixiecrats on the right, Truman shocked the nation by narrowly beating Republican challenger Thomas Dewey.[34]

The electoral revolt was a bust, but few Dixiecrats wasted time wallowing in defeat. South Carolinian James Kolb Breedin, a fierce critic of the "salt and pepper democracy of Mr. Truman," suggested that the Dixiecrats could reorganize as "the white Committee for Political Action, or the Association for the Advancement of White People." Whatever course conservative southerners adopted, Breedin considered the campaign a "fine achievement" and a precedent for the fight ahead. "The so-called practical politician may not believe it," Breedin argued, "but the States Righters have won at least a skirmish; now let us recruit our forces for the next." Speaking to Mississippi civic leaders in Jackson, James Eastland defiantly declared the Dixiecrat revolt the "opening phases of a fight" for conservative principles and racial awareness. "Governor Wright and Governor Thurmond are to be congratulated in setting up the States' Rights movement," he announced, "a movement that will never die." If Breedin advocated a regional racial crusade, Eastland envisioned a national campaign that would call the country back to white democracy.[35]

Eastland was too hotheaded to assume the leadership of such a movement, but his junior colleague was not. John Stennis came to Washington to fill the seat of the Senate's most notorious white supremacist, the late Theodore Bilbo. Considered a "dignified, conservative candidate, not given to ranting on the race question although in fundamental agreement with the Bilbo viewpoint," Stennis worked overtime to earn the respect of his colleagues. To his surprise, "virtually every Senator" welcomed the Mississippian with "very strong compliments" on his dignified campaign in the recent special election. Stennis's early days in Washington convinced him, as he explained to a political ally back home, "battles here are won . . . on friendships and calm persuasion and not by explosive statements to newspapers." So while fellow Mississippi Democrats openly plotted revolt in early 1948, Stennis laid low until critical constituents back home insisted that he fall in line. Scolding the junior senator for "Too Much Reticence," the *Jackson Daily News* demanded that Stennis should join Eastland in "valiantly fighting" Truman's civil rights program.[36]

The reaction to Stennis's restrained stance suggested that the Deep South bade farewell to "Bilboism" with more than a little ambivalence. "Mississippi did not like the *way* Bilbo fought the racial equality crowd," one constituent explained. "But every man, woman, and child down here appreciated his motives, as well as the intensity of his struggle." Even some of Stennis's closest supporters wanted the freshman senator to step up his attacks on the Truman administration. Urging Stennis to "open up on that gang with both barrels," a powerful political ally counseled: "The people of Mississippi expect and want you to give them hell, and they want to read about it in the papers."[37]

Although Stennis understood the political risks he faced back home, he recognized that white supremacist grandstanding would undermine his influence in Washington even if it garnered praise from constituents. "We have had ten years of hell-raising," Stennis argued, "and the South is definitely worse off because of it. There is a desire and a need for a new approach here, and I am at least going to try that new approach." Southern veterans of the Washington scene had learned valuable lessons in their crusade against the civil rights movement, and they looked to respectable newcomers such as Stennis to help plot a strategy for the future. "Those here who really furnish the brains for these battles have cautioned and urged me to make a careful and sound approach to this matter and not to 'pop off,'" Stennis confided to a Mississippi supporter. "They say that I can quickly ruin my chances here to be of any value in the fight." While Mississippians read few saber-rattling quotations from their freshman senator, Stennis assured his supporters that he was working overtime to thwart civil rights legislation. "I am on the go eighteen hours a day," he assured a supporter, "and I am trying to lay the foundations to have some influence in the Senate."[38]

Indeed, just two months into his first term, Stennis emerged as a leader of the revamped southern opposition. As the only southern member of the Senate Rules Committee, Stennis succeeded in delaying action on a new anti–poll tax bill by convincing his colleagues to hold public hearings. Appearing before the Judiciary Committee to argue against antilynching legislation, the former district attorney and circuit judge presented himself "not only as an advocate for our Southern viewpoint, but as a witness on the legal merits of the bill." In his maiden speech on the Senate floor, entitled "Dismantling the Constitution," Stennis took over an hour to present his legal objections to anti–poll tax amendments, antilynching legislation, the FEPC, and desegregation. While black Capitol Hill correspondent Lem Graves concluded that the senator "left no doubt that he was the successor to Senator Bilbo," he admitted that Stennis "avoided much of the demagoguery and racial name-calling" of his predecessor. But while critics pointed out that Stennis and Bilbo differed little in substance, many white southerners appreciated the tactical departure. "Thank goodness," noted Stennis's hometown newspaper, "for one man in high public office that can and did speak sensibly on the subject without calling [anyone] a nigger lover." For Stennis, the dignified approach offered the white South's last hope. Convinced that the defenders of segregation were "fighting a losing battle in the forum of public opinion," the senator made it his primary goal to "get our side of the case and our evidence before the people of the North, the East and the West."[39]

Nationalizing the problem, Stennis argued, required that southerners downplay regional appeals and racist rhetoric. "My arguments against all of this legislation have developed largely from a constitutional viewpoint, and I find that this approach has gained increasing respect for our position," Stennis informed his southern allies. "I shall make no appeals based on prejudice or passion, even if the prejudice happens to be one that I share from my natural experience of growing into maturity in the South." Stressing personal liberty and "sound American constitutional government," the reluctant Dixiecrat urged his fellow southerners to broaden and refine their critique of the Truman administration. "In thinking of States' Rights as a principle of government," Stennis announced, "we must divorce our thinking from (a) the so-called racial question, (b) the war between the States, (c) the South as a geographical region."[40]

Stennis doubted the wisdom of a southern revolt, but he shared with the Dixiecrat hardcore a desire to link states' rights to civil liberties and Deep South insurgency to a broader conservative countermovement. Only if and when cooler heads prevailed, Stennis contended, could the South reassert its influence in national affairs. "If we present our case to the rest of the nation in a calm, dispassionate manner, stressing the threat to the freedom of the whole nation that is implied in these unconstitutional attempts to abridge the freedom of the people of one section, we will make valuable friends among people who have been so misinformed as to regard the 'Civil Rights' fight as a moral issue," Stennis argued. "Only when these people see this whole program as a threat to the constitutional liberties of our entire citizenry is there any hope of this pressure campaign against the South relenting."[41]

Stennis agreed with his more militant colleagues that the ultimate salvation of the white South would come through alliance with conservatives across the nation. But while the diehards argued that the South could maximize its political power through revolt, Stennis pointed out that white southerners in Washington were not nearly as impotent as the Dixiecrats claimed. In July, he proudly reported that while Truman's civil rights proposals had made it out of committee, Senate leaders would not call them up for debate due to the certainty of a southern filibuster. With southern senators lined up in opposition to legislative encroachments on Jim Crow, Stennis believed that he and his colleagues could successfully work from within "toward getting our rights recognized and protected by the Democratic Party." When the Dixiecrats went down to defeat, neither Stennis nor Eastland spent much time mourning their demise. Unpunished for their participation in the revolt, Mississippi's senators resumed their battle from within, using their influence within Senate committees to stymie future rounds of civil rights legislation.[42]

Stennis's optimistic assessment of southern political influence relegated him to the moderate minority in Mississippi, but he nonetheless represented the majority opinion of the white South. In North Carolina, former governor Cameron Morrison reflected loyalist Democrats' confidence in their ability to stave off racial reform from within the national party. Writing off the nomination of Truman as an inevitability, the seventy-nine-year-old veteran of the state's 1898 disfranchisement campaign urged convention delegates to "step under the Democratic flag" and vote for Truman. "Then," Morrison declared, "we'll let our Congressmen and Senators beat him down when he needs beating."[43] During the 1948 presidential campaign, most southern leaders opted for Morrison's time-worn yet resilient tactic of legislative stonewalling over the drastic strategy of political defection.

Yet, for all its failures, the Dixiecrat movement had accelerated an uneven exodus of southern whites from the Democratic Party. Tracing the roots of their estrangement to the "black year" of 1936, conservative white southerners searched for a political alignment that would protect their embattled social system. In 1948, the defenders of segregation disagreed passionately about which road to take. As they moved forward, the line between Dixiecrats and Democrats blurred as southern segregationists fought civil rights advances at home and in Washington.

Just weeks after a triumphant 1946 Georgia gubernatorial campaign that sparked racial terrorism across the state, Governor Eugene Talmadge died in an Atlanta cancer ward. His supporters quickly drummed up a scheme to choose a successor through a special election in the General Assembly. Eugene's son, Herman Talmadge, a World War II veteran and the impromptu write-in candidate of his late father's loyal supporters, beat out recently elected lieutenant governor Melvin Thompson. Herman promptly stormed the office of acting governor Ellis Arnall. After a widely publicized scuffle between members of their respective entourages, Talmadge forced Arnall out of his office, changed the locks, and declared himself governor. The Georgia Supreme Court eventually ordered Herman out. Two months later, the court settled the competing claims for the governorship by naming Thompson the temporary successor to Eugene Talmadge.[44] Content to wait for a special election in September 1948, Herman had no sooner vacated his office than he began a campaign to take it back.

The younger Talmadge reflected the tension between racial militancy and economic modernization that drove postwar politics. Talmadge, like his distant cousin Strom Thurmond, served in World War II, stood firm on segregation, and promoted economic development. While Talmadge championed Jim Crow more fervently than Thurmond, he nonetheless attracted significant support from veterans, businessmen, and professionals with pledges to improve Georgia highways, hospitals, and schools. If his race-baiting overshadowed the rest of his platform, Talmadge's modernization agenda stood in stark contrast to his father's limited-government conservatism. An avowed opponent of Truman's "oppressive, communistic, anti-South legislation," the younger Talmadge nevertheless refused to steer his state into the Dixiecrat fold. Contemporary observers speculated that the incoming governor feared being branded a "bolter," a stigma that could undermine a future Senate run. With Talmadge reluctant to embrace the Dixiecrats, a *New York Times* correspondent predicted a few weeks before the 1948 election that "Georgia's Democratic leaders have ample reasons to believe they will win on party loyalty alone."[45]

For those who drew a direct line between the states' rights movement and reactionary racism, Georgia appeared out of step with its neighbors. As the Dixiecrats cut a swath through the Deep South in the 1948 presidential election, only Georgia disrupted the string of bolting states that stretched from Louisiana to South Carolina. In the formative months of the states' rights revolt, more than a few Georgia Democrats had quietly offered support and encouragement. State party chairman James Peters, Eugene Talmadge's right-hand man in the 1941 university scandal, remained publicly noncommittal while privately praising Dixiecrat efforts to undermine Truman.[46] Yet even as states' righters in neighboring states managed to take control of state party machinery, a mix of political calculus and downright confusion undermined support for a bolt.

The decision to spurn the Dixiecrat revolt was no prelude to racial moderation. To the contrary, Georgia whites' lukewarm response revealed their abiding confidence in their power to dictate the pace of racial change at home. By the presidential election of 1948, Georgia had eclipsed even Mississippi as a hotbed of racial repression. While advocates of moderation had cheered the death of Eugene Talmadge, their celebrations had been short lived. In the two months before the Georgia Supreme Court ordered him out of the governor's office, Herman Talmadge introduced legislation to privatize the state Democratic Party and purge as many previously registered black voters as possible. "If we can't have a white primary," Talmadge pledged, "we want a primary just as white as we can get it." During the 1948 gubernatorial campaign, black voters across Georgia brought suits against "a mass purge" of voting lists by Talmadge allies that required African American voters to reregister. In several counties, white officials summoned hundreds of registered black voters to appear before country registrars. In some cases, African American voters received the summons after the hearing date. In Spalding County, registrars processed summoned voters so slowly that long lines of black voters returned home empty handed. When many could not return to wait in line for a second day, country registrars struck them from the rolls.[47]

While county officials undermined black voter registration, Georgia Klansmen responded to Talmadge's campaign pledge to maintain white supremacy "by peaceful means if possible, by force if necessary." Talmadge, no stranger to the Klan, had once attended a private birthday party for Atlanta obstetrician and Georgia Grand Dragon Samuel Green. As the guest speaker, Talmadge had praised the gathered Klansmen as the foot soldiers of a postwar movement to "save America for Americans." When Talmadge began his gubernatorial campaign, Green declared the election of Talmadge the Klan's "number one job." According to undercover investigators, the Georgia Klan established Klaverns in all 159 counties by the summer of 1948. Arguing that the United States was established by and for white men, Klan recruitment literature declared, "Every effort to wrest from White Men the control of this country must be resisted." Any effort by African Americans "to share in its control," the Georgia Klan warned, was "an invasion of our scared constitutional prerogatives and a violation of divinely established laws." Throughout the gubernatorial campaign, Klansmen marched and burned crosses in dozens of Georgia towns. As the election neared, Klansmen placed miniature coffins on the doorsteps of black leaders and dropped warning leaflets from airplanes. On election day, Talmadge partisans gunned down black veteran Isaac Nixon shortly after the farmer cast his ballot.[48]

After retaking the governor's office, Talmadge rewarded his Klan supporters by naming Green a lieutenant colonel and aide-de-camp. The governor also appointed Klansman Sam Roper, a veteran Atlanta policeman and Green's eventual successor, as head of the Georgia Bureau of Investigation. With the endorsement of a grateful governor, Green continued to build his surging organization to an estimated 100,000 Klansmen. As Klan membership threatened to overtake the relatively high number of registered black voters in Georgia, statewide NAACP membership shriveled from a postwar high of 11,000 to 3,000. To further institutionalize his blend of racial intimidation and legal subterfuge, Talmadge and his legislative allies outlined plans to disfranchise 80 percent of black Georgians via a revamped "education qualification." House Speaker Fred Hand hoped to decimate the "ignorant bloc vote" while avoiding explicitly racial language. "I like to think of it that way instead of going into this color angle," Hand explained, but supporters and critics alike recognized the racial objectives of the legislation. In a particularly blunt interpretation of the new voter registration laws, registrars in one rural county required all applicants to sign a pledge declaring their support for white supremacy.[49]

White violence in Georgia erupted again just days after Truman's reelection. The same week that an all-white jury acquitted Isaac Nixon's slayers, robed men ambushed a black casket salesman in neighboring Toombs County. On the night of November 20, Robert Mallard drove home from a fundraiser at a local school with his wife, his toddler son, and two teenage relatives. The Standard Products Company had recently cited Mallard as one their top five funeral-supplies salesmen. As he cruised along the dark country road in his shiny new Fraser sedan, Mallard spotted a blockade of automobiles and several dozen robed men up ahead. After he slowed to a stop in front of Providence Church, the mob opened fire. With bullet wounds in the chest and leg, Mallard stumbled from the car and collapsed dead in the dirt. Rather than pursue Mallard's attackers, the responding police officers rifled through his wife's pocketbook.[50]

The Mallard lynching dramatized the collusion between state officials, law enforcement officers, and Klan terrorists in creating an atmosphere of racial repression. Although Mallard died on November 20, news of the murder did not reach the press for five days. When local authorities finally broke their silence, Toombs County sheriff R. E. Gray dismissed reports that white gunmen had killed Mallard for voting in the recent gubernatorial elections. Other sources cited local resentment over the salesman's flashy new car. Such extravagance earned Mallard a reputation as a "biggety nigger." According to an NAACP account, Mallard was also "a man who accorded to white persons no special deference because of their race." Regardless of the precise motive, white men had killed Mallard for forgetting his place. And despite denials from state and local officials, the press amassed substantial evidence of Klan involvement.[51]

Even in the face of unchecked white violence, white moderates seemed reluctant to admit the scope of racial backlash. While he rarely passed up the chance to take jabs at the Talmadge regime, *Atlanta Constitution* editor Ralph McGill assured readers that Klan terror was not "a real factor" in Georgia. "Most Negroes seem to enjoy watching the beer-can crosses burn," McGill editorialized. "They aren't afraid any more." But African Americans, recognizing that more refined forms of repression operated in tandem with racial terrorism, described the white backlash as a decidedly top-down affair. William A. Fowlkes, managing editor of the African American *Atlanta Daily World*, argued that "double-talk" from "Southern so-called white liberals" only obscured the broad reach of white supremacy in Georgia. "It is not so much the sheet wearing, cross burning, or casket placing activities of the Klan which is so dangerous," Fowlkes contended, "but it is the organization of prejudice and hatred and the use of systematized job and economic sanctions which mean strangulation and death for any Negro who dares compete with the supremacy system." Particularly alarming, Fowlkes declared, was the "infiltration of KKK influence and power into police, court, and prison administration."[52]

The Atlanta newspaperman could have also mentioned the state legislature, which killed an antimasking bill just days after the Mallard trial. "Pro-Klan speakers," reported one black journalist, "each in his turn professing to be a non-member of the infamous organization, invoked the Bible, extolled ancestry worship, and 'refought' the Civil War, in an effort to prove that the bed-sheet storm troopers comprise a 'noble' organization." After likening the federal government to Nazis and communists, one legislator sneered that the "only ones who are for this bill to make it unlawful to wear masks in Georgia are those from Atlanta who have to ride into office on the backs of Negroes."[53]

Despite Truman's victory over his Dixiecrat enemies, the national prospects for civil rights legislation seemed only slightly more promising than they did in the Georgia General Assembly. Hoping to build momentum for another antilynching push, the NAACP sent Robert Mallard's widow, Amy, on a nationwide speaking tour. After an enthusiastic reception in several Northeast cities, the tour succumbed to dwindling funds and a series of disputes between Mallard and her NAACP sponsors. The fate of the tour reflected the broader dilemma facing the civil rights movement. With southern leaders both inside and outside of the states' rights fold prepared to stifle dissent at home, and a Senate bloc prepared to kill civil rights bills through filibusters, the Dixiecrats' demise seemed a pyrrhic victory for advocates of racial equality.

By avoiding the states' rights revolt, Georgia conservatives remained at the vanguard of the segregationist crusade. On the national stage, Senator Richard Russell assumed the "generalship" of the southern forces on Capitol Hill, condemning Truman's civil rights program as "a crime against our civilization and a sin against nature's God." Instead of joining the Dixiecrat movement, Russell offered loyal southern Democrats a face-saving alternative at the 1948 Democratic National Convention. In a fiery nominating speech, Charles Bloch nominated Russell for president. With a Georgian in the White House, the Jewish vice president of the Georgia delegation pledged, the white South would not "be crucified on the cross of civil rights." Even though the entire Mississippi delegation and half of the Alabama delegation barged out after the adoption of the civil rights plank, Russell received over a quarter of all delegate votes in the first round of balloting. With the exception of the North Carolina delegation, which split its votes between Russell and Truman, the Georgia senator enjoyed the united support of the former Confederacy.[54]

Even as white elites back home persisted with terrorist tactics and discriminatory legislation, their representatives in Washington traded racial militancy for a rhetoric they hoped would resonate with a national audience. Building on the patriotic wartime pleas of southern white supremacists, Russell and his colleagues portrayed themselves as the real freedom fighters. As Russell announced on a national radio broadcast in 1948: "We submit that the white people of the South, though widely misunderstood and oft maligned, have some few rights as American citizens."[55] Convinced that they alone could save the Democratic Party from an alliance of hypocritical liberals, deluded minorities, and communist subversives, segregationists launched a barrage of constitutional appeals and states' rights rhetoric that would reverberate in later battles.

Despite dispiriting news from the South, national Democratic Party leaders seized on Truman's inauguration as an opportunity to showcase their commitment to civil rights. On 20 January 1949, a "Historic Cavalcade" marched down Pennsylvania Avenue. Eight of the nine black cadets enrolled at West Point marched in integrated units, as did African American midshipmen, military police, and members of the Women's Army Corps. Two soldiers, one white and one black, rode atop a tank, advertising the Army's "New Look." In the crowd, a black reporter observed, African American attendees "were everywhere, from the cheapest seats to the Presidential reviewing stand." In the first nationally televised inauguration, an estimated 10 million viewers tuned in to witness an integrated spectacle. More Americans watched the 1949 ceremonies than all previous presidential inaugurations combined, and more than a few did not like what they saw.[56]

The integrated crowd proved less than welcoming to some southern participants in the parade. As the car carrying Herman Talmadge crept along, spectators booed the Georgia governor. Even worse, the president and vice president turned away as Talmadge's car rolled past the reviewing stand. Any doubt that Truman deliberately ignored the Georgia governor, noted a delighted black reporter, disappeared when the president turned to greet the next car. "It was beyond any doubt," declared the *Atlanta Daily World*, "that the infamous Monroe Lynchings, the Mallard, Nixon and Gilbert cases, notwithstanding the current attempt to disfranchise Negro voters, figured greatly in the display accorded the state delegates." Giving Talmadge no credit for steering clear of the states' rights revolt, the *Baltimore Afro-American* referred to the Georgia governor as one of "3 Dixiecrats Snubbed." The crowd saved its loudest boos for Strom Thurmond. When the defeated Dixiecrat came into sight, those gathered around the reviewing stand shouted, "Don't speak to him, Harry!" Thurmond removed his hat as he passed by the president, but neither Truman nor Barkley returned the gesture. "They just stood and stared," noted a black correspondent, "and the crowd roared approval as Thurmond went on his way."[57]

For Georgia senator Richard Russell, the inaugural festivities confirmed the need for unrelenting southern resistance to the president's civil rights program. Arguably the most powerful southerner in Washington at midcentury, the Georgia senator embodied the mixture of angry defiance and calculated confidence that had helped the Southern bloc stymie meaningful racial reform. By early 1949, Russell's segregationist schemes reflected a larger campaign by southern lawmakers to align their struggle with fundamental American values. If nothing else, they hoped to frustrate and embarrass their northern adversaries. While they often appeared to flail desperately against the winds of change, Russell and his colleagues brushed off charges of bigoted obstructionism. They had always considered themselves conservative, white supremacist, Jeffersonian Democrats, and they resented any insinuation that their convictions were outdated or un-American. Invoking the patriotic right to segregate, Jim Crow's defenders turned the spotlight on "northern hypocrites" in an attempt to garner the sympathies of a white majority that lacked the reformist zeal of its elected representatives.[58]

With the humiliation of the integrated inaugural festivities fresh in his mind, Russell launched the 1949 legislative session with a provocative move. Just one week after the inauguration, Russell introduced a bill to establish a "Voluntary Racial Relocation Commission." Claiming that the bill would "reduce and eliminate racial tensions and improve the economic status of the American people by equitably distributing" southern blacks across the country, Russell dryly declared that the $4.5 billion program "should strongly appeal to all social-minded people." The reason for such a drastic and expensive proposal, he explained, was Truman's increasingly aggressive stand on civil rights. The president and his allies, Russell argued, were attempting to "destroy the system of segregating the races which exists in the South." The final result of the Truman civil rights program would be "the amalgamation and absorption of the minority Negro race." Since white southerners were "unalterably opposed" to integration and its ultimate outcome, "mongrelization," Russell declared his relocation scheme a humanitarian alternative to the destruction of southern civilization.[59]

Russell's appeals to "equality and justice" met with a torrent of criticism in the national press, and black newspapers dismissed the bill as a cynical political stunt. Although the Georgia senator delivered his grandiose proposal with "dead seriousness," one black correspondent reported, the relocation scheme obviously sought "to embarrass and harass the proponents of civil rights legislation." Another black journalist perceptively noted that Russell, in speaking for his bill, used the terms "civil rights" and "social equality" interchangeably. If northerners backed full civil rights for African Americans, Russell argued, they had better be prepared to welcome blacks into their communities, homes, and, eventually but inevitably, their bedrooms. "It would be manifestly unfair and un-American," the senator declared, "for the rest of the country to compel the white people of the South, by Federal fiat, to associate in the most intimate relations of life, with and perhaps eventually absorb, a much higher proportion of Negroes than they themselves will have an opportunity to accept and absorb."[60]

Russell knew, of course, that white northerners had no desire to confront the race issue at their own doorstep. He argued that the racial views of a person in a community with a tiny fraction of African Americans differed from the outlook of Deep South whites. As part of his presentation, he offered a table that listed 182 southern counties where blacks outnumbered whites. The "degree of feeling," he pointed out, varied even within the South "in accordance with the percentage of the [black] population." Thus whites in Upper South states such as North Carolina and Tennessee, Russell declared, could not be expected to oppose civil rights with the same vehemence as white Mississippians and South Carolinians.[61]

Back in Georgia, whites of various political stripes applauded Russell. As one woman reported, "I have heard people without number down here advocate shipping the negroes into those parts of the country which seem to talk most loudly about the negro's 'rights' while they have the smallest number of negroes within their own state borders." The *Atlanta Journal* predicted that the senator's relocation campaign would draw sympathetic attention to "the South's distinctive problem" while inviting "the self-righteous reformers who are far removed from the crux of this problem to share something of its realities." The city's voice of racial moderation, the *Atlanta Constitution*, predicted that the proposal would "be labeled demagogic" and "probably will not receive much attention." The paper hastened to add, however, that University of North Carolina sociologist Howard Odum had suggested during the war that voluntary black resettlement could help alleviate southern racial tension. Indeed, the southern sociologist had suggested "careful planning for the diffusion of those Negro people who wanted to move" out of Dixie. "Was it possible," Odum pondered, "that a Nation with ideals and force enough to undertake the conquest of a region could do the job better at less cost and sacrifice and in accordance with constitutional measures by providing facilities for the migration and education of Negroes, for their training and employment in areas where the people had the constitutional provisions and the will to do the job?"[62]

Apologists for the relocation scheme meshed the rhetoric of regional modernization with the "nationalization" of the race problem. The *Constitution* warned that the mechanization of southern agriculture created "a population problem of displaced farm persons." By elevating the "Negro problem" from a regional burden to a national responsibility, Russell played the part of forward-thinking southern statesman rather than reactionary demagogue. "The problem is a national one and we must think of it in national terms," argued the *Constitution*. "To persist in thinking in terms of a Dixiecrat spellbinder, is to be really disloyal to the South and its future." The editors warned against dismissing the Russell bill. "We'd like to wager," they concluded, "that about 20 years from now someone will recall the Russell proposal and the Odum suggestion, and say, 'You know, if we had started planning then we'd be better off today.'"[63]

Despite the lofty rhetoric, most supporters perceived and applauded Russell's primary motive: to portray civil rights advocates as outside agitators far removed from the everyday realities of southern race relations. Russell readily acknowledged his desire to discredit northern meddlers by launching "a counter-attack against those who attempt to run our business from other States." While the racial relocation plan languished in the Senate, segregationists wielded the proposal as a club against their northern critics. Former Louisiana governor and Dixiecrat booster Sam Jones promoted Russell's bill in the pages of *Life* magazine. Introduced as a "student of the Negro problem," Jones presented black resettlement as a "rational adaptation" of northern demands for civil rights. "We must throw out the window the idea that this is a 'states' rights' matter," Jones argued, "and we must proceed to regulate by federal legislation the complete admission, integration, and assimilation of the Negro race into our social, economic, and political fabric." When communities across the country shared the "burden" of a black minority, he predicted, "there would naturally develop a better understanding between the North and the South on the whole subject." As an example, Jones pointed out that white Minnesotans would see their black minority increase from under 10,000 to more than 300,000. "If the reader would visualize the working of the law and apply a rough approximation of it to his own community," Jones explained, "all he has to do is to take one tenth of the total population of his city or county, and that will be the number of Negroes who would ultimately live and work in his community." Since the nation was not content with the southern "solution" of segregation, Jones proposed "the nationalization of the problem" as a thinly veiled threat.[64]

Satisfied that his relocation bill had at least "put the finger on the northern hypocrites," Russell vowed to "propose it as an amendment to any civil rights bill brought before the Senate." But rhetorical jabs were only one weapon in Russell's arsenal. After opening with his relocation stunt,

Russell compiled a roster of twenty southern senators and devised a system of "guard duty" to insure that a loyal opponent of civil rights measures remained present in the Senate chamber at all times. He proposed "having one Senator from the South responsible for watching the floor each day to see that no legislative trickery is employed to secure the passage of any of these bills." Meanwhile, Russell joined with newcomers such as John Stennis to articulate an increasingly legalistic defense of Jim Crow. In the process, they impressed southern moderates who resented the perceived hypocrisy of northern liberals and the militancy of civil rights activists. As southern senators argued against civil rights measures in the spring of 1949, an Atlanta editor applauded their elevated rhetoric. "Here, at last, is the best the South has in Congress speaking for the South," declared the editor. The "Real Voice" of the region shunned "offensive vulgarity" for "integrity and logic." Hopefully, it was not too late.[65]

Within months of his triumphantly integrated inauguration, Truman's civil rights program stalled in the face of reinvigorated southern resistance. Senators stood vigil, the threat of filibuster ever present, while congressmen in the House used committee seniority to bottle up civil rights bills. But while southern lawmakers, reinforced by a growing conservative Republican contingent in both houses, stymied Truman's legislative agenda, they could not derail one of the president's top priorities. On 26 July 1948, Truman issued Executive Order 9981, demanding "equality of treatment and opportunity for all persons in the armed services without regard to race, color, religion, or national origin." Truman's order also established the President's Committee on Equality of Treatment and Opportunity in the Armed Forces, chaired by Charles Fahy, a native white Georgian deemed by the White House to be "totally reconstructed on the subject of race."[66]

Truman's executive order embarrassed southern politicians who had successfully fended off most of his civil rights agenda. Yet segregationists seized the opportunity to deploy their own vision of liberty. As Congress debated the first peacetime draft in American history in May 1948, Richard Russell introduced a "Freedom of Selection Amendment" that would require every enlistee to declare in writing whether he preferred to serve in integrated units or a unit "of his own race." Russell's proposal only recognized two racial categories, with the "principle minority race" segregated from all other American soldiers. A member of the Senate Armed Forces Committee, Russell promoted his amendment as a "true civil rights" measure. According to Russell, the proposed policy guaranteed "the inherent and fundamental right of free-born American citizens to a free choice of the type of people with whom they will live." When the amendment failed, the ordinarily hawkish southern bloc supported an amendment to shorten the life of the bill from five to two years. Disappointed by the failure of the Russell amendment and angered by conservative Republicans who supported an amendment to abolish the poll tax for enlisted men, southern senators grudgingly accepted an integrated Selective Service System.[67]

While "freedom of choice" and "freedom of association" are commonly associated with movements to preserve segregation in schools and residential areas, Russell's early deployment of this rhetoric highlighted its power and versatility. Couching a politically risky confrontation with the military brass in a refined rhetoric of individual liberty, the Georgia senator asserted the patriotic southerner's right to segregate. Guaranteeing fighting men their "freedom of choice," Russell maintained, "was fundamentally fair and in the American tradition." If military policy honored the religious beliefs of conscientious objectors, he reasoned, then it should also respect "racial instinct." Russell even criticized the "military establishment" for "violating the civil rights of our white servicemen by not giving them the right of choice which would permit them to serve with their own kind." Blasting the Truman administration for "forcing our white boys to serve in mongrelized units," South Carolina senator Burnet Maybank deemed military desegregation "a perversion of the police power of the state." While Russell evoked images of white soldiers stricken with diseases and dishonorably discharged for abandoning their posts, Maybank gloomily predicted "a conscript army of bitter malcontents."[68]

In practical terms, the fight over military desegregation posed political risks for southern Democrats who embraced Truman's aggressively anti-communist foreign policy. Although they feared the dangerous precedent of federally imposed racial reform in an institution over which they could exert only limited pressure, southern segregationists also realized the political liability of railing against the military establishment with American troops in harm's way. The fact that they persisted reveals their commitment to preserving segregation not only within their borders, but also within national institutions.

Powerless to derail comprehensive military desegregation, southern leaders in Washington soon had a more promising target for their "freedom of choice" crusade. Their critique of a federal government forcing social experiments without legislative sanction or public consent echoed in the growing conflict over school desegregation. Pleading unsuccessfully for his military segregation plan, Russell argued that segregation was ultimately a matter of "hearts and minds." Without the "voluntary cooperation" of white southerners, he warned, desegregation was a fool's errand. "They cannot be forced," Russell warned, "and efforts to coerce people by law will fail." [69]

5

THE RHETORIC OF
RESPONSIBLE RESISTANCE

Just two years after the tumultuous political season of 1948, the defenders of segregation looked to South Carolina for a glimpse of Jim Crow's future. "Of all the primary campaigns," Atlanta newspaperman Ralph McGill reported in 1950, "no other was as strange to the South as that of James Francis Byrnes." Gone were the demagogue theatrics, the "jug bands," the "hillbilly grammar," and a host of other "shabby old political props" that had plagued southern politicking for decades. Instead, McGill reported, South Carolina welcomed back a favorite son who promised a refined brand of racial politics. Byrnes, the former congressman, senator, Supreme Court justice, and secretary of state, had emerged from political retirement to run for governor of his home state. Honoring a state primary rule that required all candidates to make at least one campaign speech in each county, the seventy-one-year-old Byrnes crisscrossed the state in a chauffeured sedan. Arriving to a hero's welcome at the local rallies, the sharply dressed statesman would shake hands, make his stump speech, and promptly head for the door. Byrnes virtually ignored his three opponents, who stammered through their speeches in front of a crowd decimated by the departure of "the dapper political Pied Piper."[1]

The gubernatorial race was not so much a primary as an extended coronation. "Jimmy just walked in, with the benediction of the people," reflected one local columnist. "Remarkable, wasn't it?" The gubernatorial campaign stood in stark contrast to the bitter senatorial race between governor and erstwhile presidential candidate Strom Thurmond and former governor Olin Johnston. "Off on the far horizon one could hear the loud trumpetings of Thurmond and Johnston, whose antics were in the old mudstained pattern of recrimination," McGill noted. "But the Byrnes tour went on its antiseptic way, calm and serene, until one fancied, even, the voice of the turtle could be heard in the pleasant, pastoral land." For McGill, Byrnes embodied the dominant political trend of the primary season. "The South is freer of ranters and demagogues than it has been for a generation or more," McGill announced. For proof, he pointed to the election of moderate candidates in Alabama, Arkansas, and Louisiana. Even McGill's hometown nemesis, Georgia governor Herman Talmadge, disappointed his late father's followers with his "lack of demagogic fire" during a successful reelection campaign.[2]

The moderating trend that McGill celebrated in 1950 was already several years in the making. Postwar racial violence and the divisive Dixiecrat rebellion had convinced many committed segregationists to refine their rhetoric and tactics. From pragmatic conservatives to former firebreathers, Jim Crow's defenders invoked white supremacy less and touted segregation more. But Byrnes did more than embrace a political trend— rather, he attempted to imbue the segregationist crusade with a reform agenda by arguing that segregation's survival rested upon white southerners' ability to adapt and improve their social order. By promoting a policy of "equal educational rights," Byrnes repackaged white resistance in a reformist veneer. White southerners, he pledged, would improve the black side of Jim Crow in order to keep the color line intact. Southern liberals and moderates had made similar arguments before, but now time seemed short. Even the diehards and militants had to get on board, and Byrnes possessed the conservative credentials and political prestige necessary to rally skeptics behind a reform agenda. "He does not believe segregation can, or should, be now abolished," McGill explained, "but he fiercely insists the status quo is not the answer."[3]

Byrnes's reform program shook up Deep South politics, and his contingency plan for a federal desegregation order spread tremors as well. If the Supreme Court would allow South Carolina the necessary time, Byrnes promised, then it would bring black educational facilities up to par with those of whites. But if the federal government demanded integration, then the governor-elect would lead a campaign to abolish the public school system in South Carolina. "Whatever is necessary to continue the separation of the races in the schools of South Carolina is going to be done by the white people of the State," Byrnes pledged. That "whatever" could mean spending millions to improve black schools or abandoning state responsibility for schooling altogether. Byrnes had the power to push either plan, and he offered the carrot and the stick to black South Carolinians and federal authorities alike. Even as he advocated reform, the defiant governor-elect thus emerged as "the new symbol of the Southern revolt."[4]

Predictions of southern rebellion no longer surprised anyone, but the mix of aggressive reform and entrenched resistance that emerged in the early 1950s marked an important shift. School equalization schemes reflected the evolution of segregationist politics even as they exposed the inherent tension between moderation and militancy. White southern leaders seized on equalization not as a remedy for the injustices of the past but as a showcase for the humane and orderly future of segregation. Yet even as white elites rallied behind construction bonds and reform initiatives, they brandished the radical threat of school closings. The rhetoric of equalization, deployed simultaneously with the explicit threat of shutting down the public school system, revealed the dual character of the segregationist position even as it underscored a steadfast commitment to maintaining the color line.[5]

While equalization programs proceeded unevenly from state to state, reformist resistance developed into a regional movement. In order to stave off desegregation, prescient southern conservatives urged cooperation. Southern conservatives looked to Byrnes and South Carolina as a model for promoting segregation as responsible public policy. But as the estimated costs of "equalizing" southern schools soared above $400 million, segregationists lacked the time, the resources, and the collective will to transform reformist rhetoric into reality. When juxtaposed with the cool confidence of Byrnes, the scrambling and confusion of other southern states in the months preceding the *Brown* decision revealed the wide gap between the rhetoric of responsible segregation and the reality of crumbling black schools. Nevertheless, reformist resistance provided segregation's defenders with a veneer of respectability that helped them, in the wake of the *Brown* decision, to recast themselves as shocked and beleaguered statesmen despite years of preemptive planning. As segregationists fought federal desegregation orders and civil rights activists, they built on earlier crusades to affirm their vision of conservative Americanism.[6]

Some would feign shock and bewilderment in the wake of *Brown*, but southern politicians had argued for years that racial struggles would eventually lead to the schoolhouse door. Even when desegregated classrooms seemed a distant possibility, the defenders of segregation pointed to the public schools as the prime target of the civil rights movement. After purging suspected integrationists from the state university system in 1941, Eugene Talmadge bragged on the campaign trail that he had "scotched the snake before coils of racial equality suffocated the body of our educational institutions." Throughout the 1940s, southern conservatives denounced federal aid for education as an egalitarian Trojan horse. As one Mississippi editor warned, "camouflaged education help" was one step closer to the intertwined evils of "Hitlerized totalitarian rule" and "social equality." Just as opponents of the wartime civil rights movement fought federal aid for education with images of racially mixed classrooms, the leaders of the states' rights revolt raised the threat of school desegregation to mobilize disaffected southern Democrats. In his rousing keynote speech at the 1948 Dixiecrat convention, former Alabama governor Frank Dixon identified "the elimination of segregation in the public schools" as the primary objective of Truman's civil rights program. Like other southern conservatives, Dixon argued that the white South's devolution into "a mongrel, inferior race" ultimately led to and through the schoolhouse door.[7]

When segregationists identified education as the civil rights battleground of the future, they quickly fingered the federal courts as their enemy. Through a series of segregation cases, many dealing directly with education, southern whites could point to the slow but steady erosion of the "separate but equal" doctrine established by *Plessy v. Ferguson*. From the 1920s onward, the NAACP pursued a campaign against segregated schooling that yielded important border-state victories in the late 1930s. In 1938, in the first university segregation case to reach the federal appellate courts, NAACP lawyer Charles Hamilton Houston aided Lloyd Gaines, a twenty-three-year-old plaintiff who had applied unsuccessfully to the law school at the University of Missouri. The board rejected Gaines's application on racial grounds, offering either to provide a scholarship to attend law school out of state or to establish a law school at his alma mater, Lincoln University. The Supreme Court held that Missouri either had to provide equal legal education opportunities at black universities or admit qualified African Americans to their whites-only law school. While the decision left open the option of providing separate facilities for blacks, the Supreme Court ruled in favor of equal opportunity in practice as well as theory.[8]

By the late 1940s, the NAACP legal team filed suits claiming that segregated graduate education continued to fall far short of equality. In Texas, state officials opened a tiny law school for blacks rather than admit Heman Sweatt to the their flagship public university. The University of Oklahoma admitted G. W. McLaurin as a graduate student in education but required him to sit in separate areas of the classrooms, cafeteria, and library. NAACP officials filed suits on behalf of both plaintiffs. Briefing southern senators on the pending *Sweatt* case in early 1950, Texas attorney general and future United States senator Price Daniel warned that if the lawsuit succeeded, "the rights of States, counties, and school districts to maintain separate schools, parks, swimming pools, and eleemosynary institutions will be destroyed." Segregation suits, Daniel predicted, would be "far more tragic to the Southern States than any of the civil rights programs advocated by President Truman." While segregation's defenders had derailed most meaningful racial reforms originating in the executive and legislative branches, the judiciary posed a more sinister threat. Through litigation in increasingly sympathetic federal courts, Daniel warned, integrationists "could effectively bypass the Congress on the civil rights issues."[9]

On 5 June 1950, the Supreme Court ruled that attempts to provide "separate but equal" education in Oklahoma and Texas deprived the plaintiffs of their constitutional rights. The Supreme Court ordered the University of Texas to admit Sweatt and the University of Oklahoma to lift the restrictions imposed on McLaurin. For Deep South segregationists, the message was clear. "It means," Congressman William Colmer warned his Mississippi constituents, "that there will be an ever increasing intermingling of Negroes and whites in public places. It is the forerunner of a final decision by that court, at a not too distant date, denying segregation in all public institutions, both State and Federal." Four years before Mississippi congressman John Bell Williams supposedly coined the infamous epithet for the *Brown* decision, Texas congressman Ed Lee Gossett declared 5 June 1950, "Black Monday."[10]

As the courts eroded the legal basis for school segregation, southern conservatives redoubled their efforts to affirm the moral and constitutional basis for their crusade. On the campaign trail, Jimmy Byrnes responded resolutely to the Supreme Court rulings. "It is time for more thinking and less talking," Byrnes announced. "We will find a way out that will permit us to be just to our Negro population and at the same time preserve our system of separate schools for the races." Just one month after Supreme Court handed down the *Sweatt* and *McLaurin* decisions, Byrnes trounced his three opponents by a combined margin of 100,000 votes. The following January, the same number showed up for his inauguration. Across the state and region, newspapermen celebrated Byrnes's return to public life. The *Yorkville Enquirer* deemed it a "modern day miracle." According to veteran South Carolina newspaperman Henry Lesesne, "the man who probably has held more important public offices than any other living American" had brought his "relatively unimportant" home state "the greatest prestige it has had in modern times."[11]

Indeed, if anyone possessed the political reputation and acumen to forge a segregated future, it was the "elder statesman" of South Carolina. Byrnes had remained largely noncommittal during the states' rights revolt of 1948, but southern whites knew where he stood by 1951. "He realizes," declared a small-town newspaper editor, "that in order to halt the awesome aggrandizement of power in Washington it is necessary that our local governments stand up and fight back for the rights we have lost." This conservative stance was not novel, but the South Carolina governor gave white southerners new hope. Because of Byrnes's illustrious record of public service, particularly his Supreme Court stint, columnist John Temple Graves predicted that "he will stand before the nation a free and politically disembodied American." Unshackled by the limitations of regional identity, party affiliation, and political dogma, Byrnes could call the country back to America's "basic principles" of local government and constitutional conservatism. More than a poster boy, Byrnes possessed the prestige necessary to refine the southern critique of federal racial reform and win the sympathies of the nation. "As for what the South calls 'States' Rights,'" Graves observed optimistically, "every aspect is advanced in the prospect of James F. Byrnes. His presence gives it the liberal touch it needs, the national prestige, the countrywide scope, the broader gauge, the victory sign, and, let us believe, the margin of support to win other political races throughout the South in which Mr. Byrnes will take no part but cannot escape identification."[12]

From the outset, educational equalization was the centerpiece of Byrnes's message of responsible segregation. "If we demand respect for state rights," he announced in his inaugural address, "we must discharge state responsibilities." To finance higher salaries for black teachers, provide transportation for black children, and build new schoolhouses, Byrnes proposed the first sales tax in South Carolina history. When Byrnes declared that "preference in construction should be given where the need is greatest," he implicitly pledged the lion's share of the new funds for black schools. The new governor reminded the inaugural attendees that such unprecedented action was both a moral obligation and a political necessity. "We should do it because it is right," he continued. "For me that is sufficient reason. . . . If any person wants an additional reason, I say it is wise." The governor assured his mostly white audience that his plan would have the support of black South Carolinians. "Except for the professional agitators," Byrnes argued, "what the colored people want, and what they are entitled to, is equal facilities in their schools. We must see that they get them."[13]

Black parents in the South Carolina lowcountry had already challenged Byrnes's assumption. Less than a month before Byrnes's 1951 inauguration, the NAACP filed a class-action lawsuit challenging racial segregation in Clarendon County. While the NAACP had exposed the shortcomings of separate but equal in previous cases, this new action was the first direct challenge to the constitutionality of segregated education to be argued in a southern court since the nineteenth century. Named for the first black parents to sign on to the suit and the local white school board chairman, *Briggs v. Elliott* was a test case for four actions that the NAACP had prepared in Kansas, Delaware, Virginia, and the District of Columbia. Byrnes cited these cases directly in his inaugural address. The Truman administration, he warned, would urge the Supreme Court to endorse "socialistic programs which are certain to divide our people." With a hearing on the Clarendon County suit scheduled for late May, state leaders rallied behind their new governor. In a matter of weeks, Byrnes pushed his equalization plan through the General Assembly, which approved a 3 percent sales tax and authorized $75 million in bonds for school equalization.[14]

In addition to securing funding for educational improvements, Byrnes spearheaded other "preparedness" measures. Warning that a Supreme Court decision against segregation would "result in trouble," the governor considered it "sound governmental policy at this time to evolve a plan of action in advance in order to counteract any future hysteria." For starters, he appointed a fifteen-member committee to devise strategies for circumventing a federal desegregation order. Headed by state senator Marion Gressette, the committee maintained a relatively low profile while drafting its preemptory plans. Byrnes, on the other hand, seized headlines with his own frank warning. At the annual meeting of the state education association, Byrnes declared that South Carolina would "abandon the public school system" rather than submit to desegregation. "To do that," he declared, "would be choosing the lesser of two great evils."[15]

By threatening to abolish the public school system, Byrnes mixed paternalism with outright intimidation. If the federal government forced the state to abandon its public school system, Brynes warned, its African American residents would face dire consequences. "The white people of South Carolina would become adjusted to the situation and could pay for the education of their children," the governor explained. But the black community, he warned, "would suffer because of the irresponsible action of representatives of the National Association for the Advancement of Colored People." Insisting that southern whites had the best interests of their black neighbors at heart, Byrnes contrasted South Carolina compassion with outside opportunism. "When the Negro children are out of school and colored teachers are out of their jobs," Byrnes warned, "these misguided and irresponsible leaders are certain to desert them." Even as he raised the threat of closing black schools, Byrnes called on "the humane white people of the State, as individuals, to see that innocent Negro children are not deprived of an education because of false leaders."[16]

The mix of paternalistic promises and veiled threats resonated with many South Carolina whites. "Governor Byrnes Has A Sound And Sober Word For Southern Negroes And Their School Fight," announced a Florence newspaper. Following Byrnes's lead, the editor placed responsibility for the future of the public schools on the shoulders of black integrationists. "When the Negro, by his insistence on the end of segregation, destroys tax-supported schools," the editor warned, "he has destroyed his own best, if not only, chance of education." In striking a careful balance between respectability and resistance, Byrnes "voiced the sentiment not only of South Carolinians but of rank and file Southerners as well." According to the Florence editor, Byrnes represented "not the voice of Southern racial prejudice" but rather "the assertion of common sense" and "the utterance of moral conscience." Predicting that "every state in which the races are separated will follow Byrnes and South Carolina in their fight to preserve the segregated system," the enthusiastic editor declared Byrnes the symbol of a new segregationist crusade. "It will greatly strengthen the cause if the fight all over the South is kept on the high plane established by the Byrnes' leadership," he concluded. "It would be a pity for it to inflame the passions of the ignorant and the prejudiced who have brought and can continue to bring immeasurable damage to the cause."[17] Yet even as Byrnes offered his alternative to demagoguery and violence, resurgent radicalism threatened to steal the spotlight back from reformist resistance.

The South Carolina governor made anti-Klan measures a cornerstone of his legislative agenda. Although Byrnes had made few specific policy proposals before his inauguration, he reassured voters that "there will be no room for a government presided over by a grand dragon or a grand kleagle." By pushing antimask and anti-cross-burning bills along with school equalization projects, Byrnes presented his legislative program as an alternative to radicalism. With black militants on the one side and white hoodlums on the other, Byrnes promoted responsible segregation as the only guarantor of racial peace. Indeed, the governor portrayed Klansmen and black activists as partners in crime. Responding to a white minister who bemoaned "fascist" activity in South Carolina, Byrnes blamed Columbia's black newspaper, the *Lighthouse and Informer*, for the Klan's growth. By printing anti-Klan editorials and "pictures of white women dancing with Negroes," Byrnes argued, black editors fanned the flames of white resentment. "The attitude of the Negro press has been of wonderful assistance

South Carolina governor James F. Byrnes urged restraint in the months leading up to the Brown *decision, but some of his constituents embraced calls for militant resistance to racial change. In 1949, more than 650 robed Klansmen and -women gathered for this parade and cross burning in Denmark, South Carolina, before Byrnes pushed through anti-Klan legislation in 1951. (William D. Workman Papers, South Carolina Political Collections, University of South Carolina, Columbia, S.C.)*

to the Klan," Byrnes explained. "It makes it easy for the Grand Dragon to arouse the prejudices of the people."[18]

That Grand Dragon was Thomas Hamilton, a former grocer and veteran Georgia Klansman who relocated to South Carolina to build his own hooded empire. Operating on both sides of the state line separating North and South Carolina, Hamilton organized rallies, motorcades, and cross burnings. The Grand Dragon scorned Byrnes's refined segregationist rhetoric and vilified equalization as a capitulation to black demands. The governor responded decisively. After a series of Klan attacks in early 1951, Byrnes made good on his campaign promises by pushing antimask and anti-cross-burning bills through the state legislature. Undaunted, Hamilton's hardcore stepped up their reign of terror. In the late summer of 1951, Klansmen opened fire on a popular black nightclub in Myrtle Beach and kidnapped the proprietor. A Klansman killed during the ambush had worn his police uniform under his white robe. Less than two weeks later, Klansmen near Columbia attacked a black church. When Hamilton discovered that local white Baptists intended to teach a Vacation Bible School for black children, he mailed threatening letters that accused church leaders of "blaspheming my Lord and Saviour Jesus Christ." A few days later, Klansmen broke up the bible school by throwing a stick of dynamite out of a passing car. While state authorities kept a close watch on surging Klan activity, some South Carolina whites bemoaned "the complete lack of interest" shown by local law enforcement. "I have good reason to believe," a South Carolina merchant reported to Byrnes, "that a great many of these officers are actually members of the Klan."[19]

Despite the violent tactics of his followers, Grand Dragon Hamilton claimed common cause with Byrnes in the crusade for racial integrity and conservative principles. "The Klan is fighting for States' Rights and a Constitutional form of Government," Hamilton wrote to Byrnes just days after the Myrtle Beach nightclub raid. "I believe that when you made your Speech at Mobile, Alabama in 1950, you advocated the same thing." While Byrnes counseled moderation and reform, Hamilton blasted the governor for raising unprecedented sums for black school improvements. As one of Byrnes's top aides admitted, the Klan opposed the equalization plan "because of the preference given to Negro schools." At a Cherokee County rally, Hamilton declared that South Carolina whites "had been denied their rights" by a school reform campaign that shifted emphasis from white to black education. Railing against Byrnes for appointing a black assistant to the school finance board, the Grand Dragon alleged that state school officials had explicitly ordered surveyors "to give the negro schools the preference" in allocating funds.[20]

Despite Byrnes's popularity, more than a few South Carolinians shared Hamilton's concerns. State authorities provided Byrnes with a list of over 230 license numbers from automobiles parked at the Cherokee County rally. Other rallies attracted as many as 3,000 Klan supporters and curious locals. Ultimately, overseeing Klan activity across two states undid the Carolina Grand Dragon. After South Carolina Klansmen abducted a North Carolina couple in early 1952, federal prosecutors intervened. Convicted of abetting an interstate kidnapping, Hamilton spent four years in jail.[21]

With the Klan on the run, prominent segregationists embraced Byrnes's rhetoric of responsible segregation. When Byrnes backed anti-Klan legislation in South Carolina, Talmadge suddenly reversed his opposition to similar bills in Georgia. Only a few months earlier, Talmadge supporters had sponsored a pro-Klan bill requiring masked demonstrators to register with local authorities. Such a bill, they argued, would circumvent municipal governments that had adopted antimask ordinances. Now a new bill, introduced simultaneously with similar legislation in South Carolina, banned public cross burnings and mask wearing. Backed by Talmadge allies who had recently blocked similar measures, the anti-Klan legislation sailed through the General Assembly with only one dissenting vote.[22]

Talmadge had good reason to rally his political machine behind a reform agenda. With a local desegregation suit bearing down on him, the governor announced an ambitious equalization campaign of his own. In February 1951, the Georgia legislature approved $170 million for educational equalization and approved a 3 percent sales tax to fund the Minimum Foundation Program for Education. The next year, Talmadge issued bonds and borrowed money to launch the School Building Authority. Although African Americans accounted for approximately one-third of enrolled students, Georgia officials designated over half of the massive construction budget to black school buildings. "Most of the county school plans give top priority to Negro projects," boasted a state official, "and some counties plan to build Negro facilities only." As the national press touted the huge sums pledged to Georgia schools, Talmadge claimed leadership of the regional reform movement. "Other States have now recognized the soundness of our program here," he announced, "and are preparing to follow suit."[23]

In Georgia, as in South Carolina, the line between reaction and reform quickly blurred. Talmadge outspent Byrnes, but he also surpassed his South Carolina counterpart in outright threats. The record-breaking appropriations bill stipulated that the state would withhold education funds to any white school in Georgia that admitted a black student, "even under court order." Talmadge also consulted his legal advisers about reviving the doctrine of nullification as a possible response to future federal desegregation orders. While Byrnes preferred to downplay the more militant aspects of segregationist strategy, Talmadge taunted the federal government with the threat of public-school closures. "The people of Georgia will not submit to any co-mingling of the races in our schools," Talmadge warned. "Rather than to permit this to happen we would return to the system of private schools and subsidize the individuals that go to school." Elaborating on his plan, Talmadge advocated a state-administered "private" school system. Local school districts would lease or sell their buildings to private citizens for "nominal sums," and the state would use public funds to offset "private" school tuition. In a patriotic flourish, Talmadge likened his educational subsidy program to the GI Bill. Arguing that the private-school system would deliver the equality long denied by its public predecessor, Talmadge pledged that white and black children would receive equal amounts of aid in this system. "Everyone," the governor announced, "will be treated alike."[24]

Of all the southern states, Mississippi had the farthest to go and the fewest resources to get there. Despite the staggering costs of reversing decades of neglect, Mississippi governor and former Dixiecrat vice-presidential candidate Fielding Wright fell into line behind Georgia and South Carolina. While the governor offered no concrete proposals, he endorsed equalization as a crucial strategy for staving off desegregation. He presented the legislature with "a program designed to furnish equal opportunities" and simultaneously promised "the fullest extent of our resources" to the fight against desegregation. "We shall insist upon segregation," Wright warned, "regardless of consequences."[25]

Even as the governor pledged to protect segregation no matter the price, a biracial committee of Mississippi educators tabulated the costs of equalization. Formed in late 1950, the Mississippi Citizens Council on Education (MCCE) sent out thousands of questionnaires to gauge public support. Hoping to aid the MCCE campaign, the Mississippi Economic Council sponsored several dozen public forums to promote equalization. In Indianola, the Delta town that would soon spawn a more notorious "Citizens Council" movement, MCCE committeeman Morris Lewis admitted that "we have not done in the past what we should have done." While pledging that Mississippi would "keep the dual system of education," Lewis bluntly announced: "We've got a painful job to do financially."[26]

The MCCE's white sponsors enlisted the support of the all-black Mississippi Association of Teachers in Colored Schools in an attempt to combat black criticism of the equalization drive. For some meetings, white organizers recruited black speakers who assured the white crowd that they preferred equalization to desegregation. With white moderates, diehard segregationists, and black accommodationists seemingly united behind the equalization drive, white Mississippians across the political spectrum denounced black integrationists as irresponsible and unrepresentative. When NAACP state president W. A. Bender reaffirmed his intention "to end segregation in public education," white supporters of equalization declared him "guilty of bad timing and bad faith." Declaring that "the state's past indifference to equal school facilities has been replaced by an honest determination to remedy old wrongs," moderate Delta newspaperman

Hodding Carter accused state NAACP leaders of undermining "the great bi-racial movement for equal education." Like Carter, Governor Wright denounced the NAACP declarations as unrepresentative of "the thinking group of Mississippi Negroes."[27]

Wright's successor, Hugh White, took office in 1952 with schools on his mind. Campaigning as "the first candidate for governor to uphold and publicize the findings of Mississippi's Citizens Council on Education," White championed black school improvements as a way to safeguard the "constitutional system of equal and separate facilities." Taking White at his word, the MCCE promptly submitted their staggering equalization projections to the governor. Estimating an annual budget of $34 million and an initial outlay of $144 million for school construction, the MCCE recommended comprehensive equalization of teacher salaries, curriculum resources, and campus facilities.[28]

White, who had inherited a series of promises and stopgap measures from his predecessors, faced the daunting challenge of mobilizing an unprecedented equalization campaign. During the 1952 legislative session, state lawmakers balked at the MCCE proposals after a "padding" scandal convinced many that local districts had inflated their school rolls to get a larger share of the growing state school budget. Failing to commit the necessary funds for comprehensive school improvements, Mississippi lawmakers created a special committee to further investigate equalization. In June, the Recess Education Committee joined the governor and state school officials on a tour of Deep South state capitals. The purpose of the tour, White explained to his fellow governors, was to conduct "a complete study of what you are doing to take care of the recent court decisions on equalization of school facilities." Traveling through Alabama, Georgia, and South Carolina on a chartered bus, the Mississippians hoped to find a cure-all for their educational dilemma.[29]

The Recess Education Committee left Jackson looking for answers, but its members encountered a mix of confidence and confusion. Stopping first in Montgomery, the Mississippi delegation met with anxious Alabama officials who admitted they were "a long, long way" from equalizing school facilities. While lawmakers there had mobilized the necessary funds to equalize teacher salaries, they had not yet endorsed a comprehensive equalization plan. "There has been no real state-financed building program in this state on a big scale," admitted University of Alabama education professor Bascom Woodward, "and that is what it will take to equalize. . . . That's the big problem." When Mississippi lawmakers asked what state leaders planned to do in the event of an "unfavorable" Supreme

Court ruling, the Alabamans seemed stumped. "I wish I could answer that," Woodward admitted. "I don't know what we are going to do. . . . It's got all of us seriously worried."[30]

The South Carolina meeting was more upbeat, with state officials eager to outline their equalization efforts. Faced with the reality that most African American leaders back home wanted desegregation, the Mississippi delegation asked if state leaders involved black South Carolinians in policy decisions. Governor White wanted to know how South Carolina's equalization task force responded to "demands . . . from the black population to be represented on any of the Committees on the question of approval of equal facilities." E. Ryan Crow, head of the State Finance Commission, replied that his agency employed a former black school superintendent "to be an ambassador to the negroes." The retired black educator, Crow explained, saw "eye to eye with us on the objective of this program" and traveled the state explaining the equalization program to African Americans. As a result, Crow concluded, "We have a very wholesome sentiment among the negroes in South Carolina."[31]

At their final meeting in Georgia, the Mississippians encountered a mix of South Carolina confidence and Alabama apprehension. Georgians hoped that their school improvement efforts would sway federal sympathy. If "we show the world that we have done all we can to equalize facilities," state auditor Ed Thrasher predicted, "I believe they would have a pretty hard time condemning us." Like their counterparts across the Deep South, Georgia officials earnestly believed that the overwhelming majority of southern blacks preferred separate and equal. "Other than a few paid agitators that are stirring up trouble," declared Thrasher, who also headed the School Building Authority, "we have no big problems in Georgia with the Negro situation." When skeptical Mississippians pressed state officials on their preparations for an adverse Supreme Court decision, Georgia House Speaker Fred Hand offered few specifics. "If we give them equal facilities," Hand evaded, "I'm not worried about the colored people coming into white schools."[32]

The Mississippi committee tour revealed the cleavages and confusion that frustrated any coordinated equalization effort across the Deep South. While state officials realized the tactical and practical benefits of black school improvement, they faced varying challenges from state to state. Even as Byrnes and his allies championed local control and denounced centralization, they understood the necessity of regional cooperation. A few white southerners called state leaders on this contradiction. Carrying the ideal of "local control" to its logical conclusion, some conservative white southerners resisted the efforts of state leaders to dictate school policies and tax rates. Despite his enormous popularity, Byrnes endured public criticism from the right-wing Charleston County Citizens League. The founder and leader of the group, a diehard anticommunist named Stanley Morse, warned that equalization "would increase Columbia control of local school affairs and authorize heavy taxes in excess of educational needs, enabling politicians and their friends to enjoy a big spending spree at public expense."[33]

Notwithstanding statewide efforts to coordinate equalization initiatives, local control meant that black school improvement proceeded largely at the whim of white school boards. Despite the unprecedented state-financing efforts, a South Carolina official admitted to the Mississippi delegation that "the entire initiation of any project is in the hands of the local authorities." Even in South Carolina, the shining example of equalization in action, Finance Commission director Crow confessed that "varying degrees of progress have been made in various districts." Georgia officials bluntly informed their Mississippi guests that many counties had "absolutely not done anything towards taking care of the colored people."[34]

When equalization efforts met with local resistance, racial resentment often trumped concerns over local control. While state officials across the South realized the tactical necessity of pouring money into black schools, segregationist strategy clashed with inherited notions of white privilege. As an otherwise confident South Carolina school official confessed to his Mississippi guests, "We are meeting resistance, from the angle that community sentiment, in a lot of instances, is opposed to it." While insisting that most South Carolina whites supported the equalization strategy, he acknowledged the political liability of asking upcountry counties with small black populations to subsidize a program that devoted two-thirds of its funds to black education.[35]

The rapid shift to equalization jarred whites accustomed to having their superiority affirmed by rickety black schoolhouses. "I believe the biggest problem we are going to have is with the whites," predicted Georgia auditor Ed Thrasher, "for the simple reason that the negro schools will be newer." Similarly, House Speaker Fred Hand predicted that many Georgians would oppose equalization for undermining white privilege at white expense. "In our State, I frankly don't think the people are ready to issue any bonds, or go to any financial trouble to take care of colored people," he informed the Mississippi delegation. "That's not a nice statement, but I think it is just a statement of fact."[36]

The Mississippians returned home with more questions than answers. Governor White admitted that he had "no remedy" for a Supreme Court ruling against segregation. Rallying behind their bewildered governor, state officials offered their own segregation schemes. The commissioner of the State Department of Public Welfare proposed a system in which white students would attend school from eight to noon for eleven months per year. In the afternoon, African American students could use the same facilities. The new schools would require separate toilets, he noted, but the savings on school construction would pay for extra bathrooms, new buses, and higher teacher salaries. "At first glance we might not think well of letting Negroes use the same buildings," he concluded, "but they cook in our kitchens, eat out of our dishes, ride on the same elevators, and use the same seats in street cars and buses at times." While the governor and his advisers roundly ridiculed the proposal, they had a hard time coming up with a workable solution of their own. Delta legislator and Recess Education Committee member Ney Gore drafted a bill that would empower local school district trustees to assign individual students to schools based on "health and moral factors." A less ambitious committee member, George Howell, gloomily predicted that "voluntary segregation is all we can hope for." [37]

Skeptical African Americans had never been swayed by the upsurge in equalization rhetoric. "Has Governor Talmadge sprouted wings and halo?" quipped a black columnist. No, he continued, the committed segregationist was simply "smart enough to know that unless there is compliance with U.S. Supreme Court rulings about equalization of racial facilities, integration will come." Segregationists' mounting frustrations lent credence to black charges that "separate but equal" was a hollow promise and an untenable solution. Ultimately, integration would come because the equalization effort was too little, too late. In a series of investigative reports, the *Pittsburgh Courier* publicized the inequalities that persisted behind the success stories promoted by segregationists. In a Mississippi exposé that featured a picture of one black high school's dilapidated outhouse, reporter John Rousseau noted that nearly half of the state's black schools met in churches, tenant shacks, or other buildings. The Recess Education Committee report, released in March 1953, confirmed the "pathetic and in some cases inexcusable" conditions of Mississippi's rural black schools. "Hundreds of children of the Negro race," the legislative task force admitted, "are compelled to attend school—if they attend at all—in unpainted, unheated, and unlighted buildings that are not fit for human habitation and should have been condemned many years ago." As the legislature reconvened in November, the staunchly segregationist *Jackson Daily News* printed a picture of a crumbling black elementary school next to that of the recently completed state capitol building. In an implicit endorsement of equalization, Jackson's segregationist standard-bearer reported that the state superintendent had almost fallen through a hole in the floor during a recent inspection of the school.[38]

Even in South Carolina, widely acclaimed as a trailblazer in equalization efforts, the facts undercut the state's public relations campaign. After a trip to South Carolina, black investigative journalist Alex Rivera declared Byrnes's equalization program "a well-plotted hoax." Rivera offered numerous facts and figures to show the gaps in per capita spending, transportation, and access to the federal school lunch program. Despite the unprecedented building program, he noted, two-thirds of black pupils attended small schoolhouses staffed by one or two teachers. Arguing that African Americans had "NO VOICE in shaping policy," Rivera pointed out that a black retired superintendent served as a lowly "assistant" to the State Finance Commission director. South Carolina officials believed that they had shored up African American support by employing the distinguished educator as their "ambassador," but they declined to list his name on commission letterhead.[39]

Even as the black press panned equalization as an unworkable ploy, some worried that the movement toward responsible segregation could sway the sympathies of federal authorities. "Obviously," warned the *Pittsburgh Courier*, "the revolutionary and redoubtable efforts of rock-ribbed Confederate states like Mississippi, Georgia, and South Carolina to hasten the equalization of bi-racial educational facilities, unmindful of the cost, imperils the larger goal of racial integration." Despite considerable skepticism in the national press, the rhetoric of responsible segregation garnered sympathy from some nonsoutherners. A newspaperman in southern California informed his readers that the South Carolina equalization plan "puts an end to racial discrimination . . . while preserving the system of segregation." Governor Byrnes, the columnist argued, deserved credit for navigating his state between the "two extreme attitudes" of the Klan and the NAACP. "To some people, 'states' rights' conjures up pictures of Mint-Julep-drinking politicians who use the United States Constitution as a front for racial discrimination," the California editor reasoned. "Governor Byrnes, however, and those who are following his example, are sincere men with a strong sense of responsibility."[40]

Such praise largely evaporated after South Carolinians rallied behind Byrnes's vow to abandon public education altogether in the event of a fed-

Vote Yes
On Constitutional Amendment

On Tuesday you will have an opportunity to vote to give the Governor and our Legislature the right to act for the best interest of Education in the State of South Carolina.

Vote Yes
Protect our Children

The Supreme Court may rule on Segregated Schools this winter. They could rule against Segregation. Such a ruling would be most harmful for the best education of both the White and Colored Children.

Unless a Majority Votes Yes- The Governor and the Legislature will be handicapped in deciding what is best and carrying out a program which will provide the best education possible for every child in the State.

South Carolina can be proud that it has been blest with the most able and understanding Governor in our Nation to-day. His National and World experience has given him an understanding of our serious problems that can save us from great setbacks if we give him our support. His request is for all children both colored and white. He has fought for good schools and our support will keep good schools.

Governor Byrnes asks that we
Vote yes on the Amendment.

In anticipation of a federal desegregation ruling, Governor Byrnes urged South Carolinians to back a 1952 constitutional amendment that removed the provision for state-supported public schools. High school students in Darlington mimeographed and distributed fliers promoting the amendment, which passed by a two-to-one margin. (Gubernatorial Papers of James F. Byrnes, South Carolina Division of Archives and History, Columbia, S.C.)

eral desegregation order. From the outset, Byrnes balanced his unprecedented equalization pledge with an ominous threat. Once in office, he made good on both. In the fall of 1952, Palmetto State whites voted two to one to strike from their constitution the section mandating public schools. Afterward, Byrnes found himself lumped with less savory southern leaders. Even John Temple Graves, who had hoped Byrnes could elevate the southern cause above regional racial militancy, acknowledged "how it hurts him elsewhere to be named alongside . . . Talmadge." Alex McCullough, a Spartanburg newspaperman serving as "research secretary" to Governor Byrnes, resented northern newspapers' increasing unwillingness to say anything nice about his boss. While southern newspapers regularly printed McCullough's glowing profiles of South Carolina's "educational revolution," northern editors largely ignored the public relations campaign. Instead, McCullough complained, Byrnes's threat to abolish the public schools was being "used out of context to picture him as a relentless persecutor of Negroes."[41]

As the Deep South governors vowed to abandon public education, their critics quickly forgot the anti-Klan grandstanding of previous months.

After southern-born white journalist Stetson Kennedy infiltrated a 1952 "Klonvokation" organized by Florida Klansman Bill Hendrix, he argued that southern governors shared the blame for the resurgence of the militant Right. "With such men threatening to abolish the South's public school system rather than see it unsegregated by court order," Kennedy argued, "it is little wonder that would-be fuehrers like Hendrix conclude they can get away with anything." In Mississippi, the state NAACP denounced the abolition warning as "un-American, unchristian, and a rebellious act against the Constitution." Invoking the civil rights movement's Cold War calculus, the Mississippi NAACP argued that the abolition proposal "minimizes the effectiveness of our efforts to win allies for democracy abroad and gives additional propaganda to the Communists in their attacks on the American way of life." When the Soviet Union's delegate to the United Nations declared Governor Byrnes the "No. 1 racist in the United States," he lent credence to black warnings that international critics would not distinguish between genteel segregationists and diehard white supremacists. "Under the ever-increasing weight of world opinion being piled up," declared the northern black *Chicago Defender*, "segregated schools are as doomed as the walls of Jericho before the mighty trumpet of Joshua."[42]

As the equalization campaign failed to sway national opinion and garner federal sympathy, moderate posturing increasingly gave way to ominous threats of decay and disorder. At the November 1953 Southern Governors Conference, Herman Talmadge warned that a Supreme Court decision against school segregation would be "nothing less than a major step towards national suicide." A few weeks later, Talmadge predicted, "Blood will flow in rivers." Responding to his predictions of race war, a small-town Kansas editor pointed out that the school board in nearby Topeka had quietly abolished segregation without waiting for a Supreme Court ruling. There was no bloodshed, not even in "tiny rivulets." While Topeka was "not Georgia," the editor insisted that blood would not flow "unless the governor keeps repeating his prediction until he is sure it does."[43]

Even the unflappable Governor Byrnes sounded uncharacteristically shrill as a federal showdown inched closer. In his first speech to the South Carolina Education Association since he launched his "educational revolution," Byrnes declared that the "preservation of racial integrity" was "even dearer" than public education. "Unless we find a legal way of preventing the mixing of races in the schools," he warned the state's white school teachers, "it will mark the beginning of the end of civilization in the South as we have known it." In integrated schools, Byrnes warned, "instead of thinking about mathematics, the children would be thinking of race relations." In such a tense atmosphere, Byrnes predicted, "peaceful relations" would quickly give way to "hatred and discord."[44]

When *Brown* did come, on 17 May 1954, blood did not run in the streets. Nevertheless, segregationist leaders marked that day as a turning point in southern race relations. Before this aggressive federal intervention, they argued, the South was finally fulfilling the promise of separate but equal. By cloaking resistance in a mantle of reform, the region's leaders had nurtured the myth that meaningful racial change could happen only on a timetable dictated by white southerners. Outside intervention, they warned, would halt educational modernization across the South. After *Brown*, this narrative became an article of faith for white southerners of all political stripes. Not only had southern race relations been on the right track, but on the verge of a great leap forward.

As segregationists perpetuated the myth of their own good faith, they memorialized equalization as a largely fulfilled, if unappreciated, promise. Former Dixiecrat propagandist Tom Brady, now rallying segregationists under a new banner, argued that misguided zealots had mocked the white South's racial goodwill. Southern states had nearly bankrupted themselves building black schools, Brady argued, and black activists and northern liberals were "laughing with glee because they realize that we are going to be staggering under a terrific debt." The civil rights crowd did not care that South Carolinians had "perfectly equalized their schools," Brady claimed. They insisted, with the backing of the Supreme Court, that "you have got to sit a negro boy down by a white girl to have it equal."[45]

The portrayal of equalization as an unrequited gesture of racial goodwill became a cornerstone of segregationist mythology. Thurman Sensing, mouthpiece of the Southern States Industrial Council, argued that equalization was all but finished by the time the Supreme Court torpedoed "all the progress made in race relations" with the "inexcusable" *Brown* decision. "Rapid strides had been made—in most places the goal had been reached—in providing equal facilities of all sorts," Sensing insisted. "The rank and file of the Negroes knew these things and were satisfied." While others readily admitted that equalization had barely begun to remedy longstanding neglect of black education, they complained that egalitarian ideologues had disregarded the white South's newfound commitment to separate *and* equal. How well and how quickly equalization worked mattered little, white southerners complained, if integrationists refused to let it work. "Progress within the confines of segregation," complained a southern moderate, "was, by and large, no progress as far as they were concerned."[46]

Having lived through an era of rising tensions and looming showdowns, white southerners from across the political spectrum nevertheless transformed the postwar decade from a turbulent time to a period of comparative racial calm. In his account of the rise of Citizens' Councils, Hodding Carter III, Princeton-educated son of the Pulitzer Prize–winning Mississippi newspaperman, characterized the postwar decade as "a halcyon period" in southern race relations. The changing racial politics of the region reflected, in his words, "a mixture of passivity and troubled conscience, of acceptance of some changes and resignation to others." In this era of increasing tolerance, Carter argued, the *Brown* decision "exploded" upon "a region slowly groping its way out of the racial pattern of centuries." Portraying the postwar decade as an era of relative racial goodwill, Carter invoked not a fellow moderate but a militant segregationist. "Since the Supreme Court decision," declared Mississippi Citizens' Council leader William J. Simmons, "segregation has become inevitable." Civil rights activists made a fatal mistake, Simmons argued, by "insisting on immediate integration everywhere" and thereby uniting previously indifferent southern whites in defense of race and region. "Through the 40s and early 50s most Southerners were apathetic, resigned to what they felt was inevitable," Simmons argued, "By raising an immediate target, the integrationists hurt themselves."[47]

The notion of a squandered era of racial harmony recast advocates of integration as reckless interlopers in the slow but steady march of southern progress. This romanticized portrayal of white good faith and interracial goodwill before *Brown* bolstered the equally powerful myth of an embattled white South. As they mobilized to circumvent the Supreme Court decision, the champions of segregation argued that they were compelled to respond to unwarranted and unwise outside interference. The dual rhetoric of responsible segregation and diehard opposition persisted, not as conflicting strategies but rather as interdependent elements of the campaign to preserve segregation. Equalization served the larger goal of recasting segregationists as responsible stewards rather than reactionaries. While they faced an uphill battle convincing a skeptical nation of their newfound commitment to equal opportunity, segregationists entered the post-*Brown* years convinced that the federal government had squandered an era of growing goodwill between white and black southerners. Some invoked this rosy assessment of equalization in their attempts to paint the civil rights movement as an enemy of black progress and interracial cooperation. Convinced that they had accumulated moral capital in the equalization scramble of the early 1950s, these segregationists moved forward seeing themselves as beleaguered defenders of law and order, constitutional government, and civilization itself.

Southern denunciations of the *Brown* decision reflected the dual rhetoric honed during the equalization campaign. To stave off desegregation, white leaders made unprecedented promises. At the same time, they offered dire threats. Those who had vowed defiance before "Black Monday" did not skip a beat in its wake. "Southern people," declared Mississippi senator James Eastland, "will not surrender their dual school system and their racial heritage at the command of this crew of radical politicians in judicial robes."[48]

Many alarmed constituents applauded the headline-grabbing threats, but more than a few immediately recognized the strategic value of Eastland's junior colleague, John Stennis. The recently reelected senator couched his defiance in a language of constitutionality, law, and order. One Vicksburg resident, assessing his senators' public reactions to *Brown*, sympathized with Eastland but applauded Stennis. "Senator Eastland expressed his views, of which I approve, but some may not as they are mostly personal expressions," he explained to Stennis. "Your Radio excerpts, are founded on history, court rulings, etc., and no one can help being influenced with so much 'weight' behind them."[49]

For Eastland's junior colleague, the key to saving segregation lay in a campaign of subtle, if equally unyielding, resistance coupled with a public relations campaign. Stennis quickly concluded that "any legal subterfuge is doomed to eventual failure" due to the flood of congratulatory telegrams "coming in to the State Department and to the President from all over the world." With outside observers increasingly unsympathetic to the segregationist position, Stennis advised a mix of local compulsion and national persuasion. At home in Mississippi, Stennis argued, white elites should continue to advocate for equalization while strong-arming African Americans. After working out their plan for "unofficial separate education at the county level," local white leaders could present their terms to "a representative group of negroes." If black community leaders would not agree to this ultimatum, Stennis advised a state legislator, whites would abandon the public school system and "it would be everybody for himself."[50]

By offering unprecedented educational concessions to local blacks in exchange for allegiance to segregation, Stennis counseled Mississippi attorney general J. P. Coleman, "The responsibility could be put on them." If they did not cooperate, Stennis admitted, "we shall be driven to some sort of under-the-table devices of course." Rather than a strategic departure, this mix of promises and threats represented a refinement of long-standing tactics. "We shall just have to use some common-sense coercion, which in the final analysis is what we have been doing all the time anyway," Stennis confided to a Mississippi ally. "In a dressed up form . . . it will work again—at least, I believe for quite a number of years." Such serenity in the wake of the *Brown* decision was less a harbinger of racial moderation than a barometer of white confidence. Stennis urged Mississippi governor Hugh White not to follow grandstanding segregationists on "a crusade of defiance." Of course, Stennis assured White, "we are not going to comply with the Supreme Court decision of putting whites and blacks together, but the least we advertise that fact, the better." Instead, Stennis argued, white leaders would have to co-opt local black leadership by any means necessary.[51]

Even in the face of African American protest and unprecedented federal pressure, pragmatic conservatives such as Stennis continued to argue that southern African Americans wanted no part of integration. Despite the "tremendous pressure" put on black Mississippians by civil rights activists, Stennis advised White, "negroes will look to us first for leadership." Clinging to the paternalistic confidence that fueled the equalization campaigns across the South, the senator argued that a mixture of coercion and appeasement could stamp out black discontent and sway federal sympathy. "What the negro wants is some kind but firm leadership and some help to get better schools," Stennis concluded. "He is, I think, entitled to both."[52]

Governor White soon discovered what black Mississippians thought of "common-sense coercion." In late July, the governor invited one hundred prominent African Americans to a meeting in Jackson. Urging the gathered leaders to endorse a "voluntary" segregation plan, White pledged over $100 million additional dollars for equalization. To the consternation of the governor and his all-white Legal Education Advisory Committee, speaker after speaker urged compliance with the Supreme Court decision and endorsed a previously prepared statement calling for state officials "to consolidate and integrate the present schools on all levels." While the cautiously crafted proposal to send all Mississippi students to the school closest their homes would have minimized immediate integration, only one black leader present at the meeting pledged allegiance to segregated education. Admittedly "stunned" by the encounter, White and his allies faced the hard reality of homegrown black discontent. "I have believed sincerely that the vast majority of Negroes would go along," White declared. "Now I am definitely of the opinion that you can't put any faith in any of them on this proposition."[53]

Segregationists had lost confidence in the federal government and their black neighbors, but they remained convinced that they had the Constitution on their side. When the Supreme Court revisited the *Brown* decision in April 1955, segregationists decided that they had time on their side as well. In *Brown II*, the Supreme Court danced around any explicit timeline for school desegregation by delegating the task to southern district courts and instructing them to enforce the original decision "with all deliberate speed." Civil rights activists viewed *Brown II* as a concession to segregationists, who had swayed the court with their professions of "good faith" and predictions of bloodshed and chaos. But the vaguely worded follow-up decision did not appease segregationists. Rather, they seized on *Brown II* as a pretext for a coordinated campaign to undermine desegregation efforts and present their cause to the American public.[54]

Brown II encouraged a southern counteroffensive, but it did not signal a sudden burst of segregationist creativity. Two decades of racial skirmishing had served as a dress rehearsal for the next phase of resistance. The federal desegregation order prompted no significant departures in segregationist ideology, but it demanded that white southerners make some tough decisions. "Alabama and the South have the choice today," John Temple Graves declared, "of becoming the nation's mental case or of capitalizing on their very troubles to become the nation's economic, political and spiritual leader." Speaking across the country in the months and years after *Brown*, the veteran journalist continued his campaign to reconcile southern patriotism with regional racial practices. Massive resistance seemed to be only the latest in a string of Lost Causes, from the Dixiecrat revolt to eleventh-hour equalization, to which the "self-appointed spokesman of the South" had hitched his yoke. In the years after *Brown*, Graves never abandoned hope that the South could spark a nationwide return to the "basic American philosophy" of local government and constitutional conservatism.[55]

If such optimism seemed misplaced, Graves was not alone. Segregationists perceived themselves not simply as champions of Jim Crow but also as guardians of the American way of life. Even as zealots and propagandists whipped up racial resentment back home, prominent southern leaders attempted to elevate the segregationist defense to a higher plane. In early 1956, Strom Thurmond drafted a "manifesto" that outlined the constitutional and legal basis for segregation. He hoped such a statement, following on the heels of *Brown II*, would encourage "unity of action" among southern segregationists. Conservative Virginia senator Harry Byrd, a veteran foe of civil rights legislation, forced the freshman senator's proposal onto the southern bloc's agenda.[56]

From its inception, the Southern Manifesto emphasized legal and constitutional appeals above white supremacy. Yet veteran colleagues recognized the strategic risks of leaving the statement in the hands of the former Dixiecrat standard-bearer. Hoping to tone down Thurmond's draft, southern caucus leader Walter George tapped three senators who over three successive decades had advocated restraint in racial politics. In 1936, Richard Russell repudiated demagoguery as he fought off challenges from Eugene Talmadge. A decade later, John Stennis replaced the race-baiting Theodore Bilbo. Weeks after the *Brown* decision, the press hailed the arrival of the latest poster boy for the "soft southern approach" to racial politics. Samuel J. Ervin, a Harvard-educated state Supreme Court justice, arrived in Washington ready to lend his legal expertise and "country lawyer" charm to the segregationist cause. North Carolina governor William Umstead tapped Ervin to complete the term of Clyde Hoey, a veteran senator who died in his office just days before the *Brown* decision. Ervin privately boasted that he was as "unrepentant and unreconstructed" as Hoey, a Confederate captain's son who launched his political career in the turn-of-the-century legislature that disfranchised most black North Carolinians. Yet the leaders of the southern opposition saw in Ervin a fresh face that could elevate the segregationist defense above the white supremacist rhetoric of their father's generation.[57]

The ad hoc committee produced a "Statement of Constitutional Principles" for Walter George to present to the Senate. Twenty-eight years after fighting off FDR's attempted "purge" with a racially charged reelection campaign, Georgia's senior senator delivered the southern bloc's defiant yet measured response to *Brown* on 12 March 1956. The "unwarranted decision," George declared, represented a "clear abuse of judicial power" by the Supreme Court. Reading from the prepared statement, George declared that the 101 southern signers pledged "to use all lawful means" to resist a decision they deemed unconstitutional. Every southern senator, save Senate majority leader Lyndon B. Johnson and Tennessee moderates Estes Kefauver and Albert Gore, signed the statement.[58]

The Southern Manifesto highlighted the segregationist distinction between restraint and moderation. Speaking to civic groups across the South, John Temple Graves praised segregationist leaders for charting a course more affirming than moderation and more respectable than radicalism.

Just because the "sober South" rejected "secession" and "shooting," Graves declared, did not mean that the region accepted "surrender." "We are all going to go on being Uncle Sam's nephews," he assured a group of Virginia businessmen. "But the sober south isn't the moderate south. Moderate has been made a name for dying slowly." Comparing the segregationist countermovement to the United States' rivalry with the Soviet Union, Graves bragged in speeches across the country that segregationists were waging a "constitutional cold war" against their political enemies.[59]

Virginians did not need an Alabamian to tell them that moderation was passé. Closer to the nation's capital than to its Deep South allies, Virginia embraced a similar brand of racial politics. The state's dominant political machine, led by Democratic senator and conservative stalwart Harry F. Byrd, drew its strength from rural courthouse cliques. The Byrd Organization magnified the power of the Southside, an agricultural region that resembled the Alabama Black Belt more than the suburbs of northern Virginia. Like Richard Russell and Strom Thurmond, the veteran Virginia senator took his turn as the poster boy for southern defiance. Back in Virginia, Byrd whittled down his political opposition with poll taxes and rallied his followers against racial reform. With Byrd's reactionary regime in control, Virginia surged to the forefront of the segregationist crusade.[60]

Central to the new counteroffensive was a scheme born in Virginia yet deliberately left out of the Southern Manifesto. Interposition, an ambiguous doctrine originally promoted by James Madison in the late eighteenth century, captured the segregationist imagination in the late 1950s. The defenders of segregation declared themselves "duty bound to interpose" themselves between the citizens of the southern states and destructive federal encroachment, thus disregarding the *Brown* decision on constitutional grounds. In August 1955, Virginia attorney William Old circulated a slim pamphlet advocating "vigorous and determined state action" to resist desegregation, citing the obscure precedent of the Virginia-Kentucky Resolutions of 1798. The Citizens' Council quickly embraced the scheme. Richmond newspaperman James J. Kilpatrick, deeming the doctrine "the missing check-and-balance against the Supreme Court," promoted interposition through his editorial page and right-wing media outlets.[61]

Across the South, committed segregationists rallied behind varying interpretations and expressions of the doctrine. By the time segregationist senators presented the Southern Manifesto, governors from Georgia, South Carolina, and Mississippi had traveled to Virginia for an interposition conference. A handful of southern legislatures across the region had already endorsed the principle, and others prepared to follow suit. Th drafters of the Southern Manifesto weighed the surging popularity of inter position against the political risks of endorsing its dubious constitutional premise. John Stennis argued that the manifesto should "say something about interposition" given that it was "the subject foremost in the minds of the people." Yet at the same time, the Mississippi senator conceded that his constituents had "been led to believe that there is far greater hope in this route than is justified." In the end, the southern bloc avoided direct mention of the controversial doctrine in favor of a general declaration of defiance.[62]

Despite simmering doubts about its constitutionality, interposition offered segregationists a veneer of legal legitimacy and another slogan shorn of white supremacist rhetoric. More important, the doctrine fed segregationists' conception of their crusade as fundamentally defensive and preservationist in nature. Interposition's constitutionality, John Temple Graves contended, mattered less than the white southerners' demonstrated resolve to resist desegregation by any means necessary. "What Interposition has come to mean in the South is not nullification," Graves argued, "but the total of all the things employed, planned or imaginable for preventing mixture of the races in the public schools." More than a rallying cry, interposition symbolized the white South's commitment to pursue "every delay, obfuscation, subterfuge and multiplication the law allows." Because the *Brown* decision had "tortured the constitution," Graves argued, the South was "torturing the decision."[63]

Interposition, whether named outright or echoed in more general declarations of defiance, appealed to many because it combined the myths of responsible segregation and southern persecution with a dignified defense strategy. Its more farsighted advocates, and even some of its detractors, recognized the doctrine as another attempt to affirm the segregationist movement as a patriotic enterprise in line with the fundamental tenets of American democracy. States' rights, Graves argued, was not "moonlight and magnolia stuff" but rather the foundation for a refined rhetoric of conservative Americanism. "Let's see it as decentralized and limited government," Graves suggested, "with stress again on the individual. In other words, the American way."[64]

James J. Kilpatrick echoed Graves's optimism that the segregationist South could infuse the national conservative movement with energy and direction. In the years immediately following the *Brown* decision, Kilpatrick pled the South's case in conservative journals such as *Human Events* and William F. Buckley's fledgling *National Review*. Right-wing publishing pioneer Henry Regnery proved particularly receptive to Kilpatrick's segregationist constitutionalism. In 1957, Kilpatrick penned a treatise on interposition and coedited a collection of pro-South essays for the Chicago publishing house. "For the past several years," Kilpatrick declared, "many of us in the South have been doing our frustrated best to educate the great world outside in a few fundamental truths about the Constitution and what is happening to that beloved compact." The South, he concluded, was "the last and best hope of conservatism in the American Republic."[65]

The conflation of "conservatism" and segregation further blurred the line between radicalism and respectability. The necessity of outside sympathy rendered "white supremacy" anachronistic and insufficient. National viability demanded a broader critique of postwar liberalism, and segregationists such as Graves and Kilpatrick eagerly obliged. Yet unlike the northern sympathizers they courted, segregationists privileged race as the fundamental catalyst for a conservative reawakening. "God moves in mysterious ways," Graves declared, "and one is the way in which the Southern race problem has created the most furious force in America against a believed socialist menace." In battling the civil rights movement for the better part of two decades, southern conservatives had become "more aware than any other region of what too much government can mean, especially when it is government far from the governed."[66]

By downplaying overtly racial rhetoric in favor of patriotic pleas and constitutional arguments, segregationists accelerated a process that both predated and anticipated massive resistance. But even as they elevated the discourse, segregation's defenders clung to bedrock beliefs about race and democracy. After expending nearly 300 pages outlining the history and theory of interposition, Kilpatrick could have concluded *Sovereign States* with a parting plea to save the Constitution. Instead, the South's latest champion of respectable segregation trotted out statistical evidence of "Negro bastardy," venereal disease, and crime in his final pages. Elaborating on these "undisciplined passions" in an article for *Human Events*, Kilpatrick claimed that most southern blacks treated sex "as casually as a goodnight kiss." If the "stability of the Constitution" was the transcendent issue at stake, Kilpatrick nevertheless reminded his readers that desegregation was racial suicide.[67]

Even as segregationists tried to move beyond racial arguments, they openly affirmed their racial convictions. In pamphlets distributed by the Citizens' Council, the dignified James Byrnes and the intemperate James

Eastland both invoked Benjamin Disraeli: "No man will treat with indifference the principle of race. It is the key to history." Byrnes could wax constitutional with the best of them, and the "only living ex-Supreme Court justice" tag accompanied his every utterance. Yet Byrnes increasingly laced his rhetoric of responsible segregation with appeals to the "racial instincts" of his fellow southerners. For Byrnes, the segregated public school system represented the last line of defense in a struggle for white civilization and racial purity. In "The Supreme Court Must Be Curbed," an article that ran in *US News and World Report* before the Citizens' Council distributed it in pamphlet form, Byrnes raised the specter of high school students traveling to and from Friday night ball games on integrated buses. "Who," Byrnes asked, "can assure there will not be serious consequences?"[68]

To view this alternation between lofty constitutional rhetoric and racial anxiety as a sign of troubled conscience or inner turmoil misses the point. Byrnes himself emphatically dismissed talk of a "conflict of the soul of the South." Segregationists aligned their sense of patriotic mission with their commitment to racial integrity because they perceived no fundamental conflict between the two. For two decades, they had rallied with increasing fervor and conviction behind the only democracy they had ever known. Even as the civil rights movement declared it a sham, the defenders of segregation offered their way of life as the nation's ultimate salvation. "The fate of this Nation may rest in the hands of the Southern white people today," warned a Citizens' Council newsletter. "Segregation represents the freedom to choose one's associates, Americanism, state sovereignty, and the survival of the white race."[69]

As committed segregationists attempted to mobilize a region in defense of the racial status quo, they never fully reconciled the rhetoric of responsible segregation and the dictates of racial integrity. Indeed, some embraced the tension. "You say this is not a time for hotheads and flag-waving but for clear, cold thinking," wrote Citizens' Council founder Robert Patterson, anticipating criticism from more pragmatic segregationists. "We need those hotheads, just as we always have when our liberty is threatened." For Patterson, radicalism and respectability could coexist under the segregationist banner. "Let's let the hotheads be the forge," he proposed, "and the clear thinkers be the armorer to reforge and retemper the bright shield of segregation."[70]

By acknowledging the ideological and tactical differences that existed within the segregationist movement, even the most committed white supremacists recognized the challenge of uniting a region in defense of the color line. James Kilpatrick enjoyed access to national periodicals and conservative publishing houses that would shun a Citizens' Councilor, but he agreed with Patterson that "there is no more a single case for the South than there is a single South."[71] As diehards attempted to rally their region in defense of the racial status quo, they confronted the limits of segregationist politics.

6

THE SOUTHERN "MINORITY" & THE SILENT MAJORITY

As massive resistance gained momentum in the late 1950s, segregationist organizations seemed to sprout up overnight. The *Brown* decision shook activists out of their complacency and, in a few cases, their careers. After the Supreme Court decision, Citizens' Council founder Robert Patterson left his job managing a Mississippi Delta plantation to fight integration full-time. Describing his segregationist epiphany a few years later, the former World War II paratrooper and college football star claimed that the *Brown* decision compelled him "to lay down my life to prevent mongrelization." Patterson's racial revelation and his success as an organizer captured the attention of journalists clamoring to explain the Deep South's rebellion to the nation.[1]

For every overnight activist who rallied to the cause in the late 1950s was a veteran who took a longer view of the civil rights struggle. Looking back on three decades of racial battles, another Citizens' Council leader argued that the South had been "surrendering on the installment plan" since the New Deal. Like most Southern politicians of his generation, Georgia kingmaker Roy V. Harris cut his teeth masterminding campaigns for "straight-out New Dealers." In the late 1940s, the powerful state legislator threw his considerable political weight behind the Talmadge machine. Like the elder Talmadge, Harris used his own tabloid, the *Augusta Courier*, to fan the flames of racial reaction. Yet, despite his significant clout, Harris struggled in vain to rally Georgia behind the Dixiecrats in 1948. "Our leaders failed us in this hour of crisis and surrendered just a little bit more," Harris griped a decade later. "They shouted, 'Stay in the party and fight out your battles within the party.'" By the end of the 1950s, the lifelong Democrat and acting president of the Citizens' Councils of America had little patience for blind loyalty.[2]

Harris offered a timeline of racial betrayal for southern whites unable to shake old allegiances. The Democratic Party had abandoned the "two-thirds rule" at the 1936 national convention in favor of a simple majority vote for presidential nominees. That obscure yet ominous move eliminated the South's veto power over the nomination process and spurred the earliest forecasts of southern defection. Like Dixiecrat propagandists before him, Harris identified 1936 as the beginning of the end for the "white man's party." For those who deemed "white democracy" synonymous with one-party rule, the racial skirmishes of the New Deal era destroyed the rationale for a Solid South. By 1960, racial conservatives had battled civil rights for more than two decades, and neither party platform gave Harris any reason for optimism. Democratic and Republican presidential candidates no longer offered white southerners anything, Harris lamented, besides a choice of "which you prefer to officiate at your hanging." White southerners needed to "teach both parties a lesson" by asserting their political independence. "We must recognize that we are a minority bloc," Harris declared, "and we must wield the balance of power."[3]

During the 1950s, prominent segregationists such as Harris embraced a contradictory but compelling rhetoric of power politics. They lamented their political marginalization, yet believed they could chart a path back to national influence. For inspiration, racial conservatives looked no further than the source of their frustration. If civil rights activists could push reform with pressure politics, they reasoned, then a unified "bloc" of white southerners could employ similar tactics to derail civil rights measures. Indeed, the notion that a cabal of activists could dictate national policy appealed to southern elites who temporarily enforced conformity through state agencies and watchdog groups but failed to engineer a grassroots revolt. "Massive resistance" evoked an image of white southern unity, but committed segregationists recognized that the broad-based countermovement implied by the term did not exist. The regional coordination and racial unity that segregationists proclaimed in the Southern Manifesto belied the difficulty of uniting southern conservatives behind a coordinated plan of action. While they claimed to represent a unified regional majority, segregationists simultaneously embraced their "minority" status.[4]

Ultimately, the sympathies of a national majority determined which "minority" would hold sway—civil rights advocates or their southern opponents. On this count, segregationists believed they held a distinct advantage. White northerners, they argued, had more in common with their southern counterparts than with civil rights activists. Segregationists' success relied on their ability to outlast the civil rights surge and exploit a brewing national backlash. In the meantime, southern conservatives continued to proclaim regional unity, quash internal dissent, and stymie civil rights measures as they waited for the nation to tire of racial reform. They believed that a committed bloc could control national politics—it was simply a question of which one. While they appeared marginalized and outnumbered, the segregationist minority claimed common cause with a national majority of ignored and discontented white Americans.

Deep South states, while equally committed to maintaining the segregated status quo, diverged rhetorically and tactically in pursuing that goal. In Mississippi, the segregationist agenda of political insurgency and racial unity achieved its greatest success. Committed activists dominated state politics and embraced electoral schemes aimed at reasserting the South's minority power, but even Mississippi fell short of monolithic resistance. In South Carolina, equally committed conservatives channeled their defiant spirit into the Deep South's strongest state-level Republican Party. Yet as diehards bolted their forefathers' party for the GOP or for nowhere in particular, pragmatism and party loyalty persisted. Clinging to an older brand of minority politics, segregationist stalwarts such as Richard Russell hoped to stymie civil rights from Capitol Hill. While the Deep South's electoral schemes and increasing interest in the Republican Party marked a monumental political transformation, the Democratic Party's evolution from a haven for white supremacy to a progenitor of civil rights legislation decided Jim Crow's fate.

But new political realities did not necessarily translate to a sea change in racial politics. The arguments that segregationists deployed in the late 1950s and early 1960s were not new linguistic innovations but rather the refinement of oppositional strategies that committed southern conservatives had embraced from the earliest signs of a civil rights revolution. What had changed was the relative clout and strategic position of segregationist politicians. Southern diehards appreciated the irony of their predicament. The same "minority" power that they had once wielded through their influence in Democratic Party politics now lay in the hands of pro–civil rights forces. Rather than surrender, seasoned foes of civil rights sought new avenues and alliances to salvage what they could of their white democracy.

Like the fight over school desegregation, the politics of white southern unity predated the *Brown* decision and the rise of massive resistance. Even as they advocated equalization as a more respectable resistance strategy, southern governors such as Herman Talmadge and James Byrnes urged southern conservatives to rethink their political identity. Faced with black political challenges at home and declining influence within the Democratic Party, segregationists put a new twist on the one-party politics of white supremacy and black disfranchisement. In the wake of the Dixiecrat revolt, southern conservatives proclaimed that racial competition rather than black exclusion defined southern politics. From his 1950 gubernatorial campaign onward, Herman Talmadge urged supporters to form a "white folks' bloc" to cancel out black votes in Georgia. Two years later, South Carolina governor James Byrnes urged whites across the region to pool their pivotal electoral votes in the upcoming presidential election. "The biggest minority in this country is composed of the white people of the Southern states," Byrnes argued. "It is necessary that the minority to which we belong, in defense of ourselves, should act in concert."[5]

Byrnes, nationally recognized as "the behind-the-scenes leader of conservative Southern Democrat strategy," advocated political rebellion before large and approving crowds as the 1952 presidential election approached. None responded more enthusiastically to Byrnes's rhetoric of minority power than whites in the black-majority Mississippi Delta. Arriving to a hero's welcome, the South Carolina governor declared the Democratic Party "more antagonistic toward the South than any Republican administration since the Reconstruction Period." Echoing warnings he had made during the 1938 filibuster against the antilynching bill, Byrnes claimed that "organized minorities" controlled national politics. Just as African Americans had achieved political influence far beyond their numbers, Byrnes argued, southern whites should unite in defense of "local-self government" and states' rights. If neither national party gave "sympathetic consideration" to their pivotal bloc, Byrnes suggested a third-party revolt.[6]

The 5,000 Mississippians gathered for Byrnes's speech embraced the call to arms. Even before Byrnes endorsed political rebellion, the Mississippi Democratic Executive Committee had launched a "positive and militant program of action" to enforce white unity. Spearheaded by a 300-member committee, the People's Campaign called on every Democrat in the state to donate a dollar, wear a "Mississippi States' Rights" button, and support only "true and loyal Jeffersonian Democrats who will stand 100 percent for States' Rights and who will not count the cost in the work of protecting and continuing our sacred traditions and Southern way of life." To that end, the People's Campaign demanded that Mississippi Democrats only elect precinct delegates who would sign the "1952 Good Faith Pledge." If other southern states would follow Byrnes's advice and Mississippi's example, the insurgents predicted, a unified regional minority could beat an organized racial minority at its own game. "For the first time since 1936," announced a Mississippi Delta columnist, "the South holds the balance of political power both within the Democratic Party and in the Nation."[7]

In his calls for minority power, Byrnes revived and broadened the moribund Dixiecrat agenda with attacks on "socialized medicine," "oppressive taxation," and the "further centralization of power in Washington." But even as he expanded the segregationist critique of postwar liberalism, Byrnes maintained an explicitly racial interpretation of the national political dilemma. South Carolina fired on Fort Sumter "because we believed in the preservations of the rights and powers of the States under the Constitution," Byrnes assured a North Carolina crowd, and had overthrown Reconstruction to maintain the "integrity of the white race." With the Republican racial threat effectively muted, Byrnes argued, the South's white democracy progressed peacefully until "organized minorities of the Northern states threatened the leaders of the National Democratic Party and forced those leaders to abandon the cardinal principle of states' rights." Northern blacks left the Republican Party in droves during the Depression, Byrnes explained to a joint session of the Georgia legislature, and "voted en bloc" for unscrupulous Democrats. "These Negro politicians were interested only in race problems," Byrnes lamented. "They did not consider the effect the abandonment of the principle of the independence of States would have upon our political and economic problems." Bowing to the black bloc vote, the national Democratic Party "adopted a platform more socialistic than democratic."[8]

Byrnes spared no expense to preserve segregated schools, and he left no political option off the table in pursuit of southern power. He endorsed Richard Russell's long-shot bid for the Democratic presidential nomination in 1952 but warned that he would consider a Republican or third-party candidate if the eventual Democratic candidate proved unacceptable. Russell, like Byrnes, urged southern unity while promoting himself as a nationally viable politician. Convinced that continued clout within the Democratic Party offered the only means of maintaining segregation, Russell refused to endorse any revolt. Despite his contention that he was the only Democratic presidential hopeful who consistently outpolled the presumptive Republican nominee, General Dwight Eisenhower, in every southern state, Russell failed to attract northern and western support. Southern dissatisfaction with the national party did not derail the nomination of moderate Illinois governor Adlai Stevenson in 1952, but it compelled the national party to water down its civil rights plank and nominate Alabama senator John Sparkman for vice president.[9]

Southern conservatives remained unimpressed. After a reconvened South Carolina convention unenthusiastically endorsed the Democratic ticket, disenchanted delegates collected 53,000 signatures to place Eisen-

F. E. P. C. WILL HURT OUR WHITE TEXTILE WORKERS MORE THAN ANY OTHER GROUP OF WORKERS

Both Governor Stevenson and Senator Sparkman have made speeches to the CIO promising FEDERAL laws that will force Negroes into the white schools, hotels, restaurants, theaters, ALL MILLS & FACTORIES on equal basis with the whites, and jail penalties for violators. YOUR EMPLOYER COULD NOT PROTECT YOUR JOB.

Which Do YOU Want?

General Eisenhower and Senator Nixon have stated flatly that they favor each state handling it's own F. E. P. C. problem.

F. E. P. C. IN SOUTH CAROLINA COULD ONLY COME ABOUT AFTER YOU HAD A CHANCE TO VOTE ON IT.

Some of our South Carolina newspapers do not dare give you the TRUE news and facts. Listen to WANS every night Monday through Friday at 7 o'clock for "Fulton Lewis, Jr. and The News" and further announcements.

Before the Brown *ruling focused racial politics on school desegregation, President Truman's support for the Fair Employment Practices Commission and other civil rights measures convinced many southern conservatives to renounce their Democratic loyalty. In 1952, the independent South Carolinians for Eisenhower warned that support for the Democratic ticket would erode segregation in the workplace and public accommodations. (Gubernatorial Papers of James F. Byrnes, South Carolina Division of Archives and History, Columbia, S.C.)*

hower on the ballot as an independent. This strategy allowed South Carolina conservatives to buck the Democratic Party without voting "Republican" in the general election. In September, Byrnes endorsed Eisenhower and fulfilled his pledge to "place loyalty to my country above loyalty to a political party." Across the Deep South, many former Dixiecrats supported the Republican presidential candidate. Eisenhower-backer and former Dixiecrat-booster David Clark repackaged his attacks on the Truman administration to discredit the new Democratic standard-bearer. "Those mill employees who wish their daughters to attend school with Negro boys and girls, and work beside them in the mill," warned Clark, "should certainly vote for Adlai Stevenson."[10]

The Republican Party did not need the Deep South to retake the White House in 1952, and it did not get it. Eisenhower did pick off Texas, Florida, Tennessee, and Virginia, all states where disenchanted Democrats bolstered the Republican base. Indeed, Virginia would soon rival its Deep South counterparts as a hotbed of segregationist resistance. Yet despite Eisenhower's unprecedented success in Dixie, the Deep South states remained within the Democratic fold. Frustrated by Eisenhower's narrow defeat in South Carolina, Jimmy Byrnes declared that the Palmetto State's "Negro bloc vote" had beaten white independents at their own game. Speaking before the South Carolinians for Eisenhower shortly after the 1952 election, Byrnes warned that newly registered black voters across the South only heightened the need for white unity. Predicting that 75,000 black voters would cast ballots during the next election cycle, Byrnes urged white South Carolinians to "organize an opposing bloc in self defense." White unity would not only cancel out the growing black vote, Byrnes predicted, but also punish southern politicians who were "willing to deal . . . with Negro leaders." Just as slick Northern politicians had sold them out for black ballots, southern conservatives warned, opportunists back home would privilege party loyalty over race. Such candidates, Byrnes argued, "must be watched" and "defeated."[11]

As Byrnes's state-level strategy revealed, the "Negro bloc vote" that southern conservatives had long demonized could no longer be kept at a distance. White supremacists had raised the specter of northern big-city political machines bowing to black voters since the New Deal. Yet the postwar explosion of black voter registration forced southern leaders to concede that the "Negro bloc vote" impacted politics locally as well as nationally. In the wake of the 1952 elections, Byrnes scoured the South for black voting statistics. In Louisiana, where the number of registered black voters had risen from 10,000 in 1947 to 120,000 in 1952, a white sheriff confirmed Byrnes's fears of a swing bloc. "But for the 100,000 negro vote," the lawman reported, "Louisiana would have gone for Eisenhower." Jesse Helms, a journalist and political aide to North Carolina senator Willis Smith, fed Byrnes similar "evidence of bloc voting" in the Tar Heel State. While black registration in Louisiana had eclipsed that in North Carolina by 1952, Helms predicted that the tally could double to "200,000 Negroes registered east of Raleigh" by 1954. Those votes, Helms concluded, represented an "obvious threat" to his boss and likeminded southern conservatives.[12]

Although rattled by rapid black voter registration, Byrnes's informants agreed that a unified white electorate could defeat the "Negro bloc." The Louisiana sheriff bragged to Byrnes that whites in his parish voted "two for one for Eisenhower." While he presided over "about the only parish left where there is no negro vote," the sheriff and the majority of his white neighbors responded to a broader political threat. Back in South Carolina, Byrnes and his aides took heart in this backlash against the "Negro bloc." Their voting study suggested that southern white unity, coupled with a rightward shift nationally, could weaken black political clout. "President Eisenhower's election," an aide concluded, "proved that a candidate can win with the Negroes voting 10 to 1 against him."[13]

Eisenhower's electoral success confirmed that the black vote could be beaten, but segregationist enthusiasm for the president and his party cooled considerably after *Brown*. The unanimous decision, handed down by a Supreme Court headed by Eisenhower appointee and former Republican governor Earl Warren, convinced some segregationists that neither party deserved southern loyalty. Heading into the 1956 elections, segregationists accused both parties of pandering to black voters and ignoring white southerners. John Temple Graves, who blamed civil rights turmoil on "excessive minority power" in national politics, urged southern whites to fight fire with fire. "There are other great minorities, of course, but only the Negro one votes as a bloc," Graves explained to a Birmingham civic group. "It isn't cloak and dagger stuff, gentlemen, to speak of coming possible Negro dominance, of a 'master race' less qualified by far than the Germans whom we refused twice to let be a master race." Since civil rights advocates exploited the electoral system to undermine constitutional government, Graves reasoned, then segregationists should resort to similar means to save it. As "America's major minority," Graves explained, southern whites held the nation's destiny in their hands. But first, he argued, white southerners had to "learn to be free." They had to tell the Democrats they would "no longer stand without hitching" and inform the Republicans they would not "sign up without concessions and considerations." In short, Graves argued, white southerners had "to play one party against the other as the other minorities do."[14]

As Byrnes, Graves, and likeminded allies plotted a path back to power, their exaggerated appraisal of black political influence inspired grandiose estimations of their own clout. Like the Dixiecrats of the previous decade, segregationists looked to the Electoral College. Ever wary of third-party politics and increasingly optimistic that they could shed the provincial "Dixiecrat" stigma, southern insurgents hoped to make the nation's two-party system work in their favor. For most segregationists in the 1950s, this did not necessarily mean becoming Republicans. As suspicious of moderate "Eisenhower Republicans" as they were of the national Democratic Party's liberal northern wing, segregationists hoped to mobilize a pivotal southern bloc that could pull one or both parties back in their direction.

Buoyed by their rhetoric of minority power, diehards seized on a scheme to withhold electoral votes from any presidential candidate who failed to show sufficient sympathy for the segregationist position. The 1956 Democratic National Convention proved to be the most amicable since 1940, with liberal and moderate Democrats eager to conciliate southern segregationists. Nevertheless, some insurgents foreswore party loyalty. For the third presidential election in a row, South Carolinians led the charge. But this time, the figureheads of the 1948 and 1952 revolts, Thurmond and Byrnes, stood together. After the state Democratic Party convention narrowly endorsed the national ticket, both former governors signed a petition circulated by South Carolinians for Independent Electors. Headed by the son of former senator "Cotton Ed" Smith, the self-proclaimed "people's revolt" gathered 38,000 signatures in a week. State law required only 10,000 signatures to put an unpledged slate of electors on the ballot. Instead of choosing the Republican or Democratic candidate, South Carolina voters could simply vote to hold the state's electoral votes hostage. Anticipating a close presidential race, southern insurgents revived the Dixiecrats' electoral strategy. By withholding their electoral votes, southern states could deny either presidential candidate a majority and throw the election into the House of Representatives.[15]

Ultimately, only South Carolina, Mississippi, Louisiana, and Alabama offered voters a slate of unpledged electors. In the Palmetto State, the combined vote for independent electors and Eisenhower outnumbered the votes cast for the Democratic ticket. The unpledged-elector movement, which settled on Virginia senator Harry F. Byrd and Mississippi congressman John Bell Williams as its ticket, carried no states but racked up nearly 200,000 votes. The results revealed that the rhetoric of white "bloc" power resonated loudest and most literally in the black-majority counties of the Deep South. The South Carolina lowcountry, the Mississippi Delta, and other black-belt areas had also rallied to the Dixiecrats in 1948 and shown the most enthusiasm for Eisenhower in 1952. In 1956, they served notice that more than a few southern conservatives still believed in "minority" politics.[16]

Segregationist organizations embraced this electoral scheming with unbridled enthusiasm. Working hand in hand with state officials to promote and enforce white unity, the Citizens' Councils and other pressure groups advocated segregationist power politics as an extension of massive resistance. Committed activists believed they could dictate policy in Washington, but they struggled to rally their neighbors back home. Just as the tension between moderation and militancy frustrated segregation's defenders, so too did the chasm between segregationists and the everyday southerners they purported to represent.

The flurry of segregationist mobilization after *Brown* gave racial conservatives reason for optimism. The Citizens' Councils, founded in the Mississippi Delta town of Indianola in 1954, spread rapidly through the state and quickly spilled over its borders. Targeting professionals and businessmen, a core of able and committed organizers relied on contacts in local civic associations to launch new chapters. A tireless organizer and relentless propagandist, Mississippi Association of Citizens' Councils executive secretary Robert Patterson advocated a region-wide movement. "Forty million white Southerners, or a fraction thereof if properly organized, can be a power in this Nation," Patterson proclaimed just thirteen months after founding the first council, "but they must be thoroughly organized from the town and county level up." While no state came close to Mississippi's 85,000 members, the neighboring states of Alabama and Louisiana quickly developed thriving associations. By 1956, as southern insurgents proclaimed the power of white unity, the Citizens' Councils claimed a quarter million dues-paying members across the region.[17]

Segregationists pointed to the councils' local leadership and rapid growth as evidence of an authentic grassroots rebellion. "The Citizens' Council is not a political organization," declared Alabama state senator Sam Engelhardt. "It is an orderly and organized revolt by the white people of Alabama and the South to perpetuate life as we have known it." Yet Engelhardt, a Black Belt merchant and cotton ginner whose family had amassed several thousand acres of prime farmland, reflected the councils' elite orientation and limited appeal even as he claimed grassroots credibility. In Alabama and elsewhere, the Citizens' Councils drew their most fervent support from planters, merchants, and professionals. While their membership supported their claim to represent respectable and law-abiding advocates of states' rights and racial integrity, the councils' elite composition undercut the broader goal of white unity.[18]

Furthermore, the segregationist movement could not resolve disagreements about the nature of their rebellion. Alabama Citizens' Council leaders cringed at the antics of a militant, working-class offshoot in Birmingham, even as its membership boomed. The North Alabama Citizens Council (NACC) grabbed national headlines in April 1956 when four of its member attacked Nat King Cole during a Birmingham performance. The NACC's leader, a Navy veteran and former disc jockey named Asa Earl Carter, claimed that his organization alone spoke for everyday whites. But Engelhardt and other council leaders heaped scorn on Carter and his followers for their "fascist" extremism. Responding to Carter's exclusion of Jews from the NACC, a Selma segregationist declared, "There is no place for prejudice . . . in this movement." Another segregationist explained away such outbursts as proof of the councils' populist authenticity. "Inevitably, from time to time, perhaps in all organizations that mushroom so swiftly from the grass roots," he argued, "demagogic rabble rousers temporarily capture segments of such a group and harangue them into overt acts against the best interests of the whole community."[19]

While segregationists in Mississippi and Alabama struggled to balance popular appeal with orderly protest, leaders in other southern states poured remarkably little energy into building a movement. While political leaders in South Carolina and Georgia rivaled their southern neighbors in rhetorical militancy and tactical creativity, few whites in either state mobilized as card-carrying segregationists. Movement leaders in both states prioritized strategy and fundraising over enrollment. Roy Harris, a founder of the States' Rights Council of Georgia, conceded that the fledgling segregationist organization desired members primarily for their dues. The group, Harris announced, sought at least 150,000 Georgians who would "pay $5 a year to finance a fight to maintain segregation" but "remain silent about policy matters." At its peak, Georgia's answer to the Citizens' Councils netted only 10,000 dues-paying members. While segregationists elsewhere claimed populist credibility, some States' Rights Council leaders admitted that they had organized "a political rather that a grass roots organization."[20]

Despite their struggles to rally fellow southerners behind a segregationist crusade, committed activists exerted influence far beyond their numbers. Even in states with relatively few dues-paying segregationists, activists enjoyed significant support from state leaders. Officials who embraced segregationist organizations played pivotal roles in state-supported watchdog groups such as the Mississippi State Sovereignty Commission and the Georgia Commission on Education. Working hand in hand, public officials and independent activists plotted legal strategy, monitored civil rights supporters, and disseminated propaganda. Like the southern governors who preempted the *Brown* decision with equalization drives, these watchdog groups launched a public relations offensive. Hoping to portray segregated society as humane and orderly, the Mississippi State Sovereignty Commission monitored white extremists as well as civil rights activists. On the local level, state agents and organized segregationists used economic pressure, harassment, and blacklisting to intimidate African Americans and potential white allies.[21]

Even in states with limited segregationist organization, pressure groups pushed officials into open confrontation. In Arkansas, a state with a relatively weak Citizens' Council, segregationists' disproportionate power

Unbalanced Power

NORTHERN PUBLIC

94% DIVIDED WHITE VOTE

6% NEGRO BLOC VOTE

CITIZENS' COUNCIL, JACKSON, MISS.

By 1960, diehard segregationists argued that a small but pivotal "Negro bloc vote" controlled national politics. Southern racial conservatives claimed common cause with white northerners who, they believed, had been victimized by vote-hungry politicians and minority pressure groups. Cartoon from the Citizens' Council, *August 1960.*

spurred moderate governor Orval Faubus into one of the most dramatic confrontations of the civil rights era. With Little Rock schools on the verge of token integration in 1957 and Faubus facing reelection, the Capital Citizens' Council mobilized anxious whites and exerted considerable political pressure on the governor. Faced with the prospect of angry white demonstrators on the steps of Little Rock's Central High School, the Arkansas governor called in the National Guard to prevent the enrollment of nine black students. Faubus's concession, which forced Eisenhower to federalize the Arkansas guardsmen and ensure Central High's integration, dramatized the potential of organized segregationists to impact policy and public opinion. While segregationists could not "save" Central High, they exploited the showdown in Little Rock to discredit southern moderates and encourage resistance.[22]

Dramatic confrontations boosted segregationists' visibility, but they failed to deliver concrete victories. Segregationists deployed "Remember Little Rock!" not as a triumphant slogan but rather as an object lesson for other communities hoping to avoid similar defeats. Yet the leaders of massive resistance, whether public officials or private activists, consistently

Back In The Saddle Again!

THE SOUTH

INDEPENDENT ELECTORS

CITIZENS' COUNCIL, JACKSON, MISS.

Some segregationists argued that a larger "bloc" of white southerners could exert a similar balance of power and force concessions from both national parties on civil rights legislation. Cartoon from the Citizens' Council, *June 1960.*

failed to preserve strict segregation through schoolhouse showdowns. In 1960, state legislators and Citizens' Councilors in Louisiana mobilized to resist court-ordered desegregation in New Orleans. When four black students enrolled at two elementary schools in November, white activists staged a targeted boycott enforced by screaming mobs. Gathering daily, white mothers known as "the Cheerleaders" cursed the new black enrollees as well as white students whose families disregarded the boycott. Like Faubus before him, Louisiana's governor stepped up his segregationist rhetoric with an eye toward his political future. He would go to jail, the governor announced in the midst of the boycott, rather than accept desegregation.[23]

The New Orleans school crisis, segregationists predicted, could turn the tide in their favor. "Not since the days of the first Reconstruction Period," crowed the *Citizens' Council*, "when the white citizens of the famed Crescent City wrested control of their local government from the hands of carpetbaggers and scalawags . . . has the course of history hung so much in the balance." New Orleans, segregationists argued, followed their blueprint for white unity: "On the side of racial integrity stand the embattled people of New Orleans; the well-organized, powerful and ably-led Citizens' Councils of the area; and the government of the state of Louisiana." Despite signs that massive resistance had already peaked with the Southern Manifesto and the stand at Little Rock, professional segregationists cheered the convergence of a high-profile showdown and a national election. "Federal efforts to force racial mixing in New Orleans and the resultant violence," argued an Alabama editor, "should be enough to precipitate a revolt of all the Southern presidential electors against the candidates of both national parties." Beside headlines hailing white unity in New Orleans, the *Citizens' Council* carried a preposterous headline: "How You Can Help Elect a Southern President."[24]

Despite their failure to triumph in direct confrontations with the federal government, Deep South diehards still believed their white bloc could take the nation by storm. At twenty-five-dollar-a-plate banquets, Roy Harris, Herman Talmadge, and recently elected Mississippi governor Ross Barnett urged overflow crowds to rally behind unpledged electors in the upcoming election. Barnett, an outspoken Citizens' Council supporter, quickly emerged as an icon of diehard resistance. At a speech in South Carolina, applauding segregationists interrupted the Mississippi governor sixty-three times as he encouraged "freedom of action" in national politics. Veteran resisters such as the Southern States Industrial Council's Thurman Sensing cheered the unpledged-elector scheme as "the best weapon the South has in its struggle for States' Rights." Only through independent action, Sensing argued, could segregationists gain "a veto on party pledges to force Reconstruction II on the Southern states."[25]

In their attempts to rally their fellow southerners, diehard segregationists refused to abandon the dream of minority power politics. The Alabama editor of a white supremacist tabloid deemed the free-elector plan "a method whereby we could show the Democratic Party that we do constitute a powerful minority—quite as powerful as the Negro minorities of the Eastern states." Defining themselves explicitly in opposition to black voters, the advocates of independent electors anticipated no limits to their potential power. "National politics has deteriorated to a low standard of bloc vote control," declared Louisiana Citizens' Council leader Leander Perez. "We have in our hands, if we would but use it, the power of a bloc vote far greater than that of any other bloc or blocs in this country." Back in Mississippi, Ross Barnett took jabs at the civil rights movement and taunted national party leaders. "I look for a national election to be very close, and our eight votes and perhaps a few others may swing the pendulum," Barnett announced. "If we get the balance of power in our hands, it won't be a sit-in . . . it will be a kneel-in when the two major parties come praying for our favor."[26]

The old Dixiecrat dream of a segregationist swing vote died hard, but by 1960 most white southerners rejected these schemes as impractical at best and despicable at worst. As Barnett fed fantasies of a superhuman southern bloc, skeptical observers openly questioned the prospects for success. "It is fascinating to contemplate a close presidential race and a handful of Southern electors stepping forward and saying, 'Hold everything. We have the balance of power,'" opined Mississippi newspaperman Oliver Emmerich. Reminding his readers that "the situation in the electoral college is not as conducive to bargaining as some people seem to believe," Emmerich ridiculed Barnett's "highly fanciful" scheming. "Some people seem to think that in the event of a tight presidential vote our independent electors could face Richard Nixon and John Kennedy in a hotel room and say, 'This is it. Which one of you fellows wants to be president? We're open to bids.'" A Delta editor was more blunt. Blasting Barnett for his "egomaniac idiocy," the hometown newspaper of former Dixiecrat vice presidential candidate Fielding Wright deemed the latest revolt "just about as juvenile and ridiculous as it is possible to be."[27]

The editors ridiculed their governor not for his racial convictions but rather for his delusional political calculations. While Barnett and his ilk would not be deterred, most prominent segregationists abandoned their tentative support for the free-elector scheme. Herman Talmadge continued Georgia's tradition of flirting with revolt before lining up with fellow senator Richard Russell behind the national party nominees. South Carolina's independent-elector movement, which had led the charge in 1956 and secured nearly 30 percent of the statewide presidential vote, failed to gather enough signatures to get its slate on the 1960 ballot. Left with one viable alternative to the national party platform, disaffected South Carolina Democrats helped Republican candidate Richard Nixon secure nearly 49 percent of ballots cast in 1960. In the end, only Mississippians elected a full slate of eight unpledged electors, who joined with six of Alabama's eleven electors to cast their votes for Harry F. Byrd and Strom Thurmond. In early December, the unpledged electors pleaded with fellow southerners to join their revolt in the name of "racial and national integrity": "If we do not seize upon this opportunity . . . then we must prepare to accept . . . school integration, judicial despotism, and, finally, Federal dictation and tyranny." The plea fell on deaf ears, but the insurgents did gain a fifteenth vote from Henry Irwin, a faithless Republican elector from Oklahoma who threw his support behind Byrd for president. As for a running mate, Irwin had another candidate in mind: Arizona Republican Barry Goldwater.[28]

As southern insurgents persisted with their Electoral College schemes in the early 1960s, Goldwater's name kept popping up alongside the segregationists. Like the South's anti–New Deal insurgents, Goldwater had bucked the Democratic status quo in his native state. The second Republican senator in Arizona's history, and the first elected in three decades, the Phoenix department-store owner quickly found common ground with southern conservatives. Goldwater and other right-wing Republicans agreed with segregationist Democrats that the Electoral College no longer worked in their favor. As North Dakota Republican senator Karl Mundt explained to John Stennis, the right changes could "put the brakes on the leftists" by "diminishing the influence of pressure groups on the major parties." Some conservatives suggested dividing each state's electoral votes in proportion to the popular vote, while others advocated the direct election of Electoral College members within specially designated districts. Regardless of the particulars, the plans shared the common goal of eliminating a winner-take-all system that hinged on "big city political machines." While the unwillingness of either national party to abandon its allegedly all-consuming scramble for black votes frustrated segregationists, the rhetoric of minority power suggested that right-wing Republicans and disaffected southern Democrats shared transcendent "conservative" values. Segregationists remained hesitant to declare the GOP a safe haven by default, yet from the political wilderness of 1960 emerged voices that helped to bridge the gap between the segregationist "bloc" and the national conservative movement that was remaking the Republican Party.[29]

As militant segregationists and grandstanding politicians failed to impose unity on the white South, the GOP offered for some an alternative path to power. In South Carolina, one prominent segregationist's evolution revealed how southern whites could reconcile their racial agenda with a national conservative movement. With 1960's *The Case for the South*, newspaperman William D. Workman Jr. emerged as a leading apologist for segregation. A veteran journalist, Workman embodied the ethos of responsible segregation that had guided South Carolina's resistance campaign for over a decade. In *The Case for the South*, Workman declared his homeland under siege by black activists, northern politicians, and a reckless Supreme Court. The white South, Workman contended, was full of law-abiding and freedom-loving segregationists "who cherish state sovereignty, constitutional government, and racial integrity." Despite the excesses of a few Klansmen, the average white southerner meant no harm to his black neighbors but demanded "the right to rear his children in the atmosphere most conducive to their learning."[30]

Lamenting the "Black Shadow of Politics" looming over the South, Workman rehashed the timeworn charge that majority rule had given way to a "distressing tyranny of the numerical minority." While various pressure groups threatened the southern way of life, Workman deemed African Americans "most responsive to specialized appeals and concessions." Yet even as he rehashed the timeworn threat of the "Negro bloc," Workman spoke of segregationists not as a rival "minority" but as the core of a disfranchised national white majority. "The concurrent minority . . . thrives upon discord and disunion," Workman argued, and "seeks to pit one faction of the majority against the other." Like other defenders of segregation, Workman coupled his vilification of black voting behavior with the threat of political reprisal. "If . . . the Negroes will vote as a bloc when it is to their racial advantage to do so," Workman warned, "then there is nothing to keep the whites from voting as a bloc." Unlike earlier advocates of regional unity, Workman contended that only a national white majority could overcome "the thoroughly undemocratic leverage Negroes now exert."[31]

Segregationists other than Workman alluded to the political potential of a racially awakened and united white majority. The Citizens' Council, an organization Workman praised as an example of "responsible" racial activism, reported regularly on northern white backlash in its monthly newsletter. After both major parties endorsed civil rights planks in 1960, the *Citizens' Council* reprinted a Detroit neighborhood association's demand for "a more conservative approach to so-called 'civil rights.'" Claiming that "Negro voters" wielded unfair influence over Detroit politics, the organization's president pledged to mobilize the city's white voters "to destroy this so-called balance of power in our city by offering our support to candidates who oppose usurpation by self-styled civil righters." The neighborhood association, predicting that "our votes will outweigh those that may be controlled by the National Association for the Advancement of Colored People," invited "the beleaguered citizens of other great cities to join our political revolution." Such pronouncements, music to segregationists' ears, bolstered their claim that most white Americans shared their racial outlook.[32]

While segregationists courted northern allies, they remained wary of the Republican Party as a haven for white majority politics. Southern conservatives, Workman argued, had taken heart in Eisenhower's "seemingly genuine espousal of the principles of state sovereignty" in 1952 and 1956, but after Little Rock and the Civil Rights Act of 1957 "most of the Southerners in all those states wished they could take back those votes." Despite their overtures to southern conservatives, Workman lamented, the Republicans "had given clear, cruel, and unmistakable evidence that their concern for the South was a thing of rags and tatters, torn to shreds while they courted the Negro minority blocs of the Northern pivotal states." Openly distrustful of Republican overtures to the South, Workman wondered if the white South should attempt once again to "recapture" the Democratic Party or "establish a third party which would reflect constitutional conservatism (especially embodying states' rights)."[33]

By refusing to acknowledge the Republican Party as a viable option for southern conservatives, Workman ignored the political ferment in his own backyard. When *The Case for the South* debuted in 1960, South Carolina had already emerged as a hotbed of southern Republicanism. Hoping to consolidate the majority that split its votes almost evenly between Eisenhower and unpledged electors in 1956, South Carolina Republicans redoubled their efforts in 1960. Their renewed enthusiasm had less to do with the presumptive presidential nominee, Vice President Richard Nixon, than with the emergence of Barry Goldwater as a conservative icon. Like Workman, Goldwater churned out a manifesto in 1960, but with much more fanfare. Published and distributed by the senator's influential right-wing supporters, *The Conscience of a Conservative* shot up the summer bestseller charts. Ghostwritten by William F. Buckley's brother-in-law, L. Brent Bozell, the slim volume summed up Goldwater's stance on a variety of political issues, from government spending to "the Soviet Menace." But nothing encouraged southern conservatives more than the successive chapters on states' rights and civil rights.[34]

The subjects required separate chapters, Goldwater argued, because the civil rights struggle had both obscured and dramatized a much broader issue. Blasting attempts "to disparage the principle of States' Rights by equating it with defense of the South's position on racial integration," Goldwater championed the concept as a bulwark against growing federal power. Goldwater, who had voted for civil rights measures as a sitting senator, reassured southern conservatives by criticizing *Brown* and arguing for limits to racial reform. He criticized the "extravagant and shameless misuse" of civil rights, a blanket term he accused liberals of expanding to include "human" and "natural" rights not granted by the Constitution. So Goldwater could be for "civil" rights such as voting while still maintaining that "the federal Constitution does *not* require the States to maintain racially mixed schools." Whether or not Goldwater *liked* segregation did not matter. In a concise and carefully worded chapter, he declared white opposition to integration a perfectly legal and downright American stance. "It may be just or wise or expedient for negro children to attend the same schools as white children," Goldwater argued, "but they do not have a civil right to do so."[35]

Southern conservatives responded to Goldwater's affirmation in kind. Despite the fact that he had recently ridiculed Republican duplicity on civil rights, Workman praised *Conscience* and its author as "one of the most encouraging books—and one of the most forthright citizens—to appear on the national scene in many a year." South Carolina Republicans, having obtained advance copies of the senator's book, invited Goldwater to keynote their state convention in 1960. In spite of Richard Nixon's presumptive lock on the GOP presidential nomination, enthusiastic Palmetto State Republicans surprised Goldwater by naming him their candidate of choice. After nominating Goldwater, Republican delegates endorsed a platform comparable, in the words of the *Charleston News and Courier*, to "the party platform of the old national Democratic party before it was corrupted by the New Dealers with their socialist doctrines." By throwing their support to a sympathetic Republican, southern conservatives hoped to regain the power that three decades of civil rights struggle had stripped away. As southern conservatives caught Goldwater fever, the language of the segregationist "minority" meshed with predictions of a coalescing national majority of "politically dispossessed" white voters. Rather than operate as independents, one Goldwater supporter explained to Workman, southern conservatives could form a "formidable voting bloc within the Republican National Convention . . . thereby influencing the course of the party."[36]

Despite Goldwater's failure to derail Nixon's nomination in 1960, he reassured white southerners that they fit into his plans for a national conservative coalition. Just two months after the 1960 election, Goldwater and his congressional allies privately circulated a twenty-nine-page memo urging the Republican Party to reach out to "that dragooned and ignored individual, 'The Forgotten American.'" The Republican right wing, as conservative journalist Robert Novak explained, reached out to ordinary Americans "whose interests are not identical with those of existing political pressure groups." While this manifesto carefully avoided the question of courting southern Democrats, its rhetoric echoed the segregationist narrative of a national party corrupted and controlled by a minority bloc. The "Forgotten American" strategy hinged on attracting a national network of disenchanted Democratic constituencies, from anti-Communist Catholics to antiunion workers, but it also resonated with southern white conservatives willing to look beyond Dixie for their political salvation. For southern Democrats lamenting their wandering in the political wilderness, this new move "to brand the G.O.P. as the party of the politically dispossessed" struck a nerve.[37]

Goldwater soon made clear that southern conservatives fit into this broader vision of a "Forgotten American" coalition. At a southern Republican strategy session in Atlanta in late 1961, the Arizona senator famously admitted that "we're not going to get the Negro vote as a bloc . . . so we ought to go hunting where the ducks are." The real prize, Goldwater argued, was the emerging bloc of disaffected southern Democrats. "Why is the South turning?" Goldwater asked. "It is because liberalism has stifled . . . the southern conservative voice in the Democratic party." After his speech, Goldwater suggested to reporters that the Republican Party should water down its civil rights plank. Stepping up his criticism of federal desegregation efforts, Goldwater declared his support for a constitutional amendment to return control of education to the states.[38]

The night before Goldwater's remarks in Georgia, black Republicans attending the integrated Atlanta proceedings worried aloud that *their* forefathers' party could soon devolve into a lily-white backlash movement. Liberal Atlanta newspaperman Ralph McGill agreed. Scolding Goldwater for "pandering to Southern prejudices," McGill branded the senator "the new, and totally unexpected, hero of the klans, klaverns, and councils." In his nationally syndicated column, McGill mocked Goldwater's suspect anecdote about an early morning appearance in Savannah. Apparently, by the dawn's early light, Goldwater unknowingly pledged allegiance while facing a Confederate flag. "Senator Goldwater, of the Confederate territory of Arizona," McGill noted, won rapturous applause with this story. If he "put on a false General Lee beard, and a Confederate cap," McGill quipped, "he might do even better."[39]

While McGill mocked, southern Republicans capitalized on surging local enthusiasm for Goldwater. In early 1962, Goldwater traveled to South Carolina to keynote the largest, and whitest, Republican convention in state history. In an auditorium adorned with Confederate battle flags and a banner reading, "Welcome Barry Goldwater, Our Next President," the Arizona senator commended the convention for fielding their first serious state-level contender since Reconstruction. William Workman, two years removed from his withering critique of the Republicans in *The Case for the*

South, was running for Senate on the GOP ticket. Championing "states' rights and local self-government," Workman declared the GOP "the best hope, and perhaps the last hope, of stemming the liberal tide which has been sweeping the United States toward the murky depths of socialism." As the strains of "Dixie" died down, Goldwater implored the raucous crowd to send Workman to Capitol Hill "to help Strom Thurmond represent conservatives."[40]

Getting Workman to Washington was no mean task. Despite the enthusiasm for the Republican Party among many southern conservatives, Workman battled a South Carolina legend and a century of political tradition. In 1938, Democrat Olin D. Johnston had suffered the stigma of "purge" candidate when Roosevelt endorsed his challenge to veteran senator "Cotton Ed" Smith. Now, nearly three decades later, Johnston faced a Republican contender who argued that he could better protect the racial status quo. While the veteran senator invoked his segregationist track record, Workman argued that Johnston's party affiliation crippled his ability to defend southern sovereignty and "constitutional government." When the Kennedy administration dispatched federal troops to quell riots at the University of Mississippi in October 1962, Workman cited the "invasion" as proof that the Democratic Party was no place for a true states' righter. "When South Carolina's turn comes," Workman vowed, "she'll defend her rights." Then the band played "Dixie."[41]

Despite the undeniable momentum behind his campaign, Workman fell short of victory in November. But South Carolina's segregationist spokesman captured over 130,000 votes, 44 percent of the total, in a state where Republican challengers usually polled a few thousand at best. Workman's unprecedented showing signaled a broader shift in the thinking of "dispossessed" southern conservatives. Republican congressional candidates in the South received over three times the votes they had gotten in the previous midterm election of 1958. The party's increasingly visible "Goldwater wing" had convinced wary southerners, including Workman himself, that they had trustworthy allies in the GOP. Renouncing the "big city politics" of the Democrats, one Mississippi Delta resident declared in late 1962: "We must join with the conservatives of the North and West." When he visited South Carolina, Goldwater had lumped together Republican candidate Workman and Democratic senator Thurmond as "conservatives." The Arizona senator's southern fans agreed that party affiliation mattered less than convictions, and they increasingly lumped Goldwater together with right-wing southerners. As one Mississippian informed her senators, it was time to "get together with men like Strom Thurmond and Barry Goldwater." But first, the senators from South Carolina and Arizona had to get together with each other.[42]

Southern cooperation with sympathetic outsiders did not begin in 1962. Since they turned on the New Deal in the late 1930s, conservative southern Democrats relied on support from right-wing Republicans to block objectionable legislation. This "conservative coalition" held sway in Congress for the better part of two decades, but this marriage of convenience fell fall short of a permanent party realignment. If anything, the bipartisan cooperation among congressional conservatives reassured powerful southern Democrats that they could maintain power and influence in national politics without abandoning the party of their fathers. Insurgents regularly threatened defection, yet prominent southern Democrats held out hope that they still had a place in *their* party.[43]

None kept the faith more fervently than Richard B. Russell. In 1932, the year Russell entered the Senate, he rode through downtown Atlanta with presidential hopeful Franklin Delano Roosevelt. Perched on the back seat of a convertible, Russell and Roosevelt waved at the thousands of Georgians who spilled off the sidewalks to catch a glimpse of the next president. By the early 1960s, the political revolution that FDR had set into motion was, by Russell's own estimation, "driving the South from the house of our fathers."[44] But Russell would not leave without a fight.

Few had more to lose. As the undisputed leader of the southern senators, Russell banked segregation's future on continued influence *within* the Democratic Party. An intraparty insurgent, he balanced his racial convictions with political pragmatism. In 1948, after the entire Mississippi delegation and half of the Alabamans stormed out of the Democratic National Convention, the remaining southern delegates backed Russell as their protest candidate. When the bid failed, Russell spurned the Dixiecrats and reluctantly lined up behind the Truman ticket. In 1952, as prominent southern politicians such as Jimmy Byrnes advocated independent action, Russell made another bid for the Democratic nomination. While he failed to transcend his image as a regional protest candidate, Russell cemented his reputation as the most powerful segregationist in Washington.

Russell did not underestimate the challenges facing the segregationist cause, but as late as the early 1960s he still believed southern Democrats could stymie meaningful civil rights legislation. Russell had history on his side. The Senate had never voted to stop a southern filibuster, and national politicians wanted to avoid such long, costly standoffs on Capitol

Hill. In 1957, Russell threatened a southern filibuster to force major concessions on the first civil rights legislation enacted since Reconstruction. While southern conservatives publicly lamented the Civil Rights Act of 1957, Russell and his colleagues considered the legislation a strategic victory. Limited primarily to voting rights, the bill's lack of adequate enforcement provisions resulted in no small part from Russell's backroom dealings with Senate majority leader and fellow southerner Lyndon Johnson. Russell knew that the civil rights bill would be a huge political victory for the Texas Democrat, who eyed a presidential bid in 1960. Through strategic concessions on civil rights legislation, Russell and his fellow southern senators helped Johnson inch closer to the White House. Once he was there, segregationists hoped, he would be their ally.[45]

Racial confrontations across the South undercut Russell's strategy of subtle resistance and intraparty maneuvering. In September 1957, southern Democrats allowed Congress to pass the first civil rights act of the century only after stripping it of its most forceful provisions. Two weeks later, in a show of unprecedented force, President Eisenhower reluctantly dispatched federal troops to restore order in Little Rock. Whatever its advantages, Russell's brand of moderation posed serious political risks for southern senators. When another civil rights bill surfaced in February 1960, they filibustered. Russell organized a relay of southern senators to keep the filibuster rolling through round-the-clock sessions. By early March, southerners had filibustered for 125 hours straight in the longest continuous session in Senate history. By the time the bill came up for a final vote in April, Russell and his colleagues had once again stripped the legislation of its strongest provisions and sapped pro–civil rights senators of their will to fight.[46]

Such strategic victories hardly consoled Russell, who anticipated more confrontations ahead. "My party," he lamented, "had deviated from the past and has gone off and left me." Yet Russell and his southern colleagues clung to their strategy of obstruction and delay. The threat of a filibuster kept civil rights advocates at bay throughout the Kennedy administration, despite the fact that the civil rights movement had forced itself onto the national stage and the president's agenda. Kennedy had authorized Justice Department attorneys to draft a civil rights bill in late May 1963 after policemen turned dogs and fire hoses on marchers in Birmingham. On 11 June 1963, hours after Alabama became the last southern state to integrate its university system, the president announced his civil rights legislation on television. That same evening, a Citizens' Councilor assassinated civil rights leader Medgar Evers in Jackson, Mississippi.[47]

Despite the prominence and urgency of civil rights in 1963, Kennedy's legislative program languished. Even as Martin Luther King shared his dream with 250,000 marchers on the Washington Mall, southern defiance and liberal dejection pervaded Congress. "Rarely," the *New York Times* reported three months after the March on Washington, "has there been such a pervasive attitude of discouragement around Capitol Hill and such a feeling of helplessness to deal with it."[48] Ten days later, dejection gave way to mourning, when an assassin gunned down Kennedy in Dallas.

From the moment he took the oath of office, Lyndon Johnson considered Kennedy's civil rights program his "first priority." Johnson bitterly disappointed Russell, his Senate mentor, who had gambled that a southern president would bring an end to civil rights legislation. On the contrary, Johnson used his congressional experience to push a revamped version of Kennedy's bill through the House of Representatives. In February 1964, the Senate received the bill *Congressional Quarterly* deemed "the most sweeping civil rights measure to clear either house of Congress in the 20th Century."[49]

A southern filibuster was a foregone conclusion. But unlike in past battles, Johnson and his allies sought no compromise with southern Democrats. They aimed to garner enough votes from nonsouthern Democrats and Republicans to invoke cloture, thereby ending a filibuster by a two-thirds vote. Southern senators had filibustered civil rights bills eleven times since the inception of this rule, and their colleagues had never stopped them by force. Russell responded to the administration's aggressive strategy with an equally militant defense, pledging to fight "to the last ditch—to the death."[50] Russell quickly organized his southern bloc for another filibuster, but the 1964 Senate fight was different. For starters, pro-civil rights senators fought back. They organized relay teams to challenge the filibustering southerners with questions and rebuttals, while Democratic leaders lobbied skeptical Republicans to support cloture.

The three-month filibuster against the Civil Rights Act of 1964 encapsulated three decades of segregationist resistance. From March to June, southern senators rehashed a litany of critiques that the defenders of segregation had honed in earlier battles against racial reform. Russell and his allies presented their stand as a continuation of the campaign against big government, creeping socialism, and subversive pressure groups. Long before the civil rights confrontations of the early 1960s, segregationists had made the strategic decision to "elevate" their defense of Jim Crow above racial appeals and seek the sympathy of a national conservative audience. In 1964, this strategy undergirded the fight against the civil rights bill.

From the Senate floor, southern speakers attacked the bill's provisions as subversive and un-American. The legislation, Russell warned, would authorize "such vast governmental control over free enterprise in this country so as to commence the processes of socialism."[51] Throughout the filibuster, southern senators warned repeatedly that the civil rights bill would rob Americans of cherished liberties and constitutional government.

By downplaying white supremacist rhetoric in favor of patriotic pleas and constitutional arguments, segregationists accelerated a process that both predated and anticipated the civil rights legislation of the 1960s. Yet even in these later battles, the defenders made no secret of their bedrock racial convictions. As the leader of the filibuster, Richard Russell drew on three decades of experience fighting racial reform in the Senate. Rather than a strategic departure, Russell's rhetoric in 1964 relied on arguments he had advanced since his filibuster against the antilynching legislation in 1938. "I'm not an anthropologist, but I've studied history," Russell told a reporter. "And there is no case in history of a mongrel race preserving a civilization, much less creating one."[52] Recognizing the sheer desperation of this "last ditch" effort, Russell grew increasingly bitter and cynical. He reintroduced his 1949 "Racial Relocation" bill, which demanded government funds to "spread [blacks] more evenly over all sections of the Nation." While most newspapers, even in the South, criticized the proposal as a cynical and callous stunt, segregationist editor James J. Kilpatrick stood by Russell. "The plain truth is," Kilpatrick wrote, "that enthusiasm for integration increases by the square of the distance one is removed from the immediacy of the problem." Kilpatrick praised the doomed measure as "too simple, and too sensible, for men whose instinct is to be both complex and coercive." Russell, still confident that most northern whites shared his racial beliefs, hoped to hold out long enough for a popular backlash to turn the tide. He aimed to keep the filibuster rolling through the summer, yet by early June the pro–civil rights forces had gathered enough votes to invoke cloture. On 10 June, with all one hundred senators present and voting, the Senate ended the filibuster nearly three months and 6 million words after it began. A few days later, the Civil Rights Act of 1964 passed by a vote of nearly three to one. Accusing the civil rights forces of acting in "the spirit . . . of a lynch mob," Russell watched helplessly as seventy-three Democrats and Republicans lined up behind the bill.[53]

The 1964 civil rights showdown confirmed diehard segregationists' contention that principled independence, not party loyalty, promised a way forward. The battles of the late 1950s and early 1960s taught them that neither party deserved their allegiance. Racial conservatives may have appreciated the political influence and segregationist credentials of Democratic stalwarts such as Russell and Stennis, but insurgents stole the spotlight in the wake of the Civil Rights Act in 1964. Through nearly a decade of civil rights skirmishes, South Carolina senator Strom Thurmond had proven himself a reliable soldier for the southern bloc. At the same time, Thurmond occasionally broke ranks to bolster his segregationist credentials. Dissatisfied with Russell's compromise on the Civil Rights Act of 1957, Thurmond surprised his southern colleagues with a solo filibuster. Such grandstanding cemented his reputation as an individualist who put principles, or at least his personal priorities, above party. As one journalist covering the twenty-four-hour marathon in 1957 noted, "It never has been a sure thing that Strom Thurmond would go along with any group unless it went his way."[54]

Southern filibusters in 1960 and 1964 gave Thurmond ample opportunity to showcase "his way." When the Senate passed the Civil Rights Act of 1964, Thurmond encapsulated the segregationist mantra of patriotism, persecution, and political marginalization. "This is a tragic day for America," Thurmond declared, "when Negro agitators, spurred on by communist enticements to promote racial strife, can cause the United States Senate to be steamrolled into passing the worst, most unreasonable and unconstitutional legislation that has ever been considered by the Congress."[55]

An ally from across the aisle joined Thurmond in denouncing the bill. Barry Goldwater bucked his party leadership, and his own voting record, by opposing the Civil Rights Act of 1964. A week after the cloture vote ended the southern filibuster, the presumptive Republican nominee voiced his "constitutional" objections to the bill. Declaring his opposition to "discrimination of any sort," Goldwater warned that the bill authorized "the creation of a federal police force of mammoth proportions" and encouraged "an 'informer' psychology" among citizens. "These . . . ," Goldwater declared, "are the hallmarks of the police state and landmarks in the destruction of a free society." If the public "misconstrued" his vote as a defense of segregation, Goldwater concluded, he would accept the fallout.[56]

While Republican colleagues worried that Goldwater's vote would cost their party the White House, the Arizona senator's opposition to the Civil Rights Act of 1964 encouraged segregationists. Richard Russell, ever the loyal Democrat, nonetheless deemed Goldwater "a real states' righter." After Goldwater beat out moderate New York governor Nelson Rockefeller for the Republican presidential nomination, Charleston's conservative *News and Courier* predicted "a realignment of political power in this country, with the South, Middle West, and the Far West joined together in a new alliance."[57]

Predictions of a national conservative alliance climaxed in late summer, when Goldwater traveled to South Carolina to accept an endorsement from Strom Thurmond. The day before, Thurmond had announced his support for Goldwater on live television. Solemn and stone-faced, Thurmond declared that the Democratic Party had "abandoned the people" and "repudiated the Constitution of the United States." As Thurmond lamented the Democratic devolution from "the party of our fathers" to "the party of minority groups," the camera angle shifted upward to reveal the giant photo of Barry Goldwater hanging behind the podium. As he sang Goldwater's praises, the "D" in Thurmond's television tagline suddenly changed to an "R." The senator had not only endorsed Goldwater, he had switched parties.[58]

A well-planned stunt, Thurmond's defection punctuated segregationists' gradual estrangement from the Democratic Party. In a state where not a single Republican served in the state legislature, Thurmond's party switch rocked southern politics. Yet, as the state's Republican Party leader remarked, the senator "was just following his people"—those same southern conservatives who had debated their uncertain political future for the better part of three decades. In a fitting climax to years of political experimentation, South Carolina and its Deep South neighbors rallied behind Goldwater. For those who still questioned the demise of the South's white democracy, Thurmond offered a blunt epitaph. "The party of our fathers," he declared, "is dead."[59]

From the vantage point of 1964, it was much easier to eulogize what had supposedly died than to predict what would rise in its place. But the predictions poured forth nonetheless. The Democratic Party's betrayal of its segregationist wing, coupled with the Republican Party's overtures toward it, fueled forecasts of a race-driven realignment. Even as white democracy breathed its last breaths, contemporary observers pondered its reincarnation across the aisle. Reporting from a Republican National Committee meeting, political columnists Rowland Evans and Robert Novak encountered party insiders anxious to reap the "rich political dividends flowing from the Negrophobia of many white Americans." A surprisingly large contingent of GOP leaders, the nationally syndicated duo claimed, "want to unmistakably establish the Party of Lincoln as the white man's party."[60]

Evans and Novak saw signs of this transformation everywhere. Prominent Republican committeemen deemed African Americans "inextricably linked to the Democratic Party" and dismissed black voter outreach as "political rainbow-chasing." Predicting that "the spread of Negro demonstrations to the North" would broaden white backlash to "suburbanite" and blue-collar Americans, party insiders urged an anti–civil rights platform grounded in "established Republican principles of law-and-order, states' rights, and limited government." Southern racial conservatives had broadened their critique of liberalism beyond "segregation," and right-wing Republicans wanted to meet them halfway. "This strategy," Evans and Novak concluded, "is tailor-made for Sen. Barry Goldwater, no segregationist but the most popular politician in the South today."[61]

Some attendees lamented the rightward, and supposedly southward, drift of GOP politics. "I'm very much afraid," a National Committee member muttered, "that we're on the road to becoming the white supremacy party, and there's no turning back." When dissenters urged the committee not to write off the black vote, a proponent shot back, "This isn't South Africa. The whites outnumber the Negroes 9 to 1." Yet even many staunch conservatives doubted the wisdom of the "lily-white" strategy. Rowland and Novak agreed. With "segregation doomed," they predicted, more African Americans would enter the middle class and gravitate toward the Republican Party's economic policies. By alienating these potential voters with a thinly veiled racial ploy, the GOP's right wing was "sacrificing the future for a highly speculative present."[62]

In the short term, the trade did not pay off. Goldwater won a swath of Deep South states—Louisiana, Mississippi, Alabama, Georgia, and South Carolina—that had last voted Republican during Reconstruction. Save his home state of Arizona, the senator won no more, and he suffered the worst thrashing in presidential election history. The 1964 elections dramatized the volatility of southern politics in the civil rights era, but they did not signal a permanent, race-based party realignment. Indeed, "lily-white" Republicanism peaked even as the party's national viability ebbed. Like segregationists' dreams of southern white unity, the notion of a nationally unified white majority had its limits.

EPILOGUE A SEGREGATIONIST "SENSE OF HISTORY"

Compared to the battle over the previous year's Civil Rights Act, the congressional clash over the Voting Rights Act of 1965 was relatively tame. The real drama had already occurred in Selma, seat of an Alabama Black Belt county where less than 2 percent of the black majority had successfully registered to vote prior to the bill's passage. In some neighboring counties, no African Americans had voted since Reconstruction. The nationally televised confrontation at the Edmund Pettus Bridge, where Alabama troopers turned back civil rights marchers with clubs and tear gas, pressured Lyndon Johnson to demand passage of a new voting rights bill. The defeat of the 1964 filibuster marked a political watershed for civil rights allies and opponents alike. A year later, President Johnson's invocation of the civil rights anthem "We Shall Overcome" in his voting rights appeal, Selma's segregationist mayor remembered, "was just like you'd stuck a dagger in your heart."[1]

Despite segregationists' attempts to transform their forebears' crusade for white supremacy into a dignified defense of racial separation, the Voting Rights Act hammered home the inseparability of political equality and social inclusion. While most segregationists distinguished their commitment to the color line from enthusiasm for political repression, their fear of black ballots persisted. Months before the showdown in Selma, segregationists attempted to preempt and dilute federal voting protections. In Georgia, where white Democrats had used the specter of the "Negro bloc vote" to mobilize white opposition for two decades, the legislature passed a 1964 bill that required candidates to win primary elections by a majority vote. Reeling from the elimination of the county-unit system and an upsurge in black voter registration, Georgia conservatives hoped the majority-vote measure would dilute "bloc" power. If an African American candidate received a plurality of votes in a crowded primary field, white voters would have the opportunity to rally behind the remaining white opponent in the mandatory run-off.[2]

The bill's racial intent was dramatized by influential backers such as Denmark Groover, a seasoned legislator who had shepherded massive resistance bills through the Georgia House of Representatives in the mid-1950s. After Groover had rallied legislators behind an interposition resolution and a bill that added the Stars and Bars to the Georgia state flag, black voters in his district backed a white moderate challenger to help vote him out of office. When Groover roared back into office in the early 1960s, the self-described "segregationist" and "reactionary" backed the majority-vote rule and other measures that diluted black political power. Across the South, racial conservatives backed similar measures that redrew legislative district boundaries and manipulated voting laws to their advantage.[3]

While Democrat-dominated state legislatures attempted to preserve some semblance of white democracy, some southern Republicans sympathized with their struggle. In the midst of the battle over the 1965 Voting Rights Act, Mississippi Republican Party head Wirt Yerger denounced the pending bill for "crucifying certain states" by enfranchising "ignorant, illiterate persons." Making no apologies for race-driven party realignment, the veteran GOP organizer forfeited his chance to head the national organization of state party chairmen. Despite his yeoman's work building a viable Republican Party in the most solidly Democratic southern state, Yerger's lip service to the racial status quo hampered his national clout.[4]

Other critics of voting rights followed a different trajectory. Jim Lucier, a Detroit native and English Ph.D. who had moved to Richmond to work for segregationist editor James J. Kilpatrick, blasted the Voting Rights Act in the anticommunist John Birch Society's *American Opinion*. "The vote," Lucier warned, "is being pushed into Negro hands which, in some areas, have every reason from ignorance to avarice to destroy the Republic." Arguing that "American ideals" did not include "the notion of racial or social equality," Lucier declared, "the best system is *undemocratic* voting." Constitutional amendments that enfranchised former slaves and prohibited poll taxes in federal elections, Lucier continued, "run counter to the spirit of the body of the document and to the Bill of Rights." Lucier's anti–civil rights editorials caught the attention of conservative journalist and political operative Jesse Helms, who praised Lucier's "sense of history" as "nothing short of remarkable." When Helms headed to Washington in 1973 for his first Senate term, North Carolina's first Republican senator since Reconstruction lured Lucier away from Strom Thurmond's legislative staff.[5]

Lucier's take on history, embraced by unreconstructed Democrats and Republican converts alike, outlasted the legislative climax of the modern civil rights movement. The segregationist movement that emerged from three decades of civil rights struggles failed to unify and focus southern whites behind diehard opposition. Instead, racial change disrupted and fractured a regional political economy long dependent on domination by one race and its party of choice. Race continued to animate southern politics, but its impact was far from predictable. Goldwater's striking success in the Deep South in 1964 could not obscure his burial in a national land-slide, nor could it guarantee Republican success the next time around. Alabama governor George Wallace's foray into the 1964 Democratic primaries revealed that racial tensions transcended regional boundaries as well as party lines. Impressive showings in Wisconsin and Indiana convinced Wallace that America was ready for his blend of reactionary populism and cultural conservatism.[6] His 1968 third-party campaign also revealed the lingering distrust that many Deep South diehards harbored toward both national parties. Four out of Goldwater's five Deep South states shunned the Republicans for the segregationist icon. Only in South Carolina did Richard Nixon edge out Wallace, thanks in no small part to Republican convert Strom Thurmond.[7]

The South Carolina senator notwithstanding, the Republican Party embraced disenchanted segregationist Democrats with more ambivalence than chroniclers of the South's "Goldwater syndrome" had previously predicted. The GOP, like the party many segregationist Democrats fled, suffered its own identity crisis. Goldwater secured the 1964 presidential nomination only after a fierce primary challenge from New York governor Nelson Rockefeller, standard-bearer of the Republican Party's moderate eastern establishment. After Johnson defeated Goldwater, emboldened racial conservatives fought for control of their new party in internal struggles over fair housing, affirmative action, and welfare policy. As they argued over civil rights, Republicans echoed the earlier battles that had divided their adversaries across the aisle. Indeed, a resurgence of moderate clout in the wake of Goldwater's defeat led columnists Evans and Novak to declare "white men only" Republicanism as doomed as the white democracy that preceded it. Just two years after warning that a segregationist GOP was on the rise, the duo declared, "white backlash politics is dead, replaced by growing competition for the Negro vote." Even Yerger's successor in Mississippi, Clark Reed, echoed the sentiment. "The race issue is dead," the state party chairman announced. "The GOP won't rely on demagoguery to win elections."[8]

Yet, as southern Republicans courted disaffected Democrats, they inherited the tensions that segregationists had confronted for years. In previous decades, genteel southern statesmen had distanced themselves from racist demagogues in Democratic primaries. Now GOP moderates faced their own challenge from conservatives who capitalized on racial tensions in the South and beyond. The civil rights legislation of the mid-1960s signaled the end of the southern bloc's ability to dictate the pace of social change, but conflicts over race and rights continued. If warnings of a new

"white man's party" proved premature, so too did rosy predictions that up-
wardly mobile African Americans would gravitate to a colorblind politics of
class privilege. Recent histories of the suburban Sunbelt have amply demonstrated that the economic conservatism that fueled the rise of southern Republicanism was anything but race neutral. If the neighborhood
activists of the Sunbelt suburbs bore little resemblance to planter elites
and reactionary industrialists, they inherited a language of individualism
and privilege that white democracy's defenders had deployed in earlier
decades. That the suburban Sunbelt eclipsed the Black Belt in power and
prestige had as much to do with the South's changing political economy
as with any radical departure in racial attitudes.[9]

The idea that Deep South segregationists could graft their racial worldview onto the nation was as problematic as it was ambitious. But it was not
entirely delusional. The defenders of white democracy realized that most
Americans could not appreciate what it was like to live amid a large black
minority or, in parts of the South, an overwhelming majority. Thus they
attempted to repackage that feeling of impending powerlessness for a national audience with a persuasive narrative of political dispossession. The
reactionary populism perfected by George Wallace at campaign stops from
Mississippi to Madison Square Garden lacked the crude Negrophobia of a
Eugene Talmadge stump speech. Yet Talmadge's vilification of distant bureaucracies and subversive minorities echoed years later. Like the demagogues of the New Deal era, the Dixiecrats made more noise than history.
Yet their warnings that racial reform carried with it "the deadly virus of
statism" reemerged in right-wing ambivalence toward federal civil rights
legislation. Finally, and perhaps most pervasively, Strom Thurmond's
promise that the pursuit of prosperity could proceed unhampered by social reform resonated in Black Belt and Sunbelt alike.

From the New Deal to the legislative climax of the civil rights movement, segregation's defenders accepted and attempted to transcend the
fatal limitations of their forebears' brand of racial politics. At the same
time, they perceived fundamental continuities between their worldview
and that of the burgeoning national conservative movement. Combined,
these discoveries encouraged unrealistic expectations of regional unity
and national power even as they brought Deep South segregationists into
new alliances. The long road to the civil rights legislation of 1964 and
1965 destroyed whatever rationale remained for a Solid South, but it also
marked the high-water mark of a political coalition that had briefly overwhelmed defiant southern Democrats. In its wake, segregationist predictions of a national white backlash materialized, and northern lawmakers

backed off their commitment to civil rights even as battles over segregation and inequality raged in their own backyards. As many of the Deep South's former detractors backpedaled on civil rights, the recently routed segregationists discovered that their hostility to racial liberalism had new-found resonance.[10]

If the civil rights movement forced segregationists to adjust, it also forced them to stand firm. Their constitutional rhetoric and tactical gymnastics from the New Deal to the 1960s marked neither a strategic departure nor an attempt to recast an obstructionist agenda as a high-minded crusade. Segregationists never perceived their racial principles as incompatible with their patriotic commitments, and the civil rights movement changed few minds. Rather, the end of the Jim Crow era rendered *segregation*, like *white supremacy* before it, a doomed battle cry. But it was not a dead proposition.

NOTES

Abbreviations

ADAH	Alabama Department of Archives and History, Montgomery
CIC	Commission on Interracial Cooperation Papers, Southern Historical Collection, Louis Round Wilson Library, University of North Carolina, Chapel Hill (microfilm edition)
CUSC	Special Collections, Clemson University, Clemson, South Carolina
DUSC	Rare Books, Manuscripts, and Special Collections Library, Duke University, Durham, North Carolina
HET	Herman E. Talmadge Papers, Richard B. Russell Library for Political Research and Studies, University of Georgia, Athens
JCS	John C. Stennis Collection, Congressional and Political Research Center, Mississippi State University, Starkville
JTG	John Temple Graves Papers, Birmingham Public Library, Birmingham, Alabama
MDAH	Mississippi Department of Archives and History, Jackson
MSUSC	Special Collections, Mitchell Memorial Library, Mississippi State University, Starkville
NAACPP	Papers of the National Association for the Advancement of Colored People, Library of Congress, Washington, D.C. (microfilm edition)
NARA	National Archives and Records Administration, College Park, Maryland
RBR	Richard B. Russell Papers, Richard B. Russell Library for Political Research and Studies, University of Georgia, Athens
SCDAH	South Carolina Department of Archives and History, Columbia
SCL	South Caroliniana Library, University of South Carolina, Columbia
SCPC	South Carolina Political Collections, University of South Carolina, Columbia
SHC	Southern Historical Collection, Louis Round Wilson Library, University of North Carolina, Chapel Hill
SSIC	Southern States Industrial Council Records, Tennessee State Library and Archives, Nashville
TGB	Theodore G. Bilbo Papers, Special Collections, McCain Library, University of Southern Mississippi, Hattiesburg
WMC	William M. Colmer Papers, Special Collections, McCain Library, University of Southern Mississippi, Hattiesburg
WSP	Walter Sillers Papers, Charles W. Capps Archives and Museum, Delta State University, Cleveland, Mississippi

Introduction

1. Armbrester, "John Temple Graves," 203–13.

2. Graves, "The Southern Negro," 500, 501, 505.

3. Josephus Daniels to John Temple Graves, 21 December 1942, Box 1, Folder 5, JTG. The Wilmington race riot was the most infamous event in a white supremacy campaign orchestrated by the Democratic Party in order to overthrow a biracial fusion government of black Republicans and white Populists. For more on the Wilmington race riot and the white supremacy campaign in North Carolina, see Cecelski and Tyson, *Democracy Betrayed*; and Gilmore, *Gender and Jim Crow*. For a broader overview of the white supremacy campaign across the region, see Williamson, *The Crucible of Race* or the abridged version, *A Rage for Order*; and Kantrowitz, *Ben Tillman*.

4. Walter Sillers to James O. Eastland, 5 February 1943, Box 98, Folder 2, WSP.

5. In delineating the "long civil rights movement," historian Jacquelyn Dowd Hall acknowledges that a "wall of resistance" to racial change "arose in tandem with the civil rights offensive in the aftermath of World War II." While she refutes the "backlash" narrative of white opposition, she fails to situate the origins of its opposition in the New Deal era and wartime years even as she locates the origins of the "long civil rights movement" in "the liberal and radical milieu of the late 1930s." See Hall, "The Long Civil Rights Movement," 1235.

6. Collins, *Whither Solid South?*, vii, 246, 151.

7. W. W. Ball to Fitz Hugh McMaster, 27 June 1936, Box 26, William Watts Ball Papers, DUSC.

8. Brinkley Morton to Theodore G. Bilbo, 19 November 1942, Box 1076, Folder 1, TGB.

9. In his study of the federal government's role in southern economic development since the New Deal, Bruce Schulman has argued that the rise of the new "Whig" politicians ultimately had a moderating effect on southern race relations after 1960. Yet he notes that the "conservative, business-oriented politics" of the Whigs facilitated economic growth by discouraging interracial conflict rather than pushing for racial reform. See Schulman, *From Cotton Belt to Sunbelt*, 132, 211. Jennifer Brooks has argued that World War II veterans in Georgia rallied behind a conservative vision of progress that privileged economic modernization and "good government" at the expense of racial justice. See Brooks, *Defining the Peace*. Matthew Lassiter has also noted southern moderates' "consistent subordination of racial equality to the priority of economic growth." See Lassiter, *The Silent Majority*, 28.

10. David L. Chappell has emphasized the "fatal" divisions within the segregationist movement of the 1950s, but he does not trace them back further than the battle over school desegregation. See Chappell, "Divided Mind of Southern Segregationists," 46.

11. Earl and Merle Black have identified the defeat of the southern filibuster and subsequent passage of the 1964 Civil Rights Act as "the turning point" in southern party politics. At the same time, they demonstrate that Southern Republican

realignment was a gradual and uneven process that did not culminate until the Reagan era. Earl Black and Merle Black, *The Rise of Southern Republicans*, 74.

12. In a recent collection of essays on southern politics in the Jim Crow era, historians Jane Dailey, Glenda Gilmore, and Bryant Simon stress the "balancing act" of white supremacy: "Black resistance, not white supremacy, was continuous, while white supremacy remodeled itself to meet any challenge." Dailey, Gilmore, and Simon, *Jumpin' Jim Crow*, 4–5. For groundbreaking work on southern black resistance during the Jim Crow era, see Kelley, "We Are Not What We Seem." J. Douglas Smith has argued that the race question was never "settled" in twentieth-century Virginia but was maintained on a "daily basis." See J. Douglas Smith, *Managing White Supremacy*, 17. Several scholars have shown how black and white southerners seized opportunities to challenge Jim Crow throughout the interwar years. See Egerton, *Speak Now Against the Day*; Sullivan, *Days of Hope*; and Gilmore, *Defying Dixie*.

13. In his study of southern race relations since emancipation, Joel Williamson contends that the rise of a "Radical mentality" at the turn of the century profoundly influenced the emergence of a segregated social order. Claiming that emancipation had robbed blacks of the civilizing influence of their masters and set them on a downward spiral into savagery, white Radicals urged violent repression of African Americans in all facets of life. Profoundly pessimistic in their appraisal of black potential, Radicals fanned the flames of racial fear and helped to shape the institutional structures of segregation and disfranchisement from the late 1880s to the 1910s. Their influence then faded as racial "conservatism" imposed a "New Orthodoxy" in race relations. From World War I until the civil rights movement, Williamson argued, the white South "drifted into a racial dream world" in which segregation affirmed an organic social order rather than a white supremacist regime. See Williamson, *The Crucible of Race*, 5–7, 479.

14. This study builds on other recent work that takes seriously Charles Eagles's critique of the "asymmetrical approach" to the civil rights movement that neglects the segregationist opposition. See Eagles, "Toward New Histories," 815–16.

15. Keith M. Finley's recent study of southern senators and civil rights roughly parallels the periodization of this study but differs significantly in scope and argument. Concerned primarily with legislative tactics and rhetoric within the walls of the Senate, Finley pays little attention to segregationist resistance on the state and local level. Examining the development of the southern Senate bloc's strategy of "strategic delay," Finley's top-down approach reveals less about a broader resistance movement that rejected southern senators' resignation to the inevitable downfall of Jim Crow even as it embraced many of their justifications for its continuance. See Finley, *Delaying the Dream*.

16. In his study of South Carolina mill workers, Bryant Simon argues that the 1940s marked a turning point in state politics. "During the war," Simon states, "the focus of South Carolina politics . . . shifted away from class concerns toward issues of race and the defense of white supremacy." See Simon, *Fabric of Defeat*, 220. Glenn Feldman has also paid considerable attention to the development of white oppo-

sition to civil rights in 1940s Alabama and its relationship to political realignment and the rise of southern conservatism. See Feldman, "Race, Sex, Class" and "Southern Disillusionment."

17. In his pioneering study of southern racial politics during the 1950s, Numan Bartley connects the "neobourbon" protest politics of the black-belt Dixiecrats to the rise of massive resistance less than a decade later. See Bartley, *The Rise of Massive Resistance*, 28–46. Robert Garson's pioneering study of southern disillusionment with the Democratic Party during the 1940s ends with a brief yet important analysis of the Dixiecrat movement as a precedent for segregationist resistance and southern political realignment. See Garson, *Politics of Sectionalism*. Building on Garson's precedent, Kari Frederickson has rooted the Dixiecrat movement in the convulsions of the New Deal era and connected it to racial politics and political realignment in the 1950s and 1960s. See Frederickson, *Dixiecrat Revolt*.

18. Joseph Lowndes has located a southern precedent for modern conservatism in the writings of the Dixiecrats' chief strategist, Charles Wallace Collins. See Lowndes, *From the New Deal*, 11–44.

19. Scholars of the southern Left have offered important insights on the extent and nature of conservative opposition during the New Deal era, even if it is not their primary focus. See Egerton, *Speak Now Against the Day*; Sullivan, *Days of Hope*; and Gilmore, *Defying Dixie*. Much of the literature that emphasizes the lost opportunities of the pre-*Brown* era analyzes the role of organized labor in promoting more progressive racial politics. See Korstad and Lichtenstein, "Opportunities Found and Lost"; Korstad, *Civil Rights Unionism*.

20. As Kevin Kruse notes in his recent study of whites in postwar Atlanta, "Southern whites fundamentally understood their support of segregation as a defense of their own liberties, rather than a denial of others." See Kruse, *White Flight*, 9. For other recent studies of white southerners in the civil rights era, see Crespino, *In Search of Another Country*; Lassiter, *The Silent Majority*; and Sokol, *There Goes My Everything*.

21. In his study of white Mississippians' response to the civil rights movement of the 1950s and 1960s, Joseph Crespino has described a process of "strategic accommodation" in which white elites disavowed racial violence and conceded to basic black demands even as they worked to maintain political power and economic privilege. While Crespino provides a compelling explanation for the reemergence of white Mississippians as players in national conservative politics, he does not trace this process of reinterpreting and refining white supremacy back to its roots in the civil rights struggles before 1954. See Crespino, *In Search of Another Country*, 4.

22. Recent work on the origins of modern conservatism has emphasized the primacy of grassroots activism in shaping the American Right. For a study that pioneered this "bottom-up" approach, see McGirr, *Suburban Warriors*. Recent studies of white opposition in the civil rights era have emphasized the role of grassroots activists in the metropolitan South. See Kruse, *White Flight*; and Lassiter, *Silent Majority*.

23. In his recent study of southern conservatism, Joseph Lowndes rejects the backlash account of white resistance and its relationship to the rise of modern conservatism. Instead, Lowndes argues, "the Right that developed is better viewed as contingent, mobile, and highly adaptive, constantly responding to changing conditions on the ground." See Lowndes, *From the New Deal*, 5.

24. Johnston, *Mississippi's Defiant Years*, xiv.

25. Bartley, *The Rise of Massive Resistance*, 46. While each of these states has a robust historiography, the "long" history of white opposition to civil rights has not been addressed in a single volume.

Chapter 1

1. Herman D. Hancock, "200,000 View Colorful Parade for Nominee," *Atlanta Constitution*, 25 October 1932, 1.

2. Leuchtenburg, *The White House Looks South*, 30, 33.

3. "Roosevelt, at Atlanta, Hits 'Despair Doctrines,'" *Washington Post*, 25 October 1932, 1.

4. Fite, *Senator from Georgia*, 60–61.

5. "Roosevelt Cotton Is Sold For $1.75 Pound at Auction," *Atlanta Constitution*, 25 October 1932, 22.

6. Quoted in Leuchtenburg, *The White House Looks South*, 39.

7. Quoted in Schulman, *From Cotton Belt to Sunbelt*, 24.

8. Ibid., 22; Quoted in Tindall, *Emergence of the New South*, 71, 444.

9. Alan Brinkley has identified the southern populist tradition as the "dominant insurgent force in the depression South . . . one that could produce both radical and reactionary demands." This force "looked with equal hostility at the conservative aristocrats who dominated Southern politics and the social democratic liberals who were building a powerful and intrusive new federal bureaucracy." See Alan Brinkley, "New Deal and Southern Politics," 111.

10. Talmadge won all but three of Georgia's 159 counties and racked up over twice as many votes as his nearest rival. William Anderson, *Wild Man from Sugar Creek*, 109.

11. Quoted in Schlesinger, *The Politics of Upheaval*, 521.

12. Julian Harris, "Talmadge Attack Shocks Georgia," *New York Times*, 21 April 1935, 6E; "Calls President a Radical," ibid., 19 April 1935, 9.

13. Anderson, *Wild Man from Sugar Creek*, 137.

14. Quoted in Schlesinger, *The Politics of Upheaval*, 522; Anderson, *Wild Man from Sugar Creek*, 139; Manis, *Macon Black and White*, 118–19.

15. "Is the Junior Senator from Georgia a Rubber Stamp or Ain't He?," *Georgia Woman's World*, 14 August 1936, 1; "Should We Vote for Dick Russell, Jr. for the U.S. Senate?," ibid., 5 September 1936, 1.

16. Mrs. J. E. Andrews to Jessie Daniel Ames, n.d. [1932], reel 2, CIC; Leuchtenburg, *The FDR Years*, 122. The Women's National Association for the Preservation of the White Race was founded in 1931 in Florida, but its center of operation soon shifted to Atlanta. Members regularly contributed articles and editorials to the

Georgia Woman's World. See Executive Committee, "First Message from Our President," (Atlanta, n.d.), reel 2, CIC. For more information on the efforts of white southern women to curb lynching, see Hall, *Revolt Against Chivalry*.

17. Mrs. J. E. Andrews, "To Parents of College Students," *Georgia Woman's World*, 17 May 1938, 3. For an eyewitness account from an African American participant in the conference, see "President Willis J. King, Mediator," *Atlanta Foundation* 28 (April 1938): 4.

18. Eugene Talmadge to Richard B. Russell, 5 December 1935; n.t., n.d. (attached to Eugene Talmadge to Richard B. Russell, 5 December 1935), both in Series IV, Subseries B, Box 19, Folder 15, RBR.

19. Richard B. Russell to Eugene Talmadge, 9 December 1935, Series IV, Subseries B, Box 19, Folder 15, RBR.

20. Wilkerson-Freeman, "Creation of a Subversive Feminist Dominion," 144.

21. Richard B. Russell to Allen Reid, 4 February 1936; Richard B. Russell to Eugene Talmadge, 9 December 1935; Richard B. Russell to A. N. Brittain, 17 January 1936; all in Series IV, Subseries B, Box 19, Folder 15, RBR.

22. Gay B. Shepperson to Richard B. Russell, 1 July 1936, Series IV, Subseries B, Box 19, Folder 14, RBR; "Is the Junior Senator from Georgia a Rubber Stamp or Ain't He?," *Georgia Woman's World*, 14 August 1936, 1; "Should We Vote for Dick Russell, Jr. for the U.S. Senate?," ibid., 5 September 1936, 2.

23. Ralph McGill, "Senator Russell Lashes Talmadge," *Atlanta Constitution*, 9 August 1936, 10A; "The Negro Question," pp. 6–7, Winder Office Files, Series VI, Subseries E, Box 50, Folder 10, RBR. Howard N. Mead argues that the lack of public comment by Russell on the race issue suggested that the senator saw no need to address his own commitment to white supremacy, stating "Russell thus refused to concern himself to any extent with the race question in this campaign, and it must be assumed that the people of Georgia, by giving him their votes in such large numbers, also expressed the opinion that white supremacy was not the major question in their minds." While Russell usually avoided public comment on the race issue, he made preparations to counter Talmadge's race baiting with a defense of his own opposition to black advancement. See Mead, "Russell vs. Talmadge," 41.

24. "The Negro Question," p. 6, Winder Office Files, Series VI, Subseries E, Box 50, Folder 10, RBR.

25. Michie and Ryhlick, *Dixie Demagogues*, 266. Smith retells the story of the Philadelphia convention, including his oft-quoted denunciation of the "black, kinky-headed, blue-gummed, slew-footed Senegambian" who opened the 1936 Democratic Convention in prayer, in a 1938 campaign speech in Columbia, South Carolina. See Elison "Cotton Ed" Smith, campaign speech recording, Columbia, S.C., 26 August 1938, Box 44, Workman Papers, SCPC.

26. Quoted in Winfred B. Moore Jr., "The 'Unrewarding Stone,'" 13.

27. Ibid., 13–14; Mead, "Russell vs. Talmadge," 37.

28. W. W. Ball to "Mother," 8 June 1936; W. W. Ball to Fitz Hugh McMaster, 27 June 1936; both in Ball Papers, DUSC.

29. Turner Catledge, "Southern Bolters Block Plan of Ely to Support Landon,"

New York Times, 8 August 1936, 1; Virginius Dabney, "Democratic Doubt Vanishes in South," ibid., 30 August 1936, E6.

30. Quoted in Michie and Ryhlick, *Dixie Demagogues*, 267.

31. John Temple Graves, "South Discusses A Two-Party Plan," *New York Times*, 8 November 1936, E10.

32. Sitkoff, *A New Deal for Blacks*, 88; Freidel, *F.D.R. and the South*, 90–91; Frederickson, *Dixiecrat Revolt*, 24. While historians have noted that the dramatic political realignment of the 1930s reflected the economic appeal of the New Deal more than any firm commitment to civil rights within the Democratic Party, their focus on substance has obscured the importance of southern white perceptions of racial reform. In her study of African American political realignment, Nancy Weiss argues, "The race issue never became part of the New Deal." See Weiss, *Farewell to the Party of Lincoln*, xvi. Glenda Gilmore modifies this appraisal by rooting African American realignment in a longer process of black disillusionment with the GOP. See Gilmore, "False Friends and Avowed Enemies." Patricia Sullivan and Kevin J. McMahon have challenged the Weiss appraisal by arguing that the New Deal did signal significant political changes for the black freedom struggle. See Sullivan, *Days of Hope*; and McMahon, *Reconsidering Roosevelt on Race*. In *A New Deal for Blacks*, Sitkoff has drawn the clearest link between New Deal race politics and southern white reaction.

33. Janken, *Walter White*, 199–232. For a thorough study of the antilynching efforts of African American civil rights activists, see Zangrando, *The NAACP Crusade Against Lynching*. For the role of southern women in the fight against lynching, see Hall, *Revolt Against Chivalry*, 223–53. In a 1937 Gallup Poll, 53 percent of southerners supported federal antilynching legislation. See Tindall, *Emergence of the New South*, 552.

34. In his examination of antilynching legislation during the interwar period. George C. Rable concludes that even as southern white politicians easily blocked federal antilynching bills, they "refused to take seriously the growing black restlessness and were caught by surprise during the civil rights upheavals of the 1950s and 1960s." See Rable, "Politics of Antilynching Legislation," 201–20. However, the antilynching campaigns of the late 1930s forced southern white elites to anticipate and address the potential racial struggles that lay ahead.

35. Thompson, *Lynchings in Mississippi*, 98; "The Anti-Lynching Bill," *Jackson (Miss.) Daily News*, 11 April 1937, 6.

36. "Dual Lynching Condemned by Nation," *Winona (Miss.) Times*, 16 April 1937, 1, 4.

37. Dubay, "Mississippi and Proposed Federal Anti-Lynching Bills," 82. For the connection between the Duck Hill lynching and the looming showdown over federal antilynching legislation in Washington, see Finley, *Delaying the Dream*, 15–23.

38. "The Duck Hill Lynching," *Greenwood (Miss.) Commonwealth*, 14 April 1937, 4; "Lynching," *Biloxi Daily Herald*, 16 April 1937, 4.

39. Quoted in Tindall, *Emergence of the New South*, 552.

40. *Congressional Record*, 75th Cong., 3rd sess., 310, 305.

41. Quoted in Egerton, *Speak Now Against the Day*, 117.

42. *Congressional Record*, 75th Cong., 3rd sess., 310.

43. Manis, *Macon Black and White*, 118; *Congressional Record*, 75th Cong., 3 sess., 1102, 1098–103.

44. Bettie B. Kansler to Theodore G. Bilbo, 21 January 1938, Box 1053, Folder 13, TGB.

45. Quoted in Sitkoff, *A New Deal for Blacks*, 110.

46. "Southern States Industrial Council - Dinner Session Minutes," Washington D.C., 2 May 1938, 8, Box 1, Folder 4, SSIC. On the origins of the Conservative Manifesto and Bailey's role in drafting it, see Patterson, *Congressional Conservatism*, 198–210; and Abrams, *Conservative Constraints*.

47. Schulman, *From Cotton Belt to Sunbelt*, 15; Kennedy, *Freedom from Fear*, 346.

48. Franklin Delano Roosevelt, "The United States Is Rising and Is Rebuilding on Sounder Lines," 168; "Fireside Chat on Party Primaries," 395; both in Rosenman, *Public Papers of FDR*, vol. 7.

49. Quoted in Kennedy, *Freedom from Fear*, 347; Egerton, *Speak Now Against the Day*, 119.

50. William Anderson, *Wild Man from Sugar Creek*, 170; Michie and Ryhlick, *Dixie Demagogues*, 197; "Georgia's George Relies on Prejudice to Save His Seat," *New York Amsterdam News*, 27 August 1938, A3; Bunche, *Political Status of the Negro*, 206. James C. Cobb has argued that FDR ruined Talmadge's chances in the 1938 primary by robbing the former governor of the opportunity to paint Senator George as a New Dealer. Talmadge "might have been elected" without Roosevelt's intervention, Cobb argues, but "a Talmadge unable to bait New Dealers was hardly a Talmadge at all." Cobb's analysis of the primary suggests that New Deal liberalism was less a threat to Senator George than the reactionary racism of Talmadge. See Cobb, "Not Gone, But Forgotten," 197–209.

51. "Race Is Issue of Primaries in the South," *Chicago Defender*, 3 September 1938, 4; "Midnight in Columbia," *Time*, 12 September 1938, 26; Robertson, *Sly and Able*, 277. Smith's opponent, Olin Johnston, campaigned on a prolabor platform and a pledge of "100 percent" loyalty to the New Deal. Bryant Simon argues that the 1938 election signaled the death of working-class "liberalism" among white textile workers, who increasingly embraced reactionary race politics as the wartime civil rights movement gained momentum. See Simon, "Race Reactions," 239–59.

52. Roosevelt, "The United States Is Rising and Is Rebuilding on Sounder Lines," in Rosenman, *Public Papers of FDR*, 7:168. For a discussion of the white supremacy campaigns that codified political exclusion and legalized segregation in the South during the 1890s, see Kantrowitz, *Ben Tillman*, 198–242; and Cecelski and Tyson, *Democracy Betrayed*. For a discussion of the connection between white terrorism, disfranchisement, and segregation, see Williamson, *The Crucible of Race*, 111–258.

53. Turner Catledge, "'White Supremacy' Issue Revived in the South," *New York Times*, 28 August 1938, E7.

54. Theodore G. Bilbo to Mrs. L. W. Alford, 6 March 1939, Box 1057, Folder 15, TGB; *Congressional Record*, 75th Cong., 3rd sess., 882.

55. *Congressional Record*, 75th Cong., 3rd sess., 882; "Virginia Wants U.S. to Send Negroes Back 'Home,'" *Newsweek*, 14 March 1936, 13.

56. Fitzgerald, "'We Have Found a Moses,'" 309, 311–14.

57. Thomas Dixon, *The Flaming Sword*, xiii; Thomas Dixon to Edward Y. Clarke, 11 August 1938, Dixon Papers, DUSC.

58. Thomas Dixon, *The Flaming Sword*, xi, 83, 453.

59. K. W., "A Novel of Conflict," *New York Times Book Review*, 20 August 1939, BR10; "'Birth of a Nation' Will Have Sequel," *Raleigh News and Observer*, 22 October 1937, 8; Frank Smethurst, "Americans in Black, White, and Red," *Raleigh News and Observer*, 6 August 1939, M4; Monarch Publishing Company, "The Flaming Sword," n.d.," Dixon Papers; George Conrad, review of *The Flaming Sword* by Thomas Dixon, *New York Herald Tribune Books*, 17 September 1939, 12. In his recent introduction to the latest edition of *The Flaming Sword*, historian John David Smith emphasizes the negative and dismissive reaction to the novel and deems it an "utter failure" because most Americans ignored Dixon's "sick fantasies" of Communist takeovers and race war. At the same time, the attempts of southern conservatives and militant white supremacists to lend credence to Dixon's "final warnings" point to concerted resistance to racial reform in the prewar South. See John David Smith, "Introduction," xxv.

60. "In Issue," *Georgia Women's World*, 15 September 1937, 2; "Uncle Ralph Observe," *Hapeville (Ga.) Statesman*, 17 June 1941, 4. The Molotov-Ribbentrop Pact, historian Glenda Gilmore has noted, was a boon to southern opponents of civil rights. For the next two years, Hitler and Stalin would be allies, undercutting the claim of civil rights activists that their collaboration with leftists was part of the Popular Front struggle against right-wing totalitarianism. "The comparison of Jim Crow and Fascism," Gilmore notes, "had been the most powerful single weapon in the southern Left's arsenal." See Gilmore, *Defying Dixie*, 301. Like Gilmore, John T. Kneebone notes that the conflation of "isms" was not confined to the Talmadge camp. See Kneebone, *Southern Liberal Journalists*, 180.

61. Dies, *The Trojan Horse in America*, 118–29.

62. Norrell, "Labor at the Ballot Box," 217; Constitutional Educational League, *The Fifth Column in the South*, 5, 8.

63. Constitutional Educational League, *The Fifth Column in the South*, 34; "Uncle Ralph Observe," *Hapeville (Ga.) Statesman*, 17 June 1941, 4.

64. "Board of Regents Vote 8 to 7 to Re-elect Cocking," *Hapeville (Ga.) Statesman*, 17 June 1941, 1; Ralph McGill, "It Has Happened Here," *Survey Graphic* 30 (September 1941): 449. For other accounts of the university purge controversy, see Gilmore, *Defying Dixie*, 351–53; and Bailes, "Board of Regents Controversy."

65. "Lynching in Georgia," *Time*, 28 July 1941, 37.

66. Ibid.; "Lynching at the Capital," *Survey Midmonthly* 77 (August 1941): 240; "State Board of Education Purges Radical School Texts," *Hapeville (Ga.) Statesman*, 16 September 1941, 1.

67. "Control of Georgia South Through 'Outside' Gifts and Awards from Rosenwald and Other Funds," *Hapeville (Ga.) Statesman*, 22 July 1941, 1; "Talmadge, Phooey!," *Time*, 27 October 1941, 64.

68. "Where There's Smoke," *Hapeville (Ga.) Statesman*, 1 July 1941, 2. "Report on Inter-Racial Relations," ibid., October 28, 1941, 2.

69. Henderson, *Politics of Change in Georgia*, 49.

70. Graves, *The Fighting South*, 151.

71. Rutledge, "Negro and the New Deal," 284, 281.

72. Graves, *The Fighting South*, 151.

Chapter 2

1. NAACP, "On Guard Against Racial Discrimination" (February 1942), n.p., Folder 52, Jefferies Papers, SCL. For more on the origins and aims of the wartime civil rights movement, see Dalfiume, "The Forgotten Years"; Sitkoff, "Racial Militancy and Interracial Violence"; Finkle, *Forum for Protest*; Kellogg, "Civil Rights Consciousness in the 1940s"; Wynn, *Afro-American and the Second World War*; and Tyson, "Wars for Democracy." Harvard Sitkoff has qualified his appraisal of the wartime civil rights movement, arguing that black militancy actually waned after the United States entered World War II. See Sitkoff, "African American Militancy in the World War II South: Another Perspective."

2. W. M. Burt to Theodore G. Bilbo, 19 November 1942, Box 1076, Folder 1, TGB.

3. "Roosevelt Orders End," *Chicago Defender*, 28 June 1941, 1. For discussion of the meeting between Randolph and FDR in June 1941, see Garfinkel, *When Negroes March*, 60–62; Jervis Anderson, *A. Philip Randolph*, 257–59; Janken, *Walter White*, 253–57.

4. Gilmore, *Defying Dixie*, 361; "People Are Speaking Out," *South Today* (Winter 1942/1943): 45; Ottley, *New World A-Coming*, 305.

5. O. F. Bledsoe, "Agriculture and the Federal Government," 3, Box 29, Folder 5; Walter Sillers to James O. Eastland, 5 February 1943 and 13 May 1943, Box 98, Folder 2; all in WSP.

6. "Let's Face the Race Question," *Town Meeting*, 17 February 1944, 7.

7. Quoted in Daniel, "Going Among Strangers," 892.

8. Homer A. Legg to Richard B. Russell, 29 April 1942; R. F. Hardy to Russell, 26 June 1942; Russell to Secretary of War, 29 April 1942; John W. Martyn to Russell, 29 June 1942; all in Series X, Box 139, Folder 3, RBR.

9. John W. Martyn to Richard B. Russell, 29 June 1942, Series X, Box 139, Folder 3, RBR; Eugene Talmadge, "There Is a Race Question," *Hapeville (Ga.) Statesman*, 24 June 1943, 2.

10. Mrs. G. W. Arrington to Richard B. Russell, 8 September 1942; Alice Rogers to Russell, 17 August 1942; Giles L. Toole to Richard B. Russell, 21 September 1942; all in Series X, Box 139, Folder 2, RBR.

11. John P. Smith to J. Emile Harley, 26 February 1942, Federal Government Correspondence, Box 1, Folder "U.S. Army, 4th Corp," Jefferies Gubernatorial Papers, SCDAH.

12. C. L. West to Richard B. Russell and Walter F. George, 17 July 1942, Series X, Box 139, Folder 3, RBR.

13. "White M.P.–Sworn Statement of Corporal Wilbert H. Loesing," 12 July 1942; "White M.P.–Sworn Statement of Corporal Leonard Seidel," 12 July 1942; "Sworn Statement of Private George W. Sutton," July 12, 1942; "Sworn Statement of PFC Johnny T. Terry," 12 July 1942; "Sworn Statement of Pvt. James F. Jackson," 12 July 1942; all in Series X, Box 139, Folder 2, RBR.

14. C. L. West to Richard B. Russell and Walter F. George, 17 July 1942; "Statements Taken at a Called Meeting of Council," 21 July 1942, 3; both in Series X, Box 139, Folder 3, RBR.

15. "Statements Taken at a Called Meeting of Council," 21 July 1942, 4; "Statements Made at Call Session of Council," 30 July 1942, 2; both in Series X, Box 139, Folder 3, RBR.

16. Burnet R. Maybank to R. M. Jefferies, 28 April 1942; Jefferies to Maybank, 5 October 1942; Maybank to Frank Dixon, 30 April 1942; all in Federal Government Correspondence, Box 1, Folder "Sen. Burnet R. Maybank," Jefferies Gubernatorial Papers, SCDAH.

17. Burnet R. Maybank to R. M. Jefferies, 30 April 1942, Federal Government Correspondence, Box 1, Folder "Sen. Burnet R. Maybank," Jefferies Gubernatorial Papers, SCDAH; Richard B. Russell to J. D. NeSmith, 19 August 1942, Series X, Box 139, Folder 2, RBR; "Bankhead Says Keep Northern Soldiers North," *Chicago Defender*, 15 August 1942, 7; "Sen. Bankhead of Alabama," ibid., 15 August 1942, 14.

18. George Atwood to Theodore G. Bilbo, 10 June 1943, Box 1066, Folder 9, TGB.

19. W. J. Hall to Richard B. Russell, 25 February 1942, Series X, Box 139, Folder 3, RBR.

20. Abner Spiers to Theodore G. Bilbo, 10 February 1942, Box 1084, Folder 8, TGB; Dan Shipp to Richard B. Russell, 1 January 1942, and Carl F. Hutcheson to Russell and Walter F. George, 26 May 1942, both in Series X, Box 139, Folder 3, RBR; William E. Colley to Russell, 28 September 1942, Series X, Box 139, Folder 2, RBR.

21. V. G. Oliver to Theodore G. Bilbo, 17 June 1944, Box 1066, Folder 8, TGB.

22. Richard B. Russell to W. J. Hall, 2 March 1942; John W. Martyn to Richard B. Russell, 20 June 1942; Richard B. Russell to Dan Shipp, 13 February 1942, all in Series X, Box 139, Folder 3, RBR.

23. Fred A. Meyer, memorandum, "Policy on Negroes," 16 July 1942, Series X, Box 139, Folder 3, RBR.

24. Jason Sokol claims that some white southerners changed their racial outlook as a result of their military service, but he correctly concedes that their "transformative experiences placed them in a minority." See Sokol, *There Goes My Everything*, 19–20.

25. Roi Ottley, "Ottley Reports on Negro-White Troop Relations," *PM*, 21 September 1944, 7.

26. Ibid., 7. "U.S. Negro Troops Feted in Britain," *New York Times*, n.d., n.p., clipping in Series X, Box 139, Folder 6, RBR.

27. Roi Ottley, "Ottley Reports on Negro-White Troop Relations," *PM*, 21 September 1944, 7.

28. Lloyd H. Grandy to Richard B. Russell, 24 May 1945, Series X, Box 108,

Folder 2, RBR; Lawrence L. Massey Jr., to Theodore G. Bilbo, 20 March 1945, Box 1067, Folder 3, TGB.

29. Paul H. Green to Olin D. Johnston, 20 October 1944, Box 115, Folder "1944 Letters to Soldiers Overseas," Johnston Papers, SCPC.

30. C. B. Newman to Jerrome Daly, 8 April 1946, Box 992, Folder 12; Robert H. Lavender to Theodore G. Bilbo, 6 August 1945, Box 1067, Folder 3; both in TGB.

31. Lloyd H. Grandy to Richard B. Russell, 24 May 1945, Series X, Box 108, Folder 2, RBR; Ernest Floyd to Theodore G. Bilbo, 5 March 1946, Box 1022, Folder 13, TGB.

32. A. E. Butler to Olin D. Johnston, 17 May 1943, Subject Files, Box 3, Folder "Negro Question (1)," Johnston Gubernatorial Papers, SCDAH.

33. "To Our devoted Senator Bilbo," n.d., Box 1067, Folder 3, TGB.

34. Anonymous and untitled report in Series X, Box 139, Folder 6, RBR.

35. Sgt. Moss Simms to Theodore G. Bilbo, 22 September 1945, Box 1085, Folder 1; David M. Ditto to Bilbo, 12 September 1945, Box 1024, Folder 10; Major C. Williams to Bilbo, 5 January 1945, Box 1067, Folder 3; all in TGB.

36. William Colmer, "Congressional Sidelights," 7 April 1944, Box 421, Folder 15, WMC.

37. J. R. Bryson, "White Supremacy in the South," n.d. [1944], Box 3, Folder "Public, Legis, 1952, Civil Rights," Bryson Papers, SCPC.

38. C. L. McKinnon to S. J. Pratt, 28 September 1942; J. L. Dollard to Pratt, 26 September 1942; both in Folder 51, Jefferies Papers, SCL.

39. Stanley F. Morse to W. W. Ball, 1 August 1942, Box 37, Ball Papers, DUSC. For more on Eleanor Clubs, see Tyler, "Blood on Your Hands," 102–5; and Simon, "Introduction," in Odum, *Race and Rumors of Race*, xx–xxi.

40. T. B. Horton to S. J. Pratt, 10 September 1942, Folder 50; B. Frank Wilkes to Pratt, 29 September 1942; S. J. Pratt to R. M. Jefferies, 9 October 1942, Folder 51; Roland T. Clary to Pratt, 5 September 1942, Folder 50; all in Jefferies Papers, SCL.

41. W. W. Brown to R. M. Jefferies, 10 September 1942, Folder 50, Ibid.

42. Odum, *Race and Rumors of Race*, vii, 4, 230–34, 12. For the best discussions of *Race and Rumors of Race*, see Simon, "Introduction," in Odum, *Race and Rumors of Race*, vii–xxxii; and Gilmore, *Defying Dixie*, 372–78.

43. Graves, *The Fighting South*, 125.

44. Ibid., 125, 142–43, 140.

45. Mark Ethridge, "The Race Problem in the War," Box 6, Folder 127, Ethridge Papers, SHC; "Ethridge's Statement Compares FDR to Hitler," *Baltimore Afro-American*, 7 July 1942, 5.

46. Jonathan Daniels to Franklin Delano Roosevelt, 22 June 1943, Box 13, Folder 434; Daniels to Marvin McIntyre, 26 January 1943, Box 13, Folder 427; both in Daniels Papers, SHC. Daniels discusses his wartime tenure with the Roosevelt administration in *White House Witness*. For an examination of Daniels's wartime tenure in the White House, see Eagles, *Jonathan Daniels and Race Relations*, 83–120. Eagles portrays Daniels as a "prudent rebel" who increasingly supported African American rights throughout his life, but pays less attention to Daniels's wartime

pessimism about the prospects for racial change. Eagles also presents the idea of "Two 'Double V's,'" but his second version is a competing vision of "Double V" articulated by the Roosevelt administration, not the white South.

47. Jonathan Daniels to Marvin McIntyre, 4 February 1943, Box 13, Folder 427, Daniels Papers, SHC; Graves, *The Fighting South*, 239.

48. Jonathan Daniels to Marvin McIntyre, 4 February 1943, Box 13, Folder 427; Jonathan Daniels to Franklin Delano Roosevelt, 22 June 1943, Box 13, Folder 434; both in Daniels Papers, SHC.

49. James F. Byrnes to George Warren, 23 August 1943, Series 4, Box 7, Folder 12, Byrnes Papers, CUSC.

50. Lawson, *Black Ballots*, 56.

51. Kennedy, *Southern Exposure*, 95. Alabama, Arkansas, Florida, Georgia, Mississippi, South Carolina, Tennessee, Texas, and Virginia required the poll tax, although South Carolina waived the requirement for the white primary. For a comprehensive study of the poll tax in these states, see Ogden, *Poll Tax in the South*. For an excellent recent account of the poll tax's impact on civil rights activism and national politics, see Gilmore, *Defying Dixie*, 336–41.

52. "Poll Tax Dynasty Opposes Bill to Permit Soldier Vote," *Baltimore Afro-American*, 1 August 1942, 13; Kennedy, *Southern Exposure*, 95. For more on the disproportionate power of southern congressmen, see Katznelson, Geiger, and Kryder, "Limiting Liberalism." Dewey W. Grantham contends that the South's congressional delegations continued to wield disproportionate power during World War II, carrying out "a kind of dress rehearsal" for future battles over racial reform. See Grantham, "The South and Congressional Politics," 30.

53. "Statements of Senator Burnet R. Maybank, Governor R. M. Jefferies, Attorney General John M. Daniel, State Senator Edgar A. Brown In Opposition to United States Senate No. 1280," 13 October 1942, 19, 6–7, Folder 35, Jefferies Papers, SCL.

54. *Congressional Record*, 77th Cong., 2nd sess., 7072; "House to Act on Soldier Vote Bill Sept. 9," *Norfolk Journal and Guide*, 5 September 1942, B1.

55. "House To Act On Soldier Vote Bill Sept. 9," *Norfolk Journal and Guide*, 5 September 1942, B1; "Soldier Vote Bill Accepted By House," *New York Times*, 10 September 1942, 23. Brown quickly substituted the name of a black Tupelo pastor, James Arthur Parsons, as the write-in candidate to challenge Rankin in the general election. See "Minister to Oppose Rankin in Mississippi Election," *New York Amsterdam Star-News*, 26 September 1942, 5.

56. "This Is Utter Foolishness Which Will Do Harm Rather Than Good," *Tupelo (Miss.) Daily Journal*, 12 September 1942, 4; *Congressional Record*, 77th Cong., 2nd sess., 8078.

57. "Lynch Week," *Time*, 26 October 1942, 23–24; Walter Atkins, "Shubuta Bridge's Toll Stands at Six Lynch Victims, But Span Is Doomed," *Chicago Defender*, 7 November 1942, 1; "Two Negro Boys Lynched by Mob," *Clarke County (Miss.) Tribune*, 16 October 1942, 1.

58. "The Bitter Fruit," *Meridian (Miss.) Star*, 13 October 1942, 4; "Biddle Orders Probe Lynchings in Mississippi," ibid., 20 October 1942, 1.

59. "Defiant Dixie in Poll Tax Rout," *New York Amsterdam Star-News*, 17 October 1942, 1.

60. Graves, *The Fighting South*, 151, 120, 152, 239–40.

61. *Congressional Record*, 78th Cong., 2nd sess., A1795-A1802; A. M. Jones to Theodore G. Bilbo, 23 November 1942, Box 1076, Folder 1, TGB.

62. Hunter K. Cochran to Theodore G. Bilbo, 24 November 1942, Box 1077, Folder 2; M. W. Darby to Bilbo, 24 November 1942, Box 1077, Folder 3; both in TGB.

63. J. C. Hamilton to Theodore G. Bilbo, 17 October 1942, Box 1077, Folder 10; E. M. Pace to Bilbo, 19 November 1942, Box 1077, Folder 1; both in TGB.

64. James Robertson to Theodore G. Bilbo, 31 May 1943, Box 1076, Folder 6, TGB.

65. B. W. Morgan to Theodore G. Bilbo, n.d.; Earle C. Douglas Sr. to Theodore G. Bilbo, 29 May 1943; both in Box 1076, Folder 7, TGB.

66. E. M. Pace to Roy Porter, 19 November 1942, Box 1077, Folder 1; Charles W. Wade to Theodore G. Bilbo, 5 June 1943, Box 1084, Folder 8; both in TGB. For a discussion of the racially charged nature of the war in the Pacific from American and Japanese perspectives, see Dower, *War Without Mercy*. Penny von Eschen argues that African Americans in World War II paid attention to international anticolonial movements and offered a radical critique of American diplomacy. See von Eschen, *Race Against Empire*. For a discussion of scattered African American sympathy for the Japanese war effort, and a longer history of black-Japanese interaction, see Horne, *Race War!*, 55–59, 105–9.

67. J. W. Bradford to Walter Sillers, 2 April 1943; J. W. Bradford to the Delta Council, 2 April 1943, both in Box 11, Folder 8, WSP. Concerns over a shrinking wartime labor supply due to outmigration only heightened white elites' desire to reassert control over the Delta's black majority. See Cobb, *Most Southern Place on Earth*, 198–208; and Woodruff, "Mississippi Delta Planters."

68. J. W. Bradford to Walter Sillers, 2 April 1943; "Southern Crusaders," n.d.; both in Box 11, Folder 8, WSP. The Southern Crusaders continued to hold annual gatherings in Greenwood, Mississippi, after the war, with the stated goal of "peace and good will through racial understanding" and "work[ing] to offset any influence which tends to set our race at odds with our neighbors and throws us out of harmony with our Democratic form of government." See "Southern Crusaders Meet in Greenwood," *Atlanta Daily World*, 28 October 1949, 8.

69. Brinkley Morton to Theodore G. Bilbo, 19 November 1942, Box 1076, Folder 1, TGB; South Carolina Negro Citizens Committee, "Which Do You Want—Democracy or 'The American Way of Life,'" n.d., Folder 52, Jefferies Papers, SCL.

70. For an authoritative account of the NAACP legal campaign against the white primary, see Lawson, *Black Ballots*, 23–54.

71. "Time Bomb," *Time*, 17 April 1944, 21; Frederickson, *Dixiecrat Revolt*, 42–46.

72. "South Carolina House Backs 'Supremacy' of Whites and Warns 'Damned Agitators,'" *New York Times*, 1 March 1944, 13.

73. Untitled speech, n.d., p. 2–3, 4, 5, Subject Files, Box 3, Folder "Negro Question (2)," Johnston Gubernatorial Papers, SCDAH.

74. "Time Bomb," *Time*, 17 April 1944, 21.

75. Connor, *Case Against the New Deal*, 17 April 1944, 2–3, 16–17, 19, Box 29, Folder 5, WSP.

76. Sam Jones, "Will Dixie Bolt the New Deal?," *Saturday Evening Post*, 6 March 1943, 21; R. M. Prince, *I Can't Vote for Mr. Roosevelt in November*, n.p., copy in Series X, Box 113, Folder 1, RBR.

77. Rand delivered the speech, which was reprinted and distributed in pamphlet form, before the Alabama Lions Clubs Conference, the Mississippi Bankers Association, the Mississippi Cotton Seed Crushers Association, and the students of Southeast Louisiana College. See Rand, *New Deal and the New Slavery*, n.p.

Chapter 3

1. *Congressional Record*, 78th Cong., 2nd sess., A1795, A1798.

2. Ibid., A1802.

3. As historian Steven F. Lawson has noted, "The Mississippi Negrophobe became a vivid symbol of political repression in the South." For his account of the rise and fall of "Bilboism," see Lawson, *Black Ballots*, 98–115.

4. *Congressional Record*, 78th Cong., 2nd sess., A1798; Jaffe and Sherwood, *Dream City*, 27. While the controversial career and sensational rhetoric of Theodore Bilbo have long attracted the attention of historians, the senator's fight against civil rights in the 1940s has received less attention than his progressive, if white supremacist, political stance of earlier decades. Even historians who have discussed the final years of Bilbo's career and life have paid little attention to his chairmanship of the District Committee. A. Wigfall Green mentions the "enthusiasm" with which Bilbo worked toward municipal improvements in Washington, citing only one voice of protest, the Communist Party of the District of Columbia. Another Bilbo biographer, Chester Morgan, also emphasizes the progressive proposals for hospital construction and a modern transit system, while conceding that such plans were "overshadowed" by the senator's hostility to black residents. See A. Wigfall Green, *The Man*, 107–8; and Morgan, *Redneck Liberal*, 251–52. Other historians have focused on Bilbo's white supremacist statements during the 1940s but have either ignored the District Committee episode or emphasized its galvanizing effect for opponents of an increasingly ostracized and ineffectual Bilbo. See Bailey, "Bilbo and the Fair Employment Practices Controversy," 27–42; and Fleegler, "Bilbo and the Decline of Public Racism," 13–15.

5. Bilbo, *Take Your Choice*, 58.

6. Ibid.; "Bilbo as 'Mayor' of Washington," *Chicago Defender*, 12 February 1944, 12.

7. *Congressional Record*, 78th Cong., 2nd sess., 6252.

8. G. B. Deane to Theodore G. Bilbo, 21 February 1944; Sank Owen to Theodore G. Bilbo, 8 February 1944; both in Box 1013, Folder 10, TGB.

9. *Congressional Record*, 78th Cong., 2nd sess., 6253.

10. Constance McLaughlin Green, *The Secret City*, 247.

11. Malcolm X, *Autobiography of Malcolm X*, 75; David Brinkley, *Brinkley's Beat*, 15.

12. "Bilious Bilbo Becomes Mayor of Washington," *Baltimore Afro-American*, 12 February 1944, 3; "Bilbo Becomes Mayor of D.C.," *Chicago Defender*, 12 February 1944, 2; "Bilbo as 'Mayor' of Washington," ibid., 12.

13. "Sen. Bilbo Wants Slum Dwellers Sent to Farms," *Chicago Defender*, 25 March 1944, 4.

14. Ibid.; F. L. Mathews to T. G. Bilbo, 9 June 1945, Record Group 211, Entry 175, Box 1, Records of the War Manpower Commission, NARA.

15. Venice Tipton Spraggs, "Folks and Things 'Round Washington," *Chicago Defender*, 25 March 1944, 14; "Adventure in Bigotry," *Washington Post*, 17 March 1944, 12.

16. Bilbo, *Take Your Choice*, 133; *Congressional Record*, 78th Cong., 2nd sess., A1800.

17. Myrtis Evans to Richard B. Russell, 4 July 1942, Series X, Box 139, Folder 3, RBR; Edna Hoisington to Theodore G. Bilbo, 31 May 1944, Box 1084, Folder 9, TGB.

18. "Both Races in Revolt Against Rabid Senator," *Chicago Defender*, 22 April 1944, 1.

19. *Congressional Record*, 78th Cong., 2nd sess., 6252. While Bilbo claimed that Washington lacked restrictive housing covenants, the postwar report of the National Committee on Segregation in the Nation's Capital described the widespread use of discriminatory practices by white real estate agents. According to the Washington Real Estate Board Code of Ethics, 1948, "No property in a white section should ever be sold, rented, advertised, or offered to colored people." See Landis, *Segregation in Washington*, 30–37.

20. Sugrue, *Origins of the Urban Crisis*, 73–75. In a more recent work, Sugrue has noted that during World War II, access to housing "became the source of intense racial conflict" as well as "a major battleground for racial equality" across the urban North. See Sugrue, *Sweet Land of Liberty*, 66.

21. William B. Hartsfield to Richard Russell, 27 September 1944, Series X, Box 112, Folder 2, RBR.

22. Dorothy A. Koutnik to Theodore G. Bilbo, 7 August 1945; Mary Frances Campana to Bilbo, 14 July 1945; both in Box 1024, Folder 12; Charles L. Morey to Bilbo, 29 May 1947, Box 1115, Folder 7; all in TGB.

23. "Executive Director" to Alvin [*sic*] W. Barkley, 5 February 1944, Box 1013, Folder 11; Harry S. Wender to Theodore G. Bilbo, 10 February 1944, Box 1013, Folder 16; both in TGB.

24. Ella M. Thompson to Theodore G. Bilbo, 9 February 1944, Box 1013, Folder 10; Arthur B. McNerney to Bilbo, 27 November 1944; "*MR. AND MS. PROPERTY OWNER*," n.d.; both in Box 1014, Folder 10; all in TGB.

25. *Congressional Record*, 78th Cong., 2nd sess., 6252–53.

26. Ibid., 6250; U.S. Senate Committee on the District of Columbia, *Reorganization of the Government*, 149–51.

27. Ibid., 151–53.

28. *Congressional Record*, 78th Cong., 2nd sess., A1800, 5078.

29. For a discussion of the wartime sit-in campaign, see Flora Bryant Brown, "NAACP Sponsored Sit-ins," 274–86; and Gilmore, *Defying Dixie*, 384–93.

30. *Congressional Record*, 78th Cong., 2nd sess., 6251, A1800, 6253.

31. "Bilbo as 'Mayor' of Washington," *Chicago Defender*, 12 February 1944, 12.

32. "Should Negroes March on Washington—If So, When?," *Chicago Defender*, 3 July 1943, 13.

33. Glenda Gilmore has argued that the establishment of the FEPC "struck at the heart of Jim Crow" by calling the South's labor system and devotion to "racial integrity" into question. See Gilmore, *Defying Dixie*, 361.

34. Richard B. Russell to Cobb C. Torrance, 31 May 1944, Series X, Box 108, Folder 2, RBR.

35. Quoted in Kesselman, *The Social Politics of FEPC*, 167; Frank M. Dixon, *Crossroads Democracy*, n.p., copy in Box 3, Folder 2, Dixon Papers, ADAH.

36. Quoted in Ottley, *New World A-Coming*, 302; Gilmore, *Defying Dixie*, 363; Cobb C. Torrance to Richard B. Russell, 29 May 1944, Series X, Box 108, Folder 2, RBR.

37. Finley, *Delaying the Dream*, 78–81; Ottley, *New World A-Coming*, 304–5; Chen, *The Fifth Freedom*, 38–40.

38. William Colmer, "Congressional Sidelights," 4 May 1945, Box 421, Folder 18; "Wake up, America!: Should a Permanent Fair Employment Practice Commission Be Created by Congress," 21 May 1944, Box 421, Folder 19, WMC.

39. *Congressional Record*, 79th Cong., 1st sess., 4204; Men's Club of Trinity Methodist Church, Savannah, Georgia, "RESOLVED," 15 May 1945, Box 1024, Folder 12; Port Gibson (Miss.) Lions Club, "A RESOLUTION," Box 1022, Folder 8; both in TGB.

40. *Congressional Record*, 79th Cong., 1st sess., 4215, 4209, 4214–15.

41. "Dixie Kills FEPC," *Chicago Defender*, 7 July 1945, 1, 4; *Congressional Record*, 79th Cong., 1st sess., 6994–95. For the best discussion of Eastland's fight against the FEPC, including an insightful comparison with the senator's advocacy of leniency toward postwar Germany, see Asch, "Revisiting Reconstruction," 1–28.

42. Tyre Taylor, "To the Industrialists of the South," 9 March 1945; C. C. Gilbert, "To the Directors, Southern States Industrial Council," 16 April 1945; both in Box 4, Folder 3, SSIC.

43. Quoted in Kennedy, *Southern Exposure*, 322; Milton Murray, "Pressure Group Demands Filibuster Against FEPC," *PM*, 27 April 1945, n.p., clipping in scrapbook, SSIC.

44. Anthony Chen outlines the ad hoc alliance between conservative southern Democrats and conservative northern Republicans in the fight against the FEPC, and the motivations that fueled this coalition of convenience. See Chen, *Fifth Freedom*, 32–87. Kesselman briefly outlines business opposition to the FEPC in *The Social Politics of FEPC*, 170–73.

45. *Congressional Record*, 78th Cong., 2nd sess., 6283.

46. Benedict and Weltfish, *The Races of Mankind*, 4; Gilmore, *Defying Dixie*, 396.

47. Quoted in Kennedy, *Southern Exposure*, 86; "Plans New Edition of Race Pamphlet," *New York Times*, 8 March 1944, 11; "What South Doesn't Want Soldiers to Read About Negroes," *Chicago Defender*, 18 March 1944, 1.

48. "Modern Race Teachings Tried on Georgia Pupils," *Atlanta Journal*, 24 March

1944, 26; "Georgia Children 'Guinea Pigs' For Race-Mixing Experimentors," *Hapeville (Ga.) Statesman*, 30 March 1944, 1.

49. Irwin, *Keep the United States White*, 11; Irwin to Earnest Sevier Cox, 16 February 1945, Box 6, Folder "1945," Cox Papers, DUSC.

50. Gene Weltfish to Theodore G. Bilbo, 9 March 1944, Box 1067, Folder 2; Jewel S. Blankton to Bilbo, 19 September 1945, Box 1023, Folder 2; both in TGB.

51. Cox, *The Races of Mankind*, 22, 26–27.

52. Theodore G. Bilbo to A. S. Coody, 29 May 1945, Box 4, Folder 50, Coody Papers, MDAH; D. Foster to TGB, 21 June 1945, Box 1022, Folder 6, TGB; Mary S. Parson to Cox, June 17, 1947, Box 6, Cox Papers, DUSC; "A Southern White Friend," *The Negro Disillusioned*; Homer Loomis Jr. to Cox, n.d., Box 6, Folder "1946", Cox Papers, DUSC.

53. Landry, *The Cult of Equality*, vii, 1. For a brief discussion of Landry's book and its role in a broader effort to build an academic case for racial discrimination, see Jackson, *Science for Segregation*, 70–72.

54. Landry, *The Cult of Equality*, 42, 202–3.

55. Ibid., 233, 236, 257.

56. Ibid., 280, 269.

57. Quoted in Landry, *The Cult of Equality*, xii; Reuter, "The Cult of Equality," 348–49.

58. Bilbo, *Take Your Choice*, 3, 165.

59. Ibid., 6, 94–116, 198–282.

60. Ibid., 5, preface, n.p., 58–59.

61. Ibid., 158.

62. Key, *Southern Politics in State and Nation*, 224; D. H. Adams to Theodore G. Bilbo, 28 June 1945, Box 992, Folder 10; Sam H. Montgomery to Bilbo, September 25, 1945, Box 1023, Folder 1; both in TGB.

63. J. S. Sanders to Theodore G. Bilbo, 22 October 1945; A. B. Friend, "Mississippi's Senior United States Senator: Theodore G. Bilbo," n.d., 10; both in Box 992, Folder 11, TGB.

64. Hazel P. Lee, "Bilbo Still the Same Old Master on the Stump; Britain, Negroes Were Targets," *Webster (Miss.) Progress*, 30 May 1946, 4; Landis, *Segregation in Washington*, 88.

65. "Mississippi's Verdict," *New Orleans Times-Picayune*, 4 July 1946, 6.

66. "Bilboism," *Washington Post*, 6 December 1946, 8.

Chapter 4

1. "Grand Jury Called to Probe Race Riot in Alabama Town," *Christian Science Monitor*, 12 August 1946, 4.

2. John LeFlore, "50 Trampled in Alabama Riot," *Chicago Defender*, 17 August 1946, 1; "Militia Alert To Prevent New Alabama Riot," *Washington Post*, 12 August 1946, 1; Vincent Tubbs, "Politics Back of Athens Riot," *Baltimore Afro-American*, 24 August 1946, 1–2. The grand jury ultimately indicted seventeen white men, and nine, including Ben Massey, pled guilty and paid fines of $12.50 to $50.00 for drunkenness and unlawful assembly. Only two men faced assault charges, and

both had their cases suspended by the solicitor. See Lee E. Williams II, "Alabama Moderation," 21–22.

3. "A Call To Arms," *New York Amsterdam News*, 3 August 1946, 8. The Talmadge victory hinged on white backlash as well as on widespread attempts to discourage and dilute the black vote through fraud and terrorism. See Bernd, "White Supremacy." For more on the Monroe lynching, see Wexler, *Fire in a Canebrake*. John Egerton discusses the repressive violence of Eugene "Bull" Connor's Birmingham police force, which killed as many as five black veterans in the first six weeks of 1946. Despite divergent electoral results in Alabama and Georgia in 1946, Egerton cites the two states as "the principle killing fields" during that year. See Egerton, *Speak Now Against the Day*, 361–62, 366.

4. Gail Williams O'Brien, *The Color of the Law*; Tyson, *Radio Free Dixie*, 61; Key, *Southern Politics*, 41–46; "Statement of Gessner T. McCorvey, Chairman of the State Democratic Executive Committee of Alabama, In Reply to Statement of Senator Lister Hill in Re Proposed Amendment No. 4, Known as the Boswell Amendment," Box 82, Folder 3, Democratic Party (Ala.) State Executive Committee records, ADAH; Lawson, *Black Ballots*, 90–93 (quotation on 90).

5. Black Belt Citizens Committee for the Boswell Amendment, "Proposed Advertisement No. 4: Help Save Our Alabama Black Belt form Negro Domination," Box 106 (oversize), Democratic Party (Ala.) State Executive Committee records, ADAH. Chauncey Sparks to John Sengstacke, 14 August 1946, Alabama Governor (1943–1947: Sparks) Administrative Files, SG012515, ADAH; "No Terror Here, Says Sparks," *Chicago Defender*, 31 August 1946, 9.

6. John H. McCray, "Victim Trailed Home; Shot by White Mobbists," *Atlanta Daily World*, 27 August 1946, 2; John McCray, "The Isaac Woodard Story," n.d., box 7, McCray Papers, SCL. For a concise account of the lynching of Willie Earle and the subsequent trial, see Frederickson, *Dixiecrat Revolt*, 58–59, 61–63.

7. "Press Release [Willie Earle Case]," 18 February 1947, Speeches Series, Subseries A-General File, box 1, file 23, Thurmond Collection, CUSC; McKaine quoted in Richards, "Osceola McKaine," 261; John N. Popham, "All 28 Acquitted by Lynch Jurors in South Carolina," *New York Times*, 22 May 1947, 1.

8. Frederickson, *Dixiecrat Revolt*, 47–51.

9. Cobb, "World War II," 5; Cobb, *Industrialization and Southern Society*, 150. For a discussion of the Balance Agriculture with Industry program, see Cobb, *The Selling of the South*, 13–28. Cobb has more recently characterized the South as "a textbook example of how the forces of what we might call economic modernization may not only adapt to antidemocratic social and political institutions, such as segregation and disfranchisement, but actually help to perpetuate them." While some contemporary social scientists argued that the South had to choose between "tradition" and "progress," Cobb contends that the downfall of Jim Crow "was not an inevitable side-effect of the South's crusade for economic growth." Cobb, *The Brown Decision*, 7, 30.

10. Thurman Sensing, Memo to "Officers and Directors of the Southern States Industrial Council," 17 March 1944, Box 4, Folder 2, SSIC. Cumulative contributions to the SSIC neared $1 million in 1948, with annual contributions nearing $100,000.

See "Contributions to Southern States Industrial Council," Box 2, Folder 1, SSIC. For ranking of lobbies, see Zeller, "Federal Regulation of Lobbying Act," 258.

11. Thurman Sensing, "Southern Principles and Prosperity," press release, 6 May 1945, Scrapbook, SSIC. Kari Frederickson has noted that Strom Thurmond embraced a similar analysis of the South's "unequal, colonial status" and argued that southern prosperity would bolster racial harmony. See Frederickson, *Dixiecrat Revolt*, 2.

12. Thurman Sensing, "Southern Principles and Prosperity," press release, 6 May 1945, Scrapbook, SSIC; Thurman Sensing, *Down South*, vol. 3, preface (n.p.), 28.

13. Quoted in Cohodas, *Strom Thurmond*, 90. In her study of the impact of World War II veterans on postwar southern politics, Jennifer Brooks has shown that segregated modernization was not simply a goal of economic and political elites, but also of everyday southerners interested in "good government" and economic prosperity yet wedded to the segregated status quo. See Brooks, *Defining the Peace*, 8. Michelle Brattain argues that "traditional leaders envisioned a postwar South that maintained its boosters' appeal to business, cut short the nationalizing influence of the war, and resisted the northern and liberal impulse to reform the region's racial practices." Brattain, *The Politics of Whiteness*, 132.

14. Bruce Schulman has noted that whites claimed a disproportionate share of new jobs in southern industry during the 1940s. The wartime boom and postwar prosperity, he argues, "mainly benefited whites," especially in the Deep South. In 1950, black southerners received only 21 percent of new nonagricultural jobs in the Deep South, even though they accounted for 41 percent of the population. See Schulman, *From Cotton Belt to Sunbelt*, 83.

15. Gilmore, *Defying Dixie*, 411–13.

16. Moon, *Balance of Power*, 237–44. Clifford quoted in Sitkoff, "Harry Truman," 597.

17. *To Secure These Rights*, 147. For more on the Truman administration's sensitivity to negative press attention, see Dudziak, *Cold War Civil Rights*, 26–39.

18. Zangrando, *The NAACP Crusade Against Lynching*, 184–85; Berman, *The Politics of Civil Rights*, 70–75; *To Secure These Rights*, 137–73.

19. J. Strom Thurmond, "President Truman's So-Called Civil Rights Program," 17 March 1948, 6, Speeches Series, Subseries A-General File, box 2, file 123, Thurmond Collection, CUSC; Thurman Sensing, "Down South," 9 November 1947, Box 32, Folder 2021, Graham Papers, SHC.

20. Egerton, *Speak Now Against the Day*, 476.

21. Ibid. (first and last quotation); Nelson T. Levings to Fielding Wright, 2 February 1948, Box 318, Folder 3, WMC; Cohodas, *Strom Thurmond*, 130.

22. Charles P. Roland argues that Dixiecrat failure "indicated no change of heart on the issues of civil rights and federal authority. Rather than forfeit their rank and prestige, the region's elder political leaders such as Harry F. Byrd, James F. Byrnes, and Richard Russell preferred to wage the battle as Democrats and with weapons of their own choice." See Roland, *The Improbable Era*, 61.

23. Frederickson, *Dixiecrat Revolt*, 70; Key, *Southern Politics*, 331; Brady, *The South at Bay*, n.p.

24. Collins, *Whither Solid South?*, vii, 254.

25. Ibid., vii, 258–79. In the most comprehensive analysis of *Whither Solid South?* Joseph Lowndes argues that Collins's influence survived both the Dixiecrat revolt and massive resistance. In addition to creating an electoral strategy for southern white supremacists, Lowndes argues, Collins "provided a potent political narrative that connected white supremacy and states' rights to broader conservative trends and in doing so helped lay the groundwork for a new political identity that would reshape national politics." See Lowndes, "Southern Origins of Modern Conservatism," 24.

26. Collins, *Whither Solid South?*, 251; Brady, *The South at Bay*, n.p.; Nelson T. Levings to Fielding Wright, 2 February 1948, Box 318, Folder 3, WMC.

27. Collins, *Whither Solid South?*, x; R. Kirby Longino, "The Revolt in the South," 18 February 1948, Box 5, Folder 3, SSIC.

28. Brady, *The South at Bay*, n.p.; Collins, *Whither Solid South?*, vii. Dixiecrat strategists and recent historians are not the only ones who have noted the ambitious national vision of the States' Righters. Contemporary political scientists Emile Ader and William G. Carleton argued in the early 1950s that the Dixiecrats had their eyes on a national political realignment. Writing in 1951, Carleton claimed that the states' rights revolt "is not a sectional movement at all; it is a national movement; it is the way southern conservatives are making contact with national conservatives and orienting themselves to national conservatism." See Carleton, "The Southern Politician, 1900–1950," 221. See also Ader, "Why the Dixiecrats Failed," 356.

29. J. J. Kramer to Tyre Taylor, 26 February 1948, Box 318, Folder 3, WMC.

30. Thurman Sensing, "The Public Relations Aspects of the Southern States Industrial Council," Box 2, Folder 1, SSIC; J. J. Kramer to Tyre Taylor, 26 February 1948, Box 318, Folder 3, WMC; "The 1948 Election," *Textile Bulletin* 74 (October 1948): 16, 18.

31. "Frank M. Dixon Keynote Speech," typescript, n.p., Box 348, Folder 10, WMC.

32. Quoted in Roland, *The Improbable Era*, 61; Heard, *A Two-Party South?*, 26–27.

33. Quoted in Eagles, *Jonathan Daniels*, 136.

34. For more on the Progressive Party campaign of Henry Wallace, see Yarnell, *Democrats and Progressives*; and Culver and Hyde, *American Dreamer*, 456–503.

35. "Comments on Men and Things," 8 September 1948, 1, Box 1, Folder 8; "Comments on Men and Things," n.d. [1948], 2–3, Box 1, Folder 10; both in Breedin Papers, SCL; "States Rights' Movement Will Never Die, Declares Eastland in Talk Here," *Jackson (Miss.) Daily News*, 15 November 1948, 1; James O. Eastland to A. S. Coody, 31 May 1948, Box 5, Folder 81, Coody Papers, MDAH.

36. Key, *Southern Politics*, 252; John C. Stennis to Jas. A. McGraw, 9 February 1948, Series 29, Box 1, Folder 1, JCS; "Too Much Reticence," *Jackson (Miss.) Daily News*, 25 January 1948, 4.

37. Ben Owen to John C. Stennis, 23 January 1948, Series 29, Box 1, Folder 1; Jas. A. McGraw to Stennis, 3 February 1948, Series 29, Box 1, Folder 3; both in JCS.

38. John C. Stennis to Jas. A. McGraw, 9 February 1948, Series 29, Box 1, Folder 1, JCS.

39. Samuel A. Tower, "Action Deferred on Poll Tax Ban," *New York Times*,

11 March 1948, 30; John C. Stennis to A. E. Branch, 24 January 1948, Series 29, Box 1, Folder 1, JCS; Lem Graves Jr., "Bilbo's Successor Out-Bilbo's Bilbo," *Pittsburgh Courier*, 13 March 1948, 2; Lamar Sledge to Stennis, 15 March 1948; John C. Stennis to Oliver Emmerich, 18 February 1948, Series 29; both in Box 1, Folder 3, JCS.

40. "Memorandum on Statement Given to the Press in New Orleans," 17 September 1948, Series 29, Box 3, Folder 13, JCS.

41. John C. Stennis to A. S. Coody, 9 July 1948, Box 8, Folder 152, Coody Papers, MDAH.

42. Stennis quoted in Cohodas, *Strom Thurmond*, 134; Asch, *The Senator and the Sharecropper*, 124–25.

43. Woodrow Price, "Joyner's Keynote Address Scores Any Revolt in Party on Civil Rights Issue," *Raleigh News and Observer*, 21 May 1948, 6.

44. Egerton, *Speak Now Against the Day*, 386–89; Kytle and Mackay, *Who Runs Georgia?*

45. Brooks, *Defining the Peace*, 156–57; John N. Popham, "Close 3-Way Race Georgia Prospect," *New York Times*, 22 October 1948, 19.

46. Frederickson, *Dixiecrat Revolt*, 107.

47. "Georgia Negroes Appeal To Courts As Dixiecrats Purge Voting Lists," *Chicago Defender*, 14 August 1948, 1–2; Tuck, *Beyond Atlanta*, 76.

48. "White Supremacy in Peace or by Force—Talmadge," *Chicago Defender*, 14 August 1948, 1; Wade, *The Fiery Cross*, 283, 289; Non-Sectarian Anti-Nazi League to Champion Human Rights, "Senate Group Asked to Probe Alleged Talmadge Ku Klux Klan Interference in Elections," 2 July 1948; Association of Georgia Klans, "Ideals of the Ku Klux Klan," 5; both in Part 18, Series A, reel 4, NAACPP; "Casts Vote; Shot to Death," *Chicago Defender*, 18 September 1948, 1. For an account of the Nixon murder, see Brooks, *Defining the Peace*, 158–62.

49. Wade, *The Fiery Cross*, 294; Tuck, *Beyond Atlanta*, 74–78; "Georgia Moves To Bar Negroes At Ballot Box," *New York Amsterdam News*, 25 December 1948, 26.

50. "Mallard's Minister-Father Denies Son's Widow Guilty," *Atlanta Daily World*, 30 November 1948, 1; "Man Lynched by Robed Gang in So. Georgia," ibid., 25 November 1948, 1; "The Mallard Case," Part 7, Series A, reel 25; "Script of Interview with Mrs. Amy Mallard," 7 February 1949, Part 7, Series A, reel 26; both in NAACPP.

51. "Man Lynched by Robed Gang in So. Georgia," *Atlanta Daily World*, 25 November 1948, 1; "The Mallard Case"; "Ku Klux Klan Blocks Prosecution of Slayers of Negro in Toombs Co., League Charges," 2; both in Part 7, Series A, reel 25, NAACPP.

52. William A. Fowlkes, "Seeing and Saying," *Atlanta Daily World*, 31 October 1948, 4. See also Tuck, *Beyond Atlanta*, 79.

53. Charles Greenlea, "Klan Bill to Unmask Loses by 89–65 Vote," *Atlanta Daily World*, 21 January 1949, 1.

54. Russell quoted in Bartley, *The New South*, 95; Webb, "Charles Bloch, Jewish White Supremacist," 268–69. Macon attorney Charles Bloch would later emerge, in the words of historian David L. Chappell, as "the nation's leading legal crusader for segregation." See Chappell, "Divided Mind of Southern Segregationists," 57.

55. Webb, "Charles Bloch, Jewish White Supremacist," 268–69.

56. "Historic Cavalcade: Democracy in Action in Inaugural Parade," *Baltimore Afro-American*, 29 January 1949, 2; "New Democratic Party Blooms at Inaugural," ibid., 1; McCullough, *Truman*, 871–72.

57. "3 Dixiecrats Snubbed," *Baltimore Afro-American*, 29 January 1949, 1; "Talmadge Gets Cold Shoulder in D.C. Parade," *Atlanta Daily World*, 29 January 1949, 1.

58. Richard B. Russell to Frank Boykin, 8 February 1949, Series X, Box 143, Folder 4, RBR.

59. *Congressional Record*, 81st Cong., 1st sess., 570–71.

60. "Dixie's Rebs Open Attack to Halt Civil Rights Bills," *Pittsburgh Courier*, 5 February 1949, 4; "State Laws Prevent Mass Migration Senator Asks," *Baltimore Afro-American*, 5 February 1949, 5; *Congressional Record*, 81st Cong., 1st sess., 570.

61. *Congressional Record*, 81st Cong., 1st sess., 570.

62. Marguerite Steedman to Richard B. Russell, 28 July 1948, Series X, Box 143, Folder 6, RBR; Potenziani, "Striking Back," 272; "Senator Russell's Proposal," *Atlanta Constitution*, 29 January 1949, 10; Odum, *Race and Rumors of Race*, 215.

63. Odum, *Race and Rumors of Race*, 116, 119; "Senator Russell's Proposal," *Atlanta Constitution*, 29 January 1949, 10.

64. Richard B. Russell to Dorothy Orr, 5 October 1948, Series X, Box 143, Folder 6, RBR; Sam Jones, "A Southern Solution," *Life*, 14 March 1949, 115–16, 119.

65. Richard B. Russell to Frank Boykin, 8 February 1949, Series X, Box 143, Folder 4; Russell to Harry F. Byrd, 7 June 1949, Series X, Box 30, Folder 9; both in RBR; "Is Our Real Voice Too Late?," *Atlanta Constitution*, 2 March 1949, 10.

66. William Colmer, "Congressional Sidelights," 1 March 1950, Box 422, Folder 5, WMC; *Freedom to Serve*, xi–xii; Mershon and Schlossman, *Foxholes and Color Lines*, 189. For a detailed discussion of Executive Order 9981 and the formation of the Fahy Committee, see also Nalty, *Strength for the Fight*, 235–54; and Dalfiume, *Desegregation of the U.S. Armed Forces*, 175–200.

67. *Congressional Record*, 80th Cong., 2nd sess., 5665–66; John G. Norris, "18–25 Draft Cleared by Senate Group," *Washington Post*, 12 May 1948, 8, 1; Norris, "Two-Year Draft Law Limit Voted by Senate," ibid., 9 June 1948, 1.

68. Richard B. Russell to Thomas A. Hilton, 27 June 1950, Series X, Box 185, Folder 2, RBR; *Congressional Record*, 81st Cong., 2nd sess., 8992; Russell to Roe P. Greer, 21 June 1950, Series X, Box 185, Folder 2, RBR; *Congressional Record*, 81st Cong., 2nd sess., 8994. James H. Hershman Jr. credits Virginia newspaperman Leon Dure with introducing the phrase "freedom of choice" into the segregationist lexicon during the school desegregation battles of the 1950s and 1960s. For more on the emergence of "freedom of choice" as a rallying cry for advocates of school segregation, see Hershman, "Massive Resistance Meets Its Match," 104–33. In his recent study of white racial politics in postwar Atlanta, Kevin Kruse has shown how conservative whites deployed the rhetoric of "freedom of association" in response to black demands for segregation of public spaces. See Kruse, *White Flight*, 161–79.

69. *Congressional Record*, 81st Cong., 2nd sess., 8992–93.

Chapter 5

1. Ralph McGill, "What is Jimmy Byrnes Up to Now?," *Saturday Evening Post*, 14 October 1950, 184, 186. See also Walter J. Brown, *James F. Byrnes of South Carolina*, 185–86.

2. "Comments on Men and Things," 26 July 1950, Box 1, Folder 18, Breedin Papers, SCL; McGill, "What is Jimmy Byrnes Up to Now?," *Saturday Evening Post*, 14 October 1950, 184. McGill's characterization of Deep South politics stands in stark contrast to the contemporary and scholarly analysis of the 1950 Senate primaries in North Carolina and Florida. These campaigns, in which conservative challengers used red-baiting and race-baiting to unseat liberals Frank Porter Graham and Claude Pepper, have received more attention from historians than the relatively tame contests celebrated by McGill. See Gentry, "All That's Not Fit to Print."

3. McGill, "What is Jimmy Byrnes Up to Now?," *Saturday Evening Post*, 14 October 1950, 188.

4. Henry Lesesne, "Red Carpet Out for Gov. Byrnes," *Washington Post*, 14 January 1951, 1; McGill, "What is Jimmy Byrnes Up to Now?," *Saturday Evening Post*, 14 October 1950, 33.

5. In his study of school equalization in Mississippi during the decade before the *Brown* decision, Charles Bolton argues that "educational equalization was never a viable alternative" because of the limited funds available for the project and because white leaders settled for "minimal adjustments," believing their posturing could stave off federally mandated desegregation orders. See Bolton, "Mississippi's School Equalization Program," 783. Tony Badger has argued that equalization was "the most coherent and powerful strategy" that southern conservatives developed to fight impending desegregation. Not only did Byrnes and his allies genuinely expect their plan to work, but they also were a step ahead of white southern liberals who failed to offer any alternative public strategy before 1954. See Badger, "*Brown* and Backlash," 44.

6. "A $400 Million Baby," *Chicago Defender*, 8 September 1951, 6. Given that educational improvements required state-level authorization and funding, studies of equalization efforts have focused on individual states rather than the coordinated efforts of Deep South leaders such as Byrnes, Talmadge, and Mississippi governor Hugh White. For a comprehensive study of equalization at the state level, see Bolton, "Mississippi's School Equalization Program."

7. "People Are Speaking Out," *South Today* (Winter 1942/Spring 1943): 45; "No Thanks—Please!," *Meridian (Miss.) Star*, 6 December 1942, 8; "Frank M. Dixon Keynote Speech," typescript, 5, Box 348, Folder 10, WMC.

8. Tushnet, *The NAACP's Legal Strategy*, 70–71; McNeal, *Groundwork*, 143–45.

9. Price Daniel to J. C. Stennis, 20 February 1950, Series 29, Box 1, Folder 26, JCS.

10. William Colmer, "Congressional Sidelights," 14 June 1950, Box 422, Folder 6, WMC; Stefkovitch and Leas, "A Legal History of Desegregation," 409–10; Kluger, *Simple Justice*, 321–57.

11. Henry Lesesne, "Red Carpet Out for Gov. Byrnes," *Washington Post*, 14 Janu-

ary 1951, 1; "The Press Looks at Jimmy Byrnes and Likes What it Sees," *Winnsboro (S.C.) News and Herald*, 26 January 1951, 1.

12. Henry Lesesne, "Red Carpet Out for Gov. Byrnes," *Washington Post*, 14 January 1951, 1; "The Press Looks at Jimmy Byrnes and Likes What it Sees," *Winnsboro (S.C.) News and Herald*, 26 January 1951, 1.

13. "Inaugural Address of James F. Byrnes," 16 January 1951, 2–4, Speeches and Press Releases File, Folder "Speeches and Press Releases (1)," Byrnes Gubernatorial Papers, SCDAH. In discussing Byrnes's return to public office in 1951, historian David Chappell has noted that Byrnes "led the way in elevating the segregationist cause above racial and sectional self-interest." See Chappell, *A Stone of Hope*, 155–56.

14. Robertson, *Sly and Able*, 504–7; "Inaugural Address of James F. Byrnes," 16 January 1951, 4, Speeches and Press Releases File, Folder "Speeches and Press Releases (1)," Byrnes Gubernatorial Papers, SCDAH; John N. Popham, "South Acts to Keep Pupil Segregation," *New York Times*, 28 May 1951, 16.

15. John N. Popham, "South Acts to Keep Pupil Segregation," *New York Times*, 28 May 1951, 16; "Address of James F. Byrnes . . . to the South Carolina Education Association," 16 March 1951, Speeches and Press Releases File, Folder "Speeches and Press Releases (1)," Byrnes Gubernatorial Papers, SCDAH. Historian Numan Bartley has identified the Gressette Committee as "the first such strategy-mapping segregation group in the South." See Bartley, *Rise of Massive Resistance*, 45. See also Quint, *Profile in Black and White*, 17; and Dobrasko, "Balancing Segregation and Education."

16. "Address of James F. Byrnes . . . to the South Carolina Education Association," 16 March 1951, Speeches and Press Releases File, Folder "Speeches and Press Releases (1)," Byrnes Gubernatorial Papers, SCDAH.

17. "Governor Byrnes Has A Sound And Sober Word For Southern Negroes And Their School Fight," *Florence (S.C.) Morning News*, 18 March 1951, 4-A.

18. Henry Lesesne, "Red Carpet Out for Gov. Byrnes," *Washington Post*, 14 January 1951, 1; James F. Byrnes to R. C. Griffith, 20 November 1951, General Subjects File, Box 1, Folder "Ku Klux Klan," Byrnes Gubernatorial Papers, SCDAH.

19. Chalmers, *Hooded Americanism*, 337–38; Wade, *The Fiery Cross*, 290–91; "Dynamite Thrown at Swansea Negro Church Where Whites Conducting Bible School," *Columbia (S.C.) State*, 7 September 1951, 1; Alan H. Schafer to James F. Byrnes, n.d., General Subjects File, Box 1, Folder "Ku Klux Klan," Byrnes Gubernatorial Papers, SCDAH.

20. Thomas L. Hamilton to James F. Byrnes, 4 September 1951, General Subjects File, Box 1, Folder "Ku Klux Klan" Folder, Byrnes Gubernatorial Papers, SCDAH; Alex McCullough, "Byrnes Leads South Carolina Educational Revolution," 1 November 1953, 6, Box 14, Folder 182, Samuel Lowry Latimer Papers, SCL; "Speech Made by Thomas L. Hamilton, Grand Dragon of the Ku Klux Klan, Made in Cherokee County, South Carolina, on Wednesday Night, 12 September 1951," General Subjects File, Box 1, Folder "Ku Klux Klan," Byrnes Gubernatorial Papers, SCDAH.

21. Untitled investigative report, n.d.; R. M. Eubanks to C. R. McMillan, 27 Au-

gust 1951, both in General Subjects File, Box 1, Folder "Ku Klux Klan," Byrnes Gubernatorial Papers, SCDAH; Chalmers, *Hooded Americanism*, 338–39; Byrnes, *All in One Lifetime*, 407.

22. "House Passes Antimask Bill by 149 to 1 Vote," *Atlanta Daily World*, 16 January 1951, 1; "Senate Votes Ban On Masks," ibid., 20 January 1951, 1. Thomas O'Brien argues that *Aaron v. Cook*, the desegregation suit named for one of nearly 200 black plaintiffs and the white president of the Atlanta School Board, "set into motion a paradoxical eleven-year state policy that would force Georgians to both strengthen and threaten to abandon the public school system." See Thomas V. O'Brien, "The Dog that Didn't Bark," 79.

23. "Georgia's Last Stand," *Pittsburgh Courier*, 5 May 1951, 20; Fred Hand to Blake Clark, 21 August 1952, Series 2, Box 3, Folder 14, Hand Family and Business Records, Troup County Archives, La Grange, Georgia; "State School Building Authority," 1–2, Gubernatorial Series, Sub-series B, Box 13, Folder 10, HET.

24. John N. Popham, "South Acts to Keep Pupil Segregation," *New York Times*, 28 May 1951, 16; "White-Talmadge Exchange Blows Over Georgia Jim Crow Measure," *News from NAACP*, press release, 27 February 1951, 3, Part 18, Series C, reel 31, NAACPP; Herman Talmadge, "Why I Say the Constitution Upholds Segregation in Our Public Schools," Series 29, Box 1, Folder 31, JCS.

25. John N. Popham, "South Acts to Keep Pupil Segregation," *New York Times*, 28 May 1951, 16.

26. Bolton, "Mississippi's School Equalization Program," 806; Bob Tims, "$41 Million School Plan is Described to Audience Here," *Delta Democrat-Times*, 8 November 1951, 1.

27. "Mississippians Are Divided Over Supporting School Program," *Atlanta Daily World*, 31 October 1951, 1; "Miss. NAACP Plans to Combat Segregation in Public Schools," *Atlanta Daily World*, 9 November 1951, 1 (second and fourth quotations); "The N.A.A.C.P.'s Non-Segregation Demand," *Delta Democrat-Times*, 8 November 1951, 4.

28. "It's the Man With a Record That Counts," *Delta Democrat-Times*, 6 August 1951, 3; Bolton, "Mississippi's School Equalization Program," 806.

29. Hugh White to James F. Byrnes, 29 May 1952, RG 27, Box 1866, Folder "Recess Education," White Gubernatorial Papers, MDAH.

30. Recess Education Committee, "Transcript of Wire Recording of Conference with Alabama State Officials," 16 June 1952, 12–13, RG 27, Box 1866, Folder "Recess Education," ibid.

31. Recess Education Committee, "Transcript of Wire Recording of Conference with South Carolina State Officials," 18 June 1952, 16, ibid.

32. Ibid.; Recess Education Committee, "Transcript of Wire Recording of Conference with Georgia State Officials," 20 June 1952, 7–8, 12, ibid.

33. Stanley Morse, "To Help Education," 7 April 1951, Box 5, Folder 383, Morse Papers, SCL.

34. Recess Education Committee, "Transcript of Wire Recording of Conference with South Carolina State Officials," 18 June 1952, 7, RG 27, Box 1866, Folder "Recess Education," White Gubernatorial Papers; A. M. Rivera, "Courier Survey Bares South

Carolina Hoax," *Pittsburgh Courier*, 11 July 1953, 5; Recess Education Committee, "Transcript of Wire Recording of Conference with Georgia State Officials," 20 June 1952, 9, RG 27, Box 1866, Folder "Recess Education," White Gubernatorial Papers, MDAH. Two years after *Brown*, Crow maintained that the equalization program had been 85 percent completed but still complained of the "fatal indifference to equalizing facilities for Negroes" in some parts of South Carolina. See Quint, *Profile in Black and White*, 93.

35. Recess Education Committee, "Transcript of Wire Recording of Conference with South Carolina State Officials," 18 June 1952, 6, 8–9, RG 27, Box 1866, Folder "Recess Education," White Gubernatorial Papers, MDAH.

36. Recess Education Committee, "Transcript of Wire Recording of Conference with Georgia State Officials," 20 June 1952, 8–9, ibid.

37. "What Happens If School Segregation Is Wiped Out?," *Pittsburgh Courier*, 9 May 1953, 19; J. A. Thigpen to Hugh White, Governor of Mississippi, and Members of the Legislative Investigating Committee, 7 October 1952, RG 27, Box 1866, Folder "Recess Education," White Gubernatorial Papers, MDAH; "Sen. Gore Has 'Just In Case' School Plan," *Chicago Defender*, 21 March 1953, 2. The invocation of "health and moral factors" would continue as segregationists attempted to refine and rearticulate their critique of racial egalitarianism in the 1950s and 1960s. Anders Walker has argued that moderate southern white leaders deployed arguments about black criminal, sexual, and moral behavior in order to undermine the legitimacy of the civil rights movement. See Walker, *The Ghost of Jim Crow*.

38. "Georgia's Last Stand," *Pittsburgh Courier*, 5 May 1951, 20; John E. Rousseau, "Segregated Education In Mississippi Can Never Be Equal!," *Pittsburgh Courier*, 24 October 1953, 22; *A Report to the Mississippi State Legislature by the Recess Education Committee* (Jackson, Miss.: March 1953), 16, Owens Papers, MDAH; "From One to the Other is Less Than Two Miles," *Jackson (Miss.) Daily News*, 11 November 1953, 2.

39. A. M. Rivera, "Courier Survey Bares South Carolina Hoax," *Pittsburgh Courier*, 11 July 1953, 1, 5.

40. "Mississippi's $100 Million," ibid., 14 November 1953, 8; "Separate But Equal Southern Schools," *Santa Monica Evening Outlook*, 7 November 1953, clipping in Part 3, Series C, reel 2, NAACPP.

41. "Gov. Byrnes Urges Elimination Of Public School Requirement," *Florence (S.C.) Morning News*, 17 October 1952, 1; John Temple Graves to Lynn Landrum, 18 April 1951, Box 1, Folder 7, JTG; Alex McCullough to Editor, 28 October 1953, Box 12, Folder 674; Alex McCullough, "Byrnes Leads South Carolina Educational Revolution," 1 November 1953, Box 14, Folder 182; both in Latimer Papers, SCL.

42. Stetson Kennedy, "Inside the Confederate Army," *Baltimore Afro-American*, 13 September 1952, Magazine Section, 12; "Miss. NAACP Plans To Combat Segregation in Public Schools, *Atlanta Daily World*, 9 November 1951, 1; "Our Opinions: Stalling the Inevitable," *Chicago Defender*, 14 November 1953, 11.

43. "Talmadge Says Chaos Will Follow," *Oklahoma City Black Dispatch*, 14 November 1953, clipping in Part 3, Series C, reel 2; "School Segregation Cases: Background Materials," 3 December 1953, 21, Part 3, Series C, reel 1; both in NAACPP.

44. James Walker, "'Racial Integrity' Dearer Than Schools—Byrnes," *Greenville (S.C.) News*, 26 March 1954, 1.

45. Brady, *A Review of Black Monday*, 15.

46. Sensing, *Colored Mondays*, n.p.; Hodding Carter III, *The South Strikes Back*, 15.

47. Hodding Carter III, *The South Strikes Back*, 11–12, 14, 16.

48. Johnston, *Mississippi's Defiant Years*, xiv.

49. Joseph W. Garrett to John C. Stennis, 28 May 1954, Series 29, Box 1, Folder 32, JCS.

50. John Stennis to T. J. Tubb, 20 May 1954, Series 29, Box 1, Folder 32, JCS.

51. John Stennis to J. P. Coleman, 20 May 1954, Series 29, Box 1, Folder 32; Stennis to T. J. Tubb, 20 May 1954, Series 29, Box 1, Folder 32; Stennis to Hugh White, 4 June 1954, Series 29, Box 1, Folder 33; all in JCS.

52. John C. Stennis to Hugh White, 4 June 1954, Series 29, Box 1, Folder 33, JCS.

53. Bolton, *The Hardest Deal of All*, 64–65; Johnston, *Mississippi's Defiant Years*, 6.

54. Klarman, *From Jim Crow to Civil Rights*, 312–20.

55. John Temple Graves, "Women's Chamber of Commerce," 24 October 1956, 1–2, Box 1, Folder 14; "Citizens Councils–Selma, Ala.," 8 October 1959, 3, Box 1, Folder 15; "Lion's Club, Birmingham, Essex House, Downtown Club," 9 April 1958, Box 1, Folder 15; all in JTG.

56. Badger, "The South Confronts the Court," 127.

57. William S. White, "Rights Program Is Likely to Pass," *New York Times*, 25 March 1957, 12; Sam J. Ervin to B. B. Dougherty, 2 March 1956, Box 15, Folder 1120, Ervin Papers, SHC. For more on Hoey, see Thatcher, "A Last Gasp," 31. Historian Karl E. Campbell claims that Ervin offered a "unique strategy" by "replacing the racist rhetoric of the past with careful constitutional arguments." But as previous chapters have shown, this constitutional strategy had deeper roots in southern struggles against racial reform. Arriving in 1954, Ervin was uniquely qualified to lend unprecedented legitimacy to these arguments but was too late to craft them from scratch. As Campbell notes, Ervin's appeal was based less on his originality and more on his pedigree as a Harvard-educated former judge from a southern state with a reputation for relatively enlightened and progressive racial politics. See Campbell, *Senator Sam Ervin*, 99.

58. Badger, "The South Confronts the Court," 126.

59. "The States Won't Surrender," draft with handwritten edits, n.d., 1, 3, Box 1, Folder 11, JTG; Don Hill, "Executives Club Speaker Discusses Southern Resistance to Integration," *Norfolk Virginian-Pilot*, 25 November 1958, 11-A. Graves advocated this "constitutional cold war" in speeches across the country during the late 1950s. See Paul Dumas, "No Surrender on Segregation, Says Speaker," *Tacoma News Tribune*, 13 October 1957; "South Plans Segregation 'Cold War,' Club Is Told," *Rockford Morning Star*, 23 October 1957; and Sam Jensen, "South Waging 'Constitutional Cold War,' Dixie Newsman Says Here," *Lincoln Evening Journal and Nebraska State Journal*, 15 October 1957, 16, clippings in Box 2, Folder 2, JTG.

60. Ely, *The Crisis of Conservative Virginia*.

61. Chappell, *A Stone of Hope*, 169; Old, *The Segregation Issue*, 2–3; James J. Kilpatrick, "The Right to Interpose," *Human Events*, 24 December 1955, n.p.

62. John Stennis to Richard Russell, 24 February 1956, Series 29, Box 5, Folder 5, JCS; Bartley, *The Rise of Massive Resistance*, 136–37.

63. John Temple Graves, "The South Won't Surrender!," *American Mercury* 83 (July 1956): 41.

64. "Lion's Club, Birmingham, Essex House, Downtown Club," 9 April 1958, Box 1, Folder 15, JTG. Two years later, the publishers of South Carolina journalist William D. Workman's defense of segregation, *The Case for the South*, invoked similar language to position him as the voice of the mainstream South. Workman, promotional literature announced, was neither a "moderate" nor a "'magnolia and moonlight' romanticist." Untitled promotional broadside, Box 24, Folder "Case for the South, The: General," Workman Papers, SCPC.

65. Kilpatrick, "Conservatism and the South," 195, 188.

66. "Will the South Decide the Election?," typescript, n.d., 2, Box 1, Folder 11, JTG.

67. Kilpatrick, *The Sovereign States*, 279, 286; Kilpatrick, "The Right to Interpose," *Human Events*, 24 December 1955, n.p.

68. Byrnes, *Supreme Court Must Be Curbed*, 12–13; Eastland, *Era of Judicial Tyranny*, 5.

69. Paton, *The Negro in America Today*, n.p.; R. B. Patterson, "We Must Strengthen and Build Our Organization for a Long, Hard Fight," in Association of Citizens' Councils of Mississippi, *Annual Report* (1955), 2, Citizens' Councils Collection, MSUSC. Historian David L. Chappell has previously argued that the "fatal" division between the constitutionalists (a group to which he assigns Kilpatrick and Byrnes) and racial militants (such as Patterson) limited the popularity and effectiveness of massive resistance. While Chappell correctly points out the tactical and ideological differences among segregationists, the line separating the constitutionalist from the racial idealogue was blurred at best. See Chappell, "Divided Mind of the Southern Segregationists," 46.

70. Martin, *The Deep South Says "Never,"* 1–2.

71. Kilpatrick, *The Sovereign States*, 258.

Chapter 6

1. Martin, *The Deep South Says "Never,"* 1–2.

2. Roy V. Harris, Oral History #82, 24 February 1971, 22–23, Richard B. Russell Library for Political Research and Studies, University of Georgia, Athens; Harris, "South Is Victim of Installment Plan Surrender," *Citizens' Council* 5 (September 1960): 1.

3. Roy V. Harris, "South Is Victim of Installment Plan Surrender," *Citizens' Council* 5 (September 1960): 1; "Council Heads Renew Pledge of Dixie Unity," ibid. (May 1960): 4.

4. Kruse, "The Paradox of Massive Resistance," 1011.

5. "Talmadge Asks Whites To Bloc Vote In Macon Campaign Rally," *Atlanta Daily*

World, 23 June 1950, 1; "Address of Governor James F. Byrnes of South Carolina to the Delta Council at Cleveland, Mississippi," 15 May 1952, 16, Series 9, Box 12, Folder 18, Byrnes Papers, CUSC.

6. "Third Party Move Suggested by Byrnes," *Washington Post*, 16 May 1952, 19; John N. Popham, "Byrnes Asks Bloc of South's Whites," *New York Times*, 16 May 1952, 11; "Address of Governor James F. Byrnes of South Carolina to the Delta Council at Cleveland, Mississippi," 15 May 1952, 16, Series 9, Box 12, Folder 18, Byrnes Papers, CUSC; "Byrnes Advocates Third Party For South To Meet Challenge," *Delta Democrat-Times*, 15 May 1952, 1.

7. "People's Campaign Committee Launches Information Program," *Bolivar County (Miss.) News-Enterprise*, May 15, 1952, n.p.

8. James F. Byrnes, "The Principle of Local Government," *Vital Speeches of the Day*, 15 May 1952, 452; "Address of the Honorable James F. Byrnes . . . to the North Carolina Citizens Association," 14 March 1951, 2, Series 9, Box 12, Folder 7, Byrnes Papers, CUSC; Byrnes, "The Principle of Local Government," *Vital Speeches of the Day*, 15 May 1952, 451; "Two Addresses of Governor James F. Byrnes," 14–15, Series 9, Box 12, Folder 15, Byrnes Papers, CUSC.

9. Roscoe Drummond, "State of the Nation: Russell Looms as Strong Contender," *Christian Science Monitor*, 26 June 1952, 1; Frederickson, *Dixiecrat Revolt*, 227–28.

10. Kalk, *Origins of the Southern Strategy*, 6–7; Frederickson, *Dixiecrat Revolt*, 229–31; "Think Before Voting," *Textile Bulletin* 78 (October 1952): 46.

11. John L. Clark, "Political Picture," *Pittsburgh Courier*, 27 December 1952, 16; "Byrnes Seeks To Bar Negro," *New York Amsterdam News*, 20 December 1952, 2. Contemporary estimates of black voter registration in South Carolina confirmed Byrnes's estimate—80,000 African Americans had registered in the state by 1952. See Lawson, *Black Ballots*, 134.

12. John L. Clark, "Political Picture," *Pittsburgh Courier*, 27 December 1952, 16; Lawson, *Black Ballots*, 134; T. H. Martin to James F. Byrnes, 15 December 1952; Jesse Helms to Byrnes, 22 December 1952; both in Series 7, Box 1, Folder 4, Byrnes Papers, CUSC.

13. John L. Clark, "Political Picture," *Pittsburgh Courier*, 27 December 1952, 16; T. H. Martin to James F. Byrnes, 15 December 1952; Alex McCullough, "Analysis of Negro Bloc Voting," 1; both in Series 7, Box 1, Folder 4, Byrnes Papers, CUSC.

14. John Temple Graves, "The South to Power," 20 August 1956, 1–2; Graves, "Women's Chamber of Commerce," 24 October 1956, 2; both in Box 1, Folder 14, JTG.

15. Henry Lesesne, "South Carolina: GOP Gain?," *Christian Science Monitor*, 31 October 1956, 15. For more on independent right-wing activity during the 1956 presidential campaign, see Bartley, *Rise of Massive Resistance*, 150–69.

16. Bartley, *Rise of Massive Resistance*, 166–68.

17. R. B. Patterson, "We Must Strengthen and Build Our Organization for a Long, Hard Fight," in Association of Citizens' Councils of Mississippi, *Annual Report* (1955), 2, Citizens' Councils Collection, MSUSC; Bartley, *Rise of Massive Resistance*, 84–86.

18. Sam Engelhardt, typescript, n.t., n.d., 9, Box 4, Folder 8, Engelhardt Papers, LPR111, ADAH.

19. "Nat Cole Cancels Tour After Attack at Concert," *Washington Post–Times Herald*, 12 April 1956, 3; McMillen, *The Citizens' Council*, 50–51.

20. Bartley, *The Rise of Massive Resistance*, 102. "Office Seekers Contending Over Question of Race," *Southern School News*, September 1958, 12.

21. Kruse, "The Paradox of Massive Resistance," 1010–20; Katagiri, *The Mississippi State Sovereignty Commission*, 3–35; Crespino, *In Search of Another Country*, 26–30; McMillen, *The Citizens' Council*, 209–15; Bartley, *The Rise of Massive Resistance*, 170–89.

22. Kirk, *Beyond Little Rock*, 103–10; Bartley, *The Rise of Massive Resistance*, 251–69.

23. Claude Sitton, "Citizens' Council Fuels Louisiana Resistance," *New York Times*, 27 November 1960, E6. Lewis, *Massive Resistance*, 114–20; Inger, "The New Orleans School Crisis"; Fairclough, *Race and Democracy*, 234–64; Sokol, *There Goes My Everything*, 124–41.

24. "In New Orleans—Whites Stand Firm"; "South Has Chance to Control Outcome in Electoral College"; "How You Can Help Elect a Southern President," all in *Citizens' Council* 6 (November 1960): 1.

25. "Southern Unity Drive Gains Support," *Citizens' Council* 5 (February 1960): 1; "Free Elector Plan Picks Up Additional Southern Backing," *Citizens' Council* 5 (April 1960): 1.

26. "Free Elector Plan Picks Up Additional Southern Backing," *Citizens' Council* 5 (April 1960): 4; "'Stand Up and Fight' Policy Urged," *Citizens' Council* 5 (July 1960): 1; "State's Independents Organize for Action," *Jackson (Miss.) Clarion-Ledger*, 1 September 1960, 1A, 12A. For more on the free elector movement, see Jeansonne, *Leander Perez*, 310–35.

27. "In Our Opinion: The Independent Elector Plan," *Deer Creek Pilot* (Rolling Fork, Miss.), 5 August 1960, clipping in Series 50, Box 11, Folder 11, JCS.

28. Henderson, *Politics of Change in Georgia*, 122–23; "Statement of Unpledged Electors from Mississippi and Alabama, Dec. 12, 1960–Jackson, Miss.", Folder 7, Citizens' Council Collection, MSUSC.

29. Karl E. Mundt to John Stennis, 13 June 1955, Series 33, Box 150, Folder "Electoral College Res., 1953–55"; John C. Newman to Stennis, 27 September 1962, Series 33, Box 157, Folder "Electoral College, 1962–64," both in JCS.

30. Workman, *The Case for the South*, vii–viii.

31. Ibid., 248, 250–51, 268–69.

32. Ibid., 19; "White Voters Aroused in Detroit!," *Citizens' Council* 5 (August 1960): 1.

33. Workman, *The Case for the South*, 265–66.

34. Perlstein, *Before the Storm*, 61–68.

35. Goldwater, *The Conscience of a Conservative*, 25–28.

36. Gifford, "'Dixie is No Longer in the Bag,'" 213, 215; Perlstein, *Before the Storm*, 76.

37. Robert D. Novak, "Goldwater's Image," *Wall Street Journal*, 11 January 1961, 1.

Barry Goldwater went public with the "Forgotten American" plan in a Senate speech on 11 January 1961, in which he argued that the GOP must become the party of the "silent Americans." See Perlstein, *Before the Storm*, 138.

38. Goldfield, *Black, White, and Southern*, 195; Claude Sitton, "G.O.P. Parley Charts Campaign for a 2-Party System in South," *New York Times*, 19 November 1961, 72; Ralph McGill, "Goldwater New Hero of the Ku Klux Klan," *Hartford (Conn.) Courant*, 26 November 1961, 2B.

39. Ralph McGill, "Goldwater New Hero Of the Ku Klux Klan," *Hartford (Conn.) Courant*, 26 November 1961, 2B; McGill, "Senator Goldwater, The New Confederate," ibid., 29 November 1961, 14.

40. Claude Sitton, "Senate Race Is On In South Carolina," *New York Times*, 18 March 1962, 53.

41. Merritt, "The Senatorial Election of 1962," 294.

42. Perlstein, *Before the Storm*, 130; John C. Newman to John C. Stennis, 27 September 1962; Ethelyne Blaine to John C. Stennis, 19 September 1962; both in Series 33, Box 157, Folder "Electoral College, 1962–64," JCS.

43. Patterson, "Conservative Coalition Forms in Congress," 757–72.

44. Mann, *The Walls of Jericho*, 247.

45. Ibid., 189–224.

46. Ibid., 247–269.

47. Ibid., 317; Branch, *Parting the Waters*, 821–27; Branch, *Pillar of Fire*, 75–78, 104–17; Dittmer, *Local People*, 165–66; Payne, *I've Got the Light of Freedom*, 288–89.

48. "Many In Congress Decry Its Record," *New York Times*, 12 November 1963, 21.

49. Mann, *Walls of Jericho*, 390.

50. Ibid., 391; Whalen, *The Longest Debate*, 142.

51. *Congressional Record*, 88th Cong., 2nd sess., 4744.

52. Mann, *Walls of Jericho*, 402.

53. Potenziani, "Striking Back," 274; *Congressional Record*, 88th Cong., 2nd sess., 13329.

54. Leigh Strope, "Thurmond Set Senate Record for Filibustering: 24 Hours and 18 Minutes," 27 June 2003, Associated Press Online Archive, available at http://www.ap.org.

55. Quoted in Bass and Thompson, *Ol' Strom*, 181.

56. *Congressional Record*, 88th Cong., 2nd sess., 14319.

57. Mann, *Walls of Jericho*, 443; Cohodas, *Strom Thurmond*, 356.

58. "Notes from South Carolina," *National Review*, 6 October 1964, 852.

59. Claude Sitton, "The Old Order Falling," *New York Times*, 18 September 1964, 17.

60. Rowland Evans and Robert Novak, "The White Man's Party," *Washington Post–Times Herald*, 25 June 1963, A6.

61. Ibid.

62. Ibid.

Epilogue

1. Smitherman quoted in episode 6: "Bridge to Freedom," *Eyes on the Prize: American's Civil Rights Movement, 1954–1985*, VHS (Blackside, 1987); Lawson, *Black Ballots*, 309–12; Garrow, *Bearing the Cross*, 379–409; Branch, *At Canaan's Edge*, 44–115.

2. "Senate Wants Races Decided by a Majority," *Atlanta Daily World*, 24 May 1964, 1; Kousser, *Colorblind Injustice*, 197–206; Tuck, *Beyond Atlanta*, 218.

3. Kousser, *Colorblind Injustice*, 212–14.

4. Rowland Evans and Robert Novak, "Yerger Writes Self Off," *Washington Post–Times Herald*, 25 April 1965, E7.

5. James P. Lucier, "Civil Rites," *American Opinion* 8 (June 1965): 18–19, 20, 28; Link, *Righteous Warrior*, 204–5, 133.

6. Dan T. Carter, *The Politics of Rage*, 195–225, 294–370.

7. Perlstein, *Nixonland*, 283–85.

8. Rowland Evans and Robert Novak, "Yerger Writes Self Off," *Washington Post–Times Herald*, 25 April 1965, E7; Rowland Evans and Robert Novak, "White Men Only," *Washington Post–Times Herald*, 14 February 1966, A17; "Mississippi Official Shapes GOP Policy," *Christian Science Monitor*, 12 March 1966, 14; Crespino, *In Search of Another Country*, 215–16.

9. While he dismisses the Southern Strategy thesis that posits Deep South segregationists as the primary movers in the rise of southern Republicanism, Matthew Lassiter has concluded that the "color-blind" politics of the Sun Belt created a "suburban synthesis of racial inequality and class segregation." See Lassiter, *The Silent Majority*, 323.

10. Matthew Lassiter argues that northern leaders embraced a "color-blind" discourse that rationalized northern "de facto" segregation as distinct from "de jure" southern segregation and thus washed their hands of responsibility for integrating their own communities. In absolving themselves of responsibility for racial inequality, northern liberals and moderates deployed a rhetoric also embraced by "segregationist politicians from the Deep South." See Lassiter, "De Jure/De Facto Segregation," 27.

BIBLIOGRAPHY

Manuscript Collections

Athens, Georgia
> Richard B. Russell Library for Political Research and Studies,
> University of Georgia
>> Richard B. Russell Papers
>> Herman E. Talmadge Papers

Birmingham, Alabama
> Birmingham Public Library
>> John Temple Graves Papers

Chapel Hill, North Carolina
> Southern Historical Collection, Louis Round Wilson Library,
> University of North Carolina
>> Jonathan Daniels Papers
>> Samuel J. Ervin Papers
>> Mark Ethridge Papers
>> Frank Porter Graham Papers

Clemson, South Carolina
> Special Collections, Clemson University
>> James F. Byrnes Papers
>> Strom Thurmond Collection

Cleveland, Mississippi
> Charles W. Capps Archives and Museum, Delta State University
>> Walter Sillers Papers

College Park, Maryland
> National Archives and Records Administration
>> Records of the War Manpower Commission

Columbia, South Carolina
> South Carolina Department of Archives and History
>> Gubernatorial Papers of James F. Byrnes
>> Gubernatorial Papers of R. M. Jefferies
>> Gubernatorial Papers of Olin D. Johnston
> South Carolina Political Collections, University of South Carolina
>> Joseph R. Bryson Papers
>> Olin Dewitt Talmadge Johnston Papers
>> William D. Workman Papers
> South Caroliniana Library, University of South Carolina
>> James Kolb Breedin Papers
>> Richard Manning Jefferies Papers
>> Samuel Lowry Latimer Papers
>> John Henry McCray Papers
>> Stanley Fletcher Morse Papers

Durham, North Carolina
  Rare Books, Manuscripts, and Special Collections Library, Duke University
    William Watts Ball Papers
    Earnest Sevier Cox Papers
    Thomas Dixon Papers
Hattiesburg, Mississippi
  Special Collections, McCain Library, University of Southern Mississippi
    Theodore G. Bilbo Papers
    William M. Colmer Papers
    William D. McCain Pamphlet Collection
    Eugene Talmadge Pamphlets
Jackson, Mississippi
  Mississippi Department of Archives and History
    Archibald Coody Papers
    George W. Owens Papers
    Gubernatorial Papers of Hugh L. White
LaGrange, Georgia
  Troup County Archives
    Hand Family and Business Records
Montgomery, Alabama
  Alabama Department of Archives and History
    Alabama Governor (1943–1947: Sparks) Administrative Files
    Frank Murray Dixon Papers
    State Democratic Party (Ala.) Executive Committee Records
Nashville, Tennessee
  Tennessee State Library and Archives
    Southern States Industrial Council Records
Starkville, Mississippi
  Congressional and Political Research Center, Mississippi State University
    John C. Stennis Collection
  Special Collections, Mitchell Memorial Library, Mississippi State University
    Citizens' Council Collection

Microfilm Editions

Commission on Interracial Cooperation Papers, Southern Historical Collection,
    Louis Round Wilson Library, University of North Carolina at Chapel Hill
Papers of the National Association for the Advancement of Colored People,
    Library of Congress, Washington, D.C.

Periodicals

American Mercury

American Opinion

Atlanta Constitution

Atlanta Daily World

Atlanta Foundation

Atlanta Journal

Baltimore Afro-American

Biloxi Daily Herald

Bolivar County (Miss.) News-Enterprise

Chicago Defender

Christian Science Monitor
Citizens' Council
Clarke County (Miss.) Tribune
Columbia (S.C.) State
Delta Democrat-Times
Florence (S.C.) Morning News
Georgia Woman's World
Greenville (S.C.) News
Greenwood (Miss.) Commonwealth
Hapeville (Ga.) Statesman
Hartford (Conn.) Courant
Human Events
Jackson (Miss.) Clarion-Ledger
Jackson (Miss.) Daily News
Life
Memphis Commercial Appeal
Meridian (Miss.) Star
National Review
New Orleans Times-Picayune
Newsweek
New York Amsterdam Star-News
New York Herald Tribune
New York Times

Norfolk Journal and Guide
Norfolk Virginian-Pilot
Pittsburgh Courier
PM
Raleigh News and Observer
Rolling Fork (Miss.) Deer Creek Pilot
Ruleville (Miss.) Record
Saturday Evening Post
Savannah Morning News
Southern School News
South Today
Summit (Miss.) Sun
Survey Graphic
Survey Midmonthly
Textile Bulletin
Time
Town Meeting
Tupelo (Miss.) Daily Journal
Wall Street Journal
Washington Post
Webster (Miss.) Progress
Winnsboro (S.C.) News and Herald
Winona (Miss.) Times

Government Documents

Freedom to Serve: Equality of Treatment and Opportunity in the Armed Services. Washington, D.C.: GPO, 1950.

To Secure These Rights: The Report of the President's Committee on Civil Rights. Washington, D.C.: GPO, 1947.

U.S. Congress. Congressional Record. Washington, D.C.: GPO, 1937–64.

U.S. Congress. Senate. Committee on the District of Columbia. Reorganization of the Government of the District of Columbia: Hearings before a Subcommittee of the Committee on the District of Columbia. 78th Cong., 1st sess., 1943. Washington, D.C.: GPO, 1943.

Published Primary Sources

Benedict, Ruth, and Gene Weltfish. The Races of Mankind. 1st ed. New York: Public Affairs Committee, 1943.

Bilbo, Theodore G. Take Your Choice: Separation or Mongrelization. Poplarville, Miss.: Dream House, 1947.

Bledsoe, O. F. "Agriculture and the Federal Government." Greenwood, Miss.: n.p., 1943.

Brady, Tom P. Black Monday. Winona, Miss: Association of Citizens' Councils, 1955.

————. *A Review of Black Monday*. Winona, Miss.: Association of Citizens' Councils of Mississippi, n.d.

————. *The South at Bay*. Brookhaven, Miss.: n.p., 1948.

Byrnes, James F. *All in One Lifetime*. New York: Harper, 1958.

————. *The Supreme Court Must Be Curbed*. Greenwood, Miss.: Association of Citizens' Councils, 1956.

Collins, Charles Wallace. *Whither Solid South?: A Study in Politics and Race Relations*. New Orleans: Pelican Publishing Company, 1947.

Connor, Mike S. *The Case Against the New Deal*. N.p., 1944.

Constitutional Educational League. *The Fifth Column in the South*. New Haven: Constitutional Educational League, 1940.

Cox, Earnest Sevier. *The Races of Mankind: A Review*. Jellico, Tenn.: Arthur Daugherty, 1951.

Daniels, Jonathan. *White House Witness, 1942–1945*. Garden City, N.Y.: Doubleday, 1975.

Dies, Martin. *The Trojan Horse in America*. New York: Dodd, Mead, and Co., 1940.

Dixon, Frank M. *Crossroads Democracy*. New York: New York Southern Society, 1942.

Dixon, Thomas. *The Flaming Sword*. Edited by John David Smith. Lexington: University Press of Kentucky, 2005.

Eastland, James O. *We've Reached Era of Judicial Tyranny*. Winona: Association of Citizens' Councils of Mississippi, n.d.

Goldwater, Barry. *The Conscience of a Conservative*. Shepherdsville, Ky.: Victor, 1960.

Graves, John Temple. *The Fighting South*. New York: Putnam, 1943.

————. "The Southern Negro and the War Crisis," *Virginia Quarterly Review* 18 (Autumn 1942): 500–517.

Irwin, John R. *Let's Keep the United States White*. Sandersville, Ga.: n.p., 1945.

Kennedy, Stetson. *Southern Exposure*. New York: Doubleday, 1946.

Kilpatrick, James Jackson. "Conservatism and the South." In *The Lasting South: Fourteen Southerners Look at their Home*, ed. Louis D. Rubin and James Jackson Kilpatrick, 188–205. Chicago: Regnery, 1957.

————. *The Southern Case for School Desegregation*. New York: Crowell-Collier Press, 1962.

————. *The Sovereign States: Notes of a Citizen of Virginia*. Chicago: Regnery, 1957.

Landis, Kenesaw Mountain. *Segregation in Washington: A Report of the National Committee on Segregation in the Nation's Capital*. Chicago: National Committee on Segregation in the Nation's Capital, 1948.

Landry, Stuart Omer. *The Cult of Equality: A Study of the Race Problem*. New Orleans: Pelican Publishing Company, 1945.

Old, William. *The Segregation Issue: Suggestions Regarding the Maintenance of State Autonomy*. Chesterfield, Va.: n.p., [1955].

Paton, Alan. *The Negro in America Today: A Firsthand Report*. New York: Community Relations Service, 1955.

Prince, R. M. *I Can't Vote for Mr. Roosevelt in November*. High Point, N.C.: n.p., 1944.

Putnam, Carleton. *Race and Reason: A Yankee View*. Washington, D.C.: Public Affairs Press, 1961.

Rand, Clayton. *The New Deal and the New Slavery*. Gulfport, Miss.: Dixie Press, 1944.

Rutledge, Archibald. "The Negro and the New Deal." *South Atlantic Quarterly* 39 (July 1940): 281–89.

Sensing, Thurman. *Colored Mondays*. Nashville: Southern States Industrial Council, n.d.

———. *Down South*. Nashville: Southern States Industrial Council, 1946.

"A Southern White Friend." *The Negro Disillusioned*. Childersburg, Ala.: Crusader Publishing Company, 1944.

Talmadge, Herman E. *You and Segregation*. Birmingham: Vulcan Press, 1955.

Workman, William D. *The Case for the South*. New York: Devin-Adair, 1960.

Secondary Books and Articles

Abrams, Douglas Carl. *Conservative Constraints: North Carolina and the New Deal*. Jackson: University Press of Mississippi, 1992.

Ader, Emile. "Why the Dixiecrats Failed." *Journal of Politics* 15 (August 1953): 356–69.

Anderson, Jervis. *A. Philip Randolph: A Biographical Portrait*. New York: Harcourt Brace Jovanovich, 1972.

Anderson, William. *The Wild Man from Sugar Creek: The Political Career of Eugene Talmadge*. Baton Rouge: Louisiana State University Press, 1975.

Armbrester, Margaret E. "John Temple Graves II: A Southern Liberal Views the New Deal." *Alabama Review* 32 (July 1979): 203–13.

Asch, Chris Myers. "Revisiting Reconstruction: James O. Eastland, the FEPC, and the Struggle to Rebuild Germany, 1945-1946." *Journal of Mississippi History* 67 (Spring 2005): 1–28.

———. *The Senator and the Sharecropper: The Freedom Struggles of James O. Eastland and Fannie Lou Hamer*. New York: New Press, 2008.

Badger, Tony. "*Brown* and Backlash." In *Massive Resistance: Southern Opposition to the Second Reconstruction*, ed. Clive Webb, 39–55. New York: Oxford University Press, 2005.

———. "'Closet Moderates': Why White Liberals Failed, 1940-1970." In *The Role of Ideas in the Civil Rights Movement*, ed. Ted Ownby, 83–112. Jackson: University Press of Mississippi, 2002.

———. "The South Confronts the Court: The Southern Manifesto of 1956." *Journal of Policy History* 20, no. 1 (2008): 126–42.

———. "Southerners Who Refused to Sign the Southern Manifesto." *Historical Journal* 42 (June 1999): 517–34.

Bailes, Sue. "Eugene Talmadge and the Board of Regents Controversy." *Georgia Historical Quarterly* 53 (December 1969): 409–23.

Bailey, Robert J. "Theodore G. Bilbo and the Fair Employment Practices

Controversy: A Southern Senator's Reaction to a Changing World." *Journal of Mississippi History* 42 (February 1980): 27–42.

Barnard, William D. *Dixiecrats and Democrats: Alabama Politics, 1942–1950.* Tuscaloosa: University of Alabama Press, 1974.

Bartley, Numan V. *The New South, 1945–1980: The Story of the South's Modernization.* Baton Rouge: Louisiana State University Press, 1995.

———. *The Rise of Massive Resistance: Race and Politics in the South during the 1950s.* Baton Rouge: Louisiana State University Press, 1969.

Bass, Jack, and Marilyn W. Thompson. *Ol' Strom: An Unauthorized Biography of Strom Thurmond.* Columbia: University of South Carolina Press, 2003.

Bass, Jack, and Walter DeVries. *The Transformation of Southern Politics: Social Change and Political Consequences since 1945.* New York: Basic Books, 1976.

Berman, William C. *The Politics of Civil Rights in the Truman Administration.* Columbus: Ohio State University Press, 1970.

Bernd, Joseph L. "White Supremacy and the Disfranchisement of Blacks in Georgia, 1946." *Georgia Historical Quarterly* 66 (Winter 1982): 492–513.

Biles, Roger. *The South and the New Deal.* Lexington: University Press of Kentucky, 1994.

Black, Earl. *Southern Governors and Civil Rights: Racial Segregation as a Campaign Issue in the Second Reconstruction.* Cambridge: Harvard University Press, 1976.

Black, Earl, and Merle Black. *The Rise of Southern Republicans.* Cambridge: Harvard University Press, 2002.

Blick, David G. "Beyond 'Politics of Color': Opposition to South Carolina's 1952 Constitutional Amendment to Abolish the Public School System." *Proceedings of the South Carolina Historical Association* (1995): 179–92.

Bolton, Charles. *The Hardest Deal of All: The Battle Over School Integration in Mississippi, 1870–1980.* Jackson: University Press of Mississippi, 2005.

———. "Mississippi's School Equalization Program, 1945–1954: 'A Last Gasp to Try to Maintain a Segregated Educational System.'" *Journal of Southern History* 66 (November 2000): 781–814.

Borstelmann, Thomas. *The Cold War and the Color Line: American Race Relations in the Global Arena.* New ed. Cambridge: Harvard University Press, 2003.

Boyd, Tim. "The 1966 Election in Georgia and the Ambiguity of the White Backlash." *Journal of Southern History* 75 (May 2009): 305–40.

Branch, Taylor. *At Canaan's Edge: America in the King Years, 1965–68.* New York: Simon and Shuster, 2006.

———. *Parting the Waters: America in the King Years, 1954–63.* New York: Simon and Schuster, 1988.

———. *Pillar of Fire: America in the King Years, 1963–65.* New York: Simon and Schuster, 1998.

Brattain, Michelle. *The Politics of Whiteness: Race, Workers, and Culture in the Modern South.* Princeton, N.J.: Princeton University Press, 2001.

Brinkley, Alan. "The New Deal and Southern Politics." In *The New Deal and the South*, ed. James C. Cobb and Michael Namorato, 97–115. Jackson: University Press of Mississippi, 1984.

Brinkley, David. *Brinkley's Beat: People, Places, and Events That Shaped My Time*.
New York: Knopf, 2003.

Brooks, Jennifer E. *Defining the Peace: World War II Veterans, Race, and the
Remaking of Southern Political Tradition*. Chapel Hill: University of North
Carolina Press, 2004.

Brown, Flora Bryant. "NAACP Sponsored Sit-ins by Howard University Students
in Washington, D.C., 1943–1944." *Journal of Negro History* 85 (Autumn 2000):
274–86.

Brown, Walter J. *James F. Byrnes of South Carolina: A Remembrance*. Macon, Ga.:
Mercer University Press, 1990.

Bunche, Ralph J. *The Political Status of the Negro in the Age of FDR*. Edited by
Dewey W. Grantham. Chicago: University of Chicago Press, 1973.

Campbell, Karl E. *Senator Sam Ervin, Last of the Founding Fathers*. Chapel Hill:
University of North Carolina Press, 2007.

Carleton, William G. "The Southern Politician, 1900–1950." *Journal of Politics*
13 (May 1951): 215–31.

Carter, Dan T. *The Politics of Rage: George Wallace, the Origins of the New
Conservatism, and the Transformation of American Politics*. New York: Simon
and Schuster, 1995.

———. *Scottsboro: A Tragedy of the American South*. Baton Rouge: Louisiana State
University Press, 1969.

Carter, Hodding, III. *The South Strikes Back*. Garden City, N.Y.: Doubleday, 1959.

Cash, W. J. *The Mind of the South*. New York: Vintage Books, 1941.

Cecelski, David, and Timothy B. Tyson, eds. *Democracy Betrayed: The Wilmington
Race Riot of 1898 and Its Legacy*. Chapel Hill: University of North Carolina
Press, 1998.

Chafe, William H. *Civilities and Civil Rights: Greensboro, North Carolina and the
Black Struggle for Freedom*. New York: Oxford University Press, 1981.

Chalmers, David. *Backfire: How the Ku Klux Klan Helped the Civil Rights
Movement*. Lanham, Md.: Rowman and Littlefield, 2003.

———. *Hooded Americanism: The History of the Ku Klux Klan*. 3rd ed. Durham:
Duke University Press, 1981.

Chappell, David L. "The Divided Mind of Southern Segregationists." *Georgia
Historical Quarterly* 82 (Spring 1998): 45–72.

———. *A Stone of Hope: Prophetic Religion and the Death of Jim Crow*. Chapel Hill:
University of North Carolina Press, 2004.

Chen, Anthony S. *The Fifth Freedom: Jobs, Politics, and Civil Rights in the United
States, 1941–1972*. Princeton, N.J.: Princeton University Press, 38–40.

Cobb, James C. *The Brown Decision, Jim Crow, and Southern Identity*. Athens:
University of Georgia Press, 2005.

———. *Industrialization and Southern Society, 1877–1984*. Lexington: University
Press of Kentucky, 1984.

———. *The Most Southern Place on Earth: The Mississippi Delta and the Roots of
Regional Identity*. New York: Oxford University Press, 1992.

―――. "Not Gone, But Forgotten: Eugene Talmadge and the Purge Campaign of 1938." *Georgia Historical Quarterly* 59 (Summer 1975): 197–209.

―――. *The Selling of the South: The Southern Crusade for Industrial Development, 1936–1990*. Urbana: University of Illinois Press, 1993.

―――. "World War II and the Mind of the Modern South." In *Remaking Dixie: The Impact of World War II on the American South*, ed. Neil McMillen, 3–20. Jackson: University Press of Mississippi, 1997.

Cobb, James C., and Michael V. Namorato, eds. *The New Deal and the South*. Jackson: University Press of Mississippi, 1984.

Cohodas, Nadine. *Strom Thurmond and the Politics of Southern Change*. New York: Simon and Schuster, 1993.

Cook, James Graham. *The Segregationists*. New York: Appleton-Century-Crofts, 1962.

Crespino, Joseph. *In Search of Another Country: Mississippi and the Conservative Counterrevolution*. Princeton, N.J.: Princeton University Press, 2007.

Culver, John C., and John Hyde, *American Dreamer: The Life and Times of Henry A. Wallace*. New York: Norton, 2000.

Dailey, Jane. "Sex, Segregation, and the Sacred After *Brown*." *Journal of American History* 91 (June 2004): 119–44.

Dailey, Jane, Glenda Elizabeth Gilmore, and Bryant Simon, eds. *Jumpin' Jim Crow: Southern Politics from Civil War to Civil Rights*. Princeton, N.J.: Princeton University Press, 2000.

Dalfiume, Richard. *Desegregation of the U.S. Armed Forces: Fighting on Two Fronts, 1939–1953*. Columbia: University of Missouri Press, 1969.

―――. "The Forgotten Years of the Negro Revolution." *Journal of American History* 55 (June 1968): 90–106.

Daniel, Pete. "Going Among Strangers: Southern Reactions to World War II." *Journal of American History* 77 (December 1990): 886–911.

―――. *Lost Revolutions: The American South in the 1950s*. Chapel Hill: University of North Carolina Press, 2000.

Danielson, Chris. "'Lily White and Hard Right': The Mississippi Republican Party and Black Voting, 1965–1980." *Journal of Southern History* 75 (February 2009): 83–118.

Dittmer, John. *Local People: The Struggle for Civil Rights in Mississippi*. Champaign: University of Illinois Press, 1994.

Dower, John. *War Without Mercy: Race and Power in the Pacific War*. New York: Pantheon, 1986.

Dubay, Robert W. "Mississippi and the Proposed Federal Anti-Lynching Bills of 1937–1938." *Southern Quarterly* 7 (October 1968): 73–89.

Dudziak, Mary L. *Cold War Civil Rights: Race and the Image of American Democracy*. Princeton, N.J.: Princeton University Press, 2000.

Eagles, Charles W. *Jonathan Daniels and Race Relations: The Evolution of a Southern Liberal*. Knoxville: University of Tennessee Press, 1982.

―――. "Toward New Histories of the Civil Rights Era." *Journal of Southern History* 66 (November 2000): 815–48.

Egerton, John. *Speak Now Against the Day: The Generation Before the Civil Rights Movement in the South*. Chapel Hill: University of North Carolina Press, 1995.

Ely, James W. *The Crisis of Conservative Virginia: The Byrd Organization and the Politics of Massive Resistance*. Knoxville: University of Tennessee Press, 1976.

Fairclough, Adam. *Race and Democracy: The Civil Rights Struggle in Louisiana, 1915–1972*. Athens: University of Georgia Press, 1995.

Feldman, Glenn. *From Demagogue to Dixiecrat: Horace Wilkinson and the Politics of Race*. Lanham, Md.: University Press of America, 1995.

———. *Politics, Society, and the Klan in Alabama, 1915–1949*. Tuscaloosa: University of Alabama Press, 1999.

———. "Race, Sex, Class, and the Status Quo Society: Developing Racial, Political, and Religious Attitudes in 1940s Alabama." *History* 94 (July 2006): 360–85.

———. "Soft Opposition: Elite Acquiescence and Klan-Sponsored Terrorism in Alabama, 1946–1950." *Historical Journal* 40 (September 1997): 753–77.

———. "Southern Disillusionment with the Democratic Party: Cultural Conformity and 'the Great Melding' of Racial and Economic Conservatism in Alabama during World War II." *Journal of American Studies* 43, no. 2 (2009): 199–230.

Finkle, Lee. *Forum for Protest: The Black Press during World War II*. Rutherford, N.J.: Fairleigh Dickinson University Press, 1975.

Finley, Keith M. *Delaying the Dream: Southern Senators and the Fight against Civil Rights, 1938–1965*. Baton Rouge: Louisiana State University Press, 2008.

Fite, Gilbert C. *Richard B. Russell: Senator from Georgia*. Chapel Hill: University of North Carolina Press, 1991.

Fitzgerald, Michael W. "'We Have Found a Moses': Theodore Bilbo, Black Nationalism, and the Greater Liberia Bill of 1939." *Journal of Southern History* 63 (May 1997): 293–320.

Fleegler, Robert L. "Theodore G. Bilbo and the Decline of Public Racism, 1938–1947." *Journal of Mississippi History* 68 (Spring 2006): 1–27.

Frederickson, Kari. "'As a Man, I Am Interested in States' Rights': Gender, Race, and the Family in the Dixiecrat Party, 1948–1950." In *Jumpin' Jim Crow: Southern Politics from Civil War to Civil Rights*, ed. Jane Dailey, Glenda Elizabeth Gilmore, and Bryant Simon, 260–74. Princeton, N.J.: Princeton University Press, 2000.

———. *The Dixiecrat Revolt and the End of the Solid South, 1932–1968*. Chapel Hill: University of North Carolina Press, 2001.

———. "'The Slowest State' and 'Most Backward Community': Federal Civil Rights Legislation, 1946–1948." *South Carolina Historical Magazine* 98 (April 1997): 177–202.

Freidel, Frank. *F.D.R. and the South*. Baton Rouge: Louisiana State University Press, 1965.

Garfinkel, Harold. *When Negroes March: The March on Washington Movement in the Organizational Politics for FEPC*. Rev. ed. New York: Atheneum, 1969.

Garrow, David J. *Bearing the Cross: Martin Luther King, Jr., and the Southern Christian Leadership Conference*. 1986; reprint, New York: Morrow, 1999.

Garson, Robert A. *The Democratic Party and the Politics of Sectionalism, 1941–1948*. Baton Rouge: Louisiana State University Press, 1974.

Gentry, Jonathan. "All That's Not Fit to Print: Anticommunist and White Supremacist Campaign Literature in the 1950 North Carolina Democratic Senate Primary." *North Carolina Historical Review* 82 (January 2005): 33–60.

Gifford, Laura Jane. *The Center Cannot Hold: The 1960 Presidential Election and the Rise of Modern Conservatism*. Rockford: Northern Illinois University Press, 2009.

———. "'Dixie is No Longer in the Bag': South Carolina Republicans and the Election of 1960." *Journal of Policy History* 19, no. 2 (2007): 207–33.

Gilmore, Glenda Elizabeth. *Defying Dixie: The Radical Roots of Civil Rights, 1919–1950*. New York: Norton, 2008.

———. "False Friends and Avowed Enemies: Southern African Americans and Party Allegiances in the 1920s." In *Jumpin' Jim Crow: Southern Politics from Civil War to Civil Rights*, ed. Jane Dailey, Glenda Elizabeth Gilmore, and Bryant Simon, 219–38. Princeton, N.J.: Princeton University Press, 2000.

———. *Gender and Jim Crow: Women and the Politics of White Supremacy in North Carolina, 1896–1920*. Chapel Hill: University of North Carolina Press, 1996.

Goldfield, David R. *Black, White, and Southern: Race Relations and Southern Culture, 1940 to the Present*. Baton Rouge: Louisiana State University, 1991.

Grantham, Dewey W. "The South and Congressional Politics." In *Remaking Dixie: The Impact of World War II on the American South*, ed. Neil McMillen, 21–32. Jackson: University Press of Mississippi, 1997.

Green, A. Wigfall. *The Man: Bilbo*. Baton Rouge: Louisiana State University Press, 1963.

Green, Constance McLaughlin. *The Secret City: A History of Race Relations in the Nation's Capital*. Princeton, N.J.: Princeton University Press, 1967.

Green, Fletcher M. "Resurgent Southern Sectionalism, 1933–1955." *North Carolina Historical Review* 33 (April 1956): 222–40.

Hale, Grace Elizabeth. *Making Whiteness: The Culture of Segregation in the South*. New York: Pantheon, 1998.

Hall, Jacquelyn Dowd. "The Long Civil Rights Movement and the Political Uses of the Past." *Journal of American History* 91 (March 2005): 1233–64.

———. *Revolt Against Chivalry: Jessie Daniel Ames and the Women's Campaign Against Lynching*. New York: Columbia University Press, 1979.

Heard, Alexander. *A Two-Party South?* Chapel Hill: University of North Carolina Press, 1952.

Henderson, Harold Paulk. *The Politics of Change in Georgia: A Political Biography of Governor Ellis Arnall*. Athens: University of Georgia Press, 1991.

Hershman, James H., Jr. "Massive Resistance Meets Its Match: The Emergence of a Pro-Public School Majority." In *The Moderates' Dilemma: Massive Resistance to School Desegregation in Virginia*, ed. Matthew D. Lassiter and Andrew B. Lewis, 104–33. Charlottesville: University Press of Virginia, 1998.

Horne, Gerald. *Race War!: White Supremacy and the Japanese Attack on the British Empire*. New York: New York University Press, 2003.

Inger, Morton. "The New Orleans School Crisis of 1960." In *Southern Businessmen and Desegregation*, ed. Elizabeth Jacoway and David R. Colburn, 82–97. Baton Rouge: Louisiana State University Press, 1982.

Jackson, John P. *Science for Segregation: Race, Law, and the Case against Brown v. Board of Education*. New York: New York University Press, 2005.

Jaffe, Harry S., and Tom Sherwood. *Dream City: Race, Power, and the Decline of Washington, D.C.* New York: Simon and Schuster, 1994.

Janken, Kenneth Robert. *White: The Biography of Walter White, Mr. NAACP*. New York: New Press, 2003.

Jeansonne, Glen. *Leander Perez: Boss of the Delta*. Baton Rouge: Louisiana State University Press, 1977.

Johnston, Erle. *Mississippi's Defiant Years, 1953–1973*. Forest, Miss.: Lake Harbor Publishers, 1990.

Kalk, Bruce H. *The Origins of the Southern Strategy: Two-Party Competition in South Carolina, 1950–1972*. Lanham, Md.: Lexington Books, 2001.

Kantrowitz, Stephen. *Ben Tillman and the Reconstruction of White Supremacy*. Chapel Hill: University of North Carolina Press, 1999.

Katagiri, Yasuhiro. *The Mississippi State Sovereignty Commission: Civil Rights and States' Rights*. Jackson: University Press of Mississippi, 2001.

Katznelson, Ira, Kim Geiger, and Daniel Kryder. "Limiting Liberalism: The Southern Veto in Congress, 1933–1950." *Political Science Quarterly* 108 (Summer 1993): 283–306.

Kelley, Robin D. G. *Hammer and Hoe: Alabama Communists during the Great Depression*. Chapel Hill: University of North Carolina Press, 1990.

———. "We Are Not What We Seem: Rethinking Black Working-Class Opposition in the Jim Crow South." *Journal of American History* 80 (June 1993): 75–112.

Kellogg, Peter J. "Civil Rights Consciousness in the 1940s." *Historian* 42 (November 1979): 18–41.

Kennedy, David. *Freedom from Fear: The American People in Depression and War, 1929–1945*. New York: Oxford University Press, 1999.

Kesselman, Louis Coleridge. *The Social Politics of FEPC: A Study in Reform Pressure Movements*. Chapel Hill: University of North Carolina Press, 1948.

Key, V. O. *Southern Politics in State and Nation*. New York: Knopf, 1949.

Kirk, John A. *Beyond Little Rock: The Origins and Legacies of the Central High Crisis*. Fayetteville: University of Arkansas Press, 2007.

———. *Redefining the Color Line: Black Activism in Little Rock, Arkansas, 1940–1970*. Gainesville: University of Florida Press, 2002.

Klarman, Michael J. *From Jim Crow to Civil Rights: The Supreme Court and the Struggle for Racial Equality*. New York: Oxford University Press, 2004.

———. "How *Brown* Changed Race Relations: The Backlash Thesis." *Journal of American History* 81 (June 1994): 81–118.

———. "Why Massive Resistance?" In *Massive Resistance: Southern Opposition to the Second Reconstruction*, ed. Clive Webb, 21–38. New York: Oxford University Press, 2005.

Kluger, Richard. *Simple Justice: The History of Brown v. Board of Education and Black America's Struggle for Equality*. New York: Knopf, 1975.

Kneebone, John T. *Southern Liberal Journalists and the Issue of Race, 1920–1944*. Chapel Hill: University of North Carolina Press, 1985.

Korstad, Robert Rodgers. *Civil Rights Unionism: Tobacco Workers and the Struggle for Democracy in the Mid-Century South*. Chapel Hill: University of North Carolina Press, 2003.

Korstad, Robert, and Nelson Lichtenstein. "Opportunities Found and Lost: Labor, Radicals, and the Early Civil Rights Movement." *Journal of American History* 75 (December 1988): 787–811

Kousser, J. Morgan. *Colorblind Injustice: Minority Voting Rights and the Undoing of the Second Reconstruction*. Chapel Hill: University of North Carolina Press, 1999.

Kruse, Kevin M. "The Paradox of Massive Resistance: Political Conformity and Chaos in the Aftermath of *Brown v. Board of Education*." *St. Louis Law University Journal* 48 (Spring 2004): 1009–35.

———. *White Flight: Atlanta and the Making of Modern Conservatism*. Princeton, N.J.: Princeton University Press, 2005.

Kytle, Calvin, and James A. Mackay. *Who Runs Georgia?* Athens: University of Georgia Press, 1998.

Lassiter, Matthew D. "De Jure/De Facto Segregation: The Long Shadow of a National Myth." In *The Myth of Southern Exceptionalism*, ed. by Matthew D. Lassiter and Joseph Crespino, 25–48. New York: Oxford University Press, 2009.

———. *The Silent Majority: Suburban Politics in the Sunbelt South*. Princeton, N.J.: Princeton University Press, 2006.

Lawson, Steven F. *Black Ballots: Voting Rights in the South, 1944–1969*. Rev. ed. Lanham, Md.: Lexington Books, 1999.

Leuchtenburg, William E. *The FDR Years: On Roosevelt and His Legacy*. New York: Columbia University Press, 1995.

———. *The White House Looks South: Franklin D. Roosevelt, Harry S. Truman, Lyndon B. Johnson*. Baton Rouge: Louisiana State University Press, 2005.

Lewis, George. *Massive Resistance: The White Response to the Civil Rights Movement*. London: Hodder Arnold, 2006.

———. *The White South and the Red Menace: Segregationists, Anticommunism, and Massive Resistance, 1945–1965*. Gainesville: University Press of Florida, 2004.

Link, William A. *Righteous Warrior: Jesse Helms and the Rise of Modern Conservatism*. New York: St. Martin's, 2008.

Logan, Rayford W., ed. *What the Negro Wants*. Chapel Hill: University of North Carolina Press, 1944.

Lowndes, Joseph E. *From the New Deal to the New Right: Race and the Southern Origins of Modern Conservatism*. New Haven: Yale University Press, 2008.

Malcolm X. *The Autobiography of Malcolm X*. New York: Ballantine, 1987.

Manis, Andrew Michael. *Macon Black and White: An Unutterable Separation in the American Century*. Macon, Ga.: Mercer University Press, 2004.

Mann, Robert. *The Walls of Jericho: Lyndon Johnson, Hubert Humphrey, Richard Russell, and the Struggle for Civil Rights*. New York: Houghton Mifflin, 1996.

Marable, Manning. *Race, Reform, and Rebellion: The Second Reconstruction in America, 1945–1990*. 2nd rev. ed. Jackson: University Press of Mississippi, 1991.

Martin, John Bartlow. *The Deep South Says "Never."* New York: Ballantine Books, 1957.

McCullough, David. *Truman*. New York: Simon and Schuster, 1992.

McGirr, Lisa. *Suburban Warriors: The Origins of the New American Right*. Princeton, N.J.: Princeton University Press, 2002.

McMahon, Kevin J. *Reconsidering Roosevelt on Race: How the Presidency Paved the Road to "Brown."* Chicago: University of Chicago Press, 2004.

McMillen, Neil. *The Citizens' Council: Organized Resistance to the Second Reconstruction, 1954–1964*. Urbana: University of Illinois Press, 1994.

———. *Dark Journey: Black Mississippians in the Age of Jim Crow*. Urbana: University of Illinois Press, 1989.

McNeal, Genna Rae. *Groundwork: Charles Hamilton Houston and the Struggle for Civil Rights*. Philadelphia: University of Pennsylvania Press, 1983.

McRae, Elizabeth Gillespie. "White Womanhood, White Supremacy, and the Rise of Massive Resistance." In *Massive Resistance: Southern Opposition to the Second Reconstruction*, ed. Clive Webb, 181–202. New York: Oxford University Press, 2005.

McWhorter, Diane. *Carry Me Home: Birmingham, Alabama, the Climactic Battle of the Civil Rights Revolution*. New York: Simon & Schuster, 2001.

Mead, Howard N. "Russell vs. Talmadge: Southern Politics and the New Deal." *Georgia Historical Quarterly* 65 (Spring 1981): 28–44.

Merritt, Russell. "The Senatorial Election of 1962 and the Rise of Two-Party Politics in South Carolina." *South Carolina Historical Magazine* 98 (July 1997): 281–301.

Mershon, Sherie, and Steven Schlossman. *Foxholes and Color Lines: Desgregating the Armed Forces*. Baltimore: Johns Hopkins University Press, 1998.

Michie, Allan A., and Frank Ryhlick. *Dixie Demagogues*. New York: Vanguard, 1939.

Moon, Henry Lee. *Balance of Power: The Negro Vote*. Garden City, N.Y.: Doubleday, 1949.

Moore, John Robert. "The Conservative Coalition in the United States Senate, 1942–45." *Journal of Southern History* 33 (August 1967): 368–76.

Moore, Winfred B., Jr. "The 'Unrewarding Stone': James F. Byrnes and the Burden of Race, 1908–1944." In *The South Is Another Land: Essays on the Twentieth-Century South*, ed. Bruce Clayton and John A. Salmond, 3–27. New York: Greenwood Press, 1987.

Morgan, Chester M. *Redneck Liberal: Theodore G. Bilbo and the New Deal*. Baton Rouge: Louisiana State University Press, 1985.

Moye, Joseph Todd. *Let the People Decide: Black Freedom and White Resistance*

Movements in Sunflower County, Mississippi, 1945–1986. Chapel Hill: University of North Carolina Press, 2004.

Myrdal, Gunnar. *The American Dilemma: The Negro Problem and Modern Democracy*. New York: Harper and Row, 1944.

Nalty, Bernard C. *Strength for the Fight: A History of Black Americans in the Military*. New York: Free Press, 1986.

Newby, I. A. *Challenge to the Court: Social Scientists and the Defense of Segregation, 1954–1966*. Baton Rouge: Louisiana State University Press, 1967.

———. *The Development of Segregationist Thought*. Homewood, Ill.: Dorsey Press, 1968.

Norrell, Robert J. "Labor at the Ballot Box: Alabama Politics from the New Deal to the Dixiecrat Movement." *Journal of Southern History* 57 (May 1991): 201–34.

O'Brien, Gail Williams. *The Color of the Law: Race, Violence, and Justice in the Post–World War II South*. Chapel Hill: University of North Carolina Press, 1999.

O'Brien, Thomas V. "The Dog That Didn't Bark: *Aaron v. Cook* and the NAACP Strategy in Georgia Before *Brown*." *Journal of Negro History* 84 (Winter 1999): 79–88.

Odum, Howard W. *Race and Rumors of Race: Challenge to American Crisis*. Chapel Hill: University of North Carolina Press, 1943.

Ogden, Frederic D. *The Poll Tax in the South*. Tuscaloosa: University of Alabama Press, 1958.

Oliver, Lawrence J. "Writing from the Right during the 'Red Decade': Thomas Dixon's Attack on W. E. B. Du Bois and James Weldon Johnson in *The Flaming Sword*." *American Literature* 70 (March 1998): 131–52.

Ottley, Roi. *New World A-Coming: Inside Black America*. Boston: Houghton Mifflin, 1943.

Patterson, James T. *Congressional Conservatism and the New Deal: The Growth of the Conservative Coalition in Congress, 1933–1939*. Lexington: University of Kentucky Press, 1967.

———. "A Conservative Coalition Forms in Congress, 1933–1939." *Journal of American History* 52 (March 1966): 757–72.

Payne, Charles M. *I've Got the Light of Freedom: The Organizing Tradition and the Mississippi Freedom Struggle*. Berkeley: University of California Press, 1995.

———. " 'The Whole United States Is Southern!': *Brown v. Board* and the Mystification of Race." *Journal of American History* 91 (June 2004): 83–91.

Perlstein, Rick. *Before the Storm: Barry Goldwater and the Unmaking of the American Consensus*. New York: Hill and Wang, 2001.

———. *Nixonland: The Rise of a President and the Fracturing of America*. New York: Scribner, 2008.

Perman, Michael. *In Pursuit of Unity: A Political History of the American South*. Chapel Hill: University of North Carolina Press, 2009.

Potenziani, David D. "Striking Back: Richard B. Russell and Racial Relocation." *Georgia Historical Quarterly* 65 (Fall 1981): 263–77.

Quint, Howard H. *Profile in Black and White: A Frank Portrait of South Carolina*. Washington, D.C.: Public Affairs Press, 1958.

Rable, George C. "The South and the Politics of Antilynching Legislation, 1920–1940." *Journal of Southern History* 51 (May 1985): 201–20.

Raines, Howell. *My Soul Is Rested: Movement Days in the South Remembered.* New York: Putnam, 1977.

Rampersad, Arnold. *The Life of Langston Hughes, Vol. II: 1941–1967: I Dream a World.* New York: Oxford University Press, 1988.

Reed, Merl E. *Seedtime for the Modern Civil Rights Movement: The President's Committee on Fair Employment Practice, 1941–46.* Baton Rouge: Louisiana State University Press, 1991.

Reuter, E. B. "The Cult of Equality: A Study of the Race Problem." *American Journal of Sociology* 51 (January 1946): 348–49.

Robertson, David. *Sly and Able: A Political Biography of James F. Byrnes.* New York: Norton, 1994.

Roche, Jeff. *Restructured Resistance: The Sibley Commission and the Politics of Desegregation in Georgia.* Athens: University of Georgia Press, 1998.

Roefs, Wim. "Leading the Civil Rights Vanguard in South Carolina: John McCray and the *Lighthouse and Informer*, 1939–1954." In *Time Longer than Rope: A Century of African American Activism, 1850–1950*, ed. Charles M. Payne and Adam Green, 462–91. New York: New York University Press, 2003.

Roland, Charles P. *The Improbable Era: The South since World War II.* Lexington: University Press of Kentucky, 1975.

Rosenman, Samuel I., ed. Vol. 7 of *The Public Papers and Addresses of Franklin Delano Roosevelt.* New York: Macmillan, 1941.

Rubin, Louis D., and James Jackson Kilpatrick. *The Lasting South: Fourteen Southerners Look at Their Home.* Chicago: Regnery, 1957.

Ruchames, Louis. *Race, Jobs, and Politics: The Story of FEPC.* New York: Columbia University Press, 1953.

Savage, Sean J. "To Purge or Not to Purge: Hamlet Harry and the Dixiecrats, 1948–1952." *Presidential Studies Quarterly* 27 (Fall 1997): 773–90.

Schlesinger, Arthur M., Jr. *The Politics of Upheaval, 1935–1936.* Boston: Houghton Mifflin, 1960.

Schulman, Bruce. *From Cotton Belt to Sunbelt: Federal Policy, Economic Development, and the Transformation of the South, 1938–1980.* New York: Oxford University Press, 1991.

Simon, Bryant. *A Fabric of Defeat: The Politics of South Carolina Millhands, 1910–1948.* Chapel Hill: University of North Carolina Press, 1998.

———. "Introduction." In Howard Odum, *Race and Rumors of Race: The American South in the Early Forties*, vii–xxxii. Baltimore: Johns Hopkins University Press, 1997.

———. "Race Reactions: African American Organizing, Liberalism, and White Working-Class Politics in Postwar South Carolina." In *Jumpin' Jim Crow: Southern Politics from Civil War to Civil Rights*, ed. Jane Dailey, Glenda Elizabeth Gilmore, and Bryant Simon, 239–59. Princeton, N.J.: Princeton University Press, 2000.

Sitkoff, Harvard. "African American Militancy in the World War II South: Another

Perspective." In *Remaking Dixie: The Impact of World War II on the American South*, ed. Neil McMillen, 70–92. Jackson: University Press of Mississippi, 1997.

———. "Harry Truman and the Election of 1948: The Coming of Age of Civil Rights in American Politics." *Journal of Southern History* 37 (November 1971): 597–616.

———. *A New Deal for Blacks: The Emergence of Civil Rights as a National Issue.* New York: Oxford University Press, 1978.

———. "Racial Militancy and Interracial Violence During the Second World War." *Journal of American History* 58 (December 1971): 661–81.

Smith, Gilbert E. *The Limits of Reform: Politics and Federal Aid to Education, 1937–1950.* New York: Garland, 1982.

Smith, J. Douglas. *Managing White Supremacy: Race, Politics, and Citizenship in Jim Crow Virginia.* Chapel Hill: University of North Carolina Press, 2002.

Smith, John David. "Introduction." In *The Flaming Sword*, by Thomas Dixon, rev. ed. Lexington: University Press of Kentucky, 2005.

Sokol, Jason. *There Goes My Everything: White Southerners in the Age of Civil Rights.* New York: Knopf, 2006.

Sosna, Morton. *In Search of the Silent South: Southern Liberals and the Race Issue.* New York: Columbia University Press, 1977.

Stefkovitch, Jacqueline A., and Terrence Leas. "A Legal History of Desegregation in Higher Education." *Journal of Negro Education* 63 (Summer 1994): 406–20.

Sugrue, Thomas. *Origins of the Urban Crisis: Race and Inequality in Postwar Detroit.* Princeton, N.J.: Princeton University Press, 1996.

———. *Sweet Land of Liberty: The Forgotten Struggle for Civil Rights in the North.* New York: Random House, 2008.

Sullivan, Patricia. *Days of Hope: Race and Democracy in the New Deal Era.* Chapel Hill: University of North Carolina Press, 1996.

Thatcher, Susan Tucker. "A Last Gasp: Clyde R. Hoey and the Twilight of Racial Segregation, 1945–1954." In *The South Is Another Land: Essays on the Twentieth-Century South*, ed. Bruce Clayton and John A. Salmond, 29–48. New York: Greenwood Press, 1987.

Thompson, Julius E. *Lynchings in Mississippi: A History, 1865–1965.* Jefferson, N.C.: McFarland, 2007.

Tindall, George. *The Emergence of the New South, 1913–1945.* Baton Rouge: Louisiana State University Press, 1967.

Tuck, Stephen G. N. *Beyond Atlanta: The Struggle for Racial Equality in Georgia, 1940–1980.* Athens: University of Georgia Press, 2001.

Tushnet, Mark V. *The NAACP's Legal Strategy against Segregated Education, 1925–1950.* Chapel Hill: University of North Carolina Press, 1987.

Tyler, Pamela. "'Blood on Your Hands': White Southerners' Criticism of Eleanor Roosevelt During World War II." In *Before Brown: Civil Rights and White Backlash in the Modern South*, ed. Glenn Feldman, 96–115. Tuscaloosa: University of Alabama Press, 2004.

Tyson, Timothy B. *Radio Free Dixie: Robert F. Williams and the Roots of Black Power*. Chapel Hill: University of North Carolina Press, 1999.

———. "Wars for Democracy: African American Militancy and Interracial Violence in North Carolina during World War II." In *Democracy Betrayed: The Wilmington Race Riot of 1898 and Its Legacy*, ed. David Cecelski and Timothy B. Tyson, 253–71. Chapel Hill: University of North Carolina Press, 1998.

von Eschen, Penny. *Race Against Empire: Black Americans and Anticolonialism, 1937–1957*. Ithaca: Cornell University Press, 1997.

Wade, Wyn Craig. *The Fiery Cross: The Ku Klux Klan in America*. New York: Touchstone, 1987.

Walker, Anders. *The Ghost of Jim Crow: How Moderates Used Brown v. Board of Education to Stall Civil Rights*. New York: Oxford University Press, 2009.

Ward, Jason Morgan. "'A Richmond Institution': Earnest Sevier Cox, Racial Propaganda, and White Resistance to the Civil Rights Movement." *Virginia Magazine of History and Biography* 116 (September 2008): 262–93.

Webb, Clive. "Charles Bloch, Jewish White Supremacist." *Georgia Historical Quarterly* 83 (Summer 1999): 267–92.

Weisenburger, Steven. "The Columbians, Inc.: A Chapter of Racial Hatred from the Post-World War II South." *Journal of Southern History* 69 (November 2003): 821–60.

Weiss, Nancy. *Farewell to the Party of Lincoln: Black Politics in the Age of F.D.R.* Princeton, N.J.: Princeton University Press, 1983.

Wexler, Laura. *Fire in a Canebrake: The Last Mass Lynching in America*. New York: Scribner, 2003.

Whalen, Charles and Barbara. *The Longest Debate: A Legislative History of the 1964 Civil Rights Act*. Cabin John, Md.: Seven Locks Press, 1985.

Wilhoit, Francis M. *The Politics of Massive Resistance*. New York: George Brazlier, 1973.

Wilkerson-Freeman, Sarah. "The Creation of a Subversive Feminist Dominion: Interracialist Social Workers and the Georgia New Deal." *Journal of Women's History* 13 (Winter 2002): 132–54.

———. "The Second Battle for Woman Suffrage: Alabama White Women, the Poll Tax, and V. O. Key's Master Narrative of Southern Politics." *Journal of Southern History* 68 (Spring 2002): 333–74.

Williams, Lee E., II. "Alabama Moderation: The Athens Riot of 1946." *Griot* 16 (Fall 1997): 19–23.

Williamson, Joel. *The Crucible of Race: Black-White Relations in the American South Since Emancipation*. New York: Oxford University Press, 1982.

———. *A Rage for Order: Black-White Relations in the American South Since Emancipation*. New York: Oxford University Press, 1986.

Woodruff, Nan Elizabeth. *American Congo: The African American Freedom Struggle in the Delta*. Cambridge: Harvard University Press, 2003.

———. "Mississippi Delta Planters and Debates over Mechanization, Labor, and Civil Rights in the 1940s." *Journal of Southern History* 60 (May 1994): 263–84.

Woods, Jeff. *Black Struggle, Red Scare: Segregation and Anti-Communism in the South, 1948–1968*. Baton Rouge: Louisiana State University Press.

Woodward, C. Vann. *Origins of the New South, 1877–1912*. Baton Rouge: Louisiana State University Press, 1951.

———. *The Strange Career of Jim Crow*. 3rd ed. New York: Oxford University Press, 1974.

Wynn, Neil A. *The Afro-American and the Second World War*. Rev. ed. New York: Holmes and Meier, 1993.

Yarnell, Allen. *Democrats and Progressives: The 1948 Presidential Election as a Test of Postwar Liberalism*. Berkeley: University of California Press, 1974.

Zangrando, Robert. *The NAACP Crusade Against Lynching, 1909–1950*. Philadelphia: Temple University Press, 1980.

Zeller, Belle. "American Government and Politics: The Federal Regulation of Lobbying Act." *American Political Science Review* 42 (April 1948): 239–71.

Dissertations, Theses, and Unpublished Papers

Boyd, Tim. "'Out of the Shadows': Southern Democrats, the Civil Rights Movement, and the Shaping of the New South, 1946–1976." Ph.D. diss., Vanderbilt University, 2007.

Burran, James Albert, III. "Racial Violence in the South during World War II." Ph.D. diss., University of Tennessee, 1977.

Cook, James Frederick, Jr. "Politics and Education in the Talmadge Era: The Controversy over the University System of Georgia, 1941–1942." Ph.D. diss., University of Georgia, 1974.

Dobrasko, Rebekah M. "Balancing Segregation and Education: The Role of the Gressette Committee." Seminar paper, South Caroliniana Library, University of South Carolina, 2003.

Farmer, James O., Jr. "The End of the White Primary in South Carolina: A Southern State's Fight to Keep Its Politics White." Master's thesis, University of South Carolina, 1969.

Gentry, Jonathan Daniel. "Seeing Red: Anti-communism, Civil Liberties and the Struggle Against Dissent in North Carolina, 1949–1968." Ph.D. diss., University of South Carolina, 2003.

Lowndes, Joseph E. "The Southern Origins of Modern Conservatism, 1945–1976." Ph.D. diss., New School University, 2003.

Partin, John William. "'Assistant President' for the Home Front: James F. Byrnes and World War II." Ph.D. diss., University of Florida, 1977.

Potenziani, David Daniel. "Look to the Past: Richard B. Russell and the Defense of Southern White Supremacy." Ph.D. diss., University of Georgia, 1981.

Richards, Miles Spangler. "Osceola McKaine and the Struggle for Black Civil Rights, 1917–1946." Ph.D. diss., University of South Carolina, 1994.

Rolph, Stephanie Renee. "Displacing Race: White Resistance and Conservative Politics in the Civil Rights Era." Ph.D. diss., Mississippi State University, 2009.

Williams, Kenneth H. "Mississippi and Civil Rights, 1945–1954." Ph.D. diss., Mississippi State University, 1985.

INDEX

Aaron v. Cook, 210 (n. 22)

African Americans: service in World War II, 1, 37, 41–46, 47, 48–49, 51, 81; subordination of, 1, 41, 48; and Roosevelt's New Deal coalition, 3, 21; as threat to white women, 18, 32, 41–42, 81, 85; colonization movement, 29–32, 87, 88; gun ownership of, 52, 53, 56; and alleged women's "Eleanor Clubs," 52–53, 56; migration to Washington, D.C., 70, 71, 73; Bilbo's relocation scheme for, 71–72; migration from South, 73, 198 (n. 67); Russell's relocation scheme for, 115–17, 175; and *Brown* decision support, 143–44. *See also* Black disfranchisement; Black electorate; Black political power; Black press

Alabama: and regional identity, 8; and Roosevelt's visit to Georgia, 9; and racialized labor system, 11; and World War II, 44; and poll tax, 57, 197 (n. 51); Athens riot of 1946, 92–93, 202–3 (n. 2); vigilante violence in, 93, 203 (n. 3); and Dixiecrat revolt, 105; and southern moderates, 122; and equal educational rights, 133–34; and election of 1956, 159; and Citizens' Councils, 160, 161; and election of 1964, 178; black voter registration in, 179

Almond, J. Lindsay, Jr., 104

Americanism, 32, 40, 63, 79, 82, 123, 147

American Opinion, 180

Andrews, Mrs. J. E., 14

Arkansas, 122, 161–62, 197 (n. 51)

Armed forces: African Americans' service in World War II, 1, 37, 41–46, 47, 48–49, 51, 81; white southerners' service in World War II, 46–49, 51,

54, 85, 195 (n. 24); desegregation of, 99, 100, 119, 120; equal treatment in, 118–19

Arnall, Ellis, 36, 59, 109

Asbury Methodist Episcopal Church (Washington, D.C.), 73

Association of Southern Women for the Prevention of Lynching (ASWPL), 14, 21

Atlanta Constitution, 9, 35–36, 112, 116–17

Atlanta Daily World, 112, 114

Atlanta Journal, 84, 116

Augusta Courier, 151

Aycock, Charles Brantley, 1–2

Bailey, Josiah, 25

Balance Agriculture with Industry program, 96

Ball, William Watts, 18–19

Baltimore Afro-American, 114

Bankhead, John, 44

Barkley, Alben, 23, 114

Barnett, Ross, 164–65

Barr, John U., 103

Bartley, Numan, 7, 188 (n. 17), 209 (n. 15)

Bender, W. A., 132

Benedict, Ruth, 83, 85

Bilbo, Theodore: and white supremacy, 29, 49, 67–70, 72, 76, 88, 90, 91, 105, 199 (n. 4); and colonization movement, 29–30, 87, 88; on black soldiers, 51; and poll tax, 60; and segregationist movement, 67, 68, 72–74, 85, 87–90, 101; and Senate Committee on the District of Columbia, 68–78, 90, 199 (n. 4); and miscegenation, 76, 88; and egalitarianism, 84–85, 88; terrorism advocated by, 90, 93, 94; death of, 91; and election of 1946, 93; Stennis as successor to, 105, 107, 146

Bilboism, 68, 91, 93, 95, 106, 199 (n. 3)

The Birth of a Nation (film), 30

Black disfranchisement: and white democracy, 2, 3; federal election supervisors preventing, 21; African Americans' campaign against, 39; and poll tax, 56, 57; and white primaries, 63; and Bilbo, 75, 90; and Boswell Amendment, 93; and Herman Talmadge, 110, 111, 114; and white Radicals, 187 (n. 13); and Eugene Talmadge, 203 (n. 3); and modernization, 203 (n. 9)

Black electorate: and southern conservatives, 3; growth of, 8; and Republican Party, 18–19, 37, 98, 155, 170, 177–78, 181, 191 (n. 32); and Democratic Party, 18–21, 23, 24, 28, 98, 155, 177, 191 (n. 32); and New Deal, 28; bloc voting of, 155, 157, 158, 164, 167, 168, 170; and voter registration, 157, 214 (n. 11); and Reconstruction, 179

Black nationalists, 29–30

Black political power: and civic equality, 4, 7, 20; and New Deal, 28; Bilbo's opposition to, 74, 75–76; and poll tax, 83; Herman Talmadge's opposition to, 110–11; southern minority bloc as counter to, 154, 157–58; and segregationist movement, 166–67, 179–80. *See also* National Association for the Advancement of Colored People (NAACP)

Black press: and "Double V" campaign, 1; and Bilbo as chair of Senate Committee on District of Columbia, 71, 72; and fair employment practices, 79; on Athens, Alabama, riots of 1946, 92–93; on lynching, 93; on white supremacy in Georgia, 112; and Truman's inauguration, 114; on

Russell, 115; Byrnes on, 128–29; and equal educational rights, 136, 137

Bloch, Charles, 113, 206 (n. 54)

Boswell Amendment, 93

Bozell, L. Brent, 168

Brady, Thomas Pickens, 101, 102, 140

Breedin, James Kolb, 105

Briggs v. Elliott, 127

Brinkley, David, 70

Brooks, Abraham Lincoln, 58

Brown, Edgar, 58, 197 (n. 55)

Brown decision: and segregationist movement, 2, 4, 6, 88, 123, 125, 151, 159–60; and resistance, 4, 142, 144; southern policies preceding, 123, 141, 208 (n. 5); and southern race relations, 140–41; southern reactions to, 142–43, 145–46, 147, 151, 161; and Eisenhower, 158; Goldwater on, 168

Brown II decision, 144, 145

Bryson, Joseph, 51–52

Buckley, William F., 148

Bureau of Printing and Engraving, 72

Byrd, Harry F., 145, 146, 159, 165–66, 204 (n. 22)

Byrnes, James F.: on school desegregation, 4, 139–40, 149; and Roosevelt, 17–18, 28, 56; and Walter White, 23–24; and election of 1950, 121–22; and equal educational rights, 122, 123, 125, 126–28, 130, 134, 135, 137, 139, 155, 208 (nn. 5, 6); and constitutional conservatism, 126, 148–49; and segregationist movement, 128, 209 (n. 13); and Ku Klux Klan, 128–30; and threats to abandon public education, 137–38; international criticism of, 139; on racial integrity, 149; and political identity of southern conservatives, 153; and southern minority bloc, 154–55, 157–58; and Eisenhower endorsement, 156, 157; and election of 1956, 159; and Dixiecrat revolt, 204 (n. 22)

De facto integration: and World War II, 45–49, 52
De facto segregation, 217 (n. 10)
Delaware, 127
Delta Council, 62
Democracy: and emancipation, 58; definitions of, 63; Washington, D.C., as showcase for interracial democracy, 70; U.S. as showcase of, 98–99, 139; and segregationist movement, 147, 148, 149. *See also* White democracy
Democratic National Convention: 1936, 3, 17–18, 20, 27, 102, 108, 152, 190 (n. 25); 1948, 102, 113, 172; 1956, 158–59
Democratic Party: and white supremacy campaign, 1–2, 186 (n. 3); and segregationist movement, 2–3, 108, 159, 177; and white southerners, 5, 10, 20–21, 23, 108, 155, 158, 159, 164, 188 (n. 17); and southern conservatives, 10, 20, 33, 108, 170, 172; and black electorate, 18–21, 23, 24, 28, 98, 155, 177, 191 (n. 32); elimination of two-thirds rule for nominating candidates, 20, 102, 151–52; and lynching debate, 21–22, 23; and civil rights movement, 24, 114, 153; and demagoguery, 36; and white primaries, 63, 64, 67, 93; and New Deal, 65, 98; and Dixiecrat revolt, 101–5, 108, 109, 113, 152, 154, 155, 158, 172; Byrnes on, 154; and Russell, 155
De Priest, Oscar, 21
Detroit, Michigan, 56, 73, 83, 167
Dewey, Thomas, 105
Dies, Martin, 32–33
Disraeli, Benjamin, 149
Dixiecrat revolt, 5, 19, 100–101, 188 (nn. 17, 18)
Dixon, Frank, 79, 104, 124
Dixon, Thomas, 13, 30–32, 193 (n. 59)
"Double V" campaign: and civil rights movement, 1, 38, 69, 197 (n. 46)

Double Victory: and segregationist movement, 3, 39, 55, 66
Du Bois, W. E. B., 31
Duck Hill lynching, 22–23

Earle, Willie, 94–95
Eastland, James, 7, 81, 100, 105, 106, 108, 142, 148–49
Edgerton, John, 11
Edmund Pettus Bridge confrontation, 179
Education. *See* Public education
Egalitarianism: and World War II, 3, 37, 41, 42, 68, 84, 91; and civic equality, 4, 7, 20; and segregationist movement, 7, 83, 84–88, 89, 102; and southern conservatives, 20, 68, 83; Thomas Dixon on, 31; and poll tax, 60; and federal government, 83. *See also* Social equality
Egerton, John, 100
Eisenhower, Dwight D., 155–58, 159, 162, 167, 168, 173
Eleanor Clubs, 52
Ellender, Allen, 23
Emancipation, 58, 187 (n. 13)
Emmerich, Oliver, 165
Employment: federal fair employment initiatives, 3, 39, 78–83, 86, 89, 90, 96, 100, 107, 201 (n. 33); racialized labor system, 7, 11, 39, 78, 82, 83, 201 (n. 33); and World War II, 71, 77
Engelhardt, Sam, 160
Ervin, Joseph Wilson, 80–81
Ervin, Samuel J., 81, 145, 212 (n. 57)
Ethridge, Mark, 55
Evans, Rowland, 177–78, 181
Evers, Medgar, 173
Executive Order 8802, 39
Executive Order 9981, 118

Fahy, Charles, 118
Fair Employment Practices Committee (FEPC), 39–40, 67, 78–83, 86, 89, 90, 96, 100, 107, 201 (n. 33)

Labor unions, 12, 26, 32, 56, 188 (n. 19), 192 (n. 51)
Landon, Alfred, 31
Landry, Stuart Omer, 85–87, 101
Lang, Charlie, 58
Legal Education Advisory Committee, 143
Lesesne, Henry, 125
Levings, Nelson T., 102
Lewis, Morris, 132
Life magazine, 117
Lighthouse and Informer, 128
Little Palace cafeteria sit-in, 76
Little Rock's Central High School, 162, 164, 173
Logan-Thomas Circle Citizens' Association (Washington, D.C.), 74
Long, Huey, 12
Longino, R. Kirby, 103
Loomis, Homer, Jr., 85
Louisiana: and regional identity, 8; and Dixiecrat revolt, 104, 105; and southern moderates, 122; black voter registration in, 157; and election of 1956, 159; and Citizens' Councils, 160, 163–64; and election of 1964, 178
Louisville Courier-Journal, 55
Lucier, Jim, 180–81
Lynching: antilynching movement, 14, 21; antilynching legislation, 21, 22–25, 27, 28, 29, 60, 67, 70, 83, 99, 100, 107, 113, 154, 175, 191 (n. 34); in Mississippi, 22–23, 58–59; and interracial sexual relations, 49; and Soviet propaganda, 98; and civil rights agenda, 99

MacArthur, Douglas, 58
Madison, James, 146
Malcolm X, 70
Mallard, Amy, 113
Mallard, Robert, 111–12, 113, 114
March on Washington (1963), 174
March on Washington Movement, 39, 72

Marshall, George C., 44
Marx, Karl, 24
Massey, Ben, 92–93, 202 (n. 2)
Massey, Roy, 92–93
Maybank, Burnet, 44, 119
McCarran, Pat, 68
McCullough, Alex, 138
McDaniels, "Bootjack," 22
McGill, Ralph, 36, 112, 121–22, 170, 208 (n. 2)
McIntyre, Marvin, 55
McKaine, Osceola, 94
McKenzie, Charles, 76–77
McLaurin, G. W., 124–25
McLaurin decision, 125
Meridian Star, 59
Meyer, Fred, 46
Miscegenation, 76, 78, 85, 88
Mississippi: and segregationist movement, 7, 89, 108, 143, 153; white supremacy in, 8; and Roosevelt's visit to Georgia, 9; lynchings in, 22–23, 58–59; and New Deal, 29; and World War II, 45; and poll tax, 57, 62, 197 (n. 51); and Vigilance Committees, 62–63; migration of blacks to North, 71; and modernization, 96; and Dixiecrat revolt, 101, 105; and Bilboism, 106; NAACP in, 132–33, 139; and equal educational rights, 132–37, 142–43; and school desegregation, 146, 147; and southern minority bloc, 154; and election of 1956, 159; and election of 1960, 165; and election of 1964, 178; and Republican Party, 180; school equalization in, 208 (nn. 5, 6)
Mississippi Association of Teachers in Colored Schools, 132
Mississippi Citizens Council on Education (MCCE), 132, 133
Mississippi Democratic Executive Committee, 154
Mississippi Economic Council, 132

Mississippi State Sovereignty Commission, 161
Mitchell, Arthur, 21, 22
Moler, Dan, 43
Molotov-Ribbentrop Pact, 193 (n. 60)
Moon, Henry Lee, 98
Morrison, Cameron, 108
Morse, Stanley, 135
Mundt, Karl, 166
Mussolini, Benito, 32

National Association for the Advancement of Colored People (NAACP): Thomas Dixon on, 13; and Walter White, 21, 27; and World War II, 38; and white primaries, 63; Truman's address to, 99; in Georgia, 111; and Amy Mallard, 113; and school desegregation, 124, 127; in South Carolina, 126–27; in Mississippi, 132–33, 139; and southern threats to abolish public education, 139
National Association of Colored Women, 98
National Association of Manufacturers, 82
National Committee on Segregation in the Nation's Capital, 200 (n. 19)
National Committee to Abolish the Poll Tax, 56
National Emergency Committee against Mob Violence, 98
National Grass Roots Convention, 6, 13, 31
National Negro Council, 58
National Recovery Administration (NRA): and racialized labor system, 11–12
National Review, 148
Negro Citizens Committee of South Carolina, 63–64
Negro Nationalist Movement, 30
New Deal: and race question, 2, 10–11, 13, 14, 15–16, 18, 19, 28, 29, 191 (n. 32); and southern conservatives, 3, 5, 25–26, 32, 33, 36, 64–66, 78, 151, 183, 188 (n. 19); and Roosevelt's coalition with African Americans, 3, 21; and Eugene Talmadge, 10, 12–13, 14, 24, 192 (n. 50); and southern industrialists, 11–12, 13, 82, 96, 103; and southern modernization, 97
New Orleans Times-Picayune, 90
Newsweek, 29
New York Times, 28, 109, 174
Nixon, Isaac, 111, 114
Nixon, Richard, 103, 165, 168, 169, 181
North: segregation in, 73–74. *See also* White northerners
North Alabama Citizens Council (NACC), 160
North Carolina: white supremacy campaign in, 1–2, 186 (n. 3); and Roosevelt's visit to Georgia, 9; mob violence in, 93; Ku Klux Klan in, 129, 130; black voter registration in, 157; and election of 1950, 208 (n. 2)
Novak, Robert, 169, 177–78, 181

Odum, Howard, 54, 116, 117
Office of War Mobilization, 56
Oklahoma, 124–25
Old, William, 146
Organized labor, 12, 26, 32, 56, 188 (n. 19), 192 (n. 51)
Ottley, Roi, 39, 47

Paternalism: and Byrnes, 127–28; and Stennis, 143
Patterson, Robert, 149–50, 151, 160
Pepper, Claude, 208 (n. 2)
Perez, Leander, 164
Peters, James S., 34, 110
Pittman, Marvin, 34
Pittsburgh Courier, 136, 137
Plessy v. Ferguson, 124
Police brutality, 98, 99
Poll tax: campaign to abolish, 38, 40, 56–61, 62, 63; and southern filibusters, 38, 60, 70; Bilbo on, 67;

and threat of social equality, 78;
and black political power, 83; and
Truman's civil rights agenda, 99,
100; and Stennis, 107; and Republican Party, 119; and white primaries,
197 (n. 51)

Populists: and fusion government, 1–2,
186 (n. 3); in South, 12, 13, 189 (n. 9);
Bilbo as populist, 29; and segregationist movement, 161; and George
Wallace, 181, 182

Pratt, S. J., 53

Presidential Committee on Civil Rights
(PCCR), 98–100

President's Committee on Equality of
Treatment and Opportunity in the
Armed Forces, 118

Progressive Democratic Party (South
Carolina), 64

Progressive Party, 105

Public education: and school desegregation, 2, 4, 7, 120, 122, 123, 124,
127, 131, 139–40, 141, 144–46, 149,
162–63, 168–69, 170, 186 (n. 10), 207
(n. 68); southern threats to abolish
public school system, 4, 122, 127,
131–32, 137–39, 142; and university
segregation, 33–34, 35, 36, 110, 123,
124, 173; and equal education rights,
122–23, 208 (nn. 5, 6); and federal
aid, 123–24; and separate but equal
doctrine, 124, 125, 134, 136, 140;
Goldwater on, 170. See also *Brown*
decision

Race-baiting: and Eugene Talmadge, 6,
17, 36, 93, 190 (n. 23); and populists,
19; and Rankin, 58; and Bilbo, 93,
145; and Herman Talmadge, 109

Race question: as "settled," 1, 2, 11,
28, 187 (n. 12); and New Deal, 2,
10–11, 13, 14, 15–16, 18, 19, 28, 29, 191
(n. 32); and World War II, 37, 61

Race relations. *See* Southern race
relations

The Races of Mankind (pamphlet),
83–85

Racial discrimination: and "Double V"
campaign, 1, 38; and World War II,
38, 46, 47, 69; in workplace, 39,
72, 77, 79, 82, 83; and civil rights
agenda, 99, 100

Racialized southern labor system, 7,
11, 39, 78, 82, 83, 201 (n. 33)

Racial pessimism, 30–31

Racial Purity Law (Georgia), 17

Racial reform: and World War II, 3;
white opposition to, 7, 8, 193 (n. 59);
and Eugene Talmadge, 36; white
southerners' perceptions of, 40, 191
(n. 32); and Bilbo, 70; Truman's endorsement of, 99–100; and segregationist movement, 102, 115, 175, 212
(n. 57); and nationalization of race
problem, 102–3; federal imposition
of, 119; Goldwater on, 168

Rand, Clayton, 65–66, 199 (n. 77)

Randolph, Asa Philip, 39, 69, 77

Rankin, John, 58, 82–83

Recess Education Committee, 133, 136

Reconstruction: and threat of federal
intervention, 23, 27; and white supremacy, 27–28, 30–31, 154–55, 163–
64; civil rights movement compared
to, 54, 173; and World War II rhetoric, 60–61; and white primaries,
64–65; and Republican Party, 170,
178, 180; and black electorate, 179

Red Shirts, 27

Reed, Clark, 181

Regional coalition: and white democracy, 7–8; and New Deal, 10; and
modernization, 12, 26; and support
for Roosevelt, 19; and World War II,
44; and fair employment practices,
82; and racial retrenchment, 95, 96;
and Dixiecrat revolt, 101, 103, 104,
105; and equal educational rights,
123, 131, 134, 208 (n. 6); and southern minority bloc, 152, 154

Regnery, Henry, 148

The Report on Economic Conditions in the South, 26

Republican National Committee, 177–78

Republican Party: and fusion government, 1–2, 186 (n. 3); and black electorate, 18–19, 37, 98, 155, 170, 177–78, 181, 191 (n. 32); and southern conservatives, 25, 118, 147–48, 156–57, 158, 166, 167–72, 177–78, 181; and fair employment practices legislation, 82; in South, 153, 186–87 (n. 11); and "Forgotten American" strategy, 169–70, 216 (n. 37); and Thurmond, 177, 181; and civil rights issues, 181

Resistance: massive resistance, 2, 5, 6, 7, 144, 148, 151, 152, 153, 159, 162–63, 164, 205 (n. 25); "responsible resistance" strategies of segregationist movement, 4, 128, 130, 137, 140, 141, 147, 149, 166; and *Brown* decision, 4, 142, 144; segregationist resistance to civil rights legislation, 5, 122, 187 (n. 15); and Dixiecrat revolt, 5, 188 (n. 17); grassroots anxieties clashing with elite strategies, 52, 89; and Truman's civil rights agenda, 114, 118; and equal educational rights, 122; and interposition doctrine, 146–47, 148, 179–80

Reuter, E. B., 87

Rivera, Alex, 137

Rockefeller, Nelson, 176, 181

Roosevelt, Eleanor, 13, 14, 52–53, 69–70, 89

Roosevelt, Franklin D.: New Deal coalition with African Americans, 3, 21; and Eugene Talmadge, 6, 12–13, 31, 192 (n. 50); and election of 1932, 9–10; and Russell, 10, 12, 13–14, 172; and southern conservatives, 12, 26, 102; and election of 1936, 18, 20, 21, 25, 31; and federal judiciary, 25; and reform goals for South, 26, 28, 29; and prohibition of racial discrimination, 39; and Four Freedoms, 40; Jonathan Daniels as advisor to, 55–56, 196–97 (n. 46); downfall of white supremacy linked to, 64, 65; election of 1944, 65; and fair employment practices, 79–80; death of, 80

Roosevelt Business and Professional League (Atlanta), 10

Roper, Sam, 111

Rousseau, John, 136

Russell, Richard: and Roosevelt, 10, 12, 13–14, 172; and Eugene Talmadge, 14–17, 18, 145, 190 (n. 23); on white supremacy, 16, 17, 190 (n. 23); and antilynching legislation, 23, 24; and election of 1936, 28; and black soldiers, 41, 44, 45–46, 49; and segregation, 73, 115, 172; and employment, 78; and federal civil rights agenda, 113, 117–18, 153, 174–76, 204 (n. 22); and states' rights rhetoric, 113–14; and Truman's inauguration, 114–15; and Voluntary Racial Relocation Commission proposal, 115–17, 175; and nationalization of race problem, 117; Freedom of Selection Amendment, 118–19, 120; and election of 1952, 155; and election of 1960, 165; and Lyndon B. Johnson, 173, 174; and Goldwater, 176

Rutledge, Archibald, 37

School desegregation: and segregationist movement, 2, 4, 7, 120, 122, 124, 186 (n. 10), 207 (n. 68); Byrnes on, 4, 139–40, 149; and federal government, 122, 123, 127, 131, 144, 170; and southern moderates, 145, 146

Segregation: and white democracy, 2; and antilynching legislation, 24; and Eugene Talmadge, 34–36; and civil rights movement, 38, 39;

and World War II, 44–47, 48, 51, 54, 55; in Washington, D.C., 68, 72, 73, 74–75, 76, 77–78, 90, 127, 200 (n. 19); and modernization, 97, 203 (n. 9), 204 (n. 13); and federal civil rights agenda, 99; and Stennis, 107; de facto versus de jure segregation, 217 (n. 10)

Segregationist movement: and *Brown* decision, 2, 4, 6, 88, 123, 125, 151, 159–60; and school desegregation, 2, 4, 7, 120, 122, 124, 186 (n. 10), 207 (n. 68); and Double Victory, 3, 39, 55, 66; divisions within, 4, 5, 7, 100–101, 108–9, 149–50, 160–61, 186 (n. 10), 204 (n. 22); rhetoric of, 4, 6, 7, 78, 80–81, 82, 83, 84, 94, 113, 122, 137, 141, 158–59; and rationale for racial separation, 4, 99; and egalitarianism, 7, 83, 84–88, 89, 102; and poll tax, 60; and Bilbo, 67, 68, 72–74, 85, 87–90, 101; and Washington, D.C., 70; and law-and-order ethos, 71, 73, 94, 95, 142, 178; and fair employment practices, 78–83, 86; and freedom of association, 79, 118–19, 207 (n. 68); propaganda of, 85–86, 87, 89, 101, 104; and racial violence, 95–96, 97, 98; and federal civil rights agenda, 100, 109, 183; and Dixiecrat revolt, 100–105, 107, 109–10, 122; and constitutional conservatism, 101–3, 107–8, 113–14, 126, 130, 142, 144–45, 146, 148, 158, 166, 168, 171, 175, 212 (n. 57); and electoral votes, 102, 158, 159, 164, 165, 166, 168; and nationalization of race problem, 107, 113, 116–17; and civil rights movement, 113, 123, 140, 141–42, 149, 151, 152–53, 161, 164–65, 183, 211 (n. 37); and American values, 115, 144; and freedom of choice, 119–20, 207 (n. 68); and equal educational rights, 122–23, 135, 137, 140–42, 208 (nn. 5,

6); and federal courts, 124–25, 126, 127, 131, 133–34, 142; and Byrnes, 128, 209 (n. 13); and myth of good faith, 140–42; and health and moral factors, 148, 211 (n. 37); as minority bloc, 152–53, 158–59, 164–65, 169, 182; and freedom of action, 164; and black political power, 166–67, 179–80; and northern allies, 167–68

Selective Service System: integration of, 119

Senate Armed Forces Committee, 118

Sensing, Thurman, 96–97, 99, 140

Shepperson, Gay, 15–16

Simmons, William J., 141

Smith, Al, 21

Smith, Ellison "Cotton Ed," 17–18, 20, 26–28, 159, 171, 190 (n. 25), 192 (n. 51)

Smith, Lonnie, 63

Smith, Willis, 157

Smith v. Allwright, 63–64, 65, 90

Social equality: and civil rights legislation, 4; and New Deal, 14–16; civic equality leading to, 20, 78, 115–16; Bilbo on, 29, 67, 76–77, 89; and Eugene Talmadge, 33, 36; and World War II, 43, 49, 65, 81; in Washington, D.C., 70, 77; and fair employment practices, 78, 104; Eastland on, 81; and Dixiecrat revolt, 104; Russell on, 115–16; and federal education aid, 124; Lucier on, 180

Socialism: Thomas Dixon on, 31; and white supremacy, 32; Eugene Talmadge on, 33; and World War II, 40; and New Deal, 65, 79; Workman on, 171; Russell on, 174, 175

Soldier Voting Act of 1942, 57–58

South: and demagogues, 1, 11–12, 17–18, 28, 36–37, 51–52, 55, 59, 68, 79, 87, 90, 95, 107, 116–17, 121–22, 128, 145, 161, 181–82; Roosevelt's connection to, 9–10; modernization of, 11–12, 26, 93–94, 95, 96–97,

116, 203 (n. 9), 204 (n. 13); populist tradition in, 12, 189 (n. 9); effect of racial anxieties on, 17, 43, 53; loyalty to New Deal, 18; support for Roosevelt in, 19–20; Democratic Party in, 20–21, 57, 98, 102; and challenges to home rule, 21; Roosevelt administration's concentration on, 26; and World War II, 39–40, 54, 61; and fair employment practices, 79; colonial status of, 96, 204 (n. 11); and minority bloc, 152; Republican Party in, 153, 186–87 (n. 11); political economy of, 182. *See also* Regional coalition; White southerners; *and specific states*

South Carolina: and segregationist movement, 7, 8, 161; and Roosevelt's visit to Georgia, 9; and Byrnes's connection to Roosevelt, 17–18; and antilynching legislation, 23; and election of 1938, 27, 28; New Deal programs in, 37; and World War II, 44; and "Eleanor Clubs," 52–53; and poll tax, 57, 197 (n. 51); and white primaries, 64; mob violence in, 93, 94–95; and Dixiecrat revolt, 101, 105; primary of 1950, 121; and equal educational rights, 122, 123, 126, 127, 128, 132, 134, 135, 137–38, 140, 211 (n. 34); Ku Klux Klan in, 128–30, 131; and school desegregation, 146; and Republican Party, 153, 168, 169, 170, 171; and southern minority bloc, 154, 159; and election of 1952, 155–56, 157; black voter registration in, 157, 214 (n. 11); and election of 1956, 159, 165; and election of 1960, 165; and election of 1964, 178

South Carolina Education Association, 139

Southern Association of Colleges and Secondary Schools, 35

Southern conservatives: and defense of white democracy, 2–3; and New Deal, 3, 5, 25–26, 32, 33, 36, 64–66, 78, 151, 183, 188 (n. 19); and Dixiecrat revolt, 5, 101, 159; and Democratic Party, 10, 20, 33, 108, 170, 172; and Roosevelt, 12, 26, 102; and Republican Party, 25, 118, 147–48, 156–57, 158, 166, 167–72, 177–78, 181; and poll tax, 57–58; and segregationist movement, 66, 68, 78–79, 148; and fair employment practices, 80, 83; and federal civil rights agenda, 100; and nationalization of race problem, 103, 105, 107, 108, 205 (n. 28); and equal educational rights, 123, 134–35; and national conservative movement, 147, 166, 169, 174, 177, 182, 188 (n. 21), 205 (n. 28); as minority bloc, 152, 157, 159, 181; political identity of, 153–54; and election of 1952, 155–56; and Goldwater, 166, 168–69, 176. *See also* Southern liberals; Southern moderates

Southern Crusaders, 63, 198 (n. 68)

Southern elites: and segregationist movement, 6; and World War II civil rights movement, 63; and Boswell Amendment, 93; and federal civil rights agenda, 101; and Dixiecrat revolt, 103–4; and terrorist tactics, 113; and equal educational rights, 123, 142; and Citizens' Councils, 160

Southern filibusters: and civil rights agenda, 18, 108, 113, 172–75; and antilynching legislation, 21, 23–24, 28, 29, 70, 100, 154, 175, 191 (n. 34); and poll tax, 38, 60, 70; and fair employment practices, 82, 89; defeat of, 174, 175, 176, 179, 186 (n. 11)

Southern Governors Conference, 139

Southern industrialists: and New Deal, 11–12, 13, 82, 96, 103; and modernization, 96, 97, 203 (n. 9), 204 (n. 14); and Dixiecrat revolt, 103–4

Southern liberals, 21, 100, 122, 188
(n. 19), 193 (n. 60), 208 (n. 5). *See also*
Southern conservatives; Southern
moderates
Southern Manifesto, 145–47, 152, 164
Southern moderates: and black soldiers, 51; and segregationist movement, 55–56; and Eastland, 81;
and Bilbo, 88; and modernization,
93–94, 95, 97; and Truman's civil
rights agenda, 100; and Dixiecrat
revolt, 104; and federal civil rights
agenda, 118; and election of 1950,
122; and equal educational rights,
132–33; and school desegregation,
145, 146. *See also* Southern conservatives; Southern liberals
Southern race relations: and racial
status quo, 1, 2, 3, 4, 6, 7, 12, 15, 16,
17, 40, 66, 79, 91, 104, 122, 149, 150,
153, 171, 180; and segregated social
order, 11, 153, 187 (n. 13); federal
intervention in, 24, 117; and World
War II, 40, 53–54; and equal educational rights, 140; and *Brown* deci-
sion, 140–41; and Whig politicians,
186 (n. 9)
Southern States Industrial Council
(SSIC), 11, 25, 82, 96–97, 99, 103, 104,
140, 164, 203–4 (n. 10)
Southern University Conference, 35
Soviet Union, 5, 32, 98, 139, 146, 168
Sparkman, John, 155
Sparks, Chauncey, 94
Special House Committee on Un-
American Activities, 32
Stalin, Joseph, 32, 193 (n. 60)
Stars and Stripes, 48
Statesman, 14, 34, 84
States' rights: language of, 4; and
Roosevelt, 13; and Bailey, 25; and
World War II, 40; and poll tax, 57,
61–62; Randolph on, 77; and Dixie-
crat revolt, 101–4, 105, 107, 109–10,

113, 124; and nationalization of race
problem, 102–3, 105, 117, 205 (n. 28);
and Russell, 113–14; and threat of
school desegregation, 124; and
Byrnes, 126, 155; and Americanism,
147; and southern minority bloc,
154; and Goldwater, 168; and Work-
man, 171
States' Rights Council of Georgia, 161
Stennis, John, 105–8, 118, 142–43, 145,
147, 166, 176
Stevenson, Adlai, 155, 156
Stoney, Thomas, 17, 18
Stowe, Harriet Beecher, 34
Sullens, Frederick, 22
Sunbelt, 182, 217 (n. 9)
Sweatt, Heman, 124
Sweatt decision, 124, 125

Take Your Choice (Bilbo), 87–88
Talmadge, Eugene: and Roosevelt, 6,
12–13, 31, 192 (n. 50); political machine of, 10; and politics of localism
and resentment, 12; and Russell,
14–17, 18, 145, 190 (n. 23); and black
electorate, 24; and Americanism, 32;
and University of Georgia, 33–34, 35,
36, 110, 123; and segregation, 34–36,
37, 56, 84, 182; unsuccessful reelection campaign of, 42, 59; and poll
tax, 59; and employment discrimination, 79; terrorism advocated by, 93,
94, 109, 203 (n. 3); electoral success-
es of, 93, 189 (n. 10), 203 (n. 3); death
of, 109, 110
Talmadge, Herman: and school desegregation, 4; on Roosevelt, 10; and
modernization, 109; and white primaries, 110; and Truman's inauguration, 114; and election of 1950, 122;
and Ku Klux Klan, 130–31; and nullification doctrine, 131; and equal educational rights, 131–32, 138, 139, 208
(n. 6); and political identity of south-

ern conservatives, 153; and southern
minority bloc, 154, 164, 165
Tennessee, 9, 93, 156, 197 (n. 51)
Texas, 63–64, 124–25, 156, 197 (n. 51)
Textile Bulletin, 104
Thompson, Melvin, 109
Thrasher, Ed, 134
Thurmond, J. Strom: on mob violence,
94; and election of 1946, 97; and
modernization, 99; and Dixiecrat
revolt, 100–101, 104, 105; Herman
Talmadge compared to, 109; and
Truman's inauguration, 114; and
election of 1950, 121; and legal basis
for segregation, 144–45; and election of 1956, 159; and election of
1960, 165; and southern conservatives, 171–72, 177; and southern minority bloc, 176; and Lucier, 180; and
Nixon, 181; and pursuit of prosperity,
182; on South's colonial status, 204
(n. 11)
Tillman, Ben, 64
Tilly, Dorothy Rogers, 98
To Secure These Rights (Presidential
Committee on Civil Rights), 99, 100
Totalitarianism: white democracy contrasted with, 3, 39, 40, 61, 62, 64;
civil rights movement compared to,
36, 62; as threat to Americanism,
40, 65, 79; poll tax campaign compared to, 57; New Deal compared to,
64–66; fair employment practices
compared to, 79, 86; racial reform
compared to, 102; federal education
aid compared to, 124
Townes, Roosevelt, 22
Truman, Harry S.: civil rights agenda
of, 5, 98–101, 103, 104, 106, 108, 109,
113, 115, 117, 118, 124, 125; and Fair
Employment Practices Committee,
80; and election of 1948, 101, 104,
105, 108, 113, 172; inauguration of,
114–15

Tubbs, Vincent, 93
Tupelo Daily Journal, 58

Umstead, William, 145
United Service Organization (USO), 83
Universal Negro Improvement Associa-
tion (UNIA), 92
University of Georgia, 33–34, 35, 36,
110, 123
University of Mississippi, 171
University of Missouri, 124
Urbanization, 8, 12, 98
U.S. Department of Justice, 99
US News and World Report, 149
U.S. Supreme Court: and white pri-
maries, 63–64; and desegregation,
122; and equal education, 124, 125,
127, 134, 136, 139, 140; mobilization
to circumvent school desegregation
ruling, 141; and segregationist move-
ment, 166
U.S. War Department, 41, 42, 44, 45

Van Nuys, Frederick, 23, 68
Vigilance Committees (Mississippi),
62–63
Vigilantes, Inc. (Georgia), 59
Vigilantism: African Americans' cam-
paign against, 39, 98; violence of, 93,
95–96, 97, 98, 203 (n. 3). *See also* Ku
Klux Klan
Virginia, 8, 127, 146, 156, 197 (n. 51)
Voting Rights Act of 1965, 4, 179, 180

Wagner, Robert, 23, 24
Wallace, George, 181, 182
Wallace, Henry, 105
War Production Board, 72
Warren, Earl, 158
Wash, Howard, 58–59
Washington, D.C.: segregation in, 68,
72, 73, 74–75, 76, 77–78, 90, 127, 200
(n. 19); Bilbo as chair of Senate Com-
mittee on, 68–78, 90, 199 (n. 4); civil

rights movement in, 70, 72–73, 77; public housing in, 71; Bilbo's relocation scheme for African Americans, 71–72; housing options for black residents, 73; home rule issue, 75–76, 100; desegregation of, 99

Washington Post, 72

Weltfish, Gene, 83, 85

White, Hugh, 133, 134, 136, 143–44, 208 (n. 6)

White, Walter, 21, 23–24, 27

White democracy: defense of, 2–3, 182; Axis totalitarianism contrasted with, 3, 39, 40, 61, 62, 64; rationale for, 4; and regional coalition, 7–8; and poll tax, 60; and nationalization of race problem, 105; and one-party rule, 152, 153–54; and southern minority bloc, 153

White northerners: and resentment of African Americans, 56, 73–74; and segregation, 74; and southern minority bloc, 152

White primaries, 40, 63–65, 67, 78, 90, 93, 100, 197 (n. 51)

White southerners: and racial status quo, 1, 2, 4, 6; and Democratic Party, 5, 10, 20–21, 23, 108, 155, 158, 159, 164, 188 (n. 17); segregationist beliefs of, 6, 55, 97, 188 (n. 20); divisions over New Deal, 10–11, 19; electoral power of, 25; and black soldiers stationed in South, 38–45, 47, 51–52; perceptions of racial reform, 40, 191 (n. 32); World War II service of, 46–49, 51, 54, 85, 195 (n. 24); and modernization, 97; and federal civil rights agenda, 99, 100; and Dixiecrat revolt, 103, 104, 105, 108; and equal educational rights, 135, 140–41; as minority bloc, 152, 158; and southern industrialization, 204 (n. 14). *See also* Southern conservatives; Southern liberals; Southern moderates

White supremacy: campaign for, 1–2, 186 (n. 3); New Deal programs eroding, 3, 10, 11, 17, 25, 28, 33, 37; and Dixiecrat revolt, 5; and segregationist movement, 7, 67–68, 82, 83, 89, 90, 91, 95, 101, 115, 145, 147, 148; and critique of New Deal, 14, 32, 37; Russell on, 16, 17, 190 (n. 23); defense of, 21, 25, 28, 187 (n. 16); and antilynching legislation, 23, 24; and Ellison Smith, 27; and Reconstruction, 27–28, 30–31, 154–55, 163–64; and Bilbo, 29, 49, 67–70, 72, 76, 88, 90, 91, 105, 199 (n. 4); and Thomas Dixon, 30, 32, 193 (n. 59); and World War II, 37, 51, 60–61, 62, 69, 72, 84; and poll tax, 58, 60; and Americanism, 63; and Roosevelt equated with racial revolution, 64, 65; excesses of, 96; and moderate elites, 97; and Herman Talmadge, 110; and black disfranchisement, 111; and black minority bloc voting, 157; changes in, 187 (n. 12); reinterpretation of, 188 (n. 21)

White women: and federal employment, 15–16, 72; African Americans as threat to, 18, 32, 41–42, 81, 85; as nurses in World War II, 45; black soldiers' relationships with white European women, 48–49

Whither Solid South? (Collins), 102, 205 (n. 25)

Williams, John Bell, 125, 159

Wilmington race riot, 186 (n. 3)

Women's National Association for the Preservation of the White Race (APWR), 14, 189–90 (n. 16)

Woodard, Isaac, 94

Woodward, Bascom, 133–34

Workman, William D., Jr., 166–68, 169, 170–71, 213 (n. 64)

Works Progress Administration (WPA): in Georgia, 15–16

World War II: and civil rights movement, 1, 2, 5, 37, 38, 39, 40, 51, 54, 55, 60, 61, 66, 68, 69, 78, 88–91, 187–88 (n. 16), 194 (n. 1); African Americans' service in, 1, 37, 41–46, 47, 48–49, 51, 81; and white supremacy, 37, 51, 60–61, 62, 69, 72, 84; and segregation, 44–47, 48, 51, 54, 55; and de facto integration, 45–49, 52; white southerners' service in, 46–49, 51, 54, 85, 195 (n. 24); domestic implications of, 60; employment opportunities of, 71; and southern industrialization, 96, 97; and housing in urban North, 200 (n. 20)

Wright, Fielding, 101, 104, 105, 132–33, 165

Yerger, Wirt, 180, 181

Yorkville Enquirer, 125